Thinking Through Theatre and Performance

Thinking Through Theatre seeks to advance knowledge and understanding of theatre by exploring the questions performance itself is uniquely capable of asking, and by interrogating the ways in which it asks them. The series aims to problematize the distinction between 'making' and 'thinking' by stressing their inter-relation and by identifying in theatre and performance practices aesthetic and political forms of thought and action.

Thinking Through Theatre examines the ways in which theatre is continually rethinking the possibilities of movement, space, action, image or voice, exploring the logics of creative invention and critical investigation that enable performance to operate as a mode of thought sui generis.

Series Editors

Maaike Bleeker (Utrecht University, Netherlands), Adrian Kear (Wimbledon College of Arts, University of the Arts London, UK), Joe Kelleher (University of Roehampton, London, UK) and Heike Roms (University of Exeter, UK)

Forthcoming Titles

Nomadic Theatre: Mobilizing Theory and Practice on the European Stage
by Liesbeth Groot Nibbelink

In Solitude: The Philosophy of Digital Performance Encounters
by Eirini Nedelkopoulou

Thinking Through Theatre and Performance

Edited by
Maaike Bleeker, Adrian Kear, Joe Kelleher
and Heike Roms

methuen | drama
LONDON • NEW YORK • OXFORD • NEW DELHI • SYDNEY

METHUEN DRAMA
Bloomsbury Publishing Plc
50 Bedford Square, London, WC1B 3DP, UK
1385 Broadway, New York, NY 10018, USA

BLOOMSBURY, METHUEN DRAMA and the Methuen Drama logo are trademarks
of Bloomsbury Publishing Plc

First published in Great Britain 2019

A catalogue record for this book is available from the British Library.

A catalog record for this book is available from the Library of Congress.

ISBN: HB: 978-1-4725-7961-4
PB: 978-1-4725-7960-7
ePDF: 978-1-4725-7963-8
eBook: 978-1-4725-7962-1

Series: Thinking Through Theatre

Typeset by Deanta Global Publishing Services, Chennai, India
Printed and bound in India

To find out more about our authors and books visit www.bloomsbury.com and
sign up for our newsletters.

Contents

List of Illustrations

Notes on Contributors

Sruti Bala is Associate Professor in Theatre Studies at the University of Amsterdam. She studied German literature in Bombay, India, and theatre studies in Mainz, Germany. She became interested in the question of impact through her study of participatory practices, as well as through her own involvement as a facilitator of community-based theatre. Her other research interests include translation and performance, art and activism, and decolonial feminism. She coordinates a research project on gendered and sexual citizenship in the Dutch Caribbean in cooperation with the University of Curaçao. uva.nl/profile/s.bala/

Maaike Bleeker is Professor of Theatre Studies at Utrecht University. She has also worked as a dramaturg and costume designer. Her research is about perception and meaning-making in performance, dance, theatre and the arts, as well as in science and in public life. She combines approaches from the arts and performance with insights from philosophy, media theory and cognitive science. Her monograph *Visuality in the Theatre* was published in 2008. She has (co-)edited several volumes, including *Anatomy Live: Performance and the Operating Theatre* (2008), *Performance & Phenomenology* (2015) and *Transmission in Motion: The Technologizing of Dance* (2016). https://www.uu.nl/staff/MABleeker/0

Broderick D. V. Chow trained as an actor and singer in Vancouver, Canada, and is now Senior Lecturer in Theatre at Brunel University London. He teaches musical theatre, theatre history, performance theory and performance and sport. Current research investigates the performance of fitness and its intersection with the construction of masculinities from the late nineteenth century to the present day. He is co-editor of *Žižek and Performance* (2014) and *Performance and Professional Wrestling* (2017), and is author of the forthcoming monograph *Dynamic Tensions: Performing Fitness and Masculinities*. Broderick is an amateur Olympic weightlifter and a BWL Level 1 Qualified Weightlifting Coach. www.dynamictensions.com.

Colette Conroy teaches drama at the University of Hull. She was a theatre director before becoming an academic. She is the author of *Theatre & The Body* (2010) and has published work on disability culture, performance and sport in journals and books. She is the joint editor of the journal *RiDE: The Journal of Applied Theatre and Performance* and is currently editing a themed journal issue on access and performance and is co-editing a collection of essays about the philosopher Jacques Rancière.

Bojana Cvejić is Associate Professor of Dance and Dance Theory at the Oslo National Academy of the Arts (KHIO), and teacher at P.A.R.T.S. (Brussels) since 2002. The areas in which she teaches include continental philosophy, performance studies, European history of dance, dramaturgy and artistic methodology in dance and performance. Her current research focuses on social choreography, technologies of the self and performance poetics. She is the author of *Choreographing Problems: Expressive Concepts in European Contemporary Dance and Performance* (2015) and (together with Ana Vujanović) *Public Sphere by Performance* (2012).

Thomas F. DeFrantz received the 2017 Outstanding Research in Dance award from the Dance Studies Association. He directs SLIPPAGE: Performance, Culture, Technology, a research group that explores emerging technology in live performance applications. He has taught at the American Dance Festival, ImPulsTanz, Ponderosa and the New Waves Dance Institute, as well as at MIT, Stanford, Yale, NYU, Hampshire College, Duke and the University of Nice. He contributed a voice-over for a permanent installation at the Smithsonian African American Museum. DeFrantz believes in our shared capacity to do better, and to engage our creative spirit for a collective good that is anti-racist, anti-homophobic, proto-feminist and queer affirming.

Steve Dixon is President of LASALLE College of the Arts in Singapore. He is an actor and interdisciplinary artist, and director of the award-winning multimedia theatre company The Chameleons Group. Steve is Co-founder and Advisory Editor of the *International Journal of Performance Arts and Digital Media*, and has published over sixty book chapters and journal articles. His 800-page book *Digital Performance: A History of New Media in Theater, Dance, Performance Art and Installation* (2007) won two international awards.

Miguel Escobar Varela is a theatre scholar, web developer and translator who has lived in Mexico, the Netherlands, Singapore and Indonesia. His main interests are the digital humanities and Indonesian performance practices. His research has been published in *Digital Humanities Quarterly*, *Digital Scholarship in the Humanities*, *Theatre Research International*, *Contemporary Theatre Review*, *Asian Theatre Journal*, *Performance Research* and *New Theatre Quarterly*. He is currently Assistant Professor at the National University of Singapore and director of the Contemporary Wayang Archive (cwa-web.org). More information is available at miguelescobar.com

Liesbeth Groot Nibbelink is a lecturer and researcher in theatre studies in the Media and Culture Studies Department of Utrecht University, where she also coordinates the Master's programme in Contemporary Theatre, Dance and Dramaturgy. She is also active as a dramaturg and artistic adviser. Her research centres around relationships between dramaturgy, scenography, spatial theory and performance philosophy. She is the author of *Nomadic Theatre: Mobilizing Theory and Practice on the European Stage* (Bloomsbury, forthcoming) and has contributed to (among others) *Contemporary Theatre Review*, *Performance Research* and *Mapping Intermediality in Theatre and Performance* (Bay-Cheng et al. 2010). In 2013, she co-founded Platform-Scenography, an open-source platform for scenographers and dramaturgs that seeks to stimulate reflection on scenography.

Dominic Johnson is Reader in Performance and Visual Culture in the Department of Drama at Queen Mary University of London. He researches and writes about performance art, live art and visual art after 1960. He is the author of three books, including, most recently, *The Art of Living: An Oral History of Performance Art* (2015). He is the editor of five books, including surveys of Ron Athey, Franko B, Adrian Howells and Manuel Vason. From 2005 to 2012, his frequently bloody performances were shown around the world, in festivals, galleries, museums, theatres and clubs, a commune, a dungeon and a desert.

Adrian Kear is Director of Programme Development, Performance Arts at Wimbledon College of Arts, University of the Arts London. He is the author of numerous publications investigating the relationship between performance, politics and cultural practice. Adrian's books include *Theatre and Event: Staging the European Century* (2013); *International Politics and Performance: Critical Aesthetics and Creative Practice* (with Jenny Edkins, 2013); *Psychoanalysis and Performance* (with Patrick Campbell, 2001); and *Mourning Diana: Nation, Culture and the Performance of Grief* (with Deborah Lynn Steinberg, 1999).

Joe Kelleher is Professor of Theatre and Performance at University of Roehampton, London. His books include *The Illuminated Theatre: Studies on the Suffering of Images* (2015), *Theatre & Politics* (2009) and *The Theatre of Socìetas Raffaello Sanzio*, co-authored with Claudia and Romeo Castellucci, Chiara Guidi and Nicholas Ridout (2007).

Carl Lavery is Professor of Theatre and Performance at the University of Glasgow. His recent publications include *Rethinking the Theatre of the Absurd: Ecology, Environment and the Greening of the Modern Stage* (Bloomsbury, 2015) and a special issue of the journal *Green Letters: Studies in Ecocriticism*, 'Performance and Ecology: What Can Theatre Do?' (2017). The latter was reissued in book form in 2018. He is currently working on a new project, *Theatre and the Earth: Interrogating the Human.*

Jazmin Badong Llana teaches drama, theatre and performance studies at De La Salle University, Philippines, where she is also the dean of the College of Liberal Arts. Her research interests are on theatre and politics, activism and performance, cultural politics and cultural performance, postcoloniality, pilgrimage and religious performance. She has published in *Performance Research* and in the book *Performance Studies in Motion: International Perspectives and Practices in the Twenty-First Century* (Bloomsbury 2014). She completed her Doctor of Philosophy at Aberystwyth University, UK, on a Ford Foundation International Fellowship. Between 2014 and 2016, she was head of the Philippines' National Committee on Dramatic Arts.

Sean Metzger (UCLA School of Theater, Film, and Television) works at the intersections of performance, visual culture, Asian American, Caribbean, Chinese and sexuality studies. He has published *Chinese Looks: Fashion, Performance, Race* (2014). Metzger has also co-edited four collections of essays: *Embodying Asian/American Sexualities* (2009); *Futures of Chinese Cinema* (2009); *Race, Space, Place* (a special issue of *Cultural Dynamics*, November 2009); *Islands, Images, Imaginaries* (a special issue of *Third Text*, 2014). He co-edited an anthology of dramatic texts entitled *Awkward Stages: Plays about Growing up Gay* (2015).

Sophie Nield teaches theatre and film in the Department of Drama, Theatre and Dance at Royal Holloway, University of London. She writes on questions of space, theatricality and representation in political life and the law, and on the performance of 'borders' of various kinds. Recent work has focused on the figure of the refugee, the theatricality of protest and the political viability of the riot, and has opened interdisciplinary connections between the fields of performance studies, politics and history.

Tavia Nyong'o is Professor of Theatre Studies at Yale University in New Haven, Connecticut. He works in contemporary aesthetic and critical theory with a particular attention to the visual, musical and performative dimensions of blackness, as well as to the affective and technocultural dimensions of modern regimes of race. His first book, *The Amalgamation Waltz: Race, Performance, and the Ruses of Memory* (Minnesota, 2009), won the Errol Hill Award for best book in African American theatre and performance studies. He is also the author of *Afro-Fabulations: The Queer Drama of Black Life* (New York, 2018) and a number of essays. A fun fact: he is named after the character Tevye in *Fiddler on the Roof* (music by Jerry Bock, lyrics by Sheldon Harnick and book by Joseph Stein).

Louise Owen is lecturer in Theatre and Performance at Birkbeck, University of London. Her research examines contemporary theatre and performance in terms of economic change and modes of governance, in particular the social and cultural effects of neoliberalization. Her writing has been published in *Performance Research*, *Frakcija*, *Contemporary Theatre Review* and *TDR/The Drama Review*. Her book *Agents of the Future: Theatre, Performance and Neoliberalization* is forthcoming from Northwestern University Press. She is the co-director of Birkbeck Centre for Contemporary Theatre, and co-convenor of London Theatre Seminar.

Mike Pearson is Emeritus Professor of Performance Studies at Aberystwyth University in Wales. He was a member of RAT Theatre (1972–3), Cardiff Laboratory Theatre (1973–80) and Brith Gof (1981–97). He currently creates theatre as a solo artist; with artist/designer Mike Brookes in Pearson/Brookes; with senior performers group Good News From The Future; and for National Theatre Wales, including *The Persians* (2010), *Coriolan/us* (2012) and *Iliad* (2015). He is the co-author with Michael Shanks of *Theatre/Archaeology* (2001) and author of *In Comes I: Performance, Memory and Landscape* (2006), *Site-specific Performance* (2010), *Mickery Theater: An Imperfect Archaeology* (2011) and *Marking Time: Performance, Archaeology and the City* (2013).

Heike Roms is Professor in Theatre and Performance at the University of Exeter in the UK. She publishes on the history of performance art in a British context and on performance historiography and archiving. Her research project *What's Welsh for Performance?* won the UK's Theatre and Performance Research Association TaPRA David Bradby Award for Outstanding Research in International Theatre and Performance in 2011. She is currently working on a book arising from the project with the working title *When Yoko Ono Did Not Come to Wales – Locating the Early History of Performance Art*. www.performance-wales.org

Theron Schmidt works internationally as an artist, teacher and writer. He has published widely on contemporary theatre and performance, participatory art practices and politically engaged performance and activism. In his research and in the classroom, he is interested in exploring the ways in which theatre is not just a reflection or image of social and political structures outside the theatre, but is continuous with them – and also a place where these structures can be made visible, played with and reconfigured. In thinking about the 'work' of theatre, some other present and past artist practices that inspire him include Back to Back Theatre, Cassils, Tim Crouch, Goat Island, Richard Maxwell, Rabih Mroué, Nature Theatre of Oklahoma, Rimini Protokoll and Christoph Schlingensief.

Introduction: Thinking Through

MAAIKE BLEEKER, ADRIAN KEAR, JOE KELLEHER AND HEIKE ROMS

What Sort of Book This Is

This is a book for students. It is a book for all of us who are involved in thinking about, making, enjoying, arguing with and – above all – asking and continuing to ask certain fundamental questions of theatre and performance. To note from the start, the word 'questions' covers several bases: interrogations and investigative queries of course, but also challenges and problems, doubts and uncertainties, constructive affirmations and forceful contestations, all of which generate in turn new queries and problems and rarely anything like definitive answers. Their multiplicity and continuity are perhaps the point. We do not stop being students of this world if we continue to 'inhabit' the world inquisitively, with the sort of critical curiosity that is intent on understanding better how and why things happen. Anthropologist Tim Ingold, in his book *Being Alive*, a book that seeks to think about and describe worlds, processes and environments along with their human inhabitants at a fundamental level of enquiry, writes: 'Whether our concern is to inhabit this world or to study it – and at root these are the same, since all inhabitants are students and all students inhabitants – our task is not to take stock of its contents but to follow what is going on, tracing the multiple trails of becoming, wherever they lead' (Ingold 2011: 14). In this, Ingold sets a measure for the sort of principles and approaches that drive our own book, and that we hope will inform the seminars, lectures, workshops and discussions – and whatever occasions of collaborative and private reading and thinking – where the chapters that make up this volume are put to work. Those principles might be summarized as follows: attempts at critical description, performed by inhabitants of some of theatre's worlds within worlds, on behalf of fellow inhabitants, fellow students, and informed by questions which are capable of flowing across and between worlds, 'wherever they lead', generating new – or renewed – enquiries. This book is designed, then, for use in classrooms. Its chapters aim at once to be both introductory and explanatory. Arguments and ideas are built around closely detailed illustrative examples. Methodologies – ways of working, tools of investigation – are carefully talked through. Each of the chapters is supplemented with information about the case-study performances (with pointers towards online and other documentation) and with annotated suggestions for further reading. We think of 'classrooms', however, as typically extensive spaces, temporally, spatially and otherwise. These chapters have arguments of their own to make; but they will also – or so we hope – generate new and renewed ways of 'being alive' in theatre and performance, in theatre-making and performing, in spectating and analysis, in understanding and negotiating theatre's histories and institutions and conventions and economies, its ecologies, its politics, its manifold ways of being and doing and – as we shall seek to explore in what follows – of thinking.

It begins though with questions. You will have noticed already, if you have looked at the contents page of this book, that each of the chapters is constructed around the sort of question that might be brought to any theatre work, or theatre or performance process or experience whatsoever. The volume is not, in other words, concerned with a particular type or genre of theatre, although the reader will notice tendencies, for instance, towards works and practices that are contemporary with, or local to, the individual author's experience (although even that is by no means always the case). Nor is the book concerned with establishing or promoting a specific 'canon' of works or practitioners, although – as pointed out below in the section on 'Illustrative examples' – there is a tendency again to focus on works that have become 'exemplary' for the authors, while lending themselves to further investigation – through availability of documentation or published secondary discussion – by their readers. As for the questions themselves, in line with the classroom principle that 'there are no stupid questions', these are questions we are often coming back to, be it in transformed or recurrent or newly emergent situations and circumstances. What the reader will find are several fundamental – that is basic and long-standing – questions around, for instance, playwriting (Chapter 1), spectatorship (Chapter 2), identity and ability and inclusion (Chapter 3), or representing and understanding conventions (Chapter 4); or else scenography and its strategies (Chapter 7), stage objects and their peculiar agency (Chapter 8), media and their interrelations (Chapter 9), physical training and what it teaches of the world and of other performing bodies (Chapter 10), or the actor's work and what it teaches of others and oneself (Chapter 11). Each of these questions is inflected with a particular knot of active concerns around thinking and doing. For example: What is Black dance? What can it do? (Chapter 6) These are questions that ask not only what we can know and say about an object (What *is* Black dance?) but which immediately – to refer again to Tim Ingold's formulations – move beyond a mere stock-taking towards a more open-ended enquiry that seeks to 'follow what is going on', to 'trace the multiple trails of becoming, wherever they lead'. So, this entity, this object that a particular author is naming for now Black dance, or scenography, or the trained body, or intermediality, or theatrical labour: What can these things do? How do they act and think? How do they elaborate their images, their ideas, their politics? How are they alive in the world? And how we can we – writers and readers, makers and spectators, teachers and students together – productively think with and about them? How, indeed, are we alive in the world, through and in relation to the theatre and the practices that shape it?[1]

Which brings us to the second kind of questions that the chapters of this book take up, those that theatre asks of itself, and of us, and invites us to think about further. They are frequently questions to do with 'intervention' of one sort or another, interventions into societal structures, or into established ways of thinking and doing. What is the emancipatory

---

[1] In this respect, the book takes inspiration from and is indebted to Jenny Edkins and Maja Zehfuss's *Global Politics: An Introduction* (2013), which sets out an enquiry-driven approach to examining politics and the political. Our basic pedagogical 'set-up' of fundamental question, illustrative example, methodological exposition and challenge and critical conclusion is drawn from their innovative and influential approach to opening up key questions in international relations.

potential of performance? How, for instance, can performance disrupt institutional space? (Chapter 17) Or: How does theatre think through politics, that is the politics of its mode of representation, but also the historical political action it represents, whose impulses may still be unfinished business? (Chapter 15) Or: How does it work through historical trauma and its re-enactment? And why might theatre be a particularly good and useful place to do that? (Chapter 13) And how is theatre recognized and reconstituted – re-purposed, re-used, re-valued – through its own archival record? (Chapter 16) Interventionist as they might be, the tendency of such questions is also to provoke processes of reflective thinking that reconsider the value, the use and function, even the very nature and mode of existence of the theatrical object.

But of course, what we are referring to here as two types of questions – questions we might ask about theatre (any theatre at all), and the questions that particular theatres and performance practices ask of themselves and of us – are so closely related as to be at times indistinguishable. While they may appear to be diverse lines of pursuit, they 'lead' often enough to common and recurrent grounds of enquiry, to questions about how sense and meaning is made – by theatre makers and spectators and other interested parties – and also about relations of power, about politics and personhood. How are we ourselves 'made' in relation to theatre and performance? What kind of subjects are produced by theatre (spectators, makers, critics) and what kind of subjects are produced by thinking through it (students, teachers, researchers, experts, participants, practitioners)? And how do we *un*make and *re*make ourselves? These are then also questions about ethics and value and effective action in the world. What is an intercultural exchange, and what are the pitfalls of intercultural practice and study? (Chapter 12) What are the impacts of theatre and performance, and for whom do these impacts matter? Who is affected? And, according to whose motives and values are these effects being measured? (Chapter 13) Or else they are questions about forms of knowledge and judgement, their production and reproduction, about justice and injustice, about history and memory and trauma and repetition, and about presence and representation. For instance, what sort of show – and what sort of actions – does the authority of a societal institution such as the law depend upon? (Chapter 20) And what sort of show – and resorting to what kind of theatricality – does authoritarian power make when it represents its others to itself? (Chapter 21) And what sorts of subjects do certain economic systems make of creatures like us when they put us to work in the service of their systemic reproduction? And what sort of show is to be made of that? And to what end? (Chapter 5) And what sort of show might we make – through dancing together no less – of our own selves in motion and the ways we think, and act, socially? (Chapter 19) Questions, too, about 'being alive' in the world among others who may not be alive in quite the same ways we imagine ourselves to be, although they share this world with us. What sort of shows, what sort of actions, images and 'melting' occurrences will bring us home to that? (Chapter 18)

As these questions are being asked, each of the chapters rehearses and draws attention to its way of proceeding, its chosen method of following 'what is going on', seeking to demonstrate, step by step, how we might learn to 'inhabit' and 'study' the several worlds of theatre and performance thinking that the questions open onto. We go into more detail on these steps in the rest of this introduction, but for the moment we might summarize this procedural concern with another set of questions, again concerned with thinking and doing. How do we 'stage' ideas, both in the theatre and in our ways of writing about it? What, for instance, is an 'essay'? How does an essay articulate its ideas at the level of the sentence, paragraph, image, argument? And how does that relate to the ways that a theatrical performance articulates *its* ideas? How does an essay address its reader? What does it use for evidence, and how does it make the evidence work? Who is being spoken to and by whom? And what is *not* being spoken of? What is being masked, occluded, omitted, excluded, spoken over and generally upstaged and overlooked? What does it mean to think critically about theatre, and to think critically *with* theatre as an object of thinking? *Thinking Through Theatre and Performance* offers itself as a companion for readers in their own following of what is going on, which may well lead to other destinations than those arrived at in the essays.

How the Chapters of This Book Are Structured

Questions

The authors who have contributed to the book were set a task: not primarily to write chapters that sum up the current state of knowledge in one or other area of the discipline, but to construct *essays* – attempts, rehearsals, demonstrations, try-outs – that work through particular provocations, ideas or methods of approach. Each chapter, as noted already, is fashioned around a foundational question in theatre and performance studies (How do performances put people in the situation of being spectators? How are our ways of looking in the theatre constructed, inherited, learnt, contested?). Or else, a fundamental question in theatre-making practice (Why should it matter that theatre be 'accessible'? What sort of worlds might this or that accessibility open up, and for whom?). Questions have been our starting point because they allow us to ask what it is that we are doing when studying theatre and performance, and how we go about doing this. And, from the start, questions are staged explicitly as enabling – and requiring – further critical and creative enquiry in order to pursue their implications. So it is, then, that introductory discussions establish the critical 'problem' of the topic or phenomenon being considered, be that – to take a couple of examples from the book – the complex functioning of objects and 'things' when used and encountered within the special aesthetic conditions of theatrical performance; or the sorts of assumptions – and, for some, life choices – that inform supposed distinctions between academic 'study' and bodily 'training'; or the sort of 'work' that a working performer does. From there, the chapters unpack issues that attend upon the topic, considering the historical, cultural and political contexts that inform each enquiry, and explaining in the process some of the key approaches available. The chapters thus draw attention to and reflect on relationships between questions and methods, and how objects of research emerge from the questions asked and the approaches that are used to answer them.

Illustrative Example

Thinking Through Theatre and Performance does not pretend to universal coverage of its area of study. Nor does it aspire to an abstract summary of questions, approaches and topics. Rather, taken together, the twenty-one chapters in this book look towards an expanded and expanding field of theatrical and performance practices and concerns which – for all of the connections across the conversations – is constituted from particular, localized practices, doings, approaches. For example, a consideration of intercultural performance pedagogies in Southeast Asia stands alongside a study of the social, cultural and affective 'impact' of the work of a lesbian theatre company in Latin America, which stands alongside a discussion which starts out from another sort of impact in contemporary North American classrooms of a theatrical re-enactment of historical trauma in colonial Southwest Africa at the turn of the twentieth century. And so on. These juxtapositions and interconnections of cultures, practices, experiences and histories are a function, however, not just of the range of questions asked in the chapters, but also of the specificity of the illustrative examples that give the various enquiries distinct and material substance.

Each chapter argues through case-study examples, offering concrete analysis of performance events and materials. This allows the reader to see how the argument is developed in relation to actual theatre and performance practices, as well as through practices of evidence-gathering, analysis and argumentation. In most of the chapters, the case study will be of a particular performance or group of related performances, but occasionally the examples will extend to other sorts of materials, a high-profile courtroom trial for instance. This last is one of several chapters in the book that focus not so much on a spectatorial experience, but rather the traces left of that performance in archival documentation, in texts, images and reports (and the ways those traces have been valued, contested and put to use). Nor are the case studies meant as a canon of artists' practices. Rather, they are chosen for how they open up fields of enquiry, and for how they show theatre and performance themselves operating as investigative practices. They are chosen too with the aim that the analyses and discussions in the individual chapters may be transferable to the readers' own investigations, which will be focused on materials that are local or contemporary, or in other ways significant to their concerns and experiences. The case-study materials are, then, 'examples' in the widest sense: exemplary instances of a matter of concern, 'illustrative' of a more general materiality of performance practice that will find resonance in other contexts, and at the same time specific, located forms of critical and creative enquiry.

Investigative Methodology, Critical and Creative Challenges

In addition to articulating a foundational question or set of questions, and pursuing those questions through an illustrative case study, each chapter also reflects on its investigative methodology – the tools and methods of analysis used by the authors – and situates these methods within a broader context of ways of studying theatre and performance. What fields, what practices, what examples of critical thinking are being drawn on in order to make a point? Methodological reflections also include arguments that might operate as critical and creative challenges to the approach taken. As a chapter develops, an author will consider alternative approaches that would draw out a different, or differently inflected, set of outcomes from the enquiry. Throughout *Thinking Through Theatre and Performance*, the authors are at pains to deal – in diverse ways – with questions of what it is to make an analysis, to be critical. How does one take a critical relationship to one's field of study? How, for instance, to make one's own experiences part of writing? And how to relate an analysis to the transitory nature of the performance object? Or to the specificity of its context? How do we begin to construct an argument about a performance? Through explicit reflection on their methodological approaches, and the attention drawn to potential critical and creative challenges to the approaches taken, the chapters present historically and culturally contextualized introductions to histories of thinking about theatre and performance and a panorama of critical and analytical ways of working.

How This Book Is Organized

Thinking Through Theatre and Performance is divided into four sections, each with a specific focus of enquiry. The chapters in each section address an interrelated set of questions, although the approaches taken differ and, as such, encourage readers to engage in arguments that emerge between, as well as within, the chapters.

Part 1: Watching

Chapters in this first section interrogate ways in which theatre functions as a place for seeing and hearing. These interrogations include the questions what, and how, does an audience watch? However, it is not spectators alone who 'do' watching in the theatre (sometimes the performers and sometimes the theatre itself 'looks back'), and nor is this watching a simple business of seeing what is going on and following where it leads. It also involves making meaning of what is seen, or otherwise sensed. And – as all the chapters in this section bring out – it involves the watchers watching themselves, to the extent that we seek to understand better how our looking is constructed, provoked, enabled, not only by performances but by spaces and architectures, by habits and conventions and histories, and by economies and relations of power.

The opening chapter, Joe Kelleher's 'Why Study Drama?', identifies the business of watching theatre not only as an act of the audience, but of onstage figures (the actors and also the characters they are playing) who feel driven to ask themselves basic questions of comprehension and orientation such as: Where are we? What is going on? What does this situation want of me? What should I do? These are the sorts of questions that any spectator might ask of a drama playing out in front of them, but they are also the kinds of questions being asked just as insistently by the main personages in Tom Stoppard's 1968 comedy *Rosencrantz and Guildenstern Are Dead*, and Barrell Organ Theatre's 2014 drama, *Nothing*. Stoppard's first play and Barrell Organ's debut production are both approached, in Kelleher's chapter, as modes of 'student' drama, or dramas in which the acting out of the plot – as much as the spectators' following of the stage action – proceed as attempts to 'study' and seek out potentials for agency, emancipation and self-understanding in scripted theatre. Recent academic studies of writing for the stage are considered that extend this question of 'emancipation' beyond the spectators, or characters – or students – of the drama, to dramatic writing itself.

Theatre spectators' acts of looking and sense-making are at the centre of Maaike Bleeker's chapter 'What Do Performances Do to Spectators?', which considers some of the many ways in which theatres go about putting audiences in this state of 'being a spectator'. Bleeker's investigation is wide-ranging – historically, aesthetically, politically – in its implications, even as it remains focused on the particular example of Dries Verhoeven's 2008 performance *No Man's Land*, which did not take place in a theatre but involved, in each city where it was shown, a cast of local performers from migrant backgrounds, taking individual spectators on a walking tour through the city, which the spectators negotiate for much of the time through a voice speaking on headphones. Bleeker's core theoretical concept of 'focalization', which concerns the relation between what is seen and the point of view from which that perspective is assembled, is put to the test by Verhoeven's mobile performance. This allows ourselves, as readers, to see how an analytical concept is made to do its work, in alliance with other approaches, in similar fashion perhaps to the complex collaboration between spectator and performer, as one follows another – partly seen, uncertainly heard – around an urban environment that perhaps both call 'home' although in different ways. When performers and spectators eventually come face to face, it may be that a new analytical framework is required to comprehend the sort of 'critical intimacy' that exists between people who meet in the same space, but which is not necessarily the same 'world' for each of them.

In Colette Conroy's chapter on (dis)ability and theatrical accessibility, 'How Can the Theatre Be Fully Accessible?', acts of watching are again deeply implicated in a politics of sense-making – a matter not just of visibility but of legibility, and not just legibility but a matter of actual access to theatrical representation at all for some people, that has as much to do with strategies and decisions of theatre production as it does with the audience members' work of attention and interpretation. Conroy pursues her enquiry in part through semiotic methods of analysis, which concern at base the function and interpretation of stage signifiers, but which quickly extend – in her reading of Graeae Theatre Company's production of Lorca's *The House of Bernarda Alba* – to an explicit approach on the part of the theatre makers that draws attention to every element of the stage picture as a tactic of 'signing' (including the onstage use of British Sign Language [BSL]). Conroy also, though, works through the less academically sanctioned notion of 'aboutness', which has to do with an engaged analytical and practical concern with who gets to act and perform, and how certain performing bodies get to be seen and understood by others, as determined by a long history of systemic exclusion. This determinacy is shown in Conroy's chapter to be challenged – and broken – by the semiosis generated from Graeae's casting and staging choices, as much as by the coming together of the company's audience as an 'interpretive community' whose own semiotic labour would be the ground of a reconfigured and extended notion of 'accessibility' as such.

The critical deployment of semiotic methods of analysis are continued in Sean Metzger's chapter 'How Does Stage Performance Think Through Cultural Convention?', which focuses particularly on the concept of the 'index' – a signifying device that 'points at' something that is intended to be recognized and understood, often as founding but invisible 'cause' for the indexical signifier's apparent 'effect'. Metzger's concern is not so much with theatrical conventions, as with theatre's capacity – through actors' gestures or through elements of costume – to index cultural conventions, particularly Chinese and Asian American cultural conventions in the work of playwright David Henry Hwang, whose dramas have been seen by wide and diverse audiences. Metzger is interested in asking what it is that theatrical audiences imagine – or fantasize – that a gesture or costume choice is pointing to, if what is being represented is something that they can only grasp *through* fantasy, such as the discontinued tradition of foot-binding, and the violence and pain attendant upon it. What, Metzger asks, does a spectator have to understand – or learn – in order to be able to see? And how does such seeing and learning operate across the complexities of contemporary, intercultural discourse? Metzger pursues methods of analysis designed to enable us to ask – and to understand better – not only what a gesture, or a costume, 'means' but also how certain cultural conventions become sedimented in our understandings, even as theatre events – not unlike the flows of global capital – are ever more prone to border crossings of one sort or another.

The operations of capital and theatre's capacity to represent the predicament of some of industrial capitalism's most vulnerable subjects, is the focus of Louise's Owen's chapter 'How Does Theatre Represent Economic Systems?' Owen pursues her theme by taking us through her own attentive and detailed watching of Alexander Zeldin's 2014 play *Past Caring*, a modern 'naturalistic' drama set among a group of cleaners on 'zero hours' contracts at a British meat factory. The kind of spectator that Owen invokes is one who does not merely read the signs on stage and follow the narrative action, but who also, as it were, reads the newspapers, an informed and – as things develop – involved spectator, who notes the reference to contemporary public debates over precarious labour displayed on a notice board in the theatre foyer. This is a spectator who builds upon what she knows to inform herself further of the sort of social and economic analysis that enables her to relate the individual human stories told on stage to the specific 'means of production' that systemically generate life situations such as these. A spectator who – effectively – brings the force of her own political concern (although Owen cites a range of divergent responses to the drama, from experiential recognition to disbelief and denial) into dialogue with the representations exhibited on stage. One of the outcomes of this concern is that, even as a reading of *Past Caring* is brought into dialogue with its historical antecedents in late-nineteenth-century naturalism, there appears a divergence from the 'quasi-absent audience members' of the earlier form in the contemporary drama's engagement of 'audiences actively involved'. The watchers have, in their fashion, become actors in the world, performers of their thought. But perhaps they always were.

Part 2: Performing

This second section gathers a group of chapters that address various modes of performing, not all of which involve theatrical actors. There are discussions, for instance, of dancers and dance-makers; or of actors, dancers and performers whose 'work' appears closer to domestic or industrial labour, or the sorts of work that service industry workers such as carers do, than theatrical performing; or the sort of physical performance training that may not be for any audience at all, where the purpose is closer to training for training's sake, or for the sake anyway of the one who trains and those they train with. Furthermore, there are chapters in this section where the performing 'agents' may not even be human performers, but rather objects, architectures, sites, 'things'; elements of scenography, for instance – four hundred white plastic chairs, a firework on a cardboard box moving around the stage by remote control – that in consort with other 'things' and of their own accord (like any 'trained' and capable body) appear able to think and act for themselves.

In Thomas F. DeFrantz's chapter 'What Is Black Dance? What Can It Do?', the challenges and obligations that inform Black dance – whatever forms it takes and wherever it takes place – are not just aesthetic but social and political. Namely, as a mode of 'Black performance', it 'confirms the presence of Black people in the world', a world where 'the histories of Black people have been circumscribed by disavowal, coercion and genocide'. So, while De Frantz's study of what Black dance can 'do' involves identification of its various performance forms, his chapter looks also at how these are performed, and in what circumstances, and by – and for – whom. A crucial factor in DeFrantz's argument is that Black dance should acknowledge the historical circumstances of its making and emergence, and much of the chapter is concerned with following this challenge – this obligation – through ways in which Black dance has evolved or is being re-invented – but also dispersed and appropriated – among divergent dance situations, including theatrical dance, but also popular culture, as well as social dance and public gathering. DeFrantz's examples range from the theatre work of choreographer Donald Byrd and the writings of scholar-dancer Katherine Dunham, to impromptu group performances of the 'Electric Slide' at the first Barack Obama inauguration. From here, his questions address a range of considerations. What, for instance, might it mean for non-Black people to perform Black dance, and appear to inhabit someone else's traumatic history? But then too, how might Black dance allow for and affirm 'the revelation of Black joy' and the possibility – as DeFrantz writes – 'of collective aesthetic action', not least, modes of collective action and performing that 'centre Black people in the creative ways of the world'?

Liesbeth Groot Nibbelink's chapter 'How Does Scenography Think?' focuses on a single work by theatre director Philippe Quesne, *L'Effet de Serge* (2007, and frequently revived). The French title of the piece might be loosely translated as 'Serge's Stage Effects' and is set entirely in the simple living-room belonging to Serge, who devises small object-based performances to entertain a group of friends every Sunday evening. On the basis of this particular example – which has as much to do with the delicate attention of the individuals who make and enjoy these micro-spectacles, as it does with the seeming slightness and fragility of the materials with which such enduring effects are constructed – Groot Nibbelink extends her discussion across a wide range of scenography's 'staging strategies' and the principles that underpin them. Her investigation looks at how scenography 'sets parameters for action of all kinds', and how it creates conditions 'through which meaning and experience can emerge'. We are used, perhaps, to thinking of scenography's capacity in the theatre to create other worlds, or to inscribe on stage the settings – the parameters, the conditions – according to which such worlds can be imagined. And indeed, Groot Nibbelink keeps bringing her discussion back to the question: 'In what or which space(s) are we?' Her illustrative example – whose title is also a pun on the French phrase for 'greenhouse effect' (*effet de serre*) – provokes us to draw out the implications of our scenographic adventures taking place 'not out there but at home', implications which, as Groot Nibbelink observes, are both dramaturgical and ecological.

The performing of objects, or of 'setting' – and the sort of autonomous dialogue that can appear to be taking place between a given 'site' or location, and an 'emplaced' scenography – is also a focus of Mike Pearson's chapter, 'How Does Theatre Think Through Things?' It might be said too that the chapter seeks to enact the principle that drives this thinking, namely, 'how things make things happen'. Pearson pursues this principle through writing that is at once as analytically poised as it is rhetorically provocative, following the movement and rhythms – in action and in thought – of the theatrical performance around which the discussion revolves, an adaptation of Homer's epic poem of war, *Iliad*, co-directed by Pearson and Mike Brookes for National Theatre Wales in 2015. In part – and in company with several chapters in this book – the discussion departs from a semiotic approach to the meaning-making potential of objects and things as they are used and encountered in a theatrical framework. As things go on, however – or, keeping the Homeric example in mind, as they appear to clash and meld in a cacophony of meaning, sense and sensation – semiotic interpretation gives way to a series of metaphors, theoretical and poetic figures for thought, that attempt to take on the question, as Pearson puts it, of where to begin and end in assessing the pertinence of things. How to make sense – in the theatre, let alone an actual theatre of war – of 'all that is operating at any one time?' And how to make sense of that 'operating' as an actual agency of 'things'? Things in the sense of material objects, but also less immediately graspable agents such as sites, and experiences, and ideas. How, in the light of such thinking and making, might our own sense of what counts as 'performing' be extended?

Some of the key extensions – historical and contemporary – of performing media, beyond what we might immediately (and traditionally) think of as the live arts of the stage, are explored in Steve Dixon's chapter, 'How Does Theatre Think Through Incorporating Media?' Dixon's argument – like that of DeFrantz earlier in this section – looks beyond a single illustrative example, to examine how analogue and digital recording and projection technologies, such as film and video, have been brought into collaboration across a diverse range of theatrical staging practices, from Chameleons Group (with whom Dixon himself works) through to works by The Wooster Group, Katie Mitchell and Robert Lepage. Key to Dixon's analytical method – and comparable with other approaches in the book (see, for example, the chapters by Groot Nibbelink earlier and Lavery later) – is the establishment of a 'taxonomy', a scheme of classification for concerns, effects or ways of working, through which distinct practices can be compared. It is noticeable from the categories that Dixon brings together – for example, 'the synesthetic pleasure principle', 'semiotics and politics', 'shrinking theatre and expanding cinema' – that the frameworks for 'thinking through' such practices (we can already imagine the relevance of approaches drawn from semiotics, phenomenology, psychoanalysis and visual studies) may be as diverse as the forms of incorporated media themselves. As Dixon goes on to discuss, this diversity is not simply a matter of there being various 'options' for analysis or practice, but rather reflective of a complexity – of ideas, meanings and political messages; of people, events and times; and of distinct orders of reality – that lead into situations of transformation and the emergence of new forms (and new ways of thinking and working).

Broderick Chow's chapter 'How Does the Trained Body Think?' sets out to think through one or two specific experiences of taking on new ways of working, in Chow's own professional and – to the extent that one's body, trained or otherwise, is nothing else but – personal life. His narrative, which starts from a decision to suspend a career as a professional actor in Canada for a period of 'training' overseas, develops into a contestation of a pervasive system of values (which Chow acknowledges he once shared) that would consider the trained body as somehow removed from thinking, and as a vehicle rather for other people's creative use. As Chow notes, this value system also evokes a particular, historical complex of social power relations, which he finds himself studying – and learning to challenge – as he gets involved in specific regimes of physical training for weightlifting and professional wrestling. The doing – and the concomitant thinking – that these training regimes ask of him reveal for him also ways in which 'the body spoke back' to that system of values, whether through a 'politics of friendship' in professional wrestling or a 'community of practice' in weightlifting, whereby one learns to negotiate – through what one does with one's body – how to relate otherwise to the material world, and to the bodies of other people. As Chow puts it, one learns how to think through one's body, and how to value those ways of relating; exploring new, thoughtful and imaginative conceptions of what it means to perform.

The last chapter in this section on performing, Theron Schmidt's 'How Does Theatre Think Through Work?', returns us to the performer who acts for a living, but does so in order to ask immediately what that sort of 'living' – in the sense of professional occupation – might mean from a specifically theatrical perspective, not least, when acting and performing appears to concern itself with the very same question. This was the case in 1960s avant-garde performances that adopted ways of moving – and doing – more readily associated with forms of non-theatrical labour, industrial and domestic. The same sort of question comes up again, if differently inflected, in more recent work that negotiates ways in which certain contemporary forms of labour, for example in the service industries, appear to imitate artistic modes of performing (in the production of experiences, communications, relationality and so on). What is at stake, though, is not simply a similarity of forms, or even a cross-fertilizing of techniques of making and performing ('task-based' devising or 'durational' performance, for instance). Rather, what Schmidt identifies in his discussions of the work of choreographer Yvonne Rainer and performance artist Adrian Howells, are comparable processes of thinking – and performing – in relation to structures of social and political alienation in the world at large, and through experiences of spectatorship and encounter, of distancing and inter-relation, prevalent in the theatre situation in particular.

Part 3: Traces

We may tend to think of theatrical performances as singular events that happen, and then are gone, as if live performance were something that we may well experience intensely but feel incapable of 'grasping' as it passes. However, theatre leaves all sorts of marks and traces, and not just recordings and reports and documents, but also memories, emotions and ideas that continue to do their work in the world when the performance is over. The chapters gathered in this third section are each, in their various ways, concerned with theatre's more long-term or longitudinal existence. And, as questions are explored around documentation and 'impact' and re-enactment and such, it becomes clear that any investigation of theatre's ways of remaining in the world becomes also a consideration of attachments, loyalties, fidelities and responsibilities. In other words, the functioning of theatre as a site where – as we negotiate the traces of actions and events – we reconsider our relation not only to theatre and performance events but to other people. In this section, then, you will find chapters on teaching, politics, love, the ethics of care and remembrance, and much else.

Miguel Escobar Varela's chapter, 'What Is an Intercultural Exchange?', is a personal account of more than a decade's thinking about the possibilities and problems of intercultural work, across theatre making, teaching and – no less crucially – reading, thinking and self-reflection. The specific focus of Escobar Varela's investigation is his long-term interest in, and engagement with, Javanese theatre. His account, however, reaches back to his own setting out from a different part of the world some years ago to study in another cultural setting, and has much to say about the importance for him of the writings of other researchers and practitioners, whose traces in his own thought have been a guiding influence on this journey. He tells of lessons learnt from the work of Rustom Bharucha and Dwight Conquergood, reflections on the sorts of traps that even the most careful and enthusiastic intercultural researcher might fall into, rehearsed again in the present chapter as advice and examples for Escobar Varela's own students and readers, as much as for himself. As such, the chapter serves as a thoughtful reflection on the ethics of intercultural exchange, but also as an encouragement. Escobar Varela acknowledges the sort of 'paralysis' that can come upon us as we encounter the limitations of our knowledge, and as we recognize too the relations of power that inform those limitations. He also, though, warns against ignorance, and against stultifying reluctance to extend our engagements with the world, through informed involvement, study and dialogue.

For many of the chapters of this book, the 'illustrative example' around which the argument is constructed is a performance or theatrical event that has had 'impact' on the author in one way or another. That is the case, for instance, in the previous chapter where Escobar Varela's 'serendipitous' encounter with *wayang kulit* (a form of puppet theatre found in parts of Southeast Asia) provokes a life's engagement. Sruti Bala, in her chapter 'What Is the Impact of Theatre and Performance?', does not frame her example quite in the same way, but rather as a case study for how we might think about a range of impacts, and the several uses that may be made of them. 'Impact' has to do, Bala explains, with the mark, trace or resonance that an event might leave on an environment, beyond the immediate moment of its taking place. The sort of impact that is usually claimed for performance is a positive change brought about in people's lives, and in her discussion of *Afuera: lesbianas en escena* (Outside: Lesbians on Stage) by Teatro Siluetas from El Salvador and Guatemala, Bala discusses how Teatro Siluetas's non-hierarchical form of organization and production, and their foregrounding of lesbian subjectivity, may provoke, among people who encounter the work, all sorts of enabling recognitions, in relation to many interrelated prejudices and oppressions, along with transformative models for doing and thinking. However, Bala is concerned also with the difficulties involved in identifying and assessing impact, and these are not limited to 'methodological' difficulties, for instance, in relating a small number of audience responses to a wider conclusion. It is also important to note that particular forms of impact are inseparable from the agendas of those who have an interest in that impact, and Bala warns against unthinking reproduction of the kinds of 'neoliberal logic' that would value cultural work only for its 'utility' or, ultimately, profitability.

We might think of Tavia Nyong'o's chapter, 'Does Staging Historical Trauma Re-Enact It?', as coming from a different – but complementary – direction on some of the core questions that arise in Sruti Bala's chapter. At the heart of Nyong'o's investigation is a question of how theatre can think of its own responsibility towards the impact it has, both on those who participate in it and those who encounter it as spectators. Reflecting specifically on a student production of Jackie Sibblies Drury's 2014 play, *We Are Proud to Present ...*, Nyong'o considers how theatre might consciously extend its responsibility as regards historically and socially important – but potentially traumatic – material, by offering itself as a 'good enough holding environment' for that material to be negotiated by others. Drury's play involves an interracial theatre group, in a contemporary British or North American context, rehearsing a drama about a genocidal massacre in German colonial Southwest Africa (present-day Namibia) at the turn of the twentieth century. Nyong'o focuses on moments of disturbance in Drury's play as the young actors face up to the actions they must perform, and as he does so he finds himself in a discussion of 'trigger warnings' and art's obligations – or otherwise – to the sensibilities of its participants and consumers. However, Nyong'o does not leave the matter there, but instead – in the company of a line of thinking drawn from psychoanalytic thought – digs into theatre's inherent capacity, as a machinery of make-believe and 'fabulation', to offer itself as a very particular space for thinking through historical realities – of slavery and colonialism – that none of us can afford to be ignorant of, and whose trauma, still, to one extent or another, contributes to our constitution as subjects of history.

Theatrical re-enactment of historical violence, and – as in Nyong'o's chapter – the question of how such re-enactment might 'orient' its participants and spectators, not only in relation to history, but also towards their own political consciousness, is explored further in Jazmin Badong Llana's chapter, 'How Does Theatre Think Through Politics?' Llana's example is the annual site-specific community re-enactment by Teatro Obrero of the police 'massacre' of demonstrators, mainly local sugar industry workers, against state oppression and economic strife in Escalante, in the Philippines in 1985. Rather, though, than offering the example straightforwardly as a case study of 'political theatre', Llana is concerned to ask what sort of conceptions of politics – and of theatre – we would be dealing with if we took the Escalante re-enactment in these lights. Her argument, while recognizing the massacre itself as an event that impacted profoundly on those involved at the time, focuses on the re-enactment as no mere commemoration or representation of the historical event, but 'an event after the event' that generates its own fidelities to an 'idea' of social transformation. These subsequent and self-renewing theatrical manifestations (Llana emphasizes that they do not happen as a matter of course: they involve substantial voluntary commitment and preparation) become occasions, for all involved, for a thinking – an orientation, a 'sharing of the stakes' and a consideration of where one stands, and with whom – in relation both to the past event and in relation to the complexity of the present situation. If the theatre is able to illuminate this present with an 'idea' and an exemplary representational event, then theatre's political potential may still fire up, here and in other places, in ways as yet unimagined.

The section concludes with Heike Roms's chapter 'How and Why Are Performances Documented?', which works through the different forms of documentary traces – videos, still photographs, archival documents, memory, testament and re-imagination – of site-specific performance *Gododdin*, created by Welsh theatre company Brith Gof in collaboration with music group Test Department, and first performed in 1988. We might well, in the context of other chapters in this section, consider these several traces as 'afterlives' of the performance event, although Roms draws attention to how some of the so-called 'traces' – workbooks and set-designs, for instance, collected in the National Museum of Wales archive – relate in fact to the 'before' of the performance. What Roms goes on, then, to pursue in her chapter are the complex modes of temporality – literally, before, during and after – that 'performance documentation' establishes in relation to the performance event, which she aligns both with the specific modes of documentation that *Goddodin* has (so far) generated, and also with the development of the scholarly performance documentation debate (questions of competing literacies, of mediation, of liveness and repertoire and reproducibility of performance and the politics of the archive, pursued across the work of a number of key authors in the field). This is a debate, Roms notes, that emerged around the same time that *Gododdin* was first staged, in the late 1980s, just on the cusp of the 'digital turn'. It would be a question then – to take just one example of the issues that Roms's chapter raises – how the potentials of digital culture, unforeseen in *Gododdin*'s 'own' time, might impact on the work's continued life in the world, for those who were 'there at the time' and for the increasing number – students of performance, for instance – who were not. Pulled between these various temporalities, what sort of thing might a performance be understood to be?

Part 4: Interventions

The fourth and last section of the book considers theatre, dance, image-making and other modes of performance in specific relation to some of the larger worlds and contexts in which they have their being. These contexts include particular theatre- and performance art-relevant institutions – cultural institutions, most obviously – but also social, political, environmental and economic structures and frameworks. Several of the chapters in this section investigate ways in which theatrical performance might 'intervene' in these structures, to analyse, represent and critically reveal them, even contribute to transforming them. It is noticeable too, in this section, that several of the chapters look to 'historical' materials, events and performances from the past, to illuminate action and thinking in one's own time. Just as often, however, the authors of these chapters draw attention to ways in which, for instance, forms of 'theatrical' framing function as devices for maintaining and consolidating power, and not only in the present moment. In this and other respects, it may not just be the performance that brings about a looked-for intervention, but our own involvement – as spectators, participants, makers, performers, students and citizens – in those environments that constitute us and which we ourselves constitute.

The first chapter in this section, Dominic Johnson's 'How Can Performance Disrupt Institutional Spaces?', investigates a series of unauthorized – mainly illegal – interventions by artist Christopher D'Arcangelo in a number of major museums and galleries in the mid-1970s. Johnson draws attention to a modern history of such interventions since the 1960s and, to an extent, renewed in the present day, but goes back to D'Arcangelo's actions in particular for an example – an instructive, an exemplary instance – of how performance art can, as Johnson puts it, 'retain a glimmer of subterfuge'. Given the nature of D'Arcangelo's critical relation to cultural institutions, his early death, and the small amount of documentation of his work, Johnson's return to the archives for what can be found out and understood, enacts his own methodological intervention into the sorts of stories – art and performance histories – that have been considered worth telling and learning from. For the scholar–historian Johnson, who was not even born when D'Arcangelo took his actions into the Guggenheim and the Museum of Modern Art in New York, the anarchist artist D'Arcangelo becomes a kind of companion to help him think through the deeper assumptions that govern what we allow ourselves to say, think and do in places such as these. As this investigation is pursued, other attendant questions follow, some of which have continued to be asked since the birth of the avant-garde in the early-twentieth century, including the seeming unavailability of (some) art works for other, everyday uses, and the emancipatory potential of performance more broadly.

The extension of theatre, art and performance into the wider social and political culture, and thus also into the living – and dying – material world of nature in which and from which these practices have their being (earth and animal nature, but also machine nature, physical and phenomenal and mental nature), is addressed further in Carl Lavery's chapter, 'How Does Theatre Think Through Ecology?' The question that drives the investigation – as with other chapters in this section, and several throughout the book – is political, although it is not the direct politics of ecocritical messages or interventionist environmental actions. Lavery focuses rather on 'ecological images' – they could be images that appeal to the senses of touch, taste, thinking and hearing, as much as to the eyes – that engage or catalyse our sense of ourselves as parts of, and participants in, what he refers to as the 'dizzying adventure of matter'. Through what sort of performance images might we understand better how to exist on earth – to be alive in the world – without turning the world to either destruction or profit? Lavery's instructive example of how theatre images can operate ecologically is a 2008 work by Mike Brookes and Rosa Casado, *Some Things Happen All At Once*, which substitutes ice sculptures for human beings as the principal objects of attention, and places the spectators in a sensate – we might say calorific, literally heat-generating – relation to the materiality of the stage picture. An attendant 'impact' of such images may be to provoke in us a new set of considerations of performance's relation to anthropocentric ideas of history and time.

Questions of how theatre and performance think their relations – both historically and immediately – to the wider social order, are taken in a different direction in Bojana Cvejić's chapter 'How Does Choreography Think "through" Society?' There are resonances in Cvejić's argument with Johnson's discussion of the separation of art works and practices from objects and actions in everyday life, and also with Lavery's engagement of a pre-linguistic, 'sensate' form of perception as a ground for thinking through how we as humans inter-relate with our environment (or as Cvejić refers to it, with a more specifically social inflection, milieu). Cvejić proposes we consider a 'kinaesthetic continuum', a continuity of physicalized thinking and learning that – rather than observing an institutionalized or sacralized distinction between art and non-art activities – ranges from dancing to everyday life. She also notes choreography's potential to draw upon 'common', shared human capacities – the capacities to think and to speak, for instance – that underpin and exist between and beyond our formation as individuals or as groups, and which may inform our capacity to think, speak and – above all – embody the social differently. Cvejić's illustrative example is a work called *9x9*, developed in 2007 by Christine De Smedt alongside several other choreographers, to be performed by large groups of voluntary participants in public places, as a flexible device to explore models of social organization as gatherings of bodies in space. The 'choreography' is not so much predetermined, as it is composed of questions and tasks, to which the participants respond in real time. This is a choreography, Cvejić notes, that not only thinks and shows the social gathering in alternative ways (for instance, as collaborative action rather than stratified 'identity'), but also allows it to be seen and known differently (as felt proximity and live visibility rather than stored as governmental or marketing data). As such, performance thinking lends itself to other images and other uses for the images of ourselves we are able to perform.

The role of theatricality and the power of performance – let alone the performance of power – in public life outside the theatre, is taken up by Sophie Nield in her chapter, 'How

Does Theatricality Legitimize the Law?' Not unlike Johnson's chapter earlier in this section, Nield's chapter is built around a historical case study, the notorious 1969–70 courtroom trial in the United States of political protestors known as the Chicago Eight. Again, as in Johnson's chapter, the historical example is used to illustrate – and to think through – questions of social structure and relations of power more generally. Here, though, Nield's concern is not so much the extension of theatre and performance 'into' public life, as with the ways that social institutions, such as law and the justice system, sustain their authority – their social legitimacy, if you will – by means of a theatricality that is entirely their own. She focuses on two moments from the trial: one, a performance-based intervention by some of the defendants that played mockingly upon the court's own seemingly less nimble theatricality; the other, an incident in which the violence that underwrites the law's authority, and which its theatricality may be supposed merely to symbolize or even disavow, became immediately and starkly actual and apparent. As Nield suggests, we may be inclined to think of theatre as a mode of representation merely, its truths not 'really' true, its violence a pretend, its consequences ultimately inconsequential. The law, however, to the extent that it makes 'present' what it 'represents', operates rather differently. And perhaps, after all, seen in these lights, the theatre does too.

That last line of thought is taken up in the final chapter of this section, and of the book, Adrian Kear's 'How Does Theatre Think Through Theatricality?' Kear brings some of the questions opened in Nield's chapter – around, for instance, the function of theatricality as an operation of power – back to the actual theatre. We can also, though, note resonances with other chapters earlier in this book: for instance, with Bleeker's reflections on what the spectator sees being dependent on how the theatre 'focalizes' their way of seeing, or with Nyong'o's consideration of the theatre as a 'good enough holding environment' for representations of difficult, even traumatic, experiences that contribute towards our constitution as subjects and as citizens. For Kear, as for Nield, theatricality is polyvalent; it can have different functions and uses, both in the service of authority and as interventions against it. Specifically, though, Kear focuses upon processes of theatricalization, which involve turning people into figures in a scene, whether those people experience themselves as being 'staged' or not. He follows this process through the kind of right-wing populism associated with the US president at the time of writing, Donald Trump; but also through an authoritarian father's catastrophic theatricalizing of his daughters' professions of love in Shakespeare's *King Lear*; and finally through contemporary performance collective She She Pop's restaging of *Lear* – and the parental relation, in the onstage company of their fathers – in their 2010 work *Testament*. Kear's proposal in this chapter is to prise theatre and theatricality apart from each other, and to consider the actual theatre as a place where the slippery operations of theatricality can be made visible, studied and thought through. The need for such places has not left us, yet.

Conclusion: Making Thinking

We said this book begins with questions. It ends perhaps in the same way; or rather, it does not end but begins again – begins for the first time – in the hands of its readers and *their* questions. *Thinking Through Theatre and Performance* offers itself as a companion to study.

It shows and tells, it explains and demonstrates and – in the words of one of its authors – 'shares the stakes' with its readers. It seeks to guide – and also to provoke in its readers – an active process of thinking through theatre, which it does by introducing fundamental topics, questions, issues and their attendant modes of enquiry as these have been opened up by theatre and performance studies in recent years. Its objects of study remain the 'material practices' of theatre and performance. Yet the book seeks to show, along the way, that its modes of enquiry – from the semiosis of accessibility and the representation of economic systems, through the 'methodology of all things' and the thinking that is particular to the physically trained body, from re-enactment and the politics of theatre's 'event' through social choreography and the vicissitudes of theatricality – are in themselves material practices, critical, transformative and creative ways of thinking with, and through, theatre and performance events. It is not a matter of drawing out and giving precedence to the critical operation over the making of scenes and performances. Indeed, rather than abstracting 'theory' or regarding it as separate from 'practice', this book insists on the need to approach theatre and performance as modes of 'theoretical practice' in their own rights, but which nonetheless require critical elaboration. That elaboration – as readers of the book will discover for themselves – looks within theatre practice, aiming to meet its provocations on their own terms, but also to performative contexts beyond the limits of the theatre itself. It is on the horizon of that beyond that this introduction – at least – concludes, while the book itself begins: not, lest there be any mistake, to look beyond theatre for something more interesting out there, but to come back with renewed intellectual and creative resources to some of the questions that we have been asking of theatre – and which theatre and performance have been asking of themselves – all along, for the sake of a world that is always asking new questions of us as to what it means to be alive in it; and to provoke in the readers of this book, with whom we share this world, their own urgent and necessary investigative enquiries.

References

Edkins, Jenny, and Maja Zehfuss, eds (2013), *Global Politics: A New Introduction*, London and New York: Routledge.

Ingold, Tim (2011), *Being Alive: Essays on Movement, Knowledge and Description*, London and New York: Routledge.

Part 1 Watching

1   Why Study Drama?

JOE KELLEHER

Approaching the Questions

It is a spring evening in 2017 and I am at the theatre with a group of students. We are there to watch a play. We aren't the only ones. London's Old Vic, a nineteenth-century proscenium arch playhouse and a venerable and thriving theatre institution, just south of the River Thames in the centre of the city (it was the National Theatre of Great Britain's first home through the 1960s and much of the 1970s, and remains an important producing theatre), is packed this evening with student groups of all ages. There is something of a festive, anticipatory feeling to the evening, perhaps because it is the last week of term for many of us, just a couple of days before the Easter break. I imagine, though, the excitement also involves the fact that one of the lead actors in the production is Daniel Radcliffe, the star of the *Harry Potter* film series, and many people are looking forward to seeing him perform, as it were, in person. Anyway, here we all are – students, teachers and everyone else holding a ticket – to follow a play and to enjoy our time. And this suits me fine because I have recently been considering how to approach this essay you are now reading, about ways in which theatre and performance think through writing for the stage. I have been coming around to the view that it is not just the writing (so to speak, words on the page and words on the stage) I should be concerned with, but also the 'thinking through', as such. Or, if you will, the studying: its modes, and how it involves us. And what it is that it involves us in. On this score, the evening's programme looks like it might be instructive.

Irrespective of the famous actor in the cast, the play we are attending is well-known, having been popular on stage over the past half century (this production happens to be its fiftieth-anniversary revival), and – judging by the number of study-guides thrown up by an online search – a regular set text in recent decades in school and university classrooms. From that, via Harry Potter's school days, to the prominent student audience attending this evening, the 'study' theme is already growing on me, but there is more. Tom Stoppard's *Rosencrantz and Guildenstern Are Dead* was given its debut professional production by the National Theatre Company at the Old Vic in 1967, but was first performed in a shorter version by the student company Oxford Theatre Group a year earlier at the Edinburgh Festival Fringe. And, although Stoppard himself was not a university student – he finished formal education in his teens to work as a trainee journalist (Nadel 2004: 52–3) – I find myself thinking of the work as a 'student play', of sorts. *Rosencrantz and Guildenstern Are Dead* is, after all, a kind of experimental study of another, earlier and altogether canonical drama – one of the most-studied dramas in the Western tradition – William Shakespeare's

Hamlet. And the theme goes further. In *Hamlet*, Rosencrantz and Guildenstern are a couple of minor characters, acquaintances of the eponymous prince, maybe fellow students of his at university in Germany (Hamlet calls them 'my two schoolfellows'). In Stoppard's drama, as in Shakespeare's, they arrive at the Danish court to spy on the prince, who apparently has been behaving oddly, and to report on him to his mother and stepfather, the king and queen of Denmark. In short, there is a purpose, a project to their studies. Something they can feel called upon to do. However, they are not particularly successful spies. They hover and dither at the edge of events, clinging onto things as best they can, speaking modern English between themselves, but then running into fragments of scenes from *Hamlet* whenever the reality of the important people at court coincides – which it appears to do rather randomly – with their own. Things, then, for Rosencrantz and Guildenstern, are rather vague and confusing. Nevertheless, in contrast to their come-and-go peripheral status in Shakespeare's drama, they remain determinedly in place on Stoppard's stage. It is there, in the course of events, that they encounter a travelling theatre group who are also on their way to court (the same group of tragedians who appear in Shakespeare's play, although in Stoppard's version, the economic insecurity of the Elizabethan players is rendered more explicit). It is also from the stage that they, Rosencrantz and Guildenstern, make their claim on our (the audience's) attention, as they think through their predicament. Which is to say, as they attempt to interpret an ongoing drama that may – or may not – have something to do with them; or some part that they themselves can play in it. If ever they could work out what that is.

And how do they pursue this study? By doing the sorts of things that the students who are accompanying me to the theatre this evening are themselves already expert in. That is to say, Stoppard's protagonists take up positions – often near the stage curtains at the edge of the proscenium – from which to view the action, and they pay careful attention to what is happening. They ask questions, of the situation and of each other (they even have a competitive question-asking game that they use to pass the time, with which they hone their question-asking technique). They discuss matters between themselves (their dialogue really is one long study group). They revise their hypotheses, adjust their presumptions somewhat. They sometimes, when called upon – but also on their own initiative – get 'practically' involved, they dirty their hands, they devise scenarios and try them out, they experiment with action. Sometimes they get somewhere, or seem to; sometimes not. And then they return to their primary method: asking questions, all sorts of questions.

These include the fundamental, orienting questions. Where are we? What's going on? What does the situation want from me? What is to be done? But alongside more disinterested enquiry, there are also questions of self-interest, such as we might ask ourselves. What are we in it for? What do *we* want from *it*? Employment? Enjoyment? Wisdom? Knowledge? Are we here to *change* the situation, or try to? Will the situation change *us*? Money is involved, of course, from the very first scene, which they spend tossing a coin, again and again, betting which side it will land on, heads or tails. Famously, it keeps landing on the same side. As if the result were already written, rather than happening, well, as things happen, predictably, by seeming random chance. They attempt a theoretic-analytic-logical study of the matter ('If we postulate, and we just have, that within un-, sub- or supernatural forces, *the probability* is that … ' [Stoppard 1968: 12]). This does not get them very far, although it chimes from the off with accumulating intuitions about power and survival and responsibility, and action both of thought and deed; and about whose thoughts and deeds count for something, and whose do not; and about whose lines are already written for them and who – if anyone – gets to write their own. Meanwhile, there are a lot of jokes (Stoppard's play is a comedy), just as there are in Shakespeare's play (which is supposed to be a tragedy), some of which may be designed to deflect attention from more difficult reckonings, and some of which crack right into those reckonings, although it isn't always clear which type of joke is which, or if indeed there really is a difference. What does seem to be the case is that many of the most telling jokes (we may share an example later) have to do with being in – or attending upon – a drama, at the theatre, on one side of the stage–audience divide or another. Which, departing from the premise that what a good joke does is operate a switch between different perspectives or understandings, pulling up the roots of something to repair that same something with different roots altogether, might fashion us with a blunt methodological procedure for taking our thinking a little further 'through'.

What sort of a thing is a play or drama? Let us take the question back a step and ask: what sort of object is a 'thing'? It may sound a rather abstruse enquiry, although perhaps not if we are talking about Stoppard's *Rosencrantz and Guildenstern Are Dead*, which we shall continue to do a little while longer. To borrow a thought from outside the field of drama – but useful to our purpose, I hope – contemporary philosopher Tristan Garcia proposes that there are 'two senses of things: *that which is in a thing* and *that in which a thing is*, or that which it comprehends and that which comprehends it' (Garcia 2014: 11). As he argues, a thing 'is nothing other than the *difference* between being-inside and being-outside'. What could that mean for us? I warned that my own procedure would (unlike Garcia's, or Stoppard's) be pretty blunt, but consider a typical theatre situation – a performance of a famous play at London's Old Vic, for instance – and the ways in which that situation appears to be divided between everything that is in the drama, and everything that the drama is in. And yes, I am partly thinking of the divide between stage and auditorium, between those who act, or pretend to act, and those who study them doing so; a relation, of sorts, that can also feel like a structure of exclusion, even as it includes us in what is going on. Or so it appears when the divide is replicated in Stoppard's meta-theatrical drama (and Shakespeare's), and fatally so: Rosencrantz and Guildenstern, remember, 'are dead', and have been since we first learnt their names. So, what then does the drama 'comprehend', of itself or anything else? I would suggest our answer to this is, firstly, anything that we are capable of observing or interpreting of it: its sense of its own accomplishment, its dramaturgical strategies, its jokes, its pathos, its cleverness and – no less – its play with bewilderment and vulnerability. It's another thing that the jokes do: they tell it how it is before we have a chance to. 'At least we can still count on self-interest as a predictable factor ... I suppose it's the last to go' (Stoppard 1968: 9). Which is to say, the play comprehends us as well, and comprehends the redundancy of everything we might say that it already says about itself.

As for grasping 'that in which this thing is' (Garcia 2014: 13), we might look to the casting of Daniel Radcliffe as a kind of prospective reaching, on the part of the production, towards other relations, other forces, that would enter the theatre in unforeseeable ways: in this instance, to do with personal and collective associations on the part of audience members outside the world of the play – memories of seeing or reading those Harry Potter stories, as much as with a complex global entertainment economy that 'comprehends' this performance taking place in a 1,000-seater London theatre without, as it were, giving it too much of a second thought. As it is, though, I had a different instance in mind. The twenty-ninth of March 2017, the date I went to the Old Vic theatre with the students to see the revival of Stoppard's play, also happened to be the day on which British Prime Minister Theresa May, in the wake of a national referendum on the matter, triggered Article 50 – actually, Article 50(2) – of the Treaty on European Union, giving formal notification of the United Kingdom's intention to leave the European Union. Suffice it to say, in the country where myself and many friends, family members, colleagues and students live and work, this macropolitical situation – commonly referred to by the shorthand term 'Brexit' – has been a cause of much debate and concern: over questions of citizenship, economics, the exercise of democracy and structures – and fantasies – of social and cultural identity; let alone questions of violence and exclusion and our capacities for communal sympathy, and the seeming limits of those capacities, and of historical and futural imagining in twenty-first-century Britain.

All of this, of course, has little enough to do with a fiftieth-anniversary revival of Tom Stoppard's first play. Even so, as I watched the Old Vic production, I found myself remembering the period in my life when Stoppard's work was most important to me – he may even have been the first playwright I read – which was when I was still at school, in my early teens, maybe younger; an eager student, in the early to mid-1970s, around the time (1973) that Britain joined the European Community. Which – I suspect – was before the time when I would have been able to recognize Stoppard as a 'European' playwright, to spot the debts owed to the mid-twentieth-century 'Absurdist' playwrights (Esslin 1980), or the tribute implicitly paid to works such as Samuel Beckett's 1953 play *Waiting for Godot* (of which, more later). As I say, the one has nothing to do with the other. How could it indeed? But now I find myself thinking through, again, the sort of questions being raised by Stoppard's hapless heroes: What time is it? Where are we? What is going on? How does this involve us? What are we supposed to be doing? What is to be done? And I wonder what questions my students might want to ask tomorrow.

A Contemporary Example: *Nothing,* Much

How might these sorts of questions arise from – and inform the study of – a contemporary drama? We go from one debut work to another, keeping the student theme with us for a while. Barrel Organ Theatre's first show, *Nothing*, was performed in 2014 at Warwick University in the UK where the company members were students, and then at the UK National Student Drama Festival in Scarborough, with professional runs later that same year at the Edinburgh Festival Fringe and at Camden People's Theatre in North London, which is where I saw the work. The script for *Nothing*, authored by one of Barrel Organ Theatre's founder members, Lulu Raczka ('with additional material by the Company'), is published by Oberon Modern Plays (Raczka 2014: 3). It is, then, a drama, for sure, although the work in performance – a collection of spoken monologues woven together rhythmically, compositionally by the individual performers – struck this spectator as being not so much a 'play' 'put on' by a theatre company, but rather something song-related, like the work of a band, with songwriter credits where the author's name would go. As it is, when we arrive at the theatre there is little indication of what sort of work – or event – to expect. Camden People's Theatre is a small-scale studio, and the set-up for *Nothing* has very little of a traditional theatre about it: none of the fixed seating, raised stage and proscenium curtains of the Old Vic. We enter a bare room with some scattered chairs, a seminar or workshop room, perhaps. We each take a chair and sit, facing any direction. At some point, a young person among us stands and starts speaking a text; the work has begun. I am there with a friend, another male middle-aged theatre professor, and like a latter-day Rosencrantz and Guildenstern, the only thing we know for sure about who might be 'in' the show is that it isn't either of us. We do not know who will stand up and speak next, or how many speakers there will be. It turns out, eventually, there are eight monologues, each representing an un-named character, spoken at us from various places in the room. The performers have the licence to move around, to interrupt each other, to go back on bits and to repeat sections, to do whatever it takes to put their own monologue across, while collaborating with each other – the performers in the room – to shape the collective event for the present occasion. This means that although the actual words remain unchanged, the pattern of the speeches will fall differently every time that *Nothing* is performed.

I can't help analysing as I watch and listen. It strikes me there are various kinds of thinking at work in this theatre. Alongside the prior work of authoring, directing, devising, rehearsing – to speak schematically: the actuality is doubtless more complex, less distinct – there is the 'live' thinking of the actors, the interpreters of the text at the point of performance: making decisions, performing inflections, structuring pause and emphasis and repetition for the sake of sense, of rhythm, of musicality, to draw attention to the saying, and what is said. There is also, no less live and no less 'productive' (of sense, of meaning, of significance), the thinking of those whose attention is being engaged: the spectators, the audience, who follow what goes on, anticipating, assimilating, pulling together associations, making something of it, something we can take away. And then there is the thinking represented in the monologues themselves, each of which involves a kind of testimony, a story being told: about something that happened, and which is – to the extent that someone is thinking of it, speaking of it – happening still. The characters in Raczka's script are young adults, the same age as the performers, in their early twenties, I would say. They speak of ordinary life. One talks of her 'friend', a 'girl', still in hospital after a violent street attack by a 'guy' she was with. The words she uses – girl, guy, friend – are colloquial and at the same time abstract, as if sketching out a generality, a replaceability of social relations. The speaker's revenge fantasy on behalf of her friend, with which her monologue closes, is an imaginary act of violence – pornographic, brutal – that forgets about the girl in hospital altogether, while evoking – perhaps; it is barely a glimmer – a kind of grief and vicarious tenderness – 'He starts to cry and the guy just licks the tears away' (17) – that could be for any of them: the girl, the guy, herself. In another story, a lonely, irritable young man, walking home at night across the city after an unsatisfactory evening crashing an eighteenth birthday party, comes across a boy in an alley whose leg appears to have been cut off, below the knee. 'I was standing in it. The blood' (22). What to do? Or, how to make something of it? 'How do you tell people this? It's not like it happened to me – I don't have anything to do with it – But I am – I am involved – I just went home' (24). Another speaker, devotee of a rather self-serving sort of positivity – 'Films – They reaffirm my life' (24) – makes ill-considered attempts to connect with – or to disavow the extent to which he is disturbed by – a friend who is hospitalized with depression. 'I bought flowers – I'm just trying to decide whether that's lame' (30). In another monologue, a girl tells us of her hard-core pornography habit. She is also unimpressed with the 'opportunities' available to her. Jobs, for instance. She tells us she told her mum that 'at the moment I felt like I was throwing everything I had into a void. And it didn't seem like a fair exchange. And I think she kind of agreed'. But the point on the map being zoomed in on here is, seemingly, a small one. 'To be honest – I think I just need to hang out with my friends more' (34–5). In the last monologue of the published text a recently graduated student tells us of the next-to-nothing that is happening in their life (the script does not specify a gender). 'I imagine being middle-aged and having nothing is worse than having nothing now.' As with the others, the monologue keeps coming back to failures, absences of social connection. The thinking, for what it's worth, attempts to focus there, but as it does so, it drifts again into self-objectification, dramatizing an isolated self that can only break off, unfinished, uncontinued: 'I have never been able to relate. This is not an experience I understand. I've thought about someone screaming at me' (58).

So, what is the drama, the theatre – Raczka's drama, Barrel Organ's theatre, our theatre too now that we are there – doing with all this? As we have noted already, there is a fair amount of thinking – of study – going on, not only in the characters' self-examination (which, for all the distraction, disavowal, and numbed indifference involved, is still what the stories amount to), but also in the analytical, critical and political thinking that arises, as it were, from the drama itself. Of the latter, we might speak of the attention that is brought to the social atomization of young people's lives in places like twenty-first-century Britain, and the kinds of failures of agency – political or otherwise – that belong to that reality. But what could it mean to think of this criticality as arising 'from the drama itself'? Does it make any sense, really, to speak of how a drama 'thinks'? We could approach the question by observing that there are two images, or two scenes, happening at the same time in Barrel Organ's *Nothing*. They appear to be contradictory, but they depend on each other. At the level of the drama, the fiction, the represented actions, what we have is a composite image of young individuals who are, in all sorts of ways, isolated and lost: lost in resentment, in bewilderment, in various forms of numbed indifference, and for the most part in a kind of poverty that is as much about deprivation of imagination and sympathy and hope as it is about more tangible material resources. It is noticeable too that this drama, as far as the characters' words reveal it, is built around images, anecdotes, phrases and vocabulary that have about them something of the second-hand, the reused, the paltry and – as mentioned already – the pornographic. Perhaps all our languages are, ultimately, of that order; but here it appears part of the problem.

Meanwhile, at the level of the theatre, we participate in another scene entirely, or so it seems. This second scene is of a group, again young people, in a sense the *same* young people, but now they are together in the same room. They are a company of actors engaged in a careful and nuanced collaboration, which they share with others – listeners, spectators, attenders – who can be depended upon to bring their patience, their curiosity, their capacity for sympathetic engagement and informed critical reflection with them to the occasion. And indeed, it is a privilege to be there, not least to be taking pleasure in the pull that the writing makes on *my* imagination, between the already-happened, the witnessed, the told, and a still unfinished telling that is going on right now. And might we not, on the basis of such privilege, be inclined to suppose that this recursive showing and telling 'redeems' the drama somewhat, that its political force – or its efficacy, if you like – is to gather these already-written (already written off?), asocial and unproductive types into the more optimistic embrace of a collective and (while we are at it) intellectual practice, something like the one we are witnessing now? But then again, consider the ways in which the image of theatrical collaboration is pulled apart, tugged at and unravelled, every time, by the very material that makes up its weave. Simply put, these are voices that refuse to cooperate, that resist the redemption on offer. And was not the drama written to teach us this, first of all, and then again, and again?

Or put it this way. What the drama 'comprehends', to recall the term we were using earlier, would be all of the above, and much more. That is, it can feel as if anything that we – you, me or any others – might have to say about the work, were already understood by the work itself, already part of everything that is 'in' it: even if that everything, ultimately, finds expression in words spoken *outside* the theatre. Critic Catherine Love's concise reflection on the one-word title to Barrel Organ's theatrical debut captures, I think, the comprehensiveness of the drama's self-understanding, and the ways in which this understanding goes beyond the form and content of the drama, towards its context of production and indeed the future lives of its producers. 'The single word', she argues:

> suggests a void – emotional, ideological, physical. It is also a fierce reference to the current political landscape, in more ways than one: faced with disappearing funding, young companies such as Barrel Organ are forced to quite literally do something with nothing, while nothing is equally a fair description of what these students and recent graduates might feel the world holds for them. (Love 2014)

But if the drama already comprehends so much, what then would it be that comprehends the drama in turn? Or, to put that another way, what is it that the drama *does not know*? I suggest that the answer is not to be found in a *more*-embracing understanding: that of a director, say, or another critic, or an academic commentator, or I don't know how many spectator students. My suggestion, rather, is that what comprehends the drama is that which reaches out from it, as the expression of a predicament: a predicament of felt insignificance, of ignorance and stupidity even. But not so insignificant that it can't provoke a number of significant questions. They are the same sorts of questions as before, re-tooled for the current instance: Where are we? What sort of history am I in? What would count as an action here? What am I called on to do or think? Or, to stick with the actual questions right in front of us, on the page and in the room: 'Why would I be friends with her if she wasn't fun?' (12), and 'What if this happened to me?' (13). Or, 'I didn't ask anything – I – Why would I?' (23). Or, 'He always says the point of films is to wake us up – From what?' (25). Or, 'Get yourself out there! Ask someone out! Go on! And I just think – Who?' (56). Just for starters.

Approaches to Study

Let's broaden the view. What I want to do for a moment is focus more generally on approaches to the study of writing in theatre, as set out in a couple of recently-published books on the topic. I should emphasize that my interest here is indeed at the level of 'approaches to study', rather than with select theoretical lines of thought emerging from the work we have been looking at so far. However, it is worth noting that both of the books under discussion have extensive introductions that draw attention to significant academic debates around the often-contested relations between text and performance in the modern theatre. These include – to give only the briefest thumbnail sketch of the sort of issues involved – questions of the politics of theatrical meaning making, of literary authorship and the collaborative and multimedia practices more typical of theatrical production; or related historical questions, such as the late-twentieth-century emergence of 'postdramatic' theatrical forms; or – again, interrelated – epistemological questions (to do with ways of knowing and understanding) around immediacy and 'presence' in theatrical and other live arts in relation to writing's supposed tendency towards fixity and predetermined repetition. I indicate some of the sources for following up on these debates in the recommendations for further reading accompanying this chapter, and several of these issues will come into play in what follows. Again, though, my concern for now is with procedures and frameworks for putting these and other questions to work, and how different approaches might cast a particular light, not only on the thinking going on in the drama, but on the kind of thinking that the drama then finds itself 'in'.

Duška Radosavljević's 2013 book *Theatre-Making: Interplay Between Text and Performance in the 21st Century* situates 'writing' – the writing of plays, or writing for performance – among a number of other theatre-making processes: 'devising, directing, designing, performing and even dramaturging'. As she says, this is intended to place emphasis on 'the process (of making) rather than on the text', and as an acknowledgement of the recent trend towards 'multi-professionalization' in Western European theatre-making contexts (Radosavljević 2013: 22). The focus on processes of theatrical production, on the cultural–geographical contexts in which that production takes place, and – significantly – the cross-cultural and genealogical (relating to lines of 'family descent') connections between specific theatrical productions, becomes crucial to establishing the sort of object that the drama – a term which has much less currency in Radosavljević's account than words such as 'dramaturgy', or 'piece' or 'work' – is taken to be. Frequently, in her analyses, she begins by considering the immediate reception – as recorded in mainstream and online theatre criticism – of particular works, thereby situating the pieces in terms of their contribution to current issues of public concern, and the impact of those concerns on practices of theatre -making as such. As such, she draws attention not only to comparable methods of working in the theatre, locally and internationally, but to changing histories and traditions, noting how 'previously segregated authorial practices' are being brought into new combinations and alliances in response to specific 'economic, educational and epistemological conditions'. Radosavljević characterizes her work – her approach to study, we might say – ultimately as an 'act of recognition', a recognition that 'extends' not only to 'specific cultural and genealogical differences that influence working practices in particular contexts', but also to ways in which twenty-first-century theatre might 'emancipate itself' from inherited models of practice and analysis, 'to make history on its own terms' (2013: 196). The work of a company such as Barrel Organ, then, might be understood – with regard to the transformation of its representation of socially-atomized young people in 'Austerity Britain' into an innovative and, in one way or another, economical image of collaborative theatrical attention – as an example of that sort of emancipatory theatre-history-making.

Without necessarily contradicting that view, the discussion is taken in another direction by Julia Jarcho's 2017 book, *Writing and the Modern Stage: Theater Beyond Drama*. Jarcho's arguments will help us to think further about the written text's potential negation of the theatrical image, that apparently affirmative image of presence and attendance and togetherness that I was evoking earlier in relation to the performance of Raczka's *Nothing*. Although Jarcho focuses mainly on North American examples, one chapter in her book is dedicated to a study of the Irish author and playwright Samuel Beckett, who we have mentioned briefly already. Jarcho writes of how the characters in Beckett's dramatic texts, such as *Waiting for Godot*, seem to resist incorporation into live performance, as if seeking to escape the theatrical 'here and now' in which they – and also us, their audiences – are inextricably fixed, embedded and presented to view. She refers to 'a text that doesn't want to be performed' (Jarcho 2017: 71), or to lines spoken on stage that sound as if they belong to a 'still-unstaged script' and which 'declare their independence from that scene' (76). It is as if there were a contest – and a rather desperate contest at that – being played out between an increasingly assertive theatrical actuality, and a writing or a speaking that would be anywhere else but. Jarcho writes of how 'the shared here-and-now becomes more palpable than ever in the face of a language that, as it were, dies trying to escape it' (77). And, in getting at what is at stake in her argument, she cites the Beckett scholar Jonathan Kalb on what we might call the *predicament* of Beckett's characters, who 'can only ever be where they are, as they are; they have no "other parts" to play. In this theatre of what *cannot be otherwise*, actuality consumes the possible' (Jarcho 2017: 79, original emphasis; Kalb 1989: 47). We might recall the predicament of Stoppard's characters, in the play we visited earlier; and also – I would suggest – Raczka's characters. The point being that the 'actuality' referred to, which 'consumes' the possibility of alternative realities, is first and foremost a theatrical actuality: no matter how this extends to existential, sociological and political actualities in the world beyond the drama. As Jarcho goes on to argue, the point with respect to Beckett's dramas, the experiential problem that the plays address, is that posed by 'a monstrous persistence of the dramatic – or rather, by the perception that drama's absolute present is true to a certain modern experience of the world' (82). In this, she is echoing the mid-twentieth-century philosopher Theodor W. Adorno, whom she acknowledges as the major theoretical influence on her work, who writes of a certain enforced negation of possibility – possibilities of thought, of imagination, of radical action – in social life more generally. When Adorno writes of how 'attainable possibility' appears to present itself to people as 'radically impossible … compelling them to identify with this impossibility and make this impossibility into their own affair' – or, as Jarcho refers to it: 'the ferocity with which we have learned to attack our own longing for a different world' – then Raczka's characters don't appear to be too far away (Bloch and Adorno 1988: 4; Jarcho 2017: 82). Where Jarcho's arguments go from here – not least in her study of late-twentieth-century and early-twenty-first century writing for the theatre – is towards ways in which theatre art might attempt, as it were, to negate the negation; and how, in this context, dramatic writing might function as 'a disruptive theatrical force in its own right', not so much by 'presenting an alternative world' but rather by 'variously attacking, exploding, hyperbolizing and contesting the present as such' (xiii). For Jarcho, this is nothing less than a utopian project, aimed at escaping the 'experience' of the present, to the extent that this experience 'threatens to affirm *what is* at the expense of any radical alterity' (13, original emphasis). As she writes, it is 'a utopian desire to negate the present [that] lures writers to the theatre, and opens theatre up to writing' (8).

And as for how this thinking might help us with our study of Barrel Organ's *Nothing*? Well, there is no lack of negativity in Raczska's dramatic monologues: 'Nothing happens to me – Ever. I'd go further than that. I'd say that nothing has ever happened to me' (Raczka 2014: 54). By the same account, what the monologues do – if only by virtue of their form and structure as reflexive testimony – is they rehearse a thinking. Further, they play out as a series of attempts to think 'through', however it may be that these attempts are largely stymied, forestalled, dead-ended; as if 'radical alterity' – to borrow a phrase – were a thin, thin atmosphere, barely breathable in whatever world, whatever language these young people live their lives. We might, then, make another observation, that what these monologues largely concern themselves with are infelicities of performance: actions, gestures, attempts at involvement or communication or basic human connection that one way or another prove themselves ineffective, 'lame', enervating, pointless, self-defeating, ridiculous. As if – to borrow another formulation from Jarcho – what the characters are each coming around to recognizing is the extent to which their performance of themselves is '*too insistently* immersed' in the reality – the live and present reality, so to speak – 'that (not only has produced it, but) is producing it' (19). At the level of the drama that is a social, historical reality. Here in the room, where the drama is being played out – a little differently than the last time or the next, but essentially the same drama – it is a theatrical reality, and one in which the incapacity of performance to generate, from its immersion in the real life, some 'determinate negation of what exists' (19) is being constantly underscored. By the writing, no less; which has only just started 'thinking through'.

Conclusions, Gratuities

I promised to share a joke from Stoppard. Here it is. Deep into Act Two of *Rosencrantz and Guildenstern Are Dead*, our heroes are lost, disoriented. They don't know where they are, or even when they are. But no problem, Guildenstern puts his intelligence to work:

> **GUIL** (*clears his throat*)   In the morning the sun would be easterly. I think we can assume that.
> **ROS**   That it's morning?
> **GUIL**   If it is, and the sun is over *there* (*his right as he faces the audience*) for instance, *that* (*front*) would be northerly. (Stoppard 1968: 41)

The joke being that it is hard to work out, by such methods, which direction you are facing, or what time of day it is, if where you are is in a stage fiction, where the 'sun' can be turned on and off and moved around at will by the lighting technician. A subsequent attempt to make sense of things by determining the direction of the wind is no more successful – 'ROS: There isn't any wind. *Draught*, yes' (42, original emphasis). In short, before getting to grips with any of the big questions (Where are we? What's going on? Am I involved? etc.) it helps to know you are in a theatre. Obvious enough to us of course, but apparently less so to them. Perhaps the joke is a tip. And, big questions aside, the joke is indeed something we might think of as a gratuity, a tip, a grace note, something on top, a little extra – as pleasures and privileges are briefly re-circulated, shared out – to credit us, the audience, with being here, and for attending so assiduously. Appropriate enough too, I would say, because material need is always 'there' somehow in the theatre, if only as a reminder of how things have been. Empty pockets and purses are anyway a recurring theme of Tom Stoppard's first professional play – 'PLAYER: We have no money. (*GUIL turns to him.*) GUIL: Ah. Then what *have* you got?' (22) – and we have already noted that young companies like Barrel Organ are, as Catherine Love puts it, frequently 'forced to quite literally do something with nothing'. I often wonder if this isn't something that writing is there to teach us, how theatre shakes up its worlds – its *fictive cosmos*, if you will (Lehmann 2006: 22) – out of something less than a world, out of signifiers, 'characters', absences, deferrals and repetitions, out of all of that chiselled, inky, airy stuff. Performance, then – whether it is that of Radcliffe and his colleagues on stage at the Old Vic, or the Barrel Organ company members standing and speaking among us, or ourselves and all our diligent 'study' – we might think of as supplementing not so much the *substance* of the writing as what some might call its 'grace' (see Carson 1999: 19 and *passim*): the gift, the waste, the uncalled-for surplus, the *poetic* economy, the ultimately *gratuitous* thinking that rehearses the negation of the negation, that makes something to be said and seen where thought did not have a hope.

Performance Details

Tom Stoppard, *Rosencrantz and Guildenstern Are Dead*. First production: August 1966, by Oxford Theatre Group, at Cranston Street Hall, Edinburgh Festival Fringe. First professional production: April 1967, by the National Theatre Company at the Old Vic Theatre, London.

Barrel Organ Theatre, *Nothing*. Writer: Lulu Raczka. Productions (all UK): May 2013, University of Warwick Campus and Leamington Spa; May 2014, National Student Drama Festival, Scarborough; August 2014, Summerhall, Edinburgh Festival Fringe; November 2014, Camden People's Theatre, London. For secondary material, see the company's Education Pack (Barrel Organ 2016), containing company interviews and information, and references and links to reviews of the work.

Further Reading

In addition to the book-length studies by Radosavljević (2013) and Jarcho (2017) cited already, an invaluable collection of essays covering a range of theoretical topics and recent historical developments around writing, theatre and performance is *Performing Literatures*, edited by Stephen Bottoms, a special issue of the journal *Performance Research* (Bottoms and Gough 2009). The broader historical movement, from the canonicity of 'dramatic' thinking in the early twentieth century towards 'postdramatic' practices at the century's end, can be traced through the arguments of Szondi (1987) and Lehmann (2006). Highly recommended, for a detailed and accessible account of how drama works and can be studied, from Shakespeare to contemporary examples, is Worthen (2010). For shorter texts that raise critical and practitioner-focused questions around performed writing, both in and beyond drama, see various essays in Fuchs (1996) and Etchells (1999). The book by the poet Anne Carson (1999) cited at the end of my chapter is a recommendation from outside the Theatre and Performance field. It addresses the material 'origins' of professionalized poetic writing in questions of economy, negation and grace through the work of classical Greek poet Simonides and the modern German-language poet Paul Celan.

References

Barrel Organ (2016), *Barrel Organ Education Pack*. Available online: http://www.barrelorgan theatre.co.uk/resources (accessed 6 October 2017).

Bloch, Ernst, and Theodor W. Adorno (1988), 'Something's Missing: A Discussion Between Ernst Bloch and Theodor W. Adorno on the Contradictions of Utopian Longing', in Ernst Bloch (ed.), *The Utopian Function of Art and Literature: Selected Essays*, trans. J. Zipes and F. Mecklenburg, 1–17, Cambridge, MA: MIT Press.

Bottoms, Stephen, and Richard Gough, eds (2009), *Performing Literatures*, special issue of *Performance Research*, 14 (1).

Carson, Anne (1999), *Economy of the Unlost*, Princeton: Princeton University Press.

Esslin, Martin (1980), *The Theatre of the Absurd*, 3rd revised and expanded edn, Harmondsworth: Penguin.

Etchells, Tim (1999), *Certain Fragments*, London and New York: Routledge.

Fuchs, Elinor (1996), *The Death of Character: Perspectives on Theater after Modernism*, Bloomington: Indiana University Press.

Garcia, Tristan (2014), *Form and Object: A Treatise on Things*, trans. M. Ohm and J. Cogburn, Edinburgh: Edinburgh University Press.

Jarcho, Julia (2017), *Writing and the Modern Stage: Theater Beyond Drama*, Cambridge: Cambridge University Press.

Kalb, Jonathan (1989), *Beckett in Performance*, Cambridge: Cambridge University Press.

Lehmann, Hans-Thies (2006), *Postdramatic Theatre*, trans. K. Jürs-Munby, London and New York: Routledge.

Love, Catherine (2014), '*Nothing*, NSDF'. Available online: https://catherinelove.co.uk/2014/04/22/nothing-nsdf/ (accessed 6 October 2017).

Nadel, Ira (2004), *Double Act: A Life of Tom Stoppard*, London: Methuen.

Raczka, Lulu (2014), *Nothing*, London: Oberon Books.

Radosavljević, Duška (2013), *Theatre-Making: Interplay Between Text and Performance in the 21st Century*, Basingstoke: Palgrave Macmillan.

Stoppard, Tom (1968), *Rosencrantz and Guildenstern Are Dead*, London: Faber.

Szondi, Peter (1987), *Theory of Modern Drama*, trans. M. Hays, Minneapolis: University of Minnesota Press.

Worthen, W. B. (2010), *Drama: Between Poetry and Performance*, West Sussex: Wiley-Blackwell.

2 What Do Performances Do to Spectators?

MAAIKE BLEEKER

A railway station. A line of people standing next to each other, each holding a sheet of paper with a name on it. As if they are waiting for other people to arrive, other people they don't know yet. They wear headphones. They are waiting amid the busy crowd of travellers making their way around them. Then, another group of people materializes in front of them; one by one, an equal number of people stops and stands still, facing those waiting. The people waiting hear Dido's song 'Remember me' from Purcell's opera *Dido and Aeneas* (1688) through their headphones and see the people in front of them act as if they are singing. All of a sudden, a performance has started, right in the midst of the busy railway station. There is no theatre, no stage. There is only *mise en scène*: an arrangement of performers, spectators, actions and music. *Mise en scène* is a French term that refers to all the resources of stage performance and the activity of arranging them in a particular time and space (Pavis 1998: 363–8). It is often translated as *staging*: the activity of putting a play on stage or an event in front of a camera. In the case of the performance in the railway station, however, there is neither stage nor camera. The *mise en scène* itself sets the stage by means of the composition of the performers, their actions and the music. This arrangement also implies positions for spectators. It creates spectatorship.

The dictionary definition of spectatorship is 'the state of being a spectator'. In theatre and performance studies, the term is used to describe how performances put audiences in this state. How are audiences addressed by performances? How does the construction of performances imply positions from where to look? How do performances invite ways of seeing and interpreting? How are performances constructed to do things to spectators, to affect them? Often, performances are constructed to be seen from a particular point of view, like, for example, in the classical Western box-set stage with a proscenium arch through which the audience looks inside the world on stage. Technicians or actors waiting in the wings can see the performance from other sides; for example, they can see the back side of the scenery, yet this is not the way in which the performance is meant to be seen. The performance is directed towards the audience sitting in the auditorium and constructed to be seen from there. In the performance described above, there is no stage or auditorium directing the attention of the audience. Audience members were told to line up at this specific spot in the railway station, hold the sheets of paper and wait there for the performers to arrive. Spectatorship takes shape in the way the audience is invited to take up this position and in the way the performers address the audience with their performance, in the way they offer themselves to be seen and understood.

Fig. 2.1 *No Man's Land* by Dries Verhoeven, Utrecht 2008. Audience waiting for the performers to arrive. Photo: Maarten van Haaff.

The performance is titled *No Man's Land*. It was created by Dries Verhoeven in 2008 in Utrecht (the Netherlands) and, in the following years, recreated in (among others) Berlin, Athens, Valencia and Munich, each time with a different group of local performers from a migrant background. Their names are on the pieces of paper held by the audience. After the first encounter to the strains of Purcell's music, each of these performers approaches one spectator and takes him or her on an individual tour through the city. During this tour, spectators are invited to look at the city through the eyes of someone from elsewhere, and also to look at their guide. Via the headphones, they hear stories about what might be the life of their guides and their experiences. These stories are diverse, they sometimes contradict each other. From the beginning, it is made clear that these stories are not necessarily those of the performers met by the audience. The aim of the performance is not to reveal who these people truly are, but rather to invite reflection about being a migrant and about the projections and assumptions that are part of how they are seen. The performance confronts spectators with their own modes of looking and with being seen by others. It puts spectatorship on stage, figuratively, in they way it invites reflection about spectatorship, and also literally, in the way it makes spectators part of the performance seen by others: the passers-by in the railway station and the people on the streets watching the spectators following their guides.

In the following, I take *No Man's Land* as my guide in an exploration of how theatre and performance think through spectatorship. *No Man's Land* is an example of how theatre can trigger critical reflection about ways of showing and ways of seeing, and the relationship between them. A closer look at how *No Man's Land* is constructed to trigger such reflection, draws attention to spectatorship as fundamental to how theatre and performance operate: to how theatre and performance take their audiences along in ways of seeing, feeling, associating and interpreting what they find themselves confronted with, and how theatre and performance use ways of showing and telling to do so. Questions of spectatorship are closely connected to those of dramaturgy. Spectatorship describes how spectators and spectating are implicated within the dramaturgy of the performance. It describes how the dramaturgy of a performance invites modes of looking and interpreting, plays with them, confirms or subverts them. This happens in *No Man's Land* right from the beginning.

Tools for Analysis: Focalization and the Gaze

When the music of 'Remember Me' fades out, each performer approaches the spectator holding the paper with their name on it, looks them in the eyes, smiles and nods, turns around and walks away. Spectators have been instructed to follow the person at a little distance. Each couple leaves in a different direction and sets out for a different trajectory through the city.

After several minutes, the guide halts, turns around and looks the spectator in the eyes. A voice heard via the headphones says:

> This is me. This is my face. This isn't a theatre costume. This is not a Dutch appearance. I am a foreigner. Or migrant. That sounds better. A refugee. Political or economic. You don't know that yet. Maybe even a Muslim. Or I am just here on holiday. That is the most cheerful version. This isn't my voice. This isn't my language. This is the voice of an actor. I may still look like a stranger. Some sort of character from a comic strip from a distant country who stands in front of you a little uncomfortably. Someone who normally wouldn't speak English this fluently. Because of the English voice you will regard me differently.

'This is me', the voice says to the spectator. What you see is what you get. But what exactly is it that you see? What seems to start as an introduction to the performer turns quickly into

Fig. 2.2 *No Man's Land* by Dries Verhoeven, Athens 2014. Performer Sylla Badara and a spectator on their walk through Athens. Photo: Stavros Petropoulos.

a reflection that questions what it is that the spectator sees, and reflects back assumptions the spectator might possibly have. The text destabilizes the self-evidence of seeing and, without explicitly asking, invites the spectator to consider her own modes of looking.

The text also draws attention to the way in which what the spectator encounters is a performance ('This is the voice of an actor') and how this performance is designed with a spectator in mind ('Because of the English voice you will regard me differently'). The text exposes how performances are constructed to provide particular views on what is shown. In narratology, this is called *focalization.* Narratology is the theory of narrative and narration. The term focalization was introduced by Gérard Genette (1972) to distinguish between two agents involved in the way events are represented in stories: the agent who 'narrates' and the agent who 'sees'. The concept was further developed by Mieke Bal, who has demonstrated the usefulness of focalization for the analysis not only of literature but also of visual texts (Bal 1997, 2001). Focalization describes the relationship between what is seen and the point of view from where that which is shown is seen in a particular way. This point of view can be in concrete material space, like the chair of the spectator in the auditorium. The construction of theatre architecture and the construction of stage design are both acts of focalization in the way they stage perspectives on what is there to be seen. Focalization also involves points of view in symbolic or discursive spaces: attitudes and assumptions towards that which is shown. This perspective is part of how the construction of a performance addresses the audience and how this invites spectators to look at what is there. The English voice of the actor is part of creating such a perspective, as are the ways in which characters on stage present themselves. This is explicitly addressed when the voice of the actor observes:

> I can tell you an uncomplicated reassuring story. I can tell you about a good life. Rather plain but good. That I am an electrical engineer. Or that I own a little grocery store. That I am married and have a son. And a dog called Yuki. That I buy my clothes at Hennes & Mauritz. That I am a member of the library. What a kind man, you might think. Uncomplicated and reassuring.

The voice of the actor describes how the man should be presented to be considered kind and uncomplicated. The description draws attention to how this involves meeting culturally specific expectations, the kind of expectations that are likely part of the modes of looking of his audience. The text thus points to how ways of showing and telling (on stage or elsewhere) imply points of view and how these points of view are part of the address presented to a spectator. Getting to know whether actual audiences who attended the performance shared this point of view would require a different kind of research. It would involve reception research by means of interviews with the audience or by asking them to fill out questionnaires. Focalization, on the other hand, is an analytical tool that investigates how the construction of a performance implies points of view and how these points of view mediate ways of understanding and interpreting. These points of view can be represented on stage, for example, when a character gives an opinion or a description of something and thus (implicitly) invites the audience to look at things from their (the character's) perspective. This is called internal focalization. The way that No Man's Land implicitly invites the audience to look at the city as if through the eyes of this performer is an example of internal focalization. Performances also imply points of view that are not represented on stage or within the performance, but that are implied by how things are shown. This is called external focalization. This is, for example, the point of view implied within the description of how to pass for a kind and uncomplicated man in *No Man's Land*. This point of view is not that of the actor speaking or the performer seen but part of the perspective proposed by the text, a point of view suggested to the spectator.

The text of *No Man's Land* foregrounds how focalization works and exposes its effects. The voice seems to explain: If I present myself like this, you will see me as that. If the man presents himself this way, his presentation will meet your expectations about what a kind and uncomplicated man is like; or perhaps, what you would like a kind and uncomplicated man to be. For, how we recognize the world for what we think it is, is intimately intertwined with desires, presuppositions and fears. This is what Jacques Lacan (1981) has theorized as the *gaze*. The gaze describes culturally and historically specific patterns at work in how things come to be seen and how we recognize things for what we think they are: what appears as attractive, convincing, interesting, desirable, and what does not. In her influential article, 'Visual Pleasure and Narrative Cinema' (1975), Laura Mulvey shows how classical Hollywood cinema privileges what she terms the male gaze. The ways in which classical Hollywood cinema shows women and how it mediates in ways of looking at women corresponds to the desires and fears of a male heterosexual viewer. The construction of these films implies the point of view of such a spectator and women are shown in ways that appeal to this point of view. Mulvey shows how, in some films, this point of view is represented within the world on screen, for example, by means of a so-called over-shoulder shot, in which the camera is positioned in such a way as to give the audience the impression of looking over the shoulder of a male character at a woman. In these instances, a male character functions as an internal focalizer, as the spectator is invited to understand what is there to be seen as his view. However, Mulvey points out, even if such connection to a male perspective is absent within the world on screen, the ways in which this world is represented and the camera directs our ways of looking can still be seen to privilege male heterosexual desires. Such a view is implied within the ways things are shown.

Mulvey does not use the term focalization, yet this is what, to a considerable extent, her analysis is about. And importantly, her analysis points to the connection between focalization, as part of the construction of cinema, and culturally and historically specific modes of looking. Mulvey focuses on particular types of sexual desire, which are part of the gaze. Yet the gaze – considered as the cultural and historical specific patterns at work in how things come to be seen – is not limited to sexual desire, and also does not require the mediation of a camera. *No Man's Land* confronts its spectators with other aspects of the gaze and the way they are at work in how we see and are being seen. What do we see when we see this man standing in front of us? A foreigner? A migrant? A refugee? Or a tourist? What is it that makes us see him one way or the other? How is his appearance framed by assumptions that are part of culturally and historically specific modes of looking?

As one follows the other through the streets, spectator and guide together become a performance to others. Passers-by and people living and working in the streets that are part of the routes taken by the guides, start noticing these couples passing by at regular intervals. The looks of these others confront spectators not just with being seen by other individuals, but also with how we ourselves and our performances appear in the light of the gaze. This experience is described by Franz Fanon, a theorist who was born in 1925 in

Martinique, when this island was still a French colony. Growing up, he identified with being 'French' rather than with being 'black'. When he moved to Europe, however, he found himself increasingly confronted with being seen in a disconcerting way. This was not only a matter of the individuals looking at him. He felt himself seen through images of blackness and experiences an identity being imposed on him he did not identify with before. What he experienced was the gaze and how he was violently inscribed in racist modes of looking (Fanon 1986; Silverman 1996: 27–31).

Staging Spectatorship

I can tell you my real name. I can tell you about the prison in Spain. About the prison in Kirkuk. About the prison in Santiago. I can tell you I knocked five teeth out of someone's mouth. That a man is an ass if he can't protect his wife. I can tell you about a small white room with a panelled ceiling and a woman who judges my story. About the expectant look. That I don't have a gun. I can say that my story is implausible. A complicated story. But plain stories are more convincing.

The voice of the actor shifts the perspective on who the man in front of us might be towards the question of how to tell his story in a way that is acceptable and convincing. 'All the world is a stage', Shakespeare famously observed, and for migrants like the performers in No Man's Land, the ways in which their performance manages to convince can make the difference between being allowed to stay and having to go.

How performances should be constructed in order to convince their audiences is the subject of the oldest known reflection on making theatre in Europe, which is Aristotle's (384–322 BC) Poetics. Aristotle's treatise is based upon the plays of the ancient Greek dramatists he was acquainted with. On the basis of their work, he concludes that theatre, and in particular the type of theatre he refers to as tragedy, is an imitation of actions that are terrible and piteous and that happen to worthy men; an imitation that is 'so composed that he who hears the things that are transacted, may be seized with horror and feel pity'. This then shall result in catharsis (Part XIV). Catharsis is an intense experience of being affected by the tragic fate of the character(s) in the play. Through identification with the character(s), the audience feels along with their tragic fate, and in this way, is able to live through and be released of similar emotions.

Aristotle's observations point to how modes of showing and telling on stage have to be made with a spectator in mind. Like the actor in No Man's Land quoted above, he observes that when stories are too long, have too many parts or get too complicated, they will not be successful in convincing their audience. Aristotle also observes that not all kinds of characters and actions will do. In order to evoke horror and pity, the audience has to commiserate with the characters, and audiences will be most likely to commiserate with a character who does not deserve to be unfortunate and who one can identify with: 'a character of this kind is one who neither excels in virtue and justice, nor is changed through vice and depravity into misfortune from a state of great renown and prosperity, but has experienced this change through some [human] error such as Oedipus and Thyestes, and other illustrious men of this kind' (Part XIII).

Aristotle's ideas have greatly influenced European theatre since the Renaissance. They inspired what has come to be known as the Aristotelian unities – the unities of place, time and action – that came to serve as rules for writing plays. In the nineteenth century, Aristotle's ideas would also become the basis for the so-called well-made play. This does not mean, however, that all European theatre was and is structured according to Aristotle's ideas. Shakespeare's theatre, for example, does not follow Aristotle's ideas, and neither does much continental theatre from the Baroque, nor many other European performance traditions. And from the late-nineteenth century on, from within the theatre that developed out of the Aristotelian tradition, many of his ideas were questioned and revised, including his ideas about staging spectatorship. Why would audiences want to identify with Gods and kings like Oedipus and Thyestes and their tragic fate, authors of realist and naturalist theatre wondered, and what would be the use of that? Should theatre not rather show the reality of ordinary people and their struggles? Shouldn't theatre aim to be more real in order to truly reach its audience?

Although not realist or naturalist theatre in the strict sense, this is precisely what *No Man's Land* does. It tells the stories of ordinary people, displaced people, struggling with why they are where they are, with how to tell their story, and with how their stories will be perceived by others. 'I can tell you a different story', says the voice of the actor, and the performer suddenly halts. 'A story that makes you think: this makes sense that this person is here now. He has been through such a dreadful experience. I could put all my cards on the table. I could be open and honest.' And he continues with a story about his daughter being raped and killed in front of his eyes. It is a gruesome story 'so composed that he who hears the things that are transacted, may be seized with horror and feel pity' (Aristotle, see above) and commiserate with the characters. The description suddenly stops in the middle of the story and the voice of the actor observes, 'You'd find it absurd. Someone who opens up like that. ... I could say that three years ago I told this entire story to a woman in a white room with a panelled ceiling. How she was checking my story for gruesome details. That it would have been best if I could have shown her polaroid pictures.'

Can the real be represented or shown on stage? How does the audience recognize what is real? How could we ever recognize it other than in that which meets our beliefs and expectations about what is real? Theatre is 'a culturally conditioned mode of staging the construction of the real', writes Barbara Freedman (1991: 50). Freedman writes about Shakespearean comedy, yet her definition of theatre as a staging of the construction of the real seems to be valuable for understanding the relationship between theatre and spectators in other times and places as well. Freedman points to the relationship between theatre and the historical reality that this theatre belongs to, but without understanding theatre in terms of a representation of this reality. Rather, she argues, theatre and reality appear as parallel constructions appealing to similar ways of looking. These ways of looking are what the performers in *No Man's Land* are confronted with, not only within the performance but also in reality. And this is what the audience of their performance is confronted with too. Is this really what this person experienced? How do we tell? What do we take for real and what do we not, and why? What do we reject for being 'mere theatre', make believe?

As culturally conditioned modes of staging the construction of the real, theatre and performance correspond to the modes of looking of culturally and historically specific spectators. They respond to these modes of looking and imply points of view similar to them, but theatre and reality are not the same. This similarity and difference is a recurring motive in *No Man's Land*. From the very first line spoken, the text foregrounds the 'realness' of the person we meet. 'This is me. This is my face. This isn't a theatre costume.' Yet, only sentences later, the text also explains that the voice we hear is not that of the person we see. 'This isn't my voice. This isn't my language. This is the voice of an actor.' The text points to the difference between the voice heard through the headphones and the person seen, as well as the difference between the person standing there in front of the spectator and the 'I' of the spoken text. This difference is a structural aspect of much theatre. When an actor says 'I', this 'I' usually does not refer to him or her personally but to a character represented by him or her. Attempting to be more real, theatre and performance makers have developed strategies to minimize the difference between these two, for example, by means of acting techniques that aim towards the actor transforming as much as possible into the character – most famously the technique developed by Konstantin Stanislavski (1989), which would become the basis for what is known as method acting. Others aimed at making theatre more real by privileging the self of the actor over the character. Elinor Fuchs (1996) describes how playwrights since the late-nineteenth century have developed new dramaturgical strategies that decentre and deconstruct dramatic character, a development she proposes to term 'the death of character'. Instead of full-blown psychological characters, performances show actors presenting aspects of dramatic narrative and elements of characters. This 'death of character' contributes to a birth of the presence of the actor and is part of a shift towards increased presence of what might be described as the reality of the theatrical apparatus and staging, which is concurrent with the imaginary worlds represented. Hans-Thies Lehmann ([1999] 2006) too observes an opening up of the closed structure of dramatic theatre, based on the Aristotelian unities, fourth wall and the box-set stage, into what he terms an 'irruption of the real' (99) in the traditionally closed fictive cosmos of the theatre. This is what he terms 'postdramatic theatre': 'The postdramatic theatre is the first to turn the level of the real explicitly into "co-player"' (100). He also observes that 'in the postdramatic theatre of the real the main point is not the assertion of the real as such … but the unsettling that occurs through the undecidability whether one is dealing with reality or fiction' (101). One of his examples is Jan Fabre's *The Power of Theatrical Madness* (1982), in which at one moment;

> the house lights come on in the middle of the performance after an especially exhausting action of the performers (an endurance exercise *à la* Grotowski). Out of breath, the actors take a smoking break while looking at the audience. It remains uncertain whether their unhealthy activity is 'really' necessary or staged. The same holds true for the sweeping up of shards and other stage actions that are necessary and meaningful from a pragmatic point of view but which in the light of the theatrical signs' lack of reference to reality are perceived on an equal footing with the more clearly staged events on stage. (100)

This ambiguity and undecidability is an important difference from attempts in Body Art and Performance Art to do away with representation and show only 'the real thing': real suffering, real pain, real risk. Body Art and Performance Art are among the sources of inspiration for postdramatic theatre. However, it is precisely the undecidability (rather than the claim to show 'the real thing') that makes postdramatic theatre such a powerful tool for reflection on how theatre thinks of spectatorship and, more generally, on how seeing is not just a matter of opening one's eyes to take in what is there. 'It is not the occurrence of anything "real" as such but its self-reflexive use that characterizes the aesthetic of postdramatic theatre' (Lehmann [1999] 2006: 103). This can take the shape of a performance in a theatre, like the Fabre performance described earlier, as well as that of events that take the audience to places outside the theatre, like *No Man's Land* does. *No Man's Land* also presents an example of how this involves new ways of activating audiences that build on ideas of twentieth-century theatre innovator Bertolt Brecht (1898–1956), while also taking these ideas in new directions.

Critical Distance versus Critical Intimacy

Alerting the spectator to the difference between the 'I' of the spoken text and the person performing, *No Man's Land* deploys what might be called a Brechtian distancing effect. Brecht was a German playwright and theorist whose work marks a key moment in the twentieth-century development of Western theatre and who was very critical of Aristotle's ideas. He described his own theatre as anti-Aristotelian. Central to his critique is the Aristotelian understanding of spectatorship. Inviting the audience to commiserate with the misfortune of characters, Brecht observed, is not going to contribute much to making a change in the real world and the real life of people. Such theatre keeps the audience passive in how it invites an acceptance of misfortune as simply given, the will of God, or bad luck. What are needed instead, according to Brecht, are strategies of showing and telling that activate the audience. To achieve this, he proposes strategies of staging that remind the spectators of the performance as theatre, of its being constructed as a performance; and by drawing attention to how it is constructed, he persuades the audience to consider what the consequences of this construction are. Brecht's idea is that this will invite audiences to look at reality in a similar way as a performance, with a particular construction (what Freedman terms the cultural construction of the real) and therefore, a construction that can be changed.

In order to activate the audience, Brecht developed strategies of staging that aim to prevent the spectator from identifying with characters on stage and from taking the illusionary world and its underlying logic for granted. Instead, his theatre seeks to evoke a critical distance towards what is shown by means of what he describes (in German) as *Verfremdungseffekt*, translated as distancing effect, defamiliarization effect, estrangement effect or alienation effect. Highlighting the difference between characters and the actors performing them is one way of achieving this effect. Another strategy is that of a narrative logic that undermines the Aristotelian unities of time, place and action, and instead leaves gaps, jumps in time and space, and shifts in logic. Such a structure leaves it to the audience to make the connections between the scenes and thus activates them. *No Man's Land*, consisting of short monologues that represent fragments of different, and sometimes incompatible, stories, does precisely that. It puts the audience in the position of actively having to work out how to conceive of the relationships between these stories and between these stories and the performer.

Theatre, Brecht argues, should directly address the audience and make contact with them. It should break with the tradition of the so-called fourth wall (the convention of performing as if the audience is not there) as well as with the convention of putting audiences in a darkened auditorium from which they can look into a brightly lit other world on stage, from a distance, as if they are not really there and as if this world has nothing to do with them as spectators. This gap between stage and auditorium needs to be closed and this seems to be exactly what *No Man's Land* does. There is no stage, no auditorium. The performance directly addresses the spectators in their own, real world and makes contact with them. There is no fourth wall. Performers look the audience members in the eye and the text that the spectators hear via the headphones is directly addressing them. And yet, their world does not become one. The performance lacks the comforting promise offered by Brechtian theatre that the explicitly staged character will help us to take a distance and recognize the difference between what is real and what is not. Instead, the construction in *No Man's Land* confronts the audience with undecidability with regard to what is real and what is not. The ways in which the real is brought in as a co-performer is highly self-reflexive and draws attention to the fact that the real world that the spectator and performer seem to share is not the same for each of them.

> I can say that I have been watching Western products for years. Western commercials, Western TV, advertising vans with Coca Cola graphics riding through town. One day I gave in. I decided to accept the offer. This story about choosing your own future. Radically, optimistically, selfishly. About pursuing your dreams and that this is human and wonderful.

Once arrived in the world that promotes these values, however, it appears that what is presented as human and wonderful does not apply to everybody, and particularly, not to economic refugees. At only an arms-length distance and with no fourth wall or orchestra pit in between them, spectator and performer appear to live in different realities. They are in the same space, and at the same time they are not.

No Man's Land takes the spectator on a tour through public space to show that there is no such thing as 'the' public space that we all share; that instead, as Chantal Mouffe (2005) observes, public space is always plural and a space of contestation. The same goes for reality in general. There is no one master narrative and no outside position from where we can see it 'as it is'. Instead, we find ourselves implicated in competing narratives and competing perspectives on how things are or should be. *No Man's Land* demonstrates the potential of theatre and performance for an exploration of the complexities of this plurality and for developing sensibilities towards difference and otherness, as well as towards one's own modes of perceiving and interpreting. The performance shows how Brechtian strategies can be used to activate audiences for a critical engagement with this complexity in ways that do not evoke critical distance but rather what Gayatri Spivak (1999) terms *critical intimacy*. Instead of taking or evoking distance to see and show how things are, critical intimacy operates on the basis of intimate involvement without this implying familiarity. Critical intimacy suggests the need to employ both passion and reason while seeking understanding. *No Man's Land* evokes critical intimacy as a result of how it stages a one-to-one encounter in which personal experiences and reflections are shared. The presence of the performers and the way in which the performance requires the spectator's willingness to engage in a one-to-one encounter and follow this performer without knowing where they will go, is important to how intimacy is brought about. At the same time, the construction of the performance reminds the spectator time and again that the encounter is a performance. It is a staged event that allows for an intimate encounter with migrants. The focus is on their stories and what these tell us about the migrant experience, as well as about our own ways of relating to these experiences and to migrants. How these stories relate to the performers and who these performers really are, remains a mystery.

Media Dramaturgies of the Mind

The widespread presence and use of media has deeply affected spectatorship in theatre and performance. The development of twentieth-century theatre is intertwined with the rise of media culture. Theatre makers have incorporated other media in their work and expanded the practice of theatre to include new possibilities offered by media developments. Others have developed modes of working which precisely allowed them to distinguish and distance themselves from media like film and, later, television, video and the internet. And even when performances do not use other media on stage, they are nevertheless part of how theatre is constructed (for example in how montage and game-like structures have been incorporated in new dramaturgical structures) and perceived. Theoretical debates on the specificity of theatre, on liveness and on presence reflect how confrontation with other media has inspired a reconsideration of what the specificity of the theatre is, and how theatre differs from other media, and also, how mediatization affects our perception of liveness itself (Auslander 2002). This can also be seen in No Man's Land.

An important feature of the construction of No Man's Land is the use of headphones worn by both spectators and performers. Those of the spectators are clearly visible, those of the performers are earplugs and therefore less obvious. The use of the headphones is instrumental in setting up the ambiguous relationship of closeness and distance between the spectator and the performer. Both spectator and performer are listening to the same spoken texts by the absent actor and to a selection of different kinds of music in between the texts. Walking behind the performer, the spectator can see him or her moving to the rhythm of the music, sometimes making small dance-like movements with their hands and arms or head. Watching the performer thus move to the rhythm of the music heard through the headphones creates the sense of a shared space or bubble within the larger public space and this contributes to a sense of intimacy. Intimacy, however, towards whom? The voice-over explains right away that this voice is not that of the person the audience member is following. The spectator can see that this person he or she is following is not speaking. Yet immersed in the sound of the voice of the actor, it appears hard to mentally disconnect the 'I' of the text from the performer seen.

The effect of the headphones in No Man's Land points to how the unity of the world perceived is not given in that which is offered, but is a perceptual interpretation in response to what is offered; it points to how that which is offered affords to be perceived. Human bodies are constantly confronted with a diversity of perceptual stimuli. Processing these, they make interpretations. Our sense of the world as a unity that is both visible, audible and tangible is the result of such processing. The effect of the headphones in No Man's Land is to show that experience and expectations are part of how stimuli will be processed, and to draw attention to the ways in which media and mediatization have become part of how our bodies make sense of sensory input. The logic of understanding a technically mediated voice as being that of a person seen but not seen speaking is that of the voice-over in film, inviting us to interpret the voice heard as speaking the thoughts of the person we do see. The headphones produce a filmic experience in which that which is seen (the city and the performer in the city) is framed by a voice-over and background music.

A No-Man's Land Betwixt-and-Between

Near the end of *No Man's Land*, the couples of performers and spectators convene at a piece of no man's land in the city: a piece of wasteland amid the houses on which a row of small temporary dwellings has been erected. As couples of performers and spectators approach from different directions they can see other couples moving to the rhythm of the music that they are hearing via their headphones. For a moment it seems that the private bubble containing one spectator and one performer is expanding. What is shared is the joint condition of being absorbed in the same music and the individual experience of dwelling in one's own thoughts about the encounter with the performer. These moments near the end of the performance thus present an image of spectatorship in theatre and performance as something that takes place in public and in a situation shared with others while also being an individual experience.

No Man's Land demonstrates the potential of theatre and performance to take the audience along in experiences that are both very much here and now and somehow outside daily reality. This is what anthropologist Victor Turner (1990) describes as liminality, and which connects the experience of theatre and performance to that of rituals. His ideas are based on the notion of the limen or threshold, a term introduced by Arnold van Gennep to describe the second of three stages in rites of passage. This threshold is 'a no-man's-land betwixt-and-between' past and future (Turner 1990: 11) that allows for experiences and encounters that

Fig. 2.3 *No Man's Land* by Dries Verhoeven, Utrecht 2008. Camera Obscura projection of performer Mozjgan Lali. Photo: Maarten van Haaff.

neither could nor would take place in the reality of everyday life and that can be transformative by making the audience return to reality in a slightly different way. In *No Man's Land*, this return to reality is staged as a homecoming in which it remains ambiguous whose home is being returned to. The performers each open the door to one of the little dwellings and invite 'their' spectator inside, where they find a chair waiting for them. The performer closes the door, removes the headphones of the spectator and sings a song. Sitting in the dark, the spectator, for the first time, hears the voice of the performer and his or her own language. Then, the performer puts back the headphones and steps outside, leaving the audience member in the dark listening to 'Gute Nacht' from the *Winterreise* song-cycle of Schubert (1827) and looking at a series of *camera obscura* images created by the performers outside. In each door, a little hole has been made and light from the outside projects an image of the guides walking towards the doors on the white roof and upper part of the wall of the dwelling.

The spectators see a succession of images of different guides that ends with their 'own' performer holding a piece of paper with their name on it, thus mirroring the opening image where the audience held similar pieces of paper with the names of the performers. Having become literally a projection, the performers disappear, leaving it to the spectators to decide when to leave their temporary dwellings in no-man's land and return to reality.

Performance Details

No Man's Land. Director, text: Dries Verhoeven, local director: Marjolein Frijling (2013 and 2014), director's assistant: Hannah van Wieringen (2008), Bart van de Woestijne (2013 and 2014), dramaturgy: Judith Blankenberg (2008), sound design: Arnoud Traa, technicians: Kas van Huisstede (2012), Roel Evenhuis (2014), photography: Stavros Petropoulos and Maarten van Haaff, voices: Malou Gorter (2008), Bart Klever, Ria Marks (2013), Adam Fields (2013), in collaboration with twenty guides. Co-commissioned by Huis and Festival a/d Werf (2008), Theaterformen (2009), VEO (2010), HAU Hebbel am Ufer (2009), Stadsschouwburg Amsterdam/Frascati (2012), Call of the Mall (2013), Münchner Kammerspiele (2014) and Onassis Cultural Center (2014). For more information, images, responses and a short video exerpt, see: http://driesverhoeven.com/en/project/niemandsland/

All texts in *No Man's Land* are voice-over. Two versions are used: one spoken by a woman (this one is used for those spectators following a female performer) and one spoken by a man (used for spectators following a male performer). In the Utrecht version of the performance, the male version was translated into English (and used for spectators who did not speak Dutch but could understand English). The quotes in my text are from this English-language version.

Further Reading

For a general introduction to questions raised by the encounter between performers and audiences, and various analytical and theoretical approaches, see Bennett (1998) and Freshwater (2009). For a close reading of spectator experiences in early twenty-first-century European theatre, see Kelleher (2015). For a further explanation of the theory of focalization, see 'Focalization' and 'Visual Stories' in Bal (1997: 142–74) and Bal (2001). For an excellent discussion of the Lacanian gaze, see Silverman (1996). For more on focalization and the gaze in the theatre, the ways in which media have become part of spectating in the theatre, and the relationship between visuality and theatricality, see Bleeker (2008, 2012). For an investigation of the relationship between ethics and spectatorship, see Grehan (2009).

References

Aristotle (app. 350 BC), *Poetics*, trans. S. H. Butcher. Available online: *The Internet Classics Archive*, http://classics.mit.edu/Aristotle/poetics.html (accessed 7 May 2018).

Auslander, Philip (2002), *Liveness: Performance in a Mediatized Culture*, New York and London: Routledge.

Bal, Mieke (1997), *Narratology. Introduction to the Theory of Narrative*, 2nd edn, Toronto, Buffalo and London: University of Toronto Press.

Bal, Mieke (2001), *Looking In: The Art of Viewing*, Amsterdam: G + B Arts International.

Bennett, Susan (1998), *Theatre Audiences: A Theory of Production and Reception*, New York and London: Routledge.

Bleeker, Maaike (2008), *Visuality in the Theatre: The Locus of Looking*, Basingstoke: Palgrave Macmillan.

Bleeker, Maaike (2012), 'Media Dramaturgies of the Mind: Ivana Müller's Cinematic Choreographies', *Performance Research: On Duration* 17 (5): 61–70.

Fanon, Frantz (1986), *Black Skin, White Masks*, trans. C. L. Markmann, London: Pluto Press.

Freedman, Barbara (1991), *Staging the Gaze: Postmodernism, Psychoanalysis and Shakespearean Comedy*, Ithaca and London: Cornell University Press.

Freshwater, Helen (2009), *Theatre & Audience*, Basingstoke: Palgrave Macmillan.

Fuchs, Elinor (1996), *The Death of Character: Perspectives on Theatre after Modernism*, Bloomington: Indiana University Press.

Genette, Gérard (1972), *Figures III*, Paris: Seuil.

Grehan, Helena (2009), *Performance, Ethics and Spectatorship in a Global Age*, Basingstoke: Palgrave Macmillan.

Kelleher, Joe (2015), *The Illuminated Theatre: Studies on the Suffering of Images*, London and New York: Routledge.

Lacan, Jacques (1981), *The Four Fundamental Concepts of Psychoanalysis*, trans. A. Sheridan, New York and London: W. W. Norton & Company.

Lehmann, Hans-Thies (2006), *Postdramatic Theatre*, trans. K. Jürs-Munby, New York and London: Routledge.

Mouffe, Chantal (2005), 'Some Reflections on an Agonistic Approach to the Public', in Bruno Latour and Peter Weibel (eds), *Making Things Public: Atmospheres of Democracy*, 804–7, Karlsruhe and Cambridge, MA: ZKM Centre for Art and Media, The MIT Press.

Mulvey, Laura (1975), 'Visual Pleasure and Narrative Cinema', *Screen* 16 (3): 6–18.

Pavis, Patrice (1998), *Dictionary of the Theatre: Terms, Concepts, and Analysis*, Toronto and Buffalo: Toronto University Press.

Silverman, Kaja (1996), *The Threshold of the Visible World*, New York and London: Routledge.

Spivak, Gayatri Chakravorty (1999), *A Critique of Postcolonial Reason: Towards a History of the Vanishing Present*, Cambridge, MA: Harvard UP.

Stanislavski, Konstantin (1986), *An Actor Prepares*, New York and London: Routledge.

Turner, Victor (1990), 'Are there Universals of Performance in Myth, Ritual and Drama?' in Richard Schechner and Willa Appel (eds) *By Means of Performance*, 8–18, Cambridge: Cambridge University Press.

3 How Can the Theatre Be Fully Accessible?

COLETTE CONROY

Access

The concept at the centre of this chapter is that of *accessible* theatre. Accessible theatre has developed through the late-twentieth and early-twenty-first centuries: theatre that has fully integrated access for d/Deaf, blind and disabled spectators and performers built into the artistic structure of the play. Questions of access go beyond disability issues, of course. I might attend a performance in Mandarin and understand very little. The performance is offered to a specific language community, and the means of accessing the performance is for me to work harder in my Mandarin language classes in the future, or else to access translation via headphones or captions. Further aspects of access might be the ability to afford theatre tickets, the ability to see performances in your local area or a sense of being unwelcome or excluded from a specific venue. Accessible theatre means that you imagine your audience to be as wide a group of people as possible, anticipating that they will use the communicational apparatus of theatre in potentially different ways. An accessible theatre enables us to imagine and anticipate a wider view of who 'we' the audience may be.

In pointing towards a focus on late-twentieth-century and early-twenty-first-century theatre in the UK, I may have inadvertently implied that disability is a new concept for theatre. Nothing could be further from the truth. Throughout its entire history, theatre has been fascinated with ideas about deformity that we now think about as disability (disability as a concept may be dated back to the Industrial Revolution, along with notions of normalcy). If we extend our definition of disability to impairments caused by ageing and illness, then it seems difficult to find plays that *don't* use the idea of disability in some form or other. From classical theatre onwards, the ways that bodies are impaired, and the meanings of impairment have been important to theatregoers.

Everything the audience knows about a character comes from the stage action and appearance – what they say and do and what they look like. We might extrapolate or infer from what we observe on stage to extend our reading of the character, and sometimes this is based on intertextual and cultural readings that we bring to the theatre with us. Disability has been used as a visible shortcut to cultural signification. Hunchbacked villains and blind seers populate theatre, communicating pathos, disorder, evil or clear-sightedness and often communicate a metaphysical concept. The disability studies scholar Victoria Ann Lewis noted: 'It is not that the non-disabled theater world knows nothing about disability and is waiting to be enlightened. To the contrary, the depiction of disability is over-represented in dramatic literature' (1989: 93). *Over-represented!* It isn't completely clear what it means in this analysis to 'over-represent' disabled people, but Lewis expresses a view that disability (or rather, deformity/impairment) is more likely than not to be a crucial feature of the diegetic world of the play (the world of the onstage fiction). Deformity or impairment creates a visible index (i.e. *pointing towards* the thing it refers to, the way a knock on the door signifies the presence of a visitor or a plume of smoke indicates the presence of a fire) that connects the past and the social circumstances of the character to what the audience sees on stage. It is often a device for narrative causality. It can function as visible character indicator or as social interruption or problem. Shakespeare's Richard III is a particularly well-known disabled villain, engaging in a murderous rampage of evil because, as he explains, his deformed body means that he 'cannot prove a lover' (I'm not making any claim about the 'real' Richard III here, or accepting any arguments about the relationship between Shakespeare's eponymous villain and the political and ideological strategies of representation either. For more on this, see Freud's discussion of the character of Gloucester (Freud [1916] 2001)). Disability is woven into dramatic literature. With this in mind, it seems difficult to find any play where disability, deformity or illness is *not* present as a threat or as an overt cause of dramatic action in the play.

With this in mind, think of the number of plays or films where the disabled protagonist was played by a non-disabled actor. Or try to call to mind the numbers of disabled people who earn their livings as actors in theatre or film. (The second of these exercises is not so easy but worth trying.) So far, you will have noticed that I am arguing two things. Firstly, that disabled people have frequently been physically excluded from theatre, both as audiences and as artists. Secondly, that theatre has used disability as a rich source of communicational material to point towards cultural ideas, such as evil, exclusion or pathos. The absence of 'real' disabled bodies seems to be important here, both as an obvious injustice and also as an interesting and provoking aspect of theatre signification. 'Disability' as a stage image communicates unseen aspects of character within theatre conventions. Disability acts as a sign for concepts within a disabling society. So what is the 'reality' of disability, and how does it relate to theatre?

Since the 1980s, the articulation of disability as a political identity has become an increasingly important part of cultural discourse. Rather than using disability only as a metaphor for aspects of a generalized human condition, disability is a lived human experience, a complex perspective on the ways we live together in society. The representation of disability has therefore taken on an important political purpose. The perception of disability as a plot device or a character flaw, a social problem or a disruption seems to exist in tension with the development of disability as a political identity.

The disability rights movement targeted the barriers to equality, countering discrimination and segregation, demanding access to the spheres of social, cultural and employment activity. Access to theatres for disabled audience members is one small part of this. Another would be equal access to the mechanisms we use to produce theatre, and so, opportunities, training, space and funding for disabled actors, directors, writers, designers, musicians, etc. Attempts to increase diversity in the arts highlighted the fact that the people and bodies that make theatre don't look like or sound like the population that theatre serves. Society may be better able to think about itself in the theatre if theatre includes individuals from across its constituent groups. The demand that disabled actors should be *at least auditioned* for the role of disabled characters is an attempt to forge opportunities for inclusion and is an attempt to create opportunities for disabled actors to earn a living making theatre.

Here is an example of a glitch between audience and signifying convention. In the play *The Glass Menagerie*, the character of Laura is a young woman with an unspecified mobility impairment. Her disability functions as an individual weakness, as an expression of vulnerability that can be readily seen and understood by the audience. Her hopes for love, her isolation and her social anxiety offer a counterpoint of pathos for her brother Tom's restlessness and feelings of entrapment. This role is an interesting challenge for an actor. Nicola Miles-Wildin, a disabled actor, director and theatre maker, described to me the process of reading a blog of an audience member's response to her performance of Laura. 'They were obsessed with my disability and described the process of trying to see up my skirt to see what my legs were like.' Miles-Wildin was disturbed and upset by the detailed description and speculation about her body. The actor felt as if her performance was taken out of context, that her work as an actor was simply ignored. Instead, the spectators took her presence on stage as an invitation to stare at her and to engage in speculation about her body and its impairments. Other disabled actors I have spoken to offer similar stories, and this is but a recent example. This is puzzling. Is there something about disability that disrupts or disturbs our fluent use of convention? We can easily allow a wooden puppet or a differently aged body to stand in for any character, so what exactly is the sort of glitch or snagging that is caused by a disabled actor standing in for a disabled character?

When there is a close connection between character and actor, there is seemingly no obstacle for the easy process of reading the actor's performance as the character Laura. There is a clear problem here of the role of ostension in performance. 'Ostension' (presentation) is a way of showing without signs by way of 'showing, displaying, pointing to, exhibiting' (Osolsobe 1979: 63). The body of the disabled performer is seen as an object to be looked at, and not as a vehicle for further signification. As Ivo Osolsobe argues, theatre habitually uses ostension to communicate concepts and objects. However, the meanings carried along with the disabled performer's body are richly textured and signified and carry with them a range of cultural beliefs about normalcy and capacity. These beliefs belong neither to the body as an ostended object nor to the play as text. This experience is frequently reported by disabled performers and can be evidenced by the process of reading reviews of performances by disabled actors. It suggests that while disabled *characters* are very much part of theatre tradition, disabled *performers* are not. The implications of this idea are profound and indicate a structural exclusion of disabled bodies from the sorts of signifying practices that can be engaged with in cultural life. Disabled bodies can represent disability, but the meanings assigned by convention and the political claims of the disabled individual in society are different in significance and operate in different representational worlds. A disabled character carries meanings that work within the diegesis. The disabled actor exceeds the diegesis and makes some other claim for meaning, interrupting the ease of the process of reading an actor as a fictional character.

Ways of Reading *The House of Bernarda Alba*

The example at the centre of this chapter is a production of Lorca's *The House of Bernarda Alba*, which in February 2017 was performed at the Royal Exchange, Manchester. The production uses Jo Clifford's translation and is by Graeae Theatre Company, directed by

Jenny Sealey. Kathryn Hunter plays Bernarda Alba. Graeae Theatre Company is based in London and was founded in the 1980s. It is artistically led by disabled people and seeks to develop artistic articulations that celebrate and challenge aspects of disabled experience and also to push back the boundaries of disabled people's participation in theatre. As well as developing programmes in new writing, actor training and a variety of youth and community activities, Graeae has developed a range of adaptations of classics from the British and European theatre canon. In adapting classics, Graeae offers a cultural meeting ground for its different audiences. Deaf and visually impaired audiences gain access to some of the plays that contribute to British theatre culture. Disabled audience members get to reimagine a world in which bodies like theirs appear and make up the performance. All audiences get to engage with the aesthetic and narrative differences that disability makes. It's not just about the simple act of appearing on stage; it is also the process of sharing the story through the lens of the actors' life experiences and bodies. If the conversation that takes place through theatre occurs via a canon of Western works, then Graeae wants to position its perspective in that conversation.

Theatre can be used as a symbol of cultural engagement, protected from the implications of debate. Look around you in the theatre. Who is here? Who is not here? And what difference does this make? As we sit in the theatre, engaged in a feeling of engagement and community, we may feel that who we are is defined by who we are *not*. Imagined in this performance is a form of theatre that challenges assumptions about the bodies with which we perceive and the bodies we perceive in performance. Most mainstream theatre is not accessible to audience members with visual impairments, and very little mainstream theatre involves captioning or simultaneous performance in British Sign Language (BSL). There is a presumption in Graeae's work that as far as possible 'we' are as wide a group as can be imagined and that we all access the performance on equal terms. That doesn't mean that the performance is translated from the 'real' version to a parallel or lesser performance; the languages of the piece include BSL and audio description. As a principle and as an aesthetic practice, the performance is accessible to audiences and to performers with a range of impairments.

'Aboutness'

The House of Bernarda Alba has been performed in many translations and versions a huge number of times. In the UK alone, it has been on exam syllabuses and is performed by casts of both professional and student actors. It is not *about* disability, although Bernarda walks with a stick, which she wields to terrorize her daughters, and it includes within it notions of attractiveness and ugliness as barriers to the life chances of the daughters. On one level, it is about a woman who locks up her daughters. *The House of Bernarda Alba* is a play about tyranny and love, and most of all, how we may build prisons for those we love. Fear of poverty and reputation are at the basis of Bernarda's character. She fears losing her home and livelihood and ending up in the brothel. To have her daughters marry beneath them would be a loss of social status. After all, she says, 'The poor are like animals. They are not like us.' In the world of the play, women are vulnerable, their wealth and status is not theirs to keep, but conferred through marriage. Bernarda does the mystifying thing that we see across many political circumstances: she enforces the rules of an oppressive system in which she has a low status. In the world of the play, things can only get worse. After her husband's funeral, Bernarda gathers her daughters around her and declares: 'We will brick up the doors and board up the windows. We won't let in a breath of air from the street. That's what we did in my father's house and in my father's father's house.' The house of Bernarda Alba of the play's title is repeatedly referred to by Bernarda as 'my father's house'. Men own property and confer social status, even when dead. There is a constant threat of loss, a constant financial and reputational instability. The adversity of the class system of the play is articulated by the servant characters. Before we meet Bernarda we hear the maid say: 'I hope the day comes when it's all burnt to the ground!'

In my brief sketch above, I can see that while there are many things that the play is *about*, is certainly *not about* disability. One of the early-twentieth-century 'Prague School' theorists, Jan Mukařovský says, 'The subject of a work simply plays the role of an axis of crystallization with respect to that signification which, otherwise, would remain vague' (1976: 6–7). Here, the subject of the play acts as a hinge through which ideas take on a specific form. The hinge or axis is tyranny. Lorca has evoked a world in which tyranny is systemic, where a political system is sustained by powerful and powerless alike, and maintained through fear. Bernarda is vigilant and suspicious, and yet strangely fails to notice the evidence of the scandals she fears. The wishes of the daughters have no importance. They must sit and sew. 'That's what it is to be a woman', Bernarda tells her daughters. The play is Lorca's challenge to the systems of class and patriarchy that he saw in Spain. His poetic evocation of the domestic incarceration of a woman and her daughters is often said to have been informed by his own feelings of entrapment as a homosexual. If Lorca's own circumstances led to a deep engagement and empathy with the oppression of others, Graeae's production responds to this by engaging the experiences of disabled people; the play echoes histories of segregation and institutionalization.

Sealey's production evokes the social separation of a group of disabled people, terrified of losing what they have, locked away by their mother, who mistrusts the world outside the house. One of the things you notice immediately is the presence of an ensemble of disabled actors on stage. Disability is part of the world of the onstage reality. Every character is disabled because every actor is disabled. For example, in this production, the daughters of Bernarda play out the social and physical implications of their impairment, such as when Amelia (Phillippa Cole) secretly removes her uncomfortable prosthetic leg. This is not specified in Lorca's play, but as in all performances of plays, the meeting of role and actor create the opportunity to fill the fictional world with details inspired by the embodied lives of both the actors and characters.

The Graeae production offers two ways into the play for the audience. Firstly, it offers a set of connections between different specific examples of oppression, holding them together with the sustained study of Bernarda, the tyrant. We can find structural connections between the situation of disabled people and the histories of systemic incarceration and the role of women in society. We can find atmospheric resonances between the threat and fear of fascist power structures and the ways these are upheld through the structures of families. Finally, we can see the fear and threat involved in the prospect of shifts in power. In this way, the audience freely makes connections between ideas of power and oppression, the play enabling us to play freely with metaphor as part of our reading. Secondly, it offers a specific exploration of the situation of disabled people, but seen through the established interpretative framework of Lorca's frequently performed play. What you found in this play, thematically, in the past, may now also be applied to a history you may not know, the history of disabled people. The reference of two different onstage realities, evoked but absent. The sharing of a canonical text between groups lays a claim to access to the interpretative community.

Difference and Ostention

In the performance, difference is played across all levels, not just between disabled and non-disabled person. Meanings converge on the performance. Numerous translations are happening simultaneously. The written words of Clifford's translation are projected on screens as another mode of access. The material presence of the words in light underline the simultaneity of the different articulations of the script. The performance is made of movement and sound. Some of the movement is language, communicating information and giving detail about character, attitude, emotion. Some of the sound is descriptive information about the set. This information seems to offer a description of the visual components that make up the fictional world. On this level, it would seem that parts of the stage picture are communicating aspects of reality, albeit of a fictional world. Or else they are communicating the real appearances of objects and bodies that are making up the fictional world. Are these descriptions part of the artwork, or are they simply practical supports, like the lighting rig or the stage rostra, as opposed to 'Bernarda's chair' or 'Bernarda's table'?

In recognition of the fact that much of the visual and aural world stands for or signifies details of a fictional world, the word 'Table' is projected onto the table that stands on the stage at the start of the second half of the play. There is a real table there, and there is also a signified (fictional) table, just as there are real disabled bodies and also signified fictional disabled bodies. There are two servants, one speaks and one signs and they offer commentary and description of the action. Two things are happening here. Firstly, everything that appears on stage is a sign. Nothing is on stage because it is 'really' there: it is there because it stands for something in the world of the play. So, a disabled actor stands for a disabled character, Kathryn Hunter stands for the character Bernarda Alba, the table stands for the table in Bernarda's house (and is labelled as such). But there is another level on which this works in the complex scheme of interpretation. The play text is spoken and signed. Both of these forms of dialogue are dialogue, but they simultaneously translate for each other. The production refuses to let any of the multiple language and sign systems adopt a purely practical or 'real world' function. If it cannot be incorporated into the fiction, if it cannot be made into a non-actual sign, then it simply doesn't go into the play.

The artistic distinctiveness of this performance is that all the elements of practical communication and access are rendered into signs. We can understand some of the language systems used, but these are language systems that are part of the signified world. They stand for something beyond themselves. Labelling the table 'Table' is a gentle and humorous insistence that we are in the theatre, and the systems of communication are part of a woven fabric known as *The House of Bernarda Alba*, and also that we are participants in a world where the rules of communication are part of a socially shared set of conventions. This experience is important because those conventions are different from those we are used to, either in social reality or in the parallel social reality of the theatre. We have negotiated them together.

I was lucky to be able to attend rehearsals to see Kathryn Hunter and the cast develop the production with the director, Jenny Sealey. I watched as characters developed the motivation and the techniques for noting and describing moments of action. I listened as the translator, Jo Clifford, engaged closely in the process of working between spoken and captioned English and British Sign Language. These practices together are part of a rich cultural identity, sometimes called 'disability culture'; the articulation of modes of communicating and arts making that have grown out of the practice of working together and celebrating our differences as part of a shared identity. In development workshops, several of the actors articulated the way that they and their characters have the same or similar impairments. 'This is the first time I have played a character with the same disability as me', said Kellan Frankland, who played Martirio, in a lunchtime discussion.

The daughters of Bernarda create an ensemble, making the dialogue and action accessible to the audience by signing and voicing for each other as they would do in a family. The details of the family's communications emerged from development workshops with the creative team and the actors where they discussed upbringings in which parents didn't sign but siblings did, where relationships and power dynamics were played out in a complex system of different sorts of communication. The production reflects this; not everybody in the Alba family signs or lip-reads and the relationships and power dynamics are affected by how people communicate, moment to moment. The audience can look out for moments of tension and frustration. It's incredibly rude to turn your back on somebody who is signing. One sister voices over the BSL speech of another sister so that their mother, who can't sign, can understand. Together they facilitate or block each other's communication and in this way, enable the audience to understand the play. The dynamics of the signing and speaking sisters is as complex and nuanced as can possibly be understood. This is not a mechanistic or stylistic gloss on the performance, but is part of the depth of textual exploration and characterization that comes from the articulation of experiences of communicating and telling stories together as d/Deaf and disabled people.

Disability as Aesthetic Novelty

Disability is a relationship, a reading of bodies. We read and live our own bodies too, of course. The way we individually experience impairment or pain is a complex set of affects and sensations, mediated by language and culture. The way we understand the form of our own bodies is based on a complex relationship between the schema or pattern of generalized human bodies, our lifelong experience of others' changing bodies, and observed changes in our own bodies as they grow and mature. Bodies are not stable entities, but theoretical notions. We exist socially through systems of conventions. These please us insofar as they are hardly noticed. Art forms push these conventions or norms, but within a restricted frame. The difference with theatre is that its ingredients exist in motion and in sound, and through the way that a segment of time is unfolded in space (or vice versa). The legibility of the conventions through which we exist and think rests on social and cultural norms.

The snagging of attention caused by the appearance of a disabled body in a canonical Western theatre play is an interesting text because it enables us to negotiate a process, a time frame for the encounter that goes beyond a gaze or a stare. It is a relationship that must shift if we are to understand the play. There is a paradox implicit in what I say here. Disability may transform the way we see, but only insofar as we may transform how we see disability. The way that the play structures our attention and our responses over time may seem to be a way to organize our perceptions around a set of concepts. I think that it is a *disciplinary* structure. The point where we sit in obedience and struggle with meaning and emotional response against a backdrop of other cultural articulations is the very point. The production enables us to ask about our perception of the social body and about what we need to do (and how we might resist this) in the act of watching the real and the fictional enfolding of disabled bodies into the contingent structures of theatre.

One difficulty with the notion of *access* is that it seems to relate to the idea of freedom to use or to enter territory that exists already. To be welcomed and included seems unequivocally positive. However, there are two problems with this model of inclusion. Firstly, if you welcome somebody to partake then you lay claim to that resource. Secondly, this idea of inclusion seems to be based on a misunderstanding of theatre. Theatre is based on a dynamic interplay between the community of potential audience members and the form itself. If you change the way that the audience understands themselves and you change the way that the theatre makers understand themselves, then theatre must change.

Politics is necessarily partial and partisan. You claim space for your own identified group. If you start making space for others you can get trapped in the role of host, offering access to a pre-existing space. The difficulty of political art is that it enacts or represents politics without producing politics. One of the most exciting aspects of the production lies in a radical reframing of the body of Kathryn Hunter. Hunter is one of the most celebrated actors of her generation. By appearing as part of the cast of this production, she simultaneously ensures that many people who are uninterested in accessible theatre will go to see the production and she also claims a space as a disabled performer. Looking back at the example from Miles-Wildin's performance experience, the blogging spectator reported that basically they had become so distracted from the play they were watching simply because a real disabled person was on stage. In a world where disability is metaphor, it is not possible to think in terms of off stage impairment as this makes the performance non-theatrical. If we are used to something being a sign for something else, then it cannot and must not stand for the thing itself. This snagging of attention means that verisimilitude (faithfulness to reality) is not really part of our response to theatre. There are cultural and aesthetic conventions that enable us to see the world as straightforward, present and truthful. Kathryn Hunter's celebrated career in theatre means that for many people, theatrical experience has been heavily influenced by her work. Gently aligning herself and her body with disability performance demands that we look again at the conventions that shape our cultural expectations for which bodies make theatre and which do not.

Interpretative Community

As the audience of this performance, we are an interpretative community. As with all performance, shared space and time is the frame for all our experiences. The physical space of the Royal Exchange, Manchester is theatre in the round and it offers the experience of seeing the performance with a backdrop of other audience members, all watching as we watch. The production is crafted to enable us to each follow different aspects of the performance. One might look from the projected words to the actors as they speak the text or follow the signing actors in dialogue or perhaps engage in the aural world of the play, listening to actors' voices with the help of live audio description. Yet, beyond the attempts to follow the text, there is also a textual or interpretative experience that envelops the play. There is the aesthetic texture of the multiple communication systems and the way that they are coordinated to make the visual and aural world of the play. We might speculate about sharing an experience with people who are following the play in a very different way from us, or else enjoy the fact that we are part of a language community of users of British Sign Language. In addition, because Graeae explicitly advocates and articulates its political views about the equality of disabled people, we are likely to enjoy a sense of community with a greater proportion of disabled people, simply because of the presence of disabled people in the audience.

Theatre requires that an audience gathers together to share an experience. For the time of the performance we make a community of shared meaning. We are not required to think the same thing or to respond in the same way, but at the end of the evening we feel that we have experienced something together, across all our differences. The different communicational strands each have different grammars and vocabularies, and each has its own time frame. British Sign Language has a spatial grammar and the time frame for a specific speech needs to be coordinated with the actors who are speaking as well as the surtitles projection operator. Visual and vocal expressivity may be read from the bodies and voices of actors without directly understanding what they say. This means that while there are signifying elements within the performance that communicate Lorca's text, there are other elements that do not. Many of the linguistic signs on stage are not intended for or comprehensible by each of us, and yet they are undeniably part of what is communicated. The struggles for meaning make this a worthwhile and engaging perspective, and there is also the possibility of enjoying the performances in the different gestural vocabularies of the performers. A performance of anger in spoken English and in British Sign Language may be interesting in different ways to an audience member who understands one but not both of these languages.

This text is a bundle of related and simultaneous texts. There are nodes of shared attention, such as when Bernarda's anger creates a silent tension. These moments create a shared and unified focus. There is also a need to make clear which character is saying which line to make clear the causal relationships that lead to catastrophe in the play. The canonical status of the play ensures that there is a shared concept of 'the text' as Lorca's play, as the ultimate shared experience that all communicate and perceive. Admittedly, it would be possible to separate into different productions of *Bernarda Alba* a performance for a visually impaired audience, one for British Sign Language users and one for users of spoken English. However, the signified and unified reading available to us all is the fact that all these users are accessing the same text at the same moment, fully aware of, and able to enjoy as aesthetic, the linguistic elements that we cannot access.

The text is an idealized notion, shared and heavily individuated; singular and yet made of a bundle of signifiers and objects. We enact unanimity when we act as an audience, and yet this doesn't go anywhere close to sharing meaning or experience. Text is a performative, enacting a culture through differences. This text may carry with it social interpretations that enable the plight of the incarcerated daughters to be a reading of institutionalized and excluded disabled people. To understand the *same text at the same time* is the process of evolving a culture. 'A sign must be understood the same way by both sender and receiver' (Mukařovský 1976: 5), but there is no sense that we understand the same thing in the same way. Our divergent but simultaneous responses cohere to the point where their divergence *means* the text.

It's not that we may all take what we will from the play; we try together to understand a specific artefact as part of a specific event. This is something we work at through the play. The structure of the play takes us through an arc of action within a known and formal structure, so that where the signs shift in form we can discern the meanings that they signify. Honzl said that 'the constancy of a structure causes theatrical signs to develop complex meanings. The stability of signs promotes a wealth of meanings and associations' ([1940] 2016: 134). I suggest that the dynamics in accessible theatre adhere to the interplay of complexity and stability, making access into a two-way process. In this process, the canonical play is made accessible as the signs that enable access are placed together with other more familiar signs to widen theatre's access to modes of communication and language, and to a wider view of audience. Theatre tradition and canonicity may therefore be a way to enable theatre audiences to eventually access the creative world of disability performance.

Performance Details

The House of Bernarda Alba by Federico García Lorca. Translated by Jo Clifford. Directed by Jenny Sealey. A Royal Exchange Theatre and Graeae Theatre Company co-production. The Royal Exchange, Manchester, 3–25 February 2017
Further details and resources: http://graeae.org/our-work/house-bernarda-alba/

Further Reading

Davis (2010) is a collection of groundbreaking writings in the area of disability studies. If your habit is to think through the discipline of theatre and performance studies, then you will be challenged and exhilarated by this collection of important works by disabled scholars. Drozd et al. (2016) is a new and very exciting publication and re-translation of Czech Theatre Theory. My chapter has only dipped into the possibilities of these influential analytical approaches, but this work needs to be reread for difficult questions of theatre making and spectatorship today. Hadley (2014) is a fascinating and passionately argued book about the connections between the experience of embodied disability and performance studies. Knowles (2014) is a comprehensive introduction to systematic studies of the difficult questions about meaning and signification in theatre. He uses case studies to explore theoretical and analytical approaches in an intelligible and directly applicable way. Kuppers (2017) is a short and very readable book that guides the reader through the different parts of theatre-going and making experience; asking provocatively throughout what difference disability makes to the experience.

Acknowledgements

I would like to thank my colleagues Pavel Drábek and Lucy Nevitt for their influential commentary and advice on a draft of this chapter. I'm also very grateful to Jenny Sealey and the company of *The House of Bernarda Alba*, who generously invited me to rehearsals at the Royal Exchange in Manchester. Finally, I have enjoyed discussing the production and the play with University of Hull graduate student Sophie Hodgson and staff and students at the University of Reading. I have learnt much from them all.

References

Cohen-Almagor, Rapahel (2015), *Confronting the Internet's Dark Side: Moral and Social Responsibility on the Free Highway*, Cambridge: Cambridge University Press.

Davis, Lennard J., ed. (2010), *The Disability Studies Reader*, 3rd edn, London: Routledge.

Driedger, Diane (1989), *The Last Civil Rights Movement: Disabled Peoples' International*, London: Hurst & Co.

Drozd, David, Tomáš Kačer and Don Sparling, eds (2016), *Theatre Theory Reader: Prague School Writings*, Prague: Karolinum Press.

Freud, Sigmund ([1916] 2001), 'Some Character-Types Met with in Psycho-Analytic Work: 1. The Exceptions', in James Strachey, Anna Freud, Alix Strachey and Alan Tyson (eds and trans.), *The Standard Edition of the Complete Psychological Works of Sigmund Freud*, vol. 14, 311–5, London: Vintage.

Hadley, Bree (2014), *Disability, Public Space, Performance and Spectatorship: Unconscious Performers*, Basingstoke: Palgrave Macmillan.

Honzl, Jindřich ([1940] 2016), 'The Mobility of the Theatrical Sign', trans. I. R. Titunik, in David Drozd, Tomáš Kačer and Don Sparling (eds), *Theatre Theory Reader: Prague School Writings*, 129–46, Prague: Karolinum Press.

Knowles, Ric (2014), *How Theatre Means*, Basingstoke: Palgrave Macmillan.

Kuppers, Petra (2017), *Theatre & Disability*, Basingstoke: Palgrave Macmillan.

Lewis, Victoria Ann, ed. (1989), *Beyond Victims and Villains: Contemporary Plays by Disabled Playwrights*, New York: Theatre Communications Group.

Lorca, Federico García ([1945] 2012), *The House of Bernarda Alba*, trans. J. Clifford, London: Nick Hern Books.

Mukařovský, Jan ([1936] 1976), 'Art as Semiotic Fact', in Ladislav Matějka and Irwin R. Titunik (eds), *Semiotics of Art: Prague School Contributions*, 3–9, Cambridge, MA: MIT Press.

Osolsobe, Ivo (1979), 'On Ostensive Communication', *Studia Semiotyczne* 8: 63–75.

The House of Bernarda Alba (2017), [Live performance] Dir. Jenny Sealey, UK: Manchester Royal Exchange, 7 February.

Williams, Tennessee ([1944] 2014), *The Glass Menagerie*, London: Penguin.

4 How Does Stage Performance Think Through Cultural Convention?

SEAN METZGER

This chapter explores some of the ways in which the theatre constructs cultural conventions. By cultural convention, I mean norms associated with groups (national, ethnic, subcultural, and so forth) constituted on stage and evoked through signs like accent, behaviour, dress and locational markers. Asian American and intercultural theatre specifically foreground the creation of such norms and thus provide a useful frame for investigating the staging of cultural conventions in general. The major tool I engage for this endeavour is semiotics. 'Semiosis' (derived from the Greek word meaning 'to mark') is an activity or process that involves signs. As a field of study (semiotics), it was developed largely through philosophy and linguistics (for example, how do English-language speakers understand that the word 'cat' is a sign to denote a small feline animal). Generally speaking, we live in a world structured by such signs, although most of us do not consciously think about them on an everyday basis. Nevertheless, some professions, whether they acknowledge it or not, depend on semiotics. For example, I am typing on a computer on the outside of which is a shape recognizable to many people around the world. That image looks like an apple with a bite taken out of it. Advertisers have been very successful at linking this graphic with the word 'apple' in English and its equivalents in other languages. This example begins to demonstrate how complicated semiotics can be. 'Apple' (or its equivalent, like *pingguo* in Chinese) usually denotes a piece of fruit. Rendered as the image I described above, it conveys this information, but also, and more importantly in terms of my laptop, the word refers to a transnational corporation. One sign might have multiple interpretations, so the meaning attributed to it is arbitrary and dependent on context.

Like advertisers, theatre makers depend heavily on semiotics. People who work in stage performance depend not only on verbal signs, but also on gestural ones and those produced by images, objects and sounds in the performance space. The collection of signs might produce realist effects; for example, several tables and chairs represent a teahouse in Lao She's play *chaguan* (*Teahouse*, 1957). The costumes of the characters help viewers identify the plot's shifting time period, which moves from the late-nineteenth century to the mid-twentieth century. In a similar vein, one could imagine an actor adopting a kind of drunken stupor to portray Martha in Edward Albee's *Who's Afraid of Virginia Woolf?* (1962). In this chapter, I concentrate, although not exclusively, on sartorial semiosis and the ways that clothing and movements within these garments function as signs that convey meaning to an audience. To illustrate my analysis, I amass examples from the work of an American playwright, David Henry Hwang, who frequently stages Chinese and Chinese American cultural conventions for largely mainstream audiences.

My discussion of semiosis takes up debates about the decline of semiotic approaches in theatre broached, for example, in the 2008 special issue of *Semiotica* (Carlson 2008) concerning this topic. Because theatre so often serves as a medium of representation, it has benefited a great deal from semiotics, which, again, involves the study of signification in all of its contexts. Indeed, theatre semiotics began in earnest with the Prague School, a group of linguists and critics centred from the 1920s through the 1940s in what was then Czechoslovakia. The Prague School drew heavily on the work of Swiss linguist Ferdinand de Saussure (1857–1913) and the American philosopher, Charles Sanders Peirce (1839–1914). The semiotic enterprise that emerged from Saussure's and Peirce's respective oeuvres was wide-ranging, inflecting overlapping studies of anthropology (Claude Lévi-Strauss), film (Christian Metz), feminism (Teresa de Lauretis), literature (Roland Barthes and Umberto Eco), psychoanalysis (Jacques Lacan) and philosophy (Jacques Derrida), among other fields; in short, semiotics had a significant impact not only on, but also well beyond, the humanities and studies of expressive culture. The Prague School itself often becomes a footnote in this genealogy, perhaps because of its formal disintegration following the 1948 coup d'état. Nevertheless, theatre and performance scholars continued to draw on semiotics through the 1980s and 1990s when such lines of enquiry yielded to different methodologies.

Theatre's investment in functional material objects on stage and their simultaneous use as signs to convey meaning have long fascinated theatre semioticians (for example, the audience simultaneously recognizes the dead seagull in Chekhov's play as a prop carried and as a dead bird, as well as a symbol that might point to the character Konstantin's psychological state, among other possibilities). In light of the multiple layers of signification that occur on stage, the Saussurean model that emphasizes signifier and signified (again, 'cat' to denote a general category of feline mammals) over what Saussure called the referent (the material object) may provide less flexibility than the model of signification offered by Peirce. Certainly, I am not alone in turning towards Peirce's typology of the sign (symbol, icon, index), although studies in theatre semiotics that have used the symbol and icon have tended to bear more analytical weight than the index. My aim is to frame the ways in which the index, as an under-analysed term within theatre studies, can be recuperated to better account for the ways race, difference and gesture inter-relate in live performance – that is, the ways in which the index might offer a valuable tool to understand how stage performance signifies cultural conventions.

In order to execute this project, I begin by describing some of Hwang's plays to reveal how his productions evoke but also create cultural conventions through the deployment of specific signs on stage. First, I turn my attention to the index as a way of mediating between the actor's experience of, and engagement with, the physical world and the representations created through costume. To offer some focus to this discussion, I trace a genealogy of scholarship that facilitates thinking about the relation of physical action to semiotics through the index. As a case study, I use a production of Hwang's *Golden Child* (Hwang 1999) from 2012 in order to illuminate my more theoretical discussion. Second, I extend the possibilities of the index in relation to Hwang's two-hander called *Bondage* (first performed 1992; Hwang 1997). I conclude by reframing the importance of theatre semiotics as a particularly valuable form of critique for thinking about cultural conventions, specifically those relating to Asian American and intercultural productions.

Forms of Dress in David Henry Hwang's Theatre

David Henry Hwang is one of the most produced writers for commercial American theatre and across media platforms. His Broadway credits alone include the musicals *Aida* (1998), *Flower Drum Song* (2002) and *Tarzan* (2006), as well as the plays *Chinglish* (2011), *Golden Child* (1998) and *M. Butterfly* (1988, 2017), which has earned him the most renown and for which he has received the most scholarly attention. Although performed at venues from Hong Kong to London, Hwang's body of theatrical work most frequently appears on stages within the United States, and he has enjoyed high-profile runs in New York at the Joseph Papp Public Theater and the Signature Theatre (which hosted a residency and retrospective for Hwang in its 2012–13 season). He has also written for film on projects with directors including David Cronenberg and John Madden. His librettos have been heard at major opera houses, including collaborations with composer Bright Sheng and director Ong Keng Sen at Santa Fe Opera, composer Huang Ro and director David Paul at Washington National Opera, and composer Bright Sheng and director Stan Lai at San Francisco Opera. Hwang also works in television. Given these credits, he remains within the field of Asian American performance without rival in terms of financial returns and mainstream visibility. Looking at David Henry Hwang's work for the theatre suggests some of the ways in which his text-based work signifies Chinese and Asian American cultural conventions to a wide audience.

Hwang repeatedly returns to costume as a means to articulate transnational migratory routes that might sustain or contest ethnicized roots. The forms of dress circulating in Hwang's theatre layer historical narratives that reveal or otherwise shape erotic and political desires, as well as the norms that render those desires legible on stage (here we can think of *M. Butterfly* in which seeing and feeling feminine clothes helps the character Rene Gallimard sustain the fantasy that his male lover is a woman). A pair of Hwang's earliest plays demonstrates two of the more obvious semiotic functions of theatrical costume. *F.O.B.* (first performed 1980; Hwang 1990) begins with a monologue describing how clothing might identify the titular F.O.B., or an Asian recently arrived and 'fresh off the boat' (6). The American-Born-Chinese (or A.B.C.), Dale, decries the unfashionable look of these F.O.B.-y migrants – 'four-eyed' with 'high-water pants' or 'floods' – just after describing a litany of their ostensible personality characteristics (6). Several minutes later when Steve, Dale's nemesis, appears on stage, the F.O.B. decries the lack of cultural knowledge of the A.B.C. Steve also connects clothing to character. He laments that the people he has encountered – both the 'ChinaMan' clad in the green leisure suit and the kid in blue jeans and a t-shirt – seem to know nothing of Chinese cultural icons. In *F.O.B.*, both material clothes and linguistic references to them serve as devices that reinforce the narrative inscription of cultural difference between China and the United States. By contrast, *The Dance and the Railroad* (1981) deploys hairpieces, notably the Chinese men's long braids, or queues, to help establish movement as part of an ostensibly Chinese aesthetic that informs the play. The swinging of men's tresses codes as a part of the opera training of the protagonist Lone in the diegetic narrative; the play invents this as a cultural convention, which works to establish Chinese character. As I have discussed elsewhere, the queue marks a certain inassimilable Chineseness on the American frontier (Metzger 2014). As Hwang's work has evolved, he has continued to play with the materialization of difference and sameness through dress.

Building on this epistemology of semiotic identification that marks something Asian versus something Western, later plays frequently take up costume as a more complex semiotic sign structuring meaning and referentiality.

One example of this semiotic exploration occurs in *Golden Child*, which premiered in 1996, then appeared on Broadway in 1998, and was subsequently revised for production at New York's Signature Theatre in 2012. A memory play that transforms an expecting couple into the soon-to-be father's ancestors, *Golden Child* primarily narrates the religious conversion of Ahn, a young woman born into the household of one Eng Tien-Bing and his three wives. The production uses costume to signify three overlapping cultural systems on stage. The first is sartorially coded as Western; the second is the spirit world manifested on stage through ghostly robes and make up; and the third is what Hwang constructs as traditional China – marked through the explicit mention of items such as women's bound feet and men's *changpao*, or long robes. As might be expected, various family members clad themselves in Western clothes as they begin to convert to Christianity. The patriarch's changpao is exchanged for a suit, and his second wife exchanges her premodern attire for a Western dress and heels, which she finds herself unable to wear because of her bound feet (here it is worth noting that the usual Chinese word for suit is 'xifu', which literally means Western clothes).

When first verbalized in the play, foot-binding is immediately rendered as that which opposes China to the 'modern world' (11). The convention of bound feet is the primary physical challenge presented by this dramatic piece. The production team must solve the question of how to represent through movement, costume and/or other theatrical devices a foot whose ideal length was three and a half inches. Moreover, the audience sees the effects of foot-binding when certain characters enter a scene before its initial mention several minutes into the production. Bound feet thus raise questions in terms of the ways a performer enacts the physical constraints that help define a character. *Golden Child* raises related semiotic questions about the relation of corporeal performance to representation.

Semiotics and Indexicality

A semiotic analysis enriches the understanding of *Golden Child*, but the play also facilitates an engagement with the conundrums of the semiotic enterprise itself. Put otherwise, the play provides a case study to think about indexicality in relation to theatre and also to think through some of the theoretical complexities of indexicality. To restage this thesis yet again, *Golden Child* not only showcases cultural conventions, but also reveals how the production establishes such conventions in the first place.

The American pragmatist, Charles Peirce (1985), divided the sign into three categories: the icon (a sign that shares specific, often graphic, properties with objects: such as a pencil streak representing a geometrical line); the symbol (a sign that creates an arbitrary link between sign and object, as is the case with language); and the index (usually understood as a sign that creates a material link between sign and object, such as a bullet hole). Marvin Carlson (2008) has observed that studies of theatre semiotics have made much use of this tripartite division, although I would assert that the index remains much less theorized in theatre as opposed to, for example, film studies. Indeed, the index is perhaps the most vexing of Peirce's typology. Peirce argues the index is a sign that points to something. The index establishes a relationship between an individual object and sense of memory of the person for whom it serves as a sign (in other words, the index implies the interpretant of the sign, which Carlson has promoted as a valuable heuristic for theatre studies). For the purpose of thinking through costume, some of Peirce's (1985) provocative examples include 'a man with a rolling gait', which suggests to the author that this ambler is a sailor (13). In a similar vein, 'a man in corduroys, gaiters, and a jacket' indicates a jockey (13). Other examples of indices include a barometer and a weathervane as well as pronouns like 'this', which force a listener to 'establish a real connection between his mind and the object' (14). The status of this linkage depends on conventional understandings of cause and effect. Because the index demands this interpretation of convention, the index has often been elaborated in relationship to realism precisely because, as film scholar Mary Ann Doane has written, the 'index is sutured to its object by a physical cause, a material connection' (2007: 4). If the theatrical world suspends realism, what sets the conditions of possibility for the index?

Certainly, to think about Peirce's own examples of clothed figures pointing to a certain métier (the sailor or the jockey) poses a problem. Peirce also claims that 'indices assert nothing' (1985: 16). In and of themselves, indices do not represent content; otherwise they fall into the realm of icon or symbol. The pace and bearing of an individual in Peirce's understanding serve as indicators, but, unlike the example of a bullet hole, the gait requires continuous action. Much more like the barometer, the gait calls attention to forces normally not perceived through human eyes. Here we have a difference between theatre and film. In relation to cinema, the impression of light on celluloid partakes of a visual phenomenon and that quality has a certain property of detachability. Film does not show us what is there, but what was there. Doane writes of the 'dialectic of the empty and the full that lends the index an eeriness and uncanniness not associated with the realms of the icon or symbol' (2007: 2). Unlike electronic and digital media, live performance usually foregrounds people in the process of acting, as opposed to images or bytes. Whatever the symbolic import of, for example, a group of sailors singing 'Nothing Like a Dame' in *South Pacific* (1949), the audience sees several (usually half-naked) men dancing and singing together. Indeed, live theatre frequently plays on the layers of meaning generated between onstage actions and the connotations they produce.

Although many efforts in the area of theatre semiotics have been devoted to creating different typologies of signs, Keir Elam's relatively early study, first published in 1980, provides a very helpful lead for my chapter's concerns. In this regard, his work is worth quoting at length.

> Costume … may denote iconically the mode of dress worn by the dramatic figure but, at the same time, stand indexically for his social position or profession, just as the actor's movement across the stage will simultaneously represent some act in the dramatic world and indicate the dramatis persona's frame of mind or standing (the cowboy's swagger or, to repeat Peirce's example, the sailor's gait). The category of index is so broad that every aspect of the performance can be considered as in some sense indexical. The dramatic setting, for instance, is often represented not by means of a direct 'image' but through cause-and-effect association or contiguity. (Consider the first scene of *The Tempest*, where the storm may, according to illusionistic principles, be suggested by wind machines, stage rain and other technological paraphernalia, or simply by the actors' movements, depicting the tempest's immediate consequences.) (22–3)

Elam's analysis is useful for considering the extent of indexicality in theatrical production. For the audience to sustain belief in structures of cause and effect in a fictional onstage world, theatre makers deploy various signs that create likely causal linkages. An audience should loosely understand such connections (in Elam's Shakespearean example, the actor is rolling across the stage because he is being blown across the ship by the wind or has lost balance because of the tilt of the deck, or for some other similar reason) because the actor's action (in this case) points the spectator to a cluster of probable causes. The spectator is expected to reach those conclusions based on conventional understandings. This last point becomes apparent when one attends the theatre with a child who has never been to such a venue. The child is as likely to ask why an actor is rolling downstage as he or she is to perceive an unseen wave knocking the actor down. The lesson here? Conventional understandings of cause and effect must be learnt.

The far-reaching understanding of the index and its uses in stage production perhaps mitigates the heuristic value of indexicality in theatre semiotics. In Erika Fischer-Lichte's book *The Semiotics of Theater*, first published in German in 1983, she also writes of costumes and signs as they relate to the production of meaning through theatre. For her, the theatrical code (the system of signs in the theatre that generates meaning) works in relation to a basic formula: 'the minimum preconditions for theater to be theater are that person A represents X while S looks on' (1992: 7). Her analysis elaborates a discussion relevant for thinking through costume in particular:

> Now, in order to depict X, A (1) dons a particular external appearance, (2) acts in a certain way, and (3) does so in a certain space. ... If person A in her capacity as person A prepares her external appearance in a special way, for example, by slipping on a fur coat, then she probably does this because she is cold and wishes to warm herself. The fur coat denotes a certain utility function in which it is also used de facto. (7–8)

A costume fur coat serves as an icon of an actual fur coat insofar as the costume shares the look of the object that inspired it. In the theatrical world, putting on the coat may further indicate that the temperature has dropped (even when the temperature stays the same in the 'real' world that the audience inhabits). For Fischer-Lichte, usually the indexical function (a cause-and-effect relation) is subordinated to what Peirce would call iconic or symbolic signs. Conventional relations of cause and effect are less interesting to her than other meanings generated by different types of signs. In my case, however, I am particularly interested in what happens if we press on the idea of convention.

Carlson has also briefly discussed indexicality insofar as theatre structures and theatrical events themselves point to a historical past. One example he provides concerns Drottningholm Court Theatre in Sweden. At this site, one can see eighteenth-century court performances re-enacted for tourists in the present. Carlson explains that 'the power of this sort of icon arises from the fact that it is also an index, pointing to the absent and distanced historical reality which interests the spectator' (2008: 88). The performance promises to create the conventions of a historical period. But to what end? The implication is that something is to be gained from seeing or otherwise experiencing an embodied interpretation of history. Passion for such seemingly esoteric knowledge may seem to reside only in the fantasies of a small group of theatre historians. However, the conventions of (assumed) cultural difference have significant impact across scales from the intimate to the global.

Indeed, Carlson's ideas about the theatrical performance indexing a 'historical reality' help explain *Golden Child*.

The ambulatory qualities of *Golden Child*'s four actresses in the play's logic should help an audience access an earlier time, specifically the early years of the Chinese Republic. This era was a moment of cultural transition signified in part by the physical transformation of many women's feet. Women's corporeal movements, then, shaped this historical moment. In Hwang's theatrical world, the shift from present action to the past of memory occurs in part through the sign of the gait, or walk, of each actress. Following Mary Ann Doane's observation in the context of film and photography, we might say *Golden Child* subscribes to the 'promise of indexicality' as 'the rematerialization of time' (2002: 10). But this promise relies on a sedimentation of convention in the theatre.

The tradition of crippling young girls and women by breaking and folding in the toes and snapping the arch is a physical practice now (thankfully) lost to history. Although significant moments of pathos in the play depend on sustaining the credulity of onstage foot-binding (as in the end of act one), the misshapen bound foot is that which cannot be seen, smelled or otherwise directly perceived. An actor's real foot would simply be too large to serve as a substitute for anything close to the three-inch ideal of the bound foot. Moreover, there is, I believe, no corollary to this physical experience on which an actor might draw through some variant of realistic acting training. If the gait of these women indeed points to something, it points not to any actual referent, but to practice reconstructed through a fantasy about the experience of breaking and refusing bones, of sloughing dead skin from living tissue, of making Chinese women 'ache for beauty' (to echo poet and scholar Wang Ping; see Wang Ping 2000).

To follow the index in this case leads not to something real but instead to the conditions of possibility that found the real. Indeed, the play itself does not particularly invest in theatrical realism. Ghosts materialize on stage. The dialogue contains witty but seemingly anachronistic repartees, and broken English is used rather comically to connote a missionary's poor Chinese language skills. Only insofar as the play stages a social problem might realism seem useful as a description. The index points here less to what was than to what was imagined. That imagined past is, in turn, reconstructed through a rehearsal process that provides an imagined equivalency between women who had to move with bound feet and actresses who have to play such ladies. To put this claim another way, cause and effect are not the result of physics in this dramatic world; convention here is an imaginative reconstruction.

Indices work 'on the order of the trace' to borrow once more from Doane (2007: 2). Such a formulation need not lead to some assertions about the real, or even realism, but to the systems of knowledge that encourage and even produce a reading of present and past. What the actors and audience perceive in *Golden Child* are the traces (screams and stilted movements) produced through fantasies about women, fantasies that involve larger orientalist structures that describe the patriarchal world of feudal China.

The staging of foot-binding in *Golden Child* ultimately reveals the play's construction of feudal China. Today, foot-binding on stage can only be approximated; it cannot be replicated as a physical practice (unlike, say, an accent or a dance style appropriate to the time period). Therefore, the production evokes the cultural convention of foot-binding by indexing an ostensible cause-and-effect relationship. Again, the index of the actor's movements leads the spectator to infer that the character has bound feet. Semiotics points us to how this

Fig. 4.1 Signature Theatre's *Golden Child*, 2012. Photo: Richard J. Termine.

device reflects not 'historical reality' so much as the production team's imagination of what might have been. Rather than relying on empirical relationships of cause and effect, the index in this case leads us to consider the construction of cultural norms presumed to constitute reality.

In *Golden Child*, questions that might emerge through foot-binding are subsumed in the trajectory of past explicating the present, in telling how an oppressive feudal China can lead to surprising leaps of faith that transform a young girl with few life options available to her, because of her status in a polygamous household, into a born-again Christian who, however ironically, shapes her own destiny. This critique of feudal China tends to overshadow other possible enquiries regarding the staging of Chinese life. Rather than neatly tying things together, indexicality demands that the audience infer causation. Looking at each woman's gait helps the audience ponder a world lost. This world of the past cannot be encompassed through the singular plot of a play. Foot-binding as both a historical phenomenon and as embodied experience becomes another order of questions raised through the indexical sign of the gait. While there are many potentially fruitful directions one might pursue along these lines, allow me briefly to elaborate one. The index of the gait demands energy from the actor to sustain it. It points to something happening in the theatre right now – the continual construction of character – yet also something that has passed in terms of rehearsal. The index is of a continuous present and a past accessed as a memory of the convention of walking with bound feet. This convention has been reconstructed for the actor, rehearsed and then represented to the audience. The past temporality here thus works through not only the past of rehearsal but through recourse to conventional understandings of bound feet that set the conditions of possibility for the rehearsal.

A Historical Critique

Given Hwang's reconstruction of foot-binding, one might ask, what questions does the play fail to pose about the historical experience of women in China? Dorothy Ko has written in her revisionist history of foot-binding that it might be worth locating 'woman's agency and subjectivity not only in the world that the pain destroyed, but also in the subsequent unfolding and creation of meanings: for each woman, footbinding was an ongoing process, just as each body was located in a specific time and place' (2007: 1–2). The *fangzu*, or letting out feet, discourse from the 1900s to the 1930s is never explicitly mentioned in Hwang's play, yet it provides several possibilities for embodying the contradictions of discourses of beauty, labour and morality. For example, one scene of *Golden Child* is a dance sequence, usually staged as a moment of affection between the patriarch and his third wife, whom he chose out of love. The scene often suggests a potential transcendence available through dance for these would-be lovers, if only the woman could move appropriately. The scene stages the subjective frustration of the couple: the man trying to move into Western ideals of romantic love, the woman bound literally and figuratively by convention.

But there is a larger social commentary lurking just beyond these awkward moves. Certainly, dancing throughout the 1920s and 1930s in China ignited moral debates circulating around women's recent mobility in the literal sense, but also in the sense of a woman's place in a Confucian world view. Mobility provided greater capacity to act for some, but it also connoted licentiousness to others. And, of course, woman's movement would, beginning with the founding of the Communist Party in China during the early 1920s, also become a pivotal means of obtaining class consciousness. How bound feet create meaning for individuals and for a larger movement of women varied by numerous factors, including location, education and familial affiliation. If the index of the gait in this production points the audience to these questions, then semiotics maintains a significant role in complicating the ways that intercultural discourse moves. It points us to the sorts of cultural assertions and histories valorized by dominant American discourse and the other possibilities left unarticulated in the larger theatrical world – both actual and fantastic.

In other words, to follow the index is to see the limits of how an Asian American playwright constructs China, but also to open such expression to greater interpretation. Such a critical move echoes Carlson's call for an exploration of the relations among theatre reception, intercultural theatre and semiotics (2008: 136) and to disaggregate, as Ric Knowles has suggested, the material condition of production, the performance itself and reception (2008: 235). To follow the index through Asian American theatre specifically also allows us to rethink what and how indexicality might mean when conventions of cause and effect are dependent on always ideological reconstructions.

Gesture and Race

Another of Hwang's pieces explores further the notion of intimacy, particularly as such relationships take shape through ostensibly racialized gestures. Hwang's *Bondage* (1992) illustrates some of the ways in which indexicality might complicate understandings of intimacy as a localized feeling between people. The play takes a snapshot of the relationship between Mark and his hired dominatrix Terri. Clad completely in leather, the characters act out various sexual fantasies. The pair of leather-concealed actors on stage specifically perform racial stereotypes readily available in mainstream American media at the time. For example, in Mark's initial identification as a Chinese man, he is 'vulnerable' and questions whether 'it's Ok' for him to love Terri, who describes herself as a blonde woman. The performed relationships in *Bondage* typically begin with Terri proclaiming her character role and assigning another one to Mark. The announced routines, particularly those of Terri, who constantly confronts Mark's desire for politically correct speech in the S/M environment, thus form part of, and are shaped by, a network of hackneyed racialized types. For example, Mark initially resists the trope of white man searching for an exotic woman of colour, but he eventually capitulates to his mistress and finds himself fellating the heel of her boot.

The narrative trajectory of *Bondage* would seem to lead to a transcendence of racialized roles and the messiness of shifting power dynamics that the play otherwise explores. When the house lights come up, the characters have shorn their stereotypes along with their leather outfits. They declare desire for each other while standing exposed before the audience. From another perspective, however, this ending does not quite resolve its unsettling presentation of stereotypes. What is the professed link between the actions of a dominant, sexually aggressive woman and the racial ascription Terri gives to her character (black)? How, in other words, is the gestural vocabulary (this is the corollary to the gait of the sailor) meant to index a complicated social phenomenon like race? In this vein, one could argue that either the play or a semiotic analysis based on indexicality fails here. After all, the play's conclusion attempts to stabilize the shifting identifications of its two characters, and race is not reducible to profession or a set of physical causes and effects. Moreover, Terri and Mark tend to announce their roles, so the audience is cued to interpret individual bodily signs. With their verbal pronouncements, the duo transforms what could be indices into symbols. Nevertheless, the question for me remains, what sorts of gestural movements point to conventional understandings of race when that term has so often been conflated with a particular profession: the Chinese coolie, the Vietnamese prostitute?

Conclusion: The Index as Energizer

As my preliminary speculations throughout this chapter indicate, I am perhaps less interested in providing answers to the ways in which semiotics (particularly indexicality) and theatrical performance produce cultural conventions than raising questions that I hope will inspire further enquiries through this discourse. Certainly, one of the underlying structures that facilitates the fantasies of *Bondage* is wealth. Mark routinely 'plops down good money' for his adventures in the sex parlour (161). Little mention is made of the ways in which capitalism props up certain forms of private and public sexual practice. But certainly, performance events like fetish balls link intimate acts to circulations of global capitalism in terms of who can purchase tickets, paraphernalia or, in Mark's case, who can afford to get off. The relationships between Asia and the United States have often revolved around actual or perceived flows of capital from one region to another.

To be clear, my aim in this chapter is not to shift the whole of theatre semiotics to a focus on the index. Peirce was clear in his articulation of the index as part of a larger system of signs, a system that many scholars and theorists of the theatre have found useful. Rather, I emphasize indexicality to re-energize a certain kind of methodology in thinking through the theatre.

As more and more theatrical events cross borders, it would seem increasingly necessary to develop types of analysis that facilitate our understanding of how particular cultural conventions become sedimented. Theatre scholars must always consider the processes by which meaning is produced. David Henry Hwang's productions provide many opportunities to scrutinize how theatre produces meaning. Asian American theatre provides audiences with a number of indices that might direct us to greater cultural understanding, if we would just follow the signs.

Performance Details

F.O.B.

Premiere: 8 June 1980 at the Joseph Papp Public Theater (New York).
Directed by Mako. With Willy Corpus (Onstage Stage Manager #2/percussion); Lucia Hwong (Musician/Voice of Radio DJ); Calvin Jung (Dale); Ginny Yang (Grace); John Lone (Steve); Tzi Ma (Onstage Stage Manager #1/Percussion). Costumes: Susan Hum. www.lortel.org/Archives/Production/2231

The Dance and the Railroad

Premiere: 16 July 1981 at the Joseph Papp Public Theater (New York).
Directed by John Lone. With John Lone (Lone) and Tzi Ma (Ma). Costumes: Judy Dearing www.lortel.org/Archives/Production/2133

Bondage

Premiere: 1 March 1992 at the Actor's Theater of Louisville's Humana Festival.
Directed by Oskar Eustis. With: B. D. Wong (Mark) and Kathryn Layng (Terri)
Costumes: Laura A. Patterson
web.archive.org/web/20100917065433/actorstheatre.org/
HUMANA%20FESTIVAL%20CDROM/bondage.htm

Golden Child

Premiere: 19 November 1996 at the Joseph Papp Public Theater (New York)
Directed by James Lapine. With: Tsai Chin (Eng Siu-Yond); Stan Egi (Andrew Kwong/Eng Tieng-Bin); John Christopher Jones (Rev. Baines); Jodi Long (Eng Luan); Liana Pai (Eng Eling); Julyana Soelistyo (Eng Ahn). Costumes: Martin Pakledinaz
www.lortel.org/Archives/Production/423

Further Reading

For students interested in reading further about semiotics, a selection of articles from the Prague School has been translated into English in L. Matejka and I. R. Titunik (1976). The Prague School produced substantive semiotic studies of theatre and drama well before this time. We can see this legacy in the work of Jiří Veltruský. To my knowledge, Veltruský was not particularly interested in the question of the index, but I base my observations only on the translated work that I have read. His 1979 article (Veltruský 1979) investigates a specific play in relation to semiotics, while his 1981 (Veltruský 1981) article offers an overview of the Prague School's understanding of theatre more broadly. A more recent book details his overall contributions to theatre and semiotics (2012). Carlson (1990) provides a general introduction into theatre and semiotics.

There are many studies of semiotics that explore signification well beyond the theatre. Kaja Silverman has written a very useful overview and elaboration of the field of semiotic enquiry in her *The Subject of Semiotics* (1983). Umberto Eco is perhaps the most entertaining of writers on the subject. For example, in *Kant and the Platypus* (1999), he updates semiotic analysis for the millennium. He pursues questions such as how sign systems transform over time.

Readers interested in David Henry Hwang might begin with Esther Kim Lee's collection (2015), but his other published plays are also provocative reads. I have myself written on costume (specifically the Mao suit) in both Hwang's *M. Butterfly* and his revision of *Flower Drum Song* in my book *Chinese Looks: Fashion, Performance, Race* (2014). Other notable works include *Yellow Face* (2007) and *Chinglish* (2011).

References

Carlson, Marvin (2008), 'Intercultural Theory, Postcolonial Theory, and Semiotics: The Road Not (Yet) Taken', *Semiotica* 168 (1): 129–42.

Carlson, Marvin (1990), *Theatre Semiotics: Signs of Life*, Bloomington and Indianapolis: Indiana University Press.

Doane, Mary Ann (2007), 'Indexicality: Trace and Sign: Introduction', *Differences* 18 (1): 1–6.

Doane, Mary Ann (2002), *The Emergence of Cinematic Time: Modernity, Contingency, the Archive*, Cambridge, MA: Harvard University Press.

Eco, Umberto (1999), *Kant and the Platypus: Essays on Language and Cognition*, trans. A. McEwen, London: Harcourt.

Elam, Keir (2002), The Semiotics of Theatre and Drama, New York: Routledge, 2002.

Fischer-Lichte, Erika (1992), *The Semiotics of Theater*, trans. J. Gaines and D. L. Jones, Bloomington and Indianapolis: Indiana University Press.

Hwang, David Henry (1999), *Golden Child*, New York: Dramatists Play Service.

Hwang, David Henry (1997), *Bondage* in *Asian American Drama: Nine Plays from the Multiethnic Landscape*, ed. Brian Nelson, New York: Applause.

Hwang, David Henry (1990), *FOB and Other Plays*, New York: Plume.

Kim Lee, E., ed. (2015), *The Theatre of David Henry Hwang*, London: Bloomsbury.

Knowles, Ric (2008), 'Vital Signs', *Semiotica* 168 (1): 227–37.

Ko, Dorothy (2007), *Cinderella's Sisters: A Revisionist History of Footbinding*, Berkeley and California: University of California Press.

Matejka, Ladislav, and Irwin R. Titunik (1976), *Semiotics of Art: Prague School Contributions*, Cambridge, MA: The MIT Press.

Metzger, Sean (2014), *Chinese Looks: Fashion, Performance, Race*, Bloomington and Indianapolis: Indiana University Press.

Peirce, Charles S. (1985), 'Logic as Semiotic: The Theory of Signs', in Robert E. Innis (ed.), *Semiotics: An Introductory Anthology*, 1–23, Bloomington and Indianapolis: Indiana University Press.

Silverman, Kaja (1983), *The Subject of Semiotics*, Oxford: Oxford University Press.

Veltruský, Jiří (2012), *An Approach to the Semiotics of Theater*, trans. J. F. Veltruský, Brno: Masaryk University.

Veltruský, Jiří (1981) 'The Prague School Theory of Theater', *Poetics Today* (2, 3): 225–35.

Veltruský, Jiří (1979), 'Theatre in the Corridor. E. F. Burian's Production of "Alladine and Palomides"', *The Drama Review: TDR* 23 (4): 67–80.

Wang Ping (2000), *Aching for Beauty: Footbinding in China*, Minneapolis: University of Minnesota Press.

5 How Does Theatre Represent Economic Systems?

LOUISE OWEN

This chapter explores theatre's inextricable engagement with economic systems and their roles and structures. Economy is an expansive historical term, meaning 'the way in which something is managed; the management of resources; household management'. One of the term's roots, the ancient Greek *oikonomia*, also more broadly signifies 'administration, principles of government, arrangement of a literary work, stewardship' (*Oxford English Dictionary* 2018). Economic systems thus concern more than matters of 'wealth generation' alone, and are based on ideas concerning how societies should be organized and the functions people should assume within them; as Wendy Brown puts it, using theatrical metaphor, 'the casting of economic life' (Brown 2015: 83). And the histories studied in our classrooms demonstrate multiple concrete interactions between theatre and economy: for example, the social mandate in ancient Athens to attend theatre festivals and the display of imperial tribute that was made beforehand, the role of trade guilds in supporting mystery cycles in medieval England, or the colonial imposition and control of theatre institutions in twentieth-century Kenya (Goldhill 1997: 56; King 2006: 10–12; Wa Thiong'o 1986: 38–41). As well as what is performed on stage, theatre is implicated in the material functioning of culture and society through its institutions, the representational practices and political struggles those institutions involve, and the identities and ideologies they stage. In other words, as institution, theatre plays its part in processes of *social reproduction* both on and off stage – an emphatically economic question. As Silvia Federici argues (writing specifically on domestic labour), 'the reproduction of human beings is the foundation of every economic and political system' (2012: 2). Ric Knowles thus theorizes what he calls the *material theatre* in terms of a contextual 'triangle' of 'complex and coded systems – of production, theatrical communication and reception, all working in concert or in tension with one another' (Knowles 2004: 3). And Miranda Joseph's recommendation that we pay attention to 'sign production as well as material production ... the performativity of production, of the circulation of social formations as well as goods' (2002: 67) resonates with Knowles's critical practice.

In this sense, a particular theatre piece need not explicitly address economic issues, nor adhere to a particular aesthetic or genre, to be engaged in economic themes – just as a piece that claims to be doing so may be up to something quite different. Here, I discuss a piece that does explicitly dramatize a contemporary industrial context: Alexander Zeldin's *Beyond Caring* (2014–16), a hyper-naturalistic work set in a meat factory. For Zeldin, if the show is 'about' anything, it is about 'very tender moments of connection between isolated people' (personal interview 2016). With this statement in view, I analyse how the piece represents, and thinks through, industrial capitalism and its social relationships. Political theorist and historian Ellen Meiksins Wood offers this essential definition of capitalism: 'a system in which goods and services, down to the most basic necessities of life, are produced for profitable exchange, where even human labour-power is a commodity for sale in the market, and where all economic actors are dependent on the market' (Meiksins Wood [1999] 2002: 2). Put in Marxian terms, capitalism is a particular *mode of production*: a way of organizing society and its resources 'structured according to its class relations' (Fine & Saad-Filho 2004: 6). In what follows, I examine the techniques that *Beyond Caring* uses in representing the experience of insecure factory work in Britain under the conditions of austerity. By way of comparison, I briefly discuss *The Pajama Game* (1954), an example of mid-twentieth-century musical theatre, also set in a factory, whose plot concerns industrial action. Throughout, the chapter is geared towards a particular question: what do *Beyond Caring*'s representational strategies reveal about the continuities of the capitalist system across the decades, and how theatre makers have chosen to respond to it?

Beyond Caring in Performance

Alexander Zeldin's *Beyond Caring* was first presented at the Yard Theatre, Hackney in 2014. It then ran at the National Theatre Temporary Space in 2015, and in 2016, it undertook a UK national tour to Birmingham REP, Theatre Delicatessen in Sheffield and HOME in Manchester, also playing a European date at Les Théâtres de la Ville de Luxembourg. In 2017, Zeldin reworked the piece for a North American context with Lookingglass Theatre in Chicago. I first saw the production at the National Theatre Temporary Space on Saturday 2 May 2015. It was five days before the 2015 General Election. Between 2014 and 2015, the number of people employed on a zero hours contract – 'a colloquial term for a contract of service under which the worker is not guaranteed work and is paid only for work carried out' (Pyper and Brown 2016: 4) – had reportedly risen by 100,000 to around 697,000 (Inman 2015). In 2017, that figure rose still further, to 910,000 (Monaghan 2017). On the basis of the expansion of low-paid, insecure jobs, and the linked increase of 'underemployment' (Bell and Blanchflower 2013), Labour had made a manifesto commitment to 'ban exploitative zero hours contracts' (Labour Party 2015: 37). In the lobby of the National Theatre Temporary Space, a chalkboard bore a statement on zero hours contracts from the most recent edition of BBC Question Time – a small business owner's hostile response to Labour's proposed ban – and an annotation, presumably authored by someone at the National Theatre, attacking Labour hypocrisy concerning MPs' use of this type of contract. The chalkboard's presentation of topical information framed the production as a contribution to a live political debate whose outcome would affect the types of lives represented in *Beyond Caring* – those of people struggling to make ends meet by subsisting on insecure low-paid work – though the statements seemed to align the National Theatre both with the small business owner, whose words received no commentary, and against Ed Miliband's Labour and its moves to redress the exploitations of underemployment.

Thinking on the chalkboard and its contradictory effects, I took my seat in the Temporary Space. Arranged in a thrust configuration, with the audience on three sides both on the ground floor and in the gallery, the stage offered up the bleak, acutely realistic interior of a factory break room in 'a small loading bay area' (Zeldin 2015: 2). Its dark grey floor was

Fig. 5.1 *Beyond Caring*. Grace (Janet Etuk) and Phil (Sean O'Callaghan). Photo: Mark Douet.

stained with what resembled dried coffee, as if someone had kicked over a disposable cup a while ago and not bothered to wipe up the spillage. Some plastic office chairs were clustered around a pale grey trestle table, a few items of rubbish scattered across its surface and the surrounding floor. The back wall, a grimy shade of beige, bore large dark stains. A double door dead centre, flanked by a tall plastic bin, indicated a further room beyond, in which a health and safety poster and a fire bucket were visible. In the break room itself, two tall metal trolleys were standing against the wall behind the trestle table, filled with bin bags and folded up cardboard boxes. An adjacent noticeboard displayed a smattering of notices, all on white paper. Immediately behind the audience, on the upstage left side, was a small atrium containing coat hooks and an automatic coffee machine with a garish orange neon display – the only source of colour in the whole environment. And in the parallel spot, upstage right, was a wooden pallet, shrink-wrapped in clear plastic, upon which rested a batch of large white plastic containers of cleaning fluid. Casting my eyes to the gallery, I noticed a metal ladder and vacuum cleaner resting against a similarly grimy wall. The overall effect was drab and miserable, made all the more harsh by the cold strip lighting that illuminated the stage space, and the white floods that kept the audience in light throughout the performance. Seated in close proximity to the action, it was as if we, the audience, were in the midst of the factory break room. Another striking feature was the way in which this scenography segued seamlessly into other parts of the Temporary Theatre Space. Before the performance began, beyond the room containing the fire bucket, the cheery red of the theatre's foyer could be seen through another door, pointing to a world beyond.

In this dismal situation, we meet the characters. Three women who are employed by agencies (Grace, Becky and Susan) join a permanent, part-time member of staff (Phil, formerly a nurse) and a tyrannical middle manager (Ian) to work in the factory, which makes processed meat products. The agency workers have been recruited, as Ian explains, to 'a fourteen consecutive day position' (Zeldin 2015: 7) cleaning the factory – work that is to take place at night. The play consists dramaturgically of a series of scenic episodes, unfolding in a linear temporality, structured by the cleaning assignment. Full blackouts and a machinic bass-heavy roar separate the episodes, constructing them as fragmentary glimpses of a world. In common with many thousands of disabled people in the context of the Coalition government, Grace has been affected by changes to rules regarding disability benefit: she has been declared 'fit for work' despite suffering from rheumatoid arthritis. Becky is a young mother. Susan is a middle-aged woman whose attempt to stay in the factory to sleep at the end of one of the shifts suggests homelessness. The play does not belabour this information: these details emerge piecemeal as the drama plays out, along with others that lend texture and depth to the characters' lives – for example, that Grace needs to take two buses to and from work, and that she attends church.

Each scene takes its time. They trace out the agency workers' peremptory introduction to the job by Ian, their fifteen-minute breaks (some interrupted by work), and the beginnings and ends of their punishing shifts. The play's action is sombre, but studded with moments of dark humour. Extended silences punctuate the characters' jarring attempts at social interaction during their breaks, making the moments in which the characters do make friendly connections with one another all the more poignant and hopeful. When those relationships fail or falter – as with a moment of unpleasant irritation that sabotages a growing friendship between Grace and Phil, provoked by a manipulative divide-and-rule tactic by Ian – the effect is heart-breaking. We, the audience, witness those relationships developing in what feels like real time, which compounds the feelings of sympathy they induce. Losses pervade the characters' lives relative to this situation: Becky and Phil, of contact with their children; Grace, of disability support and contact with her church community. As the action plays out, it is not clear which day of the fourteen-day clean it is – and it is as if this really doesn't matter, that time will be felt as excruciating whatever day it is. The play's conclusion, in which 'isolated people get too close to one another, too fast' (Zeldin 2015), sees the construction of a warped familial scene. Bullied into work by Ian when she is unwell, Grace experiences a distressing seizure, and is comforted and soothed to sleep by Phil. Seemingly compelled by this evidence of his kindness, Becky reaches to Phil in desperation, and they copulate on the factory floor – an event that is witnessed by no one, and which therefore catalyses nothing within the wider world of the play. The final image is of all the workers, middle manager Ian included, furiously scrubbing a filthy piece of equipment, before a blackout plunges the scene into darkness.

Representing the Factory

The small kindnesses and cruelties of *Beyond Caring*'s characters, playing out in the hostile environment of the factory, pack a powerful emotional punch. But in what ways can we interpret the play as concerned with everyday human relationships, *and* the wider economic system? Why is it not only about the social aspects of friendship, or the abuse of power? To approach this question, it's necessary to situate the play's setting in a wider historical and material context. *Beyond Caring*'s opening stage directions describe its setting as 'a meat factory (but it could be any other kind of industry) somewhere on the edges of a city in the western world' (Zeldin 2015: 2). The point, then, is not that we are witnessing work connected with meat processing specifically, although that metaphor is highly suggestive. We are watching action in a contemporary Western factory – a systematized, machinic institution whose massive expansion during the eighteenth and nineteenth centuries was critical in the development of industrialization. The factory, and the factory system, is a crucial element of the capitalist *means of production* – that is, the 'tools and raw materials' (Fine and Saad-Filho 2004: 24) used to make products and thus to generate profit. These raw materials include waged labour – a commodity that is vulnerable to harsh exploitation to maximize returns. Discussing the early-nineteenth-century textile industry in the north of England, historian Eric Hobsbawm gives this account of the factory: 'a logical flow of processes, each with a specialized machine tended by a specialized "hand", all linked together by the inhuman and constant pace of the engine and the discipline of mechanization, gas-lit, iron-ribbed and smoking ... a revolutionary form of work' (1969: 68). He notes that many 'were pressed into the new system against their will and got nothing from it but pauperization'; further, given the loss of autonomy factory work imposed, men were more likely to decline such work where they could, entailing that it was fulfilled by 'the more tractable women and children' (1969: 66, 68).

In writing 'The Working Day', the tenth chapter of *Capital Volume I* (1867), Marx drew on the extensive reports of factory inspectors, produced in enforcing the Factory Acts imposed by the British government from 1833 onwards, which detailed unspeakable working conditions endured by adults and children in a number of industries – both in terms of physical danger and the exploitation of workers' time. According to Marx's analysis, the profit, or surplus value, generated from the sale of commodities is a function of what he calls the *socially necessary labour time* to make them: as Ben Fine and Alfredo Saad-Filho explain, 'the amount of labour time required to bake a loaf of bread when contrasted with that required to sew a shirt (and more importantly, how these labour times are determined and modified through technological and other changes)' (2004: 19). Any labour time afforded by the worker surplus to these amounts within the working day can be taken as profit – entailing sly and subtle claims on workers' spare time, which, Marx noted, were characterized by the factory inspectors as '"petty pilferings of minutes"' ([1867] 1990: 352) from their break and meal-times. In David Harvey's account, the introduction of state regulation to privately owned industry as the nineteenth century unfolded was a combined political outcome of pressure from a developing working-class movement, 'bourgeois reformism' responding to egregious factory practices, and the pragmatic requirement from the point of view of the state that the labour force not be run irretrievably into the ground (2010: 141–3). Regulation met considerable resistance from capital until factory owners recognized later in the nineteenth century that 'a healthy and efficient labour force, on a shorter working day, could be more productive than an unhealthy, inefficient, falling-apart, constantly turning over and dying off labour force' (Harvey 2010: 155).

Moving forward sixty years and crossing continents, let's turn briefly to *The Pajama Game*, a musical comedy about an industrial dispute between management and workforce in a mid-western garment factory, first staged on Broadway in 1954. It provides an interesting comparator to *Beyond Caring* not only because of its factory setting – it was revived by Chichester Festival Theatre in 2013 in a production directed by Richard Eyre and transferred to London's Shaftesbury Theatre in the West End in 2014, the same year that *Beyond Caring* was first produced. *The Pajama Game* resonates strongly with the economic conditions of the mid-twentieth century – that is, the moment following the devastation of the Second World War during which capital entered into more co-operative arrangements with organized labour in the interests of rebuilding and expansion (Harvey

1990: 125–40). Embodying this co-operation is the turbulent centrepiece love affair that takes place between trade unionist Babe and factory superintendent Sid, representatives of workforce and management. Immediately following the overture, as a musical vamp plays on underneath, factory timekeeper Hines tips his hat and announces to the audience:

> This is a very serious drama. It's kind of a problem play. It's about Capital and Labour. I wouldn't bother to make such a point of all this except later on if you happen to see a lot of naked women being chased through the woods, I don't want you to get the wrong impression. This play is full of SYMBOLISM. (Adler, Ross, Abbott and Bissell 1954: 5)

My friend Robin delivered these lines with aplomb in his performance of the role in our school production in 1996. In 2017, reading them again in my copy of the libretto, the cheeky wit of the text struck me in a manner lost on me at the time. Hines's exaggerated invocation of 'SYMBOLISM' along with the genre of the 'problem play' squarely positions The Pajama Game in a tongue-in-cheek dialogue with Henrik Ibsen – a nineteenth-century playwright whose naturalistic work explored social and cultural conflicts, especially those underpinned by class and wealth.

Ibsen was one of a number of nineteenth-century European dramatists and theatre makers contributing to the radical new transnational movement of theatrical naturalism – famous among them, Emile Zola, Anton Chekhov and August Strindberg. Naturalistic drama was paradoxically anti-theatrical: it refused received nineteenth-century stage convention and sought instead to present the authentic dynamics of everyday social interactions on stage through close observation and imitation. Of his play Ghosts (1881), Ibsen argued that its impact 'depends a great deal on making the spectator feel as if he were actually sitting, listening, and looking at events happening in real life' (Ibsen in Williams 1994: 172) – an assessment that also articulates a relationship between actors and audience wherein, as Nicholas Ridout puts it, 'one group of people spend leisure time sitting in the dark to watch others spend their working time under lights pretending to be other people' (2006: 6). This humorous description is historically specific: it conjures social constructions of work and leisure that emerged decisively in the nineteenth century, the economic positions of actors and audience, and also the genre of realism – actors are 'pretending to be other people' who might believably resemble those in the audience or elsewhere in society. Ridout points out that this is 'what we routinely understand theatre to be, in Western industrial or post-industrial modernity' (2006: 6) – that is, lights down, curtain up and audience silent in anticipation of entertainment and diversion. However, nineteenth-century naturalism was anxious to expose to public view 'the minutiae of everyday life' (Harvie and Allain 2006: 178), which also involved confronting its unpalatable aspects: corruption, violence, debt, disease. The Pajama Game's satirical nod to Ibsen tells us something about the historical position of naturalism in representing social antagonism and seems to set off its own status as a comedy in doing so.

The saucy reference to the woods, meanwhile, reminds us definitively that The Pajama Game is an example of the popular commercial genre of musical comedy. The producers of the original show clearly recognized the marketing power of sexual imagery and the double entendre of 'pajama game': the 1954 Broadway poster features a cartoon woman wearing only a man's pyjama jacket, head demurely downcast but ample cleavage exposed, being ogled by the disembodied heads of five men while a sixth averts his gaze. This sexist image bears no actual relation to the plot – though in the show's fashion parade finale, the warring protagonist lovers demonstrate their reconciliation by sporting one pyjama set between them, confirming in song that 'Married life is lots of fun / Two can sleep as cheap as one' (Adler, Ross, Abbott and Bissell 1954: 51). Contradictorily, Babe's characterization as trade unionist gently subverts normative ideas of 1950s femininity, despite the show's fundamental commitment to the nuclear family as a structure – and as Jennifer L. Borda argues, at the end 'she comes to accept patriarchal society's definition of herself' (2010: 242). Following disruptions to the factory's Fordist production line and much interpersonal conflict, the world of the drama is finally rebalanced: corporate lies about profit and loss have been exposed, and the workers' demand for a modest pay rise satisfied. The concluding reprise of the song 'Seven and a Half Cents' triumphantly proclaims that the pay rise will have each member of the workforce 'Livin' like a King!' (Adler, Ross, Abbott and Bissell 1954: 51).

First-Hand Experience

The resolution represented in this Broadway musical is a far cry from the twenty-first-century circumstances represented in *Beyond Caring* – a much smaller scale production developed initially for a fringe space, and which drew extensively on first-hand accounts of insecure work in its research and development process. Zeldin encountered French journalist Florence Aubernas's *The Night Cleaner* (2010) in formulating another, unrealized show about youth unemployment; British writer Ivor Southwood's *Non-Stop Inertia* (2011) was recommended to him by a journalist friend (personal interview 2016). Inspired by these texts, *Beyond Caring* focuses on the cleaning of the factory – in other words, *reproductive labour*, an aspect critical to its action. As Andrew Herod and Luis L. M. Aguiar write, cleaning is 'essential to ensuring that the spaces of production, consumption, and social reproduction which define the social architecture of the contemporary global economy remain sanitary and functional' (2016: 427). Despite its crucial role, this kind of work is relegated to the time of day that least interrupts production and therefore the pursuit of profit, with the use of the shift-system that Marx argued enables 'appropriation of labour throughout the whole of the 24 hours in the day' ([1867] 2010: 367).

Aubernas and Southwood provide ample evidence of exploitative 'sweatshop' (Herod and Aguiar 2016: 426) practices and the 'existential vulnerability' (Southwood 2011: 16) of insecure work. Their texts also demonstrate the ways in which austerity – the policy of 'deliberate deflation of wages and prices through cuts to public spending' (Blyth 2013: 41) imposed in Britain and across Europe in response to the financial crisis – has affected the form and availability of unskilled work. They lend support to David Harvey's conclusion that 'sad to report, Marx's analysis is all too relevant to our contemporary condition' (2010: 160). Aubernas undertook covert research into cleaning work in Basse-Normandie in northern France during the 2009 'recession'. She dyed her hair blonde, and masqueraded as a middle-aged divorcee with only a secondary qualification who was in desperate need of work. Sticking carefully to her story – 'I met a man who kept me, then ditched me' (Aubernas [2010] 2011: 21) – her mission was to be offered a permanent contract of employment. Chasing scant shifts of as little as ninety minutes, and competing for them with many other unemployed people, this is a very difficult goal. In the work she does get, overtime goes unpaid, hours of travel to and from work are completely unsubsidized, and employers place unsustainable demands on the speed of work itself in their bids to compete with other cleaning businesses. The emotional toll for workers is a constant sense of unease: 'a nagging anxiety on top of the basic tiredness that you can't get over' (Aubernas [2010] 2011: 207).

Meanwhile, Southwood suggests that this condition of anxiety about survival induces a paradoxical 'frenetic inactivity: we are caught in a cycle of non-stop inertia', concluding that the contemporary culture of work thrives on workers' 'immersive identification' (Southwood 2011: 11, 84) with it. Following Brecht's use of *Verfremdung*, or 'distantiation', he calls for the assumption of a critical stance in relation to this 'ideological theatre of employment' (Southwood 2011: 82). Brecht's translator, John Willett, explains that *verfremdung* constitutes 'not simply the breaking of illusion (though that is one means to the end); and it does not mean "alienating" the spectator in the sense of making him hostile to the play. It is a matter of detachment, of reorientation' (Willett [1959] 1977: 177). In his important essay, 'The Modern Theatre is the Epic Theatre' (1930), Brecht argued for making the spectator an 'observer' of human action represented on the stage, outlining various dramaturgical techniques to that end. He contrasted this effect with 'dramatic theatre', which, he proposed, positioned the spectator 'in the thick of it' (2001: 37). This metaphor resonates strongly with both contemporary forms of immersive theatre, which physically plunge spectators into theatrically constructed worlds, and the culture of work that Southwood critiques. Southwood argues that 'to short-circuit this cycle of inertia and truly move forward, we have to resist the pressure to go with the flow' (2011: 88) – in other words, to detach from its frenetic dynamics and to understand them not as natural or given, but as actively constructed and therefore changeable.

Beyond Caring's uses of silence and social awkwardness stage a critique of this 'ideological theatre of employment'. Its process of creation sought, as Zeldin puts it, to 'describe as intensely as possible how these fragilised people live their lives' (Zeldin quoted in Chakrabortty 2015: 33). With Athena Athanasiou, it is important to point out the depth of systemic inequality: 'the lives of those working in the cleaning sector, which is socially disdained as *par excellence* female and migrant labour, are precarious, dispensable, and disposable' (Athanasiou 2011). All *Beyond Caring*'s temporary agency workers are female, and the permanent staff members are male. But Zeldin was very clear that the aim with *Beyond Caring* was not to transmit a direct political agenda or message. Instead, his intention was to make a piece of theatre that 'works on the frame of a moment: inside that moment is contained all of a bigger moment, a bigger structure' (personal interview 2016). In developing material about exploitation, he observes that 'it's more interesting for us to look at what the *effect* of the pay cut is' (personal interview 2016) than take a didactic political line. Focusing on the complexity of human relationships, Zeldin proposes that 'the economics seep into it' (personal interview 2016) in a more understated manner. Ian's sexism and casual racism correspond with his individualistic arrogance and assertion of power, but they also register dramatically as a form of defensive unhappiness with his own situation. Phil's depression and distress compel him periodically to seek refuge in the toilets, while Ian yells threats of non-payment of wages through the wall. These elements of context and character subtly allude to the gendered and racialized aspects of insecure work, and its emotional consequences; the pace of the piece formally reflects the distance between the rhetoric of 'flexibility' and abrasive lived realities.

Zeldin describes the 'heartbeat' of *Beyond Caring* as 'the contact between the inner sensation of an actor, and the person they're meeting' (personal interview 2016) in the research process – a sympathetic encounter that finds its way into the rehearsal room, and thereby into the work itself. Thus, as well as drawing on published accounts, Zeldin spent some time working as a night cleaner himself. Additionally, as Zeldin and actor Janet Etuk explained to me, the company met with workers, campaigners and union activists, who described to them conditions beset with inadequate equipment, insufficient time to complete the work required, and very little recourse. Though *Beyond Caring* is a fiction, in its methods we can see parallels with documentary theatre research and development based on actors' re-enactment (Merlin 2007: 41). It must be emphasized that Zeldin is the author of his works, but the mode of each piece's development is a 'porous process'; and, as he puts it, 'it's not just about actors. The core creativity in every new production comes from the selves of the people that I'm working with' (personal interview 2016). This is a very striking conceptual statement regarding the process of artistic research with people from other walks of life, theatrical mediation of experience, and the relationship between the material conditions of life and human subjectivity. It refuses an idea of acting as solely a form of technical artifice and proposes that creative practice and human subjectivity are entwined. In this understanding, theatre is one manifestation of human action in a larger life-world and is not cordoned off from it.

Similarly, *Beyond Caring*'s scenography conceives of the industrial spaces of the theatre and the factory as inter-articulated. One constructed space, the factory, seamlessly becomes another, the theatre foyer. In its naturalism, the production implicitly proposes that it permits theatrical access to a workplace that would otherwise be inaccessible to most of us. Bathed in light along with the performers, audiences are actively implicated in the social situation that *Beyond Caring* represents: as Zeldin insists, 'there is nowhere to hide' (personal interview 2016). In this scenario, theatre is not a place of fantasy or escape. Subverting what Brecht called the 'culinary' theatre of consumerism, it also departs from a mode of naturalism whereby quasi-absent audience members gaze voyeuristically upon a private space through a 'fourth wall'. In this sense, *Beyond Caring* offers a kind of meta-theatrical commentary on normative conditions of theatrical representation and reception – and in its fragmentary dramaturgy and naturalistic aesthetic, as critic Andrew Haydon suggests, 'there's so much more than "naturalism" at work in the piece. Really, it's more of a meditation than a play' (*Postcards from the Gods* 2016). It does not employ a Brechtian mode of distantiation exactly, but it does challenge its audience to encounter the onstage situation reflexively.

And audiences reacted to that situation in a range of ways. During break times, as the workers are seated around the table, Phil reads Dick Francis's thriller *Blood Sport* (1967), which becomes the object of stilted conversation. In the second of these moments, about a third of the way through the piece, Grace (Janet Etuk) tentatively asks Phil (James Doherty [at HOME]) what is happening in the story. He explains, but not in detail. A silence falls. After a very lengthy pause, she asks him again: 'What's happening now?' (Zeldin 2015: 24). It is as if the story that Phil is reading silently is taking place with them in real time. He offers another brief summary. Then she sidles over slightly, and subtly tries to look at the book. He tilts the book, just as subtly, almost as if he isn't really doing it, so that she can see. At the performance I saw at HOME in Manchester, this moment of offering, of friendship forming, prompted a spontaneous 'ohhh!' of delight in the audience. This instance of generosity contrasts strongly with the miserable performance review Ian (Luke Clarke) conducts with Susan (Kristin Hutchinson) in the penultimate scene of the play, inspired by a questionnaire Southwood discusses in *Non-Stop Inertia* (personal interview 2016). His patronizing observations of her work and brusque tone elicited a loud 'pffffffffffft' from more than one audience member that evening at the National Theatre. And, returning to HOME, the end of that performance witnessed one of the most extraordinary moments I've seen in the theatre. During the curtain call, following the performance's merciless concluding moment of frenzied cleaning, a woman on the front row a few seats down from me stood up and approached Etuk. As the applause tailed off and the other actors began to leave the stage, the audience member held Etuk's hand and earnestly affirmed that her performance of the arthritic seizure truly reflected her own experience.

The production also engendered anger. Zeldin and Etuk describe audience members in Sheffield shouting out during the show:

AZ This is shit.
JE This isn't theatre.
LO What?!
JE This is an observation. This doesn't happen in this country any more.
AZ This is not British. Britain's got labour laws, this couldn't happen. (personal interview 2016)

Following another performance at the National Theatre, a dissatisfied audience member confronted Etuk: 'he found me and tapped me on the back afterwards, just said "rubbish" and walked off' (personal interview 2016). The strength of these responses speaks to the performative workings of the production – the precision of its realism, its disruption of theatre-as-entertainment, and its representation of experiences to which some might respond with ambivalence or agitation in the deeply embattled, unequal context of austerity. They resonate with Erin Hurley's gloss of psychologist William James: emotion is 'inevitably influenced by a person's expectations and interpretative lens; the shape of the expectations and the curvature of the lens are forged in experience and cultural norms that vary across geography and period' (Hurley 2010: 19). The expectations in these examples relate to the clash between assumptions regarding workplace protections and the lived contemporary realities represented in the performance, and between notions of what does and does not count as 'good' or 'legitimate' theatre. These aspects again are intrinsically linked to the relationship between theatre and economic system. Questions of class and income disparity are unavoidably raised by a performance that sensitively represented lives encumbered by poverty, but which itself cost the equivalent of two hours minimum-waged work in the UK to attend, and substantially more in the United States – a barrier addressed in Chicago with the offer of free tickets to temporary workers (Vitali 2017).

Past and Present

As I was preparing this chapter, I discussed *Beyond Caring* with a friend who had not seen the production. She made a valuable observation: that it was noteworthy that the piece concerned itself with a factory, and not with digital culture, 'immaterial labour' or other forms of work engaged with telecommunications and the management of information. In this sense, the piece represents a kind of refusal of one narrative about the transformation of work in the rich Western world. Manufacturing jobs as a proportion of economic activity have diminished substantially since the 1970s (Berry 2016). But manual labour, and exploitation based not on wireless connectivity's blurring of work and leisure time but on highly systematized, low-paid, insecure work are lived daily realities. Although consumers may experience online communications and commerce as weightless and instantaneous, back-breaking assiduously timetabled work at 'fulfilment centres' for global organizations like Amazon still facilitates the provision of goods in a service economy, as investigative reporting attests (Cadwalladr 2013). Aditya Chakrabortty writes that the rare example of *Beyond Caring* demonstrates 'how poorly the theatre and the arts more broadly have handled the crisis', congratulating the piece 'for putting down the microscope and picking up the widescreen lens' (Chakrabortty 2015: 33) – that is, for departing from narratives about powerful executives, and paying attention to the wider context of insecure work and its environments.

The cinematic metaphor of 'widescreen lens' seems an unusual one, but is apt for *Beyond Caring's* painstaking realism, and reflects the uptake of tropes of the screen in other criticism. Time and again critics drew attention to the piece's naturalism – speaking of its 'rare quality of gripping authenticity' (Cavendish 2015), the performative details 'so faultlessly convincing that you almost feel you are spying via CCTV' (Marlowe 2015), its 'unostentatious naturalism' (Hemming 2015), and its 'Mike Leigh-esque social realism with pinches of heightened theatricality' (Anon 2015). While close attention to visual detail is a time-honoured realist strategy, its uncompromising use of lengthy silence made the piece feel to me to be bold and newly experimental. And strangely, its experimentalism resonated with Martin Esslin's thoughts, written in 1968, on the emergence of naturalism in the nineteenth century and its subsequent development. Esslin proposed then that nineteenth-century naturalism, 'an iconoclastic, revolutionary onslaught against the establishment has now turned into the embodiment of "squareness", conservatism and the contemporary concept of the well-made play' (Esslin 1968: 67). Both these perceptions of naturalism, and the proximity between 'sign-vehicle and content' (States 1985: 20) in theatrical representation might also account for critical hostility to non-naturalistic approaches to economic questions. For example, Caroline Horton's *Islands* (2015), a magnificently scatological *buffon* treatment of tax havens, alienated several critics, who felt that the economic content and clownish form of the piece were mismatched (for example, Billington 2015).

For me, like *Islands*, *Beyond Caring* succeeded brilliantly in producing apt '*feeling*' (*Postcards from the Gods* 2015) – in this case, desolation, joy, hope and anger befitting the situation on stage. And *Beyond Caring's* naturalistic representations were the precise opposite of jaded aesthetic conservatism, nonetheless echoing critical images from nineteenth-century theatre. Gazing upon *Beyond Caring's* factory for the first time, I thought more and more of the boots resting in the kitchen in Strindberg's *Miss Julie* (1888), and the portrait of Hedda Gabler's father in Ibsen's 1891 play, hanging portentously in the background – symbols of profoundly effective patriarchal dominance and hierarchy. The equivalent in *Beyond Caring* of these absent-but-present fathers is the unseen boss Richard, whom Ian toadyingly mentions has lately celebrated his marriage with a big white wedding. While in *Miss Julie*, the revelation of private sex sabotages public respectability, in the interaction between Phil and Becky, we see sex pushed from home into work, with no reputational consequences but

Fig. 5.2 *Beyond Caring*. Victoria Moseley, Sean O'Callaghan, Hayley Carmichael, Janet Etuk. Photo: Mark Douet.

profound psychic ones. As a title, *Beyond Caring* evokes the abandonment of the state and the characters' ensuing forced abandonment of their own children, as well as the emotional extremity of the situation, which Chakrabortty characterizes as an 'acid bath' (Chakrabortty 2015). Raymond Williams argues that in naturalism, 'environments are integral parts of the dramatic action, indeed, in a true sense, are themselves actors and agencies' (Williams [1980] 1997: 128). We can absolutely see that principle reflected in *Beyond Caring*, and also, with its lighting decisions, a dramaturgical critique, where 'action is seen not only within an environment but as itself, within certain limits and pressures, producing an environment' (127). In his discussion of nineteenth-century naturalism in England, Williams asks after 'the relations between forms and social formations' (147). Despite their many differences, the dramaturgical affinity between *Beyond Caring* and much earlier socially critical plays suggests a strong connection between the socioeconomic and industrial conditions of the late-nineteenth century and the early twenty-first.

Performance Details

The Pajama Game: A Musical Comedy, premiere St James Theatre, New York 1954, music and lyrics by Richard Adler and Jerry Ross, book by George Abbott and Richard Bissell, directed by George Abbott and Jerome Robbins. For more information, see 'The Pajama Game' broadwaymusicalhome.com/shows/pajama.htm (accessed March 2018).

Beyond Caring, premiere Yard Theatre, London 2014, written and directed by Alexander Zeldin, designer: Natasha Jenkins, sound designer: Josh Anio Grigg, lighting designer: Marc

Williams, assistant director: Grace Gummer. With Sean O'Callaghan (Phil), Luke Clarke (Ian), Victoria Mosley (Becky), Hayley Carmichael (Susan) and Janet Etuk (Grace). In subsequent productions in Britain, the roles of Susan and Phil were performed by Kristin Hutchinson and James Edward Doherty.

These interviews with Alexander Zeldin provide great insights into the research and development process:

Catherine Love, 'Alexander Zeldin: "The Director as God is Bullshit"', *Exeunt Magazine*, 21 April 2015. Available online: http://exeuntmagazine.com/features/the-director-as-god-is-bullshit/ (accessed January 2018).

'Director Alexander Zeldin talks Beyond Caring', *HomeMCR*, 12 July 2016. Available online: https://homemcr.org/article/director-alexander-zeldin-talks-beyond-caring (accessed January 2018).

Max McGuinness, 'Playwright Alexander Zeldin on the power – and limitations – of theatre', *Financial Times*, 29 March 2017, Available online: https://www.ft.com/content/48303ffe-13d4-11e7-b0c1-37e417ee6c76 (accessed January 2018).

And this review of *Beyond Caring* in Chicago and video interview with Alexander Zeldin and David Schwimmer (Lookingglass Theatre co-founder) offer fascinating comparison and contrast between the European and North American contexts:

Chris Jones, 'Review: "Beyond Caring" is about the work, done right in your face', *Chicago Tribune*, 2 April 2018. Available online: http://www.chicagotribune.com/entertainment/theater/reviews/ct-beyond-caring-review-ent-0403-20170402-column.html (accessed January 2018).

Marc Vitali, 'David Schwimmer on "Beyond Caring" at Lookingglass', *Chicago Tonight*, 5 April 2017. Available online: http://chicagotonight.wttw.com/2017/04/05/david-schwimmer-beyond-caring-lookingglass (accessed January 2018).

Further Reading

For a close reading and contextualization of Marx's *Capital, Volume 1*, see Harvey (2010 and 2008–17). David Harvey's lectures on *Capital, Volume 2* and *Marx and Capital* can also be accessed at his website. For an analysis of the intersection between sexual identity and capitalism from a materialist feminist standpoint, see Hennessy (2000). For an account of the class politics of the theatre industry and representations of poverty on stage, see Gardner (2016). And for a contextualization of zero hours contracts departing from a visit to *Beyond Caring*, see Mason (2014).

References

Abbott, George, and Richard Bissell (1954), *The Pajama Game*, London: Warner Chappell Music.

Allain, Paul, and Jen Harvie (2006), *The Routledge Companion to Theatre and Performance*, Abingdon and New York: Routledge.

Anon (2018), 'The Pajama Game'. Available online: http://broadwaymusicalhome.com/shows/pajama.htm (accessed March 2018).

Anon (2015), 'Also Showing', *The Sunday Times*, 10 May.

Athanasiou, Athena (2011), 'Becoming Precarious through Regimes of Gender, Capital, and Nation', *Hot Spots: Cultural Anthropology*, 28 October. Available online: https://culanth.org/fieldsights/250-becoming-precarious-through-regimes-of-gender-capital-and-nation (accessed January 2018).

Aubernas, Florence ([2010] 2011), *The Night Cleaner*, Cambridge and Malden, MA: Polity Press.

Bell, David, and David Blanchflower (2013), 'Underemployment in the UK Revisited', *National Institute Economic Review*, 229: F8–F22. Available online: https://www.dartmouth.edu/~blnchflr/papers/bell&blanchflower2013.pdf (accessed January 2018).

Berry, Craig (2016), 'SPERI British Political Economy Brief No. 25: UK Manufacturing Decline Since the Crisis in Historical Perspective', *Sheffield Political Economy Research Institute*, October. Available online: http://speri.dept.shef.ac.uk/wp-content/uploads/2016/10/Brief-25-UK-manufacturing-decline-since-the-crisis.pdf (accessed January 2018).

'Beyond Caring – HOME, Manchester [seen 14/07/16]', *Postcards from the Gods*, 16 July 2016. Available online: https://postcardsgods.blogspot.co.uk/2016/07/beyond-caring-home-manchester.html (accessed January 2018).

Blyth, Mark (2013), 'The Austerity Delusion: Why a Bad Idea Won Over the West', *Foreign Affairs*, May/June: 41–56.

Borda, Jennifer L. (2010) 'Working-class Women, Protofeminist Performance, and Resistant Ruptures in the Movie Musical The Pajama Game', *Text and Performance Quarterly*, 30 (3): 227–46.

Brecht, Bertolt (2001), *Brecht on Theatre: The Development of an Aesthetic*, ed. and trans. J. Willett, London: Methuen.

Brown, Wendy (2015), *Undoing the Demos: Neoliberalism's Stealth Revolution*, New York: Zone Books.

Cadwalladr, Carol (2013) 'My Week as an Amazon Insider', *The Observer*, 1 December.

Cavendish, Dominic (2015), 'Beyond Caring, National Theatre, Review: 'Gripping Authenticity', *Daily Telegraph*, 3 May.

Chakrabortty, Aditya (2015), 'In Praise of… Beyond Caring', *The Guardian*, 15 May: 33.

'economy, n.', OED Online, *Oxford University Press*. Available online: http://0-www.oed.com.catalogue.libraries.london.ac.uk/view/Entry/59393 (accessed January 2018).

Esslin, Martin (1968), 'Naturalism in Context', *TDR: The Drama Review*, 13 (2): 67–76.

Federici, Silvia (2012), *Revolution at Point Zero: Housework, Reproduction, and Feminist Struggle*, Oakland: PM Press.

Fine, Ben, and Alfredo Saad-Filho (2004), *Marx's Capital*, 4th edition, London and Ann Arbor: Pluto Press.

Gardner, Lyn (2016) '"Poverty Porn": How Middle-Class Theatres Depict Britain's Poor', *The Guardian: Theatre Blog*, 15 April. Available online: https://www.theguardian.com/stage/theatreblog/2016/apr/15/poverty-porn-theatre-boy-yen-rehome (accessed January 2018).

Goldhill, Simon (1997), 'The Audience of Athenian Tragedy', in P. E. Easterling (ed.), *The Cambridge Companion to Greek Tragedy*, 54–68, Cambridge: Cambridge University Press.

Harvey, David (2010), *A Companion to Marx's Capital*, London and New York: Verso.

Harvey, David (1990), *The Condition of Postmodernity: An Enquiry into the Origins of Cultural Change*, Oxford: Blackwell.

Harvey, David (2008–17) 'Reading Capital with David Harvey', *DavidHarvey.org*. Available online: http://davidharvey.org/reading-capital/ (accessed January 2018).

Hemming, Sarah (2015) 'Beyond Caring, National Theatre, London – Review', *Financial Times*, 5 May.

Hennessy, Rosemary (2000), *Profit and Pleasure: Sexual Identities in Late Capitalism*, New York and London: Routledge.

Herod, Andrew, and Luis L. M. Aguiar (2016), 'Introduction: Cleaners and the Dirty Work of Neoliberalism', *Antipode*, 38 (3): 425–34.

Hobsbawm, Eric (1969), *Industry and Empire*, London: Pelican.

Hurley, Erin (2010), *Theatre and Feeling*, Basingstoke: Palgrave Macmillan.

Inman, Philip (2015), 'Almost 700,000 People in UK Have Zero-hours Contract as Main Job', *The Guardian*, 25 February. Available online: https://www.theguardian.com/uk-news/2015/feb/25/zero-hours-contract-rise-staff-figures (accessed January 2018).

Joseph, Miranda (2002), *Against the Romance of Community*, Minneapolis: University of Minnesota Press.

King, Pamela M. (2006), *The York Mystery Cycle and the Worship of the City*, Cambridge: D. S. Brewer.

Knowles, Ric (2004), *Reading the Material Theatre*, Cambridge: Cambridge University Press.

Labour Party (2015), 'The Labour Party Manifesto 2015'. Available online: http://action.labour.org.uk/page/-/A4%20BIG%20_PRINT_ENG_LABOUR%20MANIFESTO_TEXT%20LAYOUT.pdf (accessed January 2018).

Marlowe, Sam (2015), 'Beyond Caring, NT Temporary', *The Times*, 5 May.

Marx, Karl ([1867] 1990), *Capital: A Critique of Political Economy, Volume One*, trans. B. Fowkes, London: Penguin.

Mason, Paul (2014) 'There Are no Heroes on the Zero-Hours Borderline', *Channel 4 News*, 11 July. Available online: https://www.channel4.com/news/by/paul-mason/blogs/heroes-zerohours-borderline (accessed January 2018).

Meiksins Wood, Ellen ([1999] 2002), *The Origin of Capitalism: A Longer View*, London: Verso.

Merlin, Bella (2007), '*The Permanent Way* and the Impermanent Muse', *Contemporary Theatre Review*, 17 (1): 41–9.

Monaghan, Angela (2017), 'Record 910,000 UK Workers on Zero-Hours Contracts', *The Guardian*, 3 March. Available online: https://www.theguardian.com/business/2017/mar/03/zero-hours-contracts-uk-record-high (accessed January 2018).

Personal interview with Alexander Zeldin and Janet Etuk, September 2016.

Postcards from the Gods (2015), 'Islands – Bush Theatre', 24 January. Available online: https://postcardsgods.blogspot.co.uk/2015/01/islands-bush-theatre.html (accessed January 2018).

Pyper, Doug, and Jennifer Brown (2016), *House of Commons Library: Briefing Paper Number 06553, 13 April 2016: Zero-hours contracts*. Available online: http://researchbriefings.parliament.uk/ResearchBriefing/Summary/SN06553 (accessed January 2018).

Ridout, Nicholas (2006), *Stage Fright, Animals and Other Theatrical Problems*, Cambridge: Cambridge University Press.

Southwood, Ivor (2011), *Non-Stop Inertia*, Winchester and Washington: Zero Books.

States, Bert O. (1985), *Great Reckonings in Little Rooms: On the Phenomenology of Theatre*, Berkeley and Los Angeles: University of California Press.

Vitali, Marc (2017), 'David Schwimmer on "Beyond Caring" at Lookingglass', *Chicago Tonight*, 5 April. Available online: http://chicagotonight.wttw.com/2017/04/05/david-schwimmer-beyond-caring-lookingglass (accessed January 2018).

Wa Thiong'o, Ngugi (1986), *Decolonising the Mind: The Politics of Language in African Literature*, London: James Currey.

Willett, John (1977), *The Theatre of Bertolt Brecht*, London: Methuen Drama.

Williams, Raymond ([1980] 1997), *Problems in Materialism and Culture*, London and New York: Verso.

Williams, Simon (1994), 'Ibsen and the Theatre, 1877–1900', in James McFarlane (ed.), *The Cambridge Companion to Ibsen*, 165–82, Cambridge: Cambridge University Press.

Zeldin, Alexander (2015), *Beyond Caring*, London: Bloomsbury.

Part 2 Performing

6   What Is Black Dance? What Can It Do?

THOMAS F. DEFRANTZ

What are the terms of dance that allow for the emergence of Black dance? How are identity and culture implicated in the articulation of genres of dance? How is it that televisual dance – music video dance – inevitably seems to refer to Black dance and its aesthetic values? What are the foundational modes of gesture, rhythm, musicality and social relationship that produce Black dance? This chapter considers the formation of Black dance as a critical category created by dancers, and the terms of address that produce that same category among researchers and critics. An assessment of historical becomings of Black dance allows us to think through the different sorts of access that insiders and outsiders have to its contents. The chapter will consider examples of dance to suggest divergent, but related, forms of Black dance: theatrical and social. The terms of a 'doing' for Black dance as resistant demonstration and embodied aesthetic protest will be discussed through the examples. We will also consider cultural appropriation as an urgent mode of analysis relevant to the construction of Black performance theory and Black dance.

What's at Stake?

Again and again, we notice that performers who claim relationship to an African diaspora dance differently than others. There may be more of a sense of rhythmic attack; a stronger sense of release in the lower back and the hips. There may be a willingness to kick higher or bounce lower throughout a movement sequence. There may seem to be something 'extra' in the execution of the phrases; some sort of authoritative panache that makes the dancing seem to be of the dancer herself, right now, in immediate gestural relief.

But how can we attribute an approach to performance to a group bound by ethnicity or even race? To do this, we will have to engage the possibilities of a strategic essentialism, one that will allow us to make claims for Black dance and Black people. We must remain aware of the limitations of essentialisms here. But we must also be willing to explore techniques that might hold together performances born of African diasporic approaches to creative practice. So, let's pursue, together, this mode of performative address that we call Black dance.

At stake in Black performance and Black dance are possibilities for group communion and a group articulation of aesthetic and social priorities. Black performance brings into being the possibility of Black people making and doing: creating intentional gestures in order to register, distinctively, as Black people. In this definition, Black performance circles back to its emergence as something created for the purpose of expressing itself aesthetically and socially. Black performance exists to confirm the presence of Black people in the world.

If we begin here, we can see that Black performance arrives as a form of social engagement, and its production confirms creative borders, boundaries and remains. Black performance doesn't include every sort of performative action ever done by a Black person; rather it encompasses those creative actions that allow people to recognize Black presence. This includes some forms of performance and dance practice, and some approaches to dancing, but – obviously – not all of them. In defining Black performance in this way, we allow it to emerge for itself among those who create it as an aesthetic and social confirmation of a possibility of Black life.

Why do we need such confirmation? Frankly, because the histories of Black people have been circumscribed by disavowal, coercion and genocide. Black life emerges in the global abjection created by capitalism and driven by racism. We find endless examples of the ways that Black people have been consistently disavowed in the annals of Western thought and literature; in the context of the United States, Black people have been relentlessly policed, incarcerated and disenfranchised. The music and dance that emerged within this bleak context for social life answered the call for creative expression and corporeal resistance, even as it demonstrated unanticipated possibilities for Black performance and its importance.

Black dance, then, allows for a recovery of an animated body of people rising up in resistance and demonstrating strength and possibility through art making. When we consider dance in this manner, we begin by acknowledging the terms of its production in social life. Black dance does not float aimlessly in a sea of 'aesthetics' that are of, or for, some sort of detached 'art for art's sake'. These dances emerge as intentional art that seeks to satisfy a basic human need for affirmation through the expressive movement of the body.

How Are Identity and Culture Implicated in the Articulation of Genre?

Large theoretical claims may seem to universalize Black dance, by imagining an ontological ground for its practice as a system of knowing-being in the world. But this is exactly what might be produced by Black dance; this might be what it can *do*. Black dance can stabilize aesthetic liveliness in the creative practices of Black people who might be engaged in music and dance for many reasons; Black dance allows us to appreciate Black people in musical motion as foundational to understanding Black life.

Of course, we acknowledge that Black identities are multiple and complex. They may be multi-racial, queer, cis-gendered, working-class, creative-class, varied religiously and geographically distributed. They are not one thing, or singular. And yet we call on Black dance as a category of engagement, a mode of address to bring together practices that produce particular sorts of effects in the world. As with any art, we cannot narrow the possible effects of Black dance with any usefulness; it will arrive and disperse with unexpected results depending on its frames and contexts. But we can call Black dance forward, as a signal for Black expression that erupts when and where it is needed; where it might be valued and useful. Black dance surely answers a need for expressive motion.

But what is Black dance? Our willingness to call out Black dance supports thinking of it as a recognizable gesture, so that we can identify some of its possibilities and productivities. Black dance calls on approaches to aesthetic gesture that converge to suggest a continuum of embodiment. But, of course, it is not a single thing or a single mode of performance.

Rather, Black dance arrives as an approach to moving and being in relationship to others. So then, to dance Black: move with intention; remain attentive to rhythm and conscious of ways that it shifts time and space. Cast your weight downward into the ground and earth, to physically consecrate gravity and the fact of body and its presence here and now. Bend the arms and knees; bend at the waist, bend the neck and tilt the torso, bend the feet back towards their flexion. In bending, create the possibility to extend and propel; to create the possibility of a release that can be reset. Twist and circle the hips; twist the wrists, circle the head; create centrifuges at several movement centres simultaneously. Twist, and bend, release and explode; vary the rhythm in surprising manners; share energy by elaborating on the nature of time. Play the rhythmic break.

In this description of the manner of Black dance, we can understand not particular movements, but rather, approaches to moving. These approaches might be deployed in all sorts of genres of dance: tap dance, b-girling and capoeira, modern dance or contemporary dance, ballet or Senegalese Sabar, South African gumboot dancing, line dancing, or partner dancing. And these approaches arrive and disperse within these forms of dance across time, as forays inherently unstable and unsustainable. These approaches are not particular sequences of movements, but ways to structure movement. They are engaged by dancers in various contexts and tend to arrive in bursts, or nodules. And they need to be identified at least by the dancers performing through them, if not through their attendant witnesses, or their audiences.

Black dance, then, is a complex approach of movement bound by relationship to its own recognition. This depiction of dance may be quite different from a generic description of theatrical dance forms, such as 'ballet' or 'modern dance', which depend on particular rules of physical line or volume that might be achieved through training. In this chapter, Black dance emerges as an intentional deployment of energy designed to achieve recognition within its practices. Circling back to what Black dance *does*, we assert that Black dance arrives in order to confirm a liveliness of Black possibility, by means of these gestural approaches.

Some genres of dance rely more heavily on the physical approaches to Black dance mentioned above. B-girling and B-boying, sometimes referred to as 'hip hop dance', and the capacious category of 'jazz dance', which might include all manner of dance in music videos, are two modes that rely almost entirely on approaches to manipulating rhythm and bending the body in an unexpected manner. To consider these forms of theatricalized social dance, we come into direct contact with the extended possibilities of Black dance method. In hip hop or jazz dance, we witness the body challenged to its extremes: whirling, twisting and bending on the ground, balancing against itself, catapulting in the air. In jazz dance, the twist and bend of the hips; the rhythmic pulsations and accenting that clarify divisions of meter; and the aggressive pushing of energy from dancer towards their witnessing audience all bind the form to aspects of Black dance.

Some dance researchers might assert that these two genres – hip hop dance and jazz dance – along with certain social dances and dance practices crafted in explicitly African and African diaspora contexts, constitute Black dance. But this narrow defining would discount the approaches to, say, experimental contemporary performance or modern dance that some Black artists engage. These artists might intend for their work to register as Black dance, recognizable to their witnesses and performers as such, even as their work also fits into other genre categories. A ballet performed *en pointe*, for example, might be conceived and received as Black dance. Our challenge here, then, is to identify Black dance on its own terms, and allow it to do its work, first for the Black people who create it and share it, and then with the audiences that gather around it. By prioritizing Black people in relationship to Black dance, we will centre its discussion, assessments and achievements in terms of engagement that speak back to the social circumstances of making dance and art; circumstances that are particular. Even as the creative expressions of Black dance might speak out to a global audience, they speak from particular social histories and aesthetic concerns that allow the emergence of Black dance to do its work in the world.

Particular Forms of Black Dance

We turn now to explore some examples of Black dance. Because Black life has emerged in relationship to flows of capital and power that repeatedly denigrate its potency, Black dance arrives with at least two distinctive modes of analysis important to its discourse. Social dances, meant to be shared among other dancers, and theatrical dances, intended to be viewed by witnesses and audiences who needn't dance themselves. (An expansive category of sacred dances will stand outside of the terms of this chapter.) The distinction between these modes matters: social dances assume a dancing populace already in motion, and in relationship to the dancing at hand. Theatrical dances assume a familiarity with Black forms of address and aesthetic practices on the part of the performers, but not necessarily on the part of the audience. These two modes mirror an insider/outsider experience of Black life. The experience of dancing within an embodied knowledge of histories that have constructed the category of Black dance arrives with distinction from other sorts of dancing and spectatorship. Dancing Black dance while identifying as a Black person is quite different from dancing Black dance styles while identifying in other ways. And watching Black dance forms without dancing alongside them, from across the room, creates fissures in expressive analysis. What the dances 'look like' is often quite different from what they have meant, historically, or what they feel like for the dancers performing them.

Thinking in these two modes of social dance and theatrical dance, allows us to structure discourse of what Black dance can do. We begin with social dance, and a consideration of the Electric Slide. The Slide arrives among all sorts of group 'called dances', that is, line dances that offer simple instructions to be undertaken by the gathered group of dancers. These dances continue in unbroken sequence from the earliest days of American social affairs. For African Americans, the line dances demonstrate a fleeting social mobility, in the gathering of people to dance together in joyful rhythmic motion and, historically, outside of the all-seeing eyes of the church clergy. Because enslaved Black Americans had little recourse to 'free' social time, traditions of group dancing were largely constrained, historically, to church services which were, ironically, negative towards dancing. Restrictions on African American assemblies – whether enslaved or not – lessened slightly in the nineteenth century, and dancing together became possible in some US locations.

Line dancing follows traditions of social dance adapted from European forms, including the quadrille, which deployed a musician and a caller. But where white American adaptations of European forms tended to stress the ability of the dancers to follow complex instructions, or to learn dances in advance of the social event, Black line dances tended to arrive with easy-to-learn, rhythmically flexible arrangements of steps that change facing towards all four cardinal points in space. Where the quadrille calls for an even number of participants who dance in pairs, line dances, including the Electric Slide, can accommodate any number of participants. And where the quadrille might require all sorts of instruction and preparation, the Electric Slide can be learnt by a wide swathe of dancers of varying ages and abilities.

The Electric Slide emerged in the 1970s in concert with a musical recording that suited its contours. The dance has remained among the most recognizable forms of group celebration, practised at any number of social events. The basic form of the dance is very simple, and can be learnt quickly. But the Electric Slide encourages improvisation and the insertion of personal style into its contents. Variations and elaborations on the basic steps keep the dance lively and interesting for participants; the dance encourages the pleasurable moving alongside others in similar directions, but with individualized approaches and variations to each passage through its contents.

> *Electric Slide at Obama Inauguration*, YouTube video, January 2009. A loose crowd among a large crowd on the Mall in Washington DC. People are wrapped up in blankets, winter coats, heads covered against the drizzling cold. A recording of Stevie Wonder and Usher – two important figures in African American R&B who represent inter-generational affiliation – bleeds into the air. The duo sings 'Higher Ground', a song by Wonder about finding the way towards something better. The YouTube video begins *in medias res* with a few dancers in motion, but quickly twenty dancers are visible. To perform the dance: they move to the right for four counts, to the left for four, to the back for four, lean down towards the ground with their left shoulders in the front, then rebound back away towards the right. A two-count quarter-turn to face a different front. Others join in quickly, dancing in celebration and against the cold. They carry their bags – purses, knapsacks and book bags; they dance to explore the formation; the uneven, eighteen-count rhythmic structure; and to share energy in a common physical text enlivened by their individuality. Several videos of the inauguration event reveal the Slide as an embodied touchstone of connection, gathering dancers of many ages, ethnicities, gender presentations and abilities to share their creative address to its contents. (See 'Further Reading'.)

The Electric Slide follows many other line dances that served similar creative functions for African Americans: allowing for joyful rhythmic expression and self-actualization through dance. To better understand what the Electric Slide *does* as a Black dance, we return to a social context for Black life. If our context for understanding Black life stems from its general disavowal, within the political structures of slavery, the practices of social dance that encourage individual expression within a group dynamic become obvious barometers of enlivened social lives. Dancing the Electric Slide alongside others who identify as Black creates a possibility of communion, a sharing of social gesture and creative expression. Dancing elaborates social possibility for the group, opening outward from a moving-together-in-motion towards the possibility of an expressive self, embedded within a mobilized group.

> *Tongues Untied* (1989). An imaginative documentary created by Marlon Riggs (1957–1994) that poetically aligns text with imagery of queer Black men in various states of community. Thirty-seven minutes into the film, we see a group of Black men dancing the Electric Slide together. They move as a group, but not as one; gliding across the ground in an outdoor park; a group of at least ten men move through, varying the choreography as they need to. Are there more than ten? The camera fails to reveal boundaries to the

group; the dancing extends, in slow motion, beyond the time or space of the camera's frame. Even as we only glimpse the Slide shared among the men, briefly, we sense its capacious variety. Some turn even as they travel while others don't; some punch the ground with heavy weight while others float and shimmy above its facticity. The short sequence bristles with diversity: small men, tall and juicy, thick men; skinny men in polo shirts and possibly fem-men in shorts all dance together. The Slide calls them together in a social dance of communal variety, and the men share joy through their act of intentional, embodied choice-making in the service of physical musicality.

Of course, the Electric Slide is also enjoyed by participants of many social identifiers; it is not contained exclusively as a Black social dance. In this, the form demonstrates a useful social productivity stemming from Black cultural expression. That the dance enjoyed by Black people could be enjoyed by others allows for a social mobility among Black culture; this feeds back into a pleasurable function within the dance itself as an emblem of shareable creativity.

Theatrical dance forms raise questions of watching and judging; evaluation and scrutiny within the practice of an audience's search for inspiration or meaning. These modes of address arrive with complex tensions for Black people. The afterlives of slavery suggest that Black people being scrutinized by others for their physical form and for their value as agents of work will be bound up in the complex histories of global capital and the disavowal of Black humanity. This historical background persists well into the twenty-first century. Often, performances by Black artists on stages are viewed by audiences as exotica rather than as valid creative expression.

Still, theatrical dance allows for repeated engagement with principles of Black dance. Choreographer Donald Byrd, artistic director of the Spectrum Dance Company of Seattle, has made dozens of works that explicitly engage aesthetic suppositions of Black dance. Byrd, who claims African American ancestry and choreographs through a studied respect for principles of African diaspora art making, created *Short Dances/Little Stories* in 2003 to music by Southern pop-rap musical artist Mystikal.

Short Dances engages the gestural attributes of Black dance referred to earlier: weighted movements that push through the stage floor; angular flexion of limbs in unexpected orderings; a propulsive and playful manipulation of rhythmic accents in phrasing that confidently stresses the dynamics of the musical accompaniment. As is often true in Byrd's choreography, the performers here are encouraged to *bend* the movement beyond its obvious physical and rhythmic ends, at times: pushing an extended limb past expectations, or holding a difficult balance longer, and with more obvious risk, than might seem necessary. These extensions of phrasing and stance confirm a Black aesthetic approach to timing, weight, phrasing and capacity; they bring forward the sensibility of dynamic resistance as a mode of theatrical address.

Theatrical dance offers more semiotic information to a viewer that can be discussed and interpreted from a distance. An audience, gathered to witness the event of the performance, can gain all sorts of clues to help determine value and meaning from the evidence on stage. In the case of *Short Dances*, we note the simple chic, form-fitting black costumes that accentuate the musculature of the dancers. Outfitted like superheroes, the costuming encourages us to notice every tensioned pulling of muscle as well as the extraordinary fitness of the dancers performing the work. Theatrical lighting reveals areas of bright intensity and darkness, creating shadows that allow dancers to seemingly appear and recede at will.

Fig. 6.1 Allison Keppel in Donald Byrd's *Short Dances/Little Stories*, 2003. Photo: Gabriel Bienczycki.

The dancers jump and land with an otherworldly sort of authority, commanding sections of the stage through their presence in blistering pools of light. A scenic element of a wall in the background covered in abstract graffiti art sets the work in an unquestionably urban centre; a part of a city where young residents took matters of community decoration into their own hands to create visions of a world beyond the one at hand. (This scenic element changed in several performances of the work, at times painted during the performance by collaborating visual artists, and at other times simply revealed as a backdrop to the stage action.)

While setting, lighting and costumes tend to support the unified vision of a stage event, music and movement offer their own shifting paradigms of information for the audience to consider. The musical score here, by Mystikal, rides through New Orleans hip hop sound, a sort of bouncing dance music built around distinctive sample materials that stutter and hesitate even as they cohere to a steady, duple-metre beat. Mystikal's voice conjures an old-fashioned, country preacher masculinity. He leans into a gruff, hardened animated growl for most of his 'hooks' – the refrains of different songs used to accompany this particular dance. His rapping, though, vacillates between quick, rhythmically playful passages and slower, gravelly assertions. Like many rap artists, Mystikal works with a chorus of background singers and 'hype men'; voices included in the recording who encourage the leading artist and offer preferred responses to the song as it unfolds. Generally, Mystikal strikes an assertive, aggressive sound of exhortation as he rhymes, claiming the sonic space that his music encounters unapologetically, as his own domain.

A woman roots herself into the stage, legs wide apart, partially concealed by shadows bouncing off her all-black dance costume. Her feet are bare, and they grip the black stage floor with a palpable intensity. She gestures in a mysterious sequence of roiling muscularity: circling her hands and arms intently in front of her body, sometimes with arms long, or with arms bent and fists hitting into each other or along her forearms and biceps. Feet planted, she whirls with her torso and shoulders; gestures that might convey something about hunger? Something about addiction and pain? Something about needing love? She bends her knees to reach down to the ground but rebounds with hands against her mouth: was she not allowed to say something? Is she holding something back, with hand against face? She reaches down toward the floor with arms extended together, divining for an unknowable something, then completes the gestural sequence with an unfolding of the hand from high above her head towards the floor, as if in a formal greeting of thanks, to be viewed at a distance. The thirty-second sequence arrives full of mystery and grounded intensity: these gestures *mean* something for this dancer. We, in the audience, are drawn into her commitment and the possibility of self-actualization evident in her forceful manner.

Short Dances emerges as Black dance because of its setting, musical score and the harsh attack of the dancing performed by Byrd's collaborators of the Seattle-based Spectrum Dance Company. Surprisingly, none of the dancers in the performance claimed a singular Black identity. The performers are mostly white, with one or two-mixed race artists. Donald Byrd does claim Black identity in the world, of course, and he coaches his collaborators towards a take-no-prisoners, fierce attitude that reads to audiences as Black affect. This affect allows the audiences of *Short Dances* to recognize its intentions as Black dance. The dance engages a nearly indecipherable assemblage of movement ideas, performed at the absolute ends of their possibility. In pushing the dancers to perform at their expressive extremes, the work demands that the dancers physicalize and embody the sorts of burning impossibilities that surround Black social life. Joy, desperation, anguish and hard-edged aggressions pepper the work and its performance.

Also, surprisingly, the movement vocabulary for *Short Dances* derives largely from ballet and contemporary modern dance exercises. But in this context, with this *mise en scène* of scenery, with the music of Mystikal, and with the physical attack of these performances, the dance movements arrive as sharp as knives and as potent as the outrage of civil uprisings or social protest.

The fact that Byrd creates Black dance without Black people dancing on stage speaks to a possibility of affect that might be contained by Black dance as a craft and approach to performance. This possibility is crucial to our understanding of Black dance as a process in and of itself, a mode of performance that might be engaged by many, but speaks from and towards a particular sensibility. The sensibility of Black dance as a creative liveliness in relationship to Black social death becomes a standard for understanding the undeniable attractiveness of Black dance. Many people want to dance in this way, because the dancing clearly speaks to possibilities of humanity that are difficult to imagine.

Past Approaches to Analyses

Indeed, Black dance tends to look powerful, freeing, fun and outrageous. This has led many critics and commentators to note only these most obvious dimensions of these modes of dance. Taken in and of itself, as phenomenal gesture, Black dance seems to answer a call of uniqueness in the social spaces where it lands: in North America and Europe. Black dance is not necessarily articulated or idolized in the Caribbean, Latin America or on the African continent where people of colour enjoy rich varieties of corporeal expression. Again, we note that Black dance as we define it here has grown within the peculiar crucible of chattel slavery that produced a seemingly coherent Black identity in the United States and then in Europe. So, while there are many forms of dance engaged by Black people, people of colour and others, our enquiry here focuses on the approaches to performance that have been gathered beneath a banner of Black dance. That banner gathers an approach to dancing and expertise that underscores an expressive and resistant possibility in its foundational appeal.

Historically, Black dance has been discussed by white critics as an accessible, vernacular mode of movement. Its techniques and achievements have rarely been considered art, or even art-like. Racism has fuelled the dismissal of Black dance as an urgent mode of art making. When considered as vernacular performance, Black dance could be undervalued as childish, unstructured or spontaneous. Black dance has been consistently discussed in terms of a 'natural' achievement, something somehow bred into Black communities and realized without effort. Of course, these sorts of assertions arrive without merit and are entirely untrue. Expert Black dancers practise, rehearse, risk failure and achieve unique performances through persistent effort. But the legacies of demeaning Black dance as unintellectual or underdeveloped persist and surround creativity in this mode.

Explorations of Black dance that arrive within recognized modes of artistry – as modern dance or ballet – have been consistently undervalued as derivative or second-rate. For example, the formation of the Dance Theatre of Harlem in 1969 answered a call to explore the presence of Black dancers within classical and neo-classical ballet, a challenge that had not been effectively answered in the United States at that time. The company achieved grudging success among white critics, always circumscribed by the novelty of Black artists performing work presumably made for white dancers. Black dance historians and critics tended to value the company's work and its realization of an urgent possibility for Black dance. But when the company slowed its operations in 2004, laying off most of its staff and taking a hiatus from performing, general financial support for the company could not be bolstered (see Kaufman 2004).

To write about Black dance with some understanding of its subtleties of execution and approach requires an appreciation for vernacular cultures, that is, cultures of the everyday, including the cultures of social survival, and their extension into the realms of expertise as art. Black dance may indeed be available to many, but its most expert practitioners move it squarely into a realm as artistic practice worthy of consideration for its unique, crafted achievement. Few writers have taken the time to create worthy documents in this area, but we can look to the sublime writings of Katherine Dunham to understand a potential in this area. Dunham's career included dancing in Hollywood and on Broadway, as well as studying dance as an anthropologist in several sites in the Caribbean. Her performances and her development of a dance practice/technique provide embodied evidence of Black dance retention and creativity.

Dunham combined aspects of dance that she observed during her study to create the Katherine Dunham technique, an approach to dancing that emphasizes relationships to rhythm, stretch and balance, and detailed understandings of how movement and sound correspond and relate to each other. Dunham technique, unlike other modes of theatrical dance forms, such as modern dance or ballet, is built around its relationship to drumming and musicianship, and the careful awareness of music in motion. Dunham technique can be constantly referred to as Black dance, as its terms of engagement arise in relation to the embodied musical practices of Black people in diaspora: in Martinique, Haiti, Jamaica, Trinidad and Tobago, and other spaces that Dunham researched.

Dunham's writings assume a continuity among the dances of the islands and the dancing of Black Americans in the context of the United States. While she recognized stark differences of social life in the United States and in the Caribbean, she focused on the aesthetic approaches to dance that suggested shared concerns and physical explorations. In Dunham's writing, we find evidence of diasporic affinities that place dances in familial relationship to each other.

In this, Black dance can affirm presence across geography and time. Obvious creative connections among North American stepping and South African gumboot dancing, or the 'wining' dances of the Virgin Islands and the 'twist' of the United States confirm black communities in creative motion, dancing through differing social circumstances. The dances mean differently across location and era: for example, the Running Man constructs dispersed narratives of relation to commerce when performed at a party in Brooklyn, circa 1989, or in Budapest at a nightclub in 2009. But these dances remain related, and thrive in their relationality as evidence of perseverance. In this, Black dance operates beyond affinities of form; its practice provides embodied evidence of possibility.

Researching Black Dance: Critical and Creative Challenges

We have outlined many challenges surrounding Black dance as a mode of address, the largest being that the category strains against its own impossible boundaries. Black dance arrives as a hailing of Black life, a reminding practice of creative expression that incites Black joy by way of Black corporeality. But Black dance may be enacted by dancers who do not claim Black identity. And Black dance has not been valued with much nuance by writers, historians or theorists who do not claim Black identity.

What might it mean for whites, Asians, aboriginals and Latin people to dance Black? What is it to inhabit the creative remains of someone else's traumatic history? How can we make sense of finding physical pleasure and creative expression within gestures born within the crucibles of social coercion and disavowal?

Creatively, Black dance makes less sense when it is engaged without any Black people present. And yet, this sort of appropriation has haunted theatrical performances since Black dance could be named. The desire to move in the manners available to Black dance has chased artists all over the world, resulting in expert Korean hip hop dance crews; white European ballet experiments that combine improvisation and a 'get down' approach to performance; and any number of swing dance festivals with few Black participants.

The questions that loom in these dance encounters have to do with whether the dancing actually speaks in any way to Black people in the world. Again, if we are willing to imagine Black dance as the affirmation of Black possibility, then it would seem urgent to encounter Black people in its practices. Black dance might be best engaged to speak of and to Black people. When others dance Black, though, with an expectation to be recognized for their ability in these modes of address, Black people might be confused, annoyed or distressed. Sharing culture might be something done in proximity, as when dancers teach each other moves and approaches to movement in circumstances where people dance. But to approach the shapes and rhythms of Black dance without any intention to engage Black people who have nurtured and burnished these movement practices can too often seem crass, supremacist and ethically unfortunate.

When Donald Byrd coaches his white and Asian dancers into the complex approaches to Black modern dance that appeal to him, he brings his many years of experience as a Black man into the rehearsal hall. Even when the work being rehearsed might seem to have little to do with his always-shifting identity markers, his experiences and familial relationships become part of the tapestry of art making that he engages. *Short Dances* succeeds as a demonstration of modes of Black dance because of its direct access to foundational physical understanding of how Black dance operates, emerges, and what it can do in the theatrical space.

But when white choreographers attempt to copy a sort of downward-directed ferocity of rhythmic attack, or a loose-limbed, improvisational-seeming 'do your own thing' choreography without the creative collaboration of Black artists, their work often seems false, odd or just confusing to its audiences. At times, these explorations might seem patently rude or embarrassing, as when Miley Cyrus tried to 'twerk' in a television special, or when the Chicago-based Joffrey Ballet tried to stage a ballet to the music of Prince with choreography that referenced Black social dances made by white choreographers. Most often, Black dance is referenced by white performers as a mode of playful, sexy 'fun' that might allow them to be momentarily 'free' from the embodied strictures of everyday whiteness. But of course, this possible outcome has little to do with the formation of Black dance that we have discussed here. Cynicism emerges at this intersection, where dancers seem willing to act out someone else's traumatic history in the mode of dance practice.

Conclusion: Making-Thinking Black Dance

Ultimately, if we are all able to acknowledge the depth of experience that produces Black dance, then we might be able to acknowledge its urgency, profundity and special value as creative address. We understand Black dance as a system of address that operates in several modes simultaneously. Black dance allows for resistant demonstration and embodied aesthetic protest; a working through of identity and its varied affects; the exploration of excellence; an improvisational address of rhythm and rhythmic phrasing; and the channelling of desire into the realm of an aesthetically-engaged body in motion. Black dance makes space for the thinking through of the great social disavowal that produced Black identities in the world. Black dance contains its history as a remains of the Atlantic slave trade – as a creative response to a world without equal opportunities and in need of unexpected gesture and rhythmic layering.

And Black dance allows for an intricate urgent process: a system of address, a rendering of rhythm and relationship, a dancing beyond disavowal towards Black joy. In the twenty-first century, the revelation of Black joy surely might be one of our shared common ambitions in performance. In a world wrought with dissent and fragmentations, we might collect ourselves around expressions that speak of, and towards, communities of colour in particular ways, often crafted by artists who identify themselves as Black no matter their ethnicity or country of origin. In this, Black dance offers us a possibility of collective aesthetic action, moving ourselves into the lines of action that centre Black people in the creative ways of the world.

Performance Details

Short Dances/Little Stories, choreographed by Donald Byrd, was first presented at Spectrum Dance Theater, Seattle, WA, in October 2003. The music from the dance was drawn from *Tarantula* by Mystikal, Jive Records, 2001; *Ghetto Fabulous* by Mystikal, No Limit Records, 1998; and *Let's Get Ready* by Mystikal, Jive Records, 2000.

Further Reading

For a discussion of nomenclature, and distinctions among African American dance and Black dance, see my essay, 'African American Dance: A Complex History' in Thomas F. DeFrantz (2002: 2–35). For videos of the Electric Slide at the Obama Inauguration see *Electric Slide* (2009). For more on Marlon Riggs's work, including classroom resources, articles, interviews and clips of *Tongues Untied*, see the *Marlon Riggs Critical Resource Page* at California Newsreel (online). For a recent scholarly overview of Katherine Dunham's achievement see Das (2017). Dunham published several studies of dance and memoirs, see Dunham (1946, 1959, 1969 and 1983) and Clark and Johnson (2006). For further reading on issues discussed in this chapter, see DeFrantz and Willis (2016), Gottschild (2003) and DeFrantz and Gonzalez (2014).

References

Clark, VèVè A., and Sara E. Johnson, eds (2006), *Kaiso! Writings by and about Katherine Dunham*, Madison and London: University of Wisconsin Press.

Das, Joanna Dee (2017), *Katherine Dunham: Dance and the African Diaspora*, Oxford: Oxford University Press.

DeFrantz, Thomas F., ed. (2002) *Dancing Many Drums: Excavations in African American Dance*, Madison and London: University of Wisconsin Press.

DeFrantz, Thomas F., and Anita Gonzalez, eds (2014), *Black Performance Theory: An Anthology of Critical Resources*, Durham, NC: Duke University Press.

DeFrantz, Thomas F., and Tara Aisha Willis, eds (2016), 'Black Moves: New Research in Black Dance Studies', special issue of *The Black Scholar*, 46 (1).

Dunham, Katherine (1946), *Journey to Accompong*, New York: H. Holt and Company. Re-issued in 2013 as *Katherine Dunham's Journey to Accompong*, Literary Licensing, LLC.

Dunham, Katherine (1959), *A Touch of Innocence*, New York: Harcourt. Reissued 1994 as *A Touch of Innocence: Memoirs of Childhood*, Chicago: Chicago University Press.

Dunham, Katherine ([1947] 1983), *Dances of Haiti*, Los Angeles: Center for Afro-American Studies, UCLA.

Dunham, Katherine ([1969] 1994), *Island Possessed*, Chicago: University of Chicago Press.

Electric Slide (n.d.), available online: https://www.youtube.com/watch?v=KdVdsXsajK8 *and* https://www.youtube.com/watch?v=BTe5oG-ZOM4 (accessed 14 February 2018).

Gottschild, Brenda Dixon (2003), *The Black Dancing Body: A Geography from Coon to Cool*, New York: Palgrave Macmillan.

Kaufman, Sarah (2004), 'Dance Theatre of Harlem Cancels Season', *Washington Post*, 22 September: C02. Available online: http://www.washingtonpost.com/wp-dyn/articles/A401 30-2004Sep21.html (accessed 14 February 2018).

Marlon Riggs Critical Resource Page (n.d.), Available online: http://newsreel.org/Riggs.asp (accessed 14 February 2018).

Tongues Untied (1989), [Film] Dir. Marlon T. Riggs, with Steve Langley and Alex Langford (composers), USA: Frameline and California Newsreel.

7 How Does Scenography Think?

LIESBETH GROOT NIBBELINK

Setting the Stage – or Staging the Set?

A stunningly purple carpet covers the entire floor of the living room, likely to catch the eye of anyone viewing the set of Philippe Quesne's *L'Effet de Serge* (Vivarium Studio, 2007). This performance is all about attention: attention to detail, to apparently trivial objects, to theatre making itself. During the performance, we become acquainted with Serge, the inhabitant of this living room. We see how he spends his time while at home, and the ways in which he uses various materials and tools to produce small 'effects' or micro-spectacles: projections, fireworks, experimental robotics. Each Sunday, he invites a few 'friends' (actually local residents from the city where the show is being presented) into his living room for a miniature performance lasting no more than three minutes.

L'Effet de Serge is not only a show about a man in his living room, but also a performance about scenography; about how to use tools, conventions and materials to create scenes and situations ('effects'), and how to stage them for an audience. On stage, we see a set, a set that suggests a living room, a living room which changes into a theatre when Serge presents his mini spectacles. The Latin 'spectare' means looking or watching. This is what the spectacle is all about: to show, to put on display, to present in order to be seen, to draw the attention of the audience. Usually, a spectacle achieves this through large-scale, awe-inspiring effects. In the course of history, such spectacles (flying ballerinas, simulated rain and thunder, deus ex machina appearances) were closely associated with scenography and stage machinery (Baugh 2014). *L'Effet de Serge*, however, deals with micro-spectacles: they are incredibly small, they are very brief – we might even say they are extremely *un*spectacular. By changing the scale of the spectacle and, as we shall see, by shifting perspectives on the living room, Philippe Quesne invites us into a peculiar universe in which we encounter a range of theatre conventions and art-making practices in a slightly twisted way. Via Serge, he analyses those conventions and practices, and by deconstructing or altering them, he shows how scenography works. *L'Effet de Serge* is thus an excellent starting point for asking how theatre thinks scenography and, vice versa, how we can understand theatre's effects via the lens of scenography.

By playing with ideas related to set, stage, setting, spectacle and spectatorship, *L'Effet de Serge* provides a tour through scenography's toolbox. Yet, if scenography is so closely connected to staging and spectatorship, how does scenography differ from the work of a theatre director or, in the case of an artists' collective, from the collaborative work of theatre

Fig. 7.1 Serge presents one of his effects, in *L'Effet de Serge*. Courtesy Vivarium Studio. Photo: Martin Argyroglo.

makers? What is the difference between scenography and *mise-en-scène* or staging? What is specifically scenographic about staging? To rephrase that question: what kind of sensitivity does scenography bring to the theatre? What knowledge about staging is implicated in scenography?

Scenography, briefly put, involves performance design, and more specifically, the design of spaces for performance. In this chapter, *L'Effet de Serge* will be my companion in exploring how scenography is engaged with (de)constructing and dissecting the theatre, while choosing a distinctively *spatially* oriented perspective to do so. This spatial perspective provides us with another question that serves as a stepping stone to the larger issues raised earlier. This is a question that plays a role in much, perhaps all, scenographic design: in what or which space(s) are we, exactly?

What or Which Spaces?

The question of what or which space(s) are created by scenography seems a concrete and 'easy' question. It is a question, however, that can generate an extremely wide range of answers. Scenography not only creates spaces that refer to other spaces (a living room, a forest, a street) but also addresses the affective qualities of space (a bright room, a confining place, a damp spot). Scenography produces spatial relationships and conditions (inside, outside, isolated, included, around, dispersed) and in doing so, often relies on and plays with the codes and conventions of theatre (the stage, the 'fourth wall', word scenery and so on).

The plurality of space is somehow 'incarnated' in the word 'scenography' itself. Scenography, in its most literal and simplest definition, means the writing or drawing of the scene (McKinney and Palmer 2017: 4). The 'scene', in turn, relates to a variety of meanings and, again, an amalgam of spaces. Etymologically, scenography describes the writing of the 'skene', referring to the back wall which in a Greek amphitheatre divided the pro-skene and the orchestra from the backstage (McKinney and Butterworth 2009: 105–6). A 'scene', however, also has come to refer to the playing area or the stage itself – think of the use of the word, for example, in the term *mise-en-scène*. Scenography, therefore, has also been translated as 'scenic writing', a writing on the scene (Collins and Nisbet 2010: 140; Aronson 2005: 7). Closely connected to this, in her essay 'The Written Space' (1992), Flemish dramaturg Marianne van Kerkhoven describes scenography as the writing of and the writing *with* spaces, which exposes scenography's engagement with temporality and transformation. Spaces (and texts) unfold in time and change through use; they materialize through what we do in space and how we interact with them. A 'scene', lastly, is also a staged *situation*. When actors play and interact with each other – whether impersonating a character or not – they are involved in a scene; in fact, any situation that is deliberately staged might be called a scene. This latter reading is highly relevant for contemporary forms of scenography, which move into the realm of public space, site-specific performance or immersive theatre. From back wall to playing area to transformational spaces to staged situations, one word – scenography – opens up a myriad of spaces and spatial perspectives to the stage, asking the question: in what or which space(s) are we?

In contemporary approaches to scenography, another set of spaces comes to the fore. Sodja Lotker and Richard Gough, in their introduction to a special issue on scenography of *Performance Research* (2013), argue that scenography can happen anywhere. Scenography is to be found not only in the theatre but equally in our homes, public spaces, airports, television shows, courts of justice or politics, in fashion and advertising, on social media and in video games. Such expanding forms of scenography involve a literal change of scenery as well as a conceptual widening of the spaces that scenography creates. These spaces are increasingly seen as spaces for *performance* and consequently, as spaces for (self) presentation, encounters and (social) interaction. They can be called performative spaces as they are not only spaces for performance, but are being performed themselves; they materialize as a result of our interactions with and responses to space (for a reflection on performative versus geometric space, see Fischer-Lichte 2008: 105–6).

Many recent publications on scenography emphasize this process-character of scenography and performance design. Joslin McKinney and Philip Butterworth, for instance, regard scenography as the 'manipulation and orchestration of the performance environment' (2009: 4). In *Scenography Expanded* (2017), editors Joslin McKinney and Scott Palmer approach scenography as 'a mode of encounter and exchange founded on spatial and material relations between bodies, objects and environments' (2017: 2). In his foreword to that volume, Arnold Aronson likens scenography to a set of 'visual and spatial organizing principles' (xiv). All these authors note, in one way or another, that scenography is not (and never has been) a mere backdrop for the action, or an illustration of the world depicted in a play, or the visual translation of a director's concept, but rather plays a much more prominent role in any staged event.

To summarize, scenography can be regarded as primarily concerned with the design of spaces *and* spatial relationships; with the spatial and material conditions for performance that shape the interactions between humans, objects, materials and environments. Yet, one element of scenography seems a little overshadowed in these reflections, which is the rather obvious but still relevant observation that scenography is rooted in the theatre. When expanding or travelling, this theatre-based luggage – full of concepts, histories and practical experience – is taken along. This chapter therefore moves back into the theatre, to ask how theatre has shaped scenographic thinking and to reflect on the specific ingredients of the scenographic toolbox. So, let's return to a space that is probably the most represented space in the history of (Western) scenography, at least since the rise of realism, that is, the living room–very special living room, the room of Serge, our specialist in micro-spectacles.

L'Effet de Serge

On first sight, there is nothing strange about portraying a living room on a stage. Over the course of (Western) theatre history, scenographers must have created hundreds of thousands of living rooms. Due to its persistent reappearance in history, we might even call a living room a 'scenographic trope'. Christopher Balme notes that the living room is the 'quintessential space of Western realistic drama', a carrier of Western bourgeois ideology (2008: 57). Such living rooms tend to include one or more couches, tables and chairs and a variety of props to support the conflicts, misunderstandings, shattered appearances or any other large-scale battles that are fought out on an individual (psychological) level. The living room in *L'Effet de Serge*, however, is half empty. The left side of the stage is left bare, leaving the carpet to appear in all its magnificent purpleness. There are no couches. There is only one table and one chair. This could be a first hint that something else is at stake here – this will probably not be a performance about families or (broken) relationships.

In between presenting his micro-spectacles, we see Serge in his house, totally at ease, as if he was not on a stage and not watched by an audience. We see how he drinks a glass of wine, orders a pizza or listens to music, while tinkering with electric wires and remote-control devices as he prepares his effects. We may think that we are dealing with another well-known theatre convention, that of the (closed) fourth wall. Yet, in this performance, the audience is not placed in the position of a voyeur. We are not ignored at all. The opening scene in particular makes this explicitly clear, providing the audience with a lesson in scenographic thinking, so to speak, since it uses close observation – the scenographic equivalent of close reading – as a starting point for analysing how the material and spatial conditions of performance create meaning and experience.

At the start of the performance, Serge is not yet on stage. The stage is lit, which provides the audience with time to take in the room, observe its height and depth, to notice the carpet, to see that the table is actually a ping-pong table, covered with books, toys, electric wires and a television set, to discover boxes, bags and knick-knacks stacked against the wall (Allen 2013; Bosch et al. 2013). A little later, a man dressed as a cosmonaut appears behind the glass window in the back wall. Like a true adventurer, he starts exploring the house's interior, first from the outside, then from inside the living room. The room is dark now. With the help of a search light, he points at the things to be seen in the room. By lighting

Fig. 7.2 Opening scene, *L'Effet de Serge*. **Courtesy Vivarium Studio. Photo: Pierre Grosbois.**

and describing the space and the objects he informs the audience about the life and habits of Serge, the inhabitant of this room. He tells us about Serge's effects and the presentations on Sunday evenings, he leafs through some books (comics, manuals, a Beckett play), he points at 'l'espace vide' on the left, explaining how Serge likes to use this empty space for walking around, or standing still. He demonstrates how Serge enjoys lying on the carpet, or even, at times, likes to crawl *under* the carpet. This attention to trivial details characterizes Philippe Quesne's oeuvre. French scholar Chloé Déchery situates Quesne's work within a development of contemporary French theatre in which (staged) reality is treated as an 'archeological site', disclosing 'the presence of "things" whose proximity, everydayness and banality usually prevent them from being seen' (2011: 122).

Through the cosmonaut's excavations, the room and its objects are now (literally) seen in a different light. Anne Karin ten Bosch observes that by showing them *again*, we are likely to watch them more closely and perceive them afresh (Bosch et al. 2013: 103). Simultaneously, the space gets connected to a fictional character named Serge. While learning to observe the set, we gradually enter a theatrical reality, that of Serge's living room (103). The following moment, a voice-over takes over from the cosmonaut, who disappears through a door on the left, while 'he' continues telling us what is to be 'seen' offstage (a kitchen, a corridor, a bathroom, the front door), further opening the scenographic toolbox, since here again we are invited to imagine a space that is actually not there.

This play with the relation between presented and imaginary spaces is a fine example of writing with spaces; it also activates a history of dramatic theatre and related conventions of staging illusionary worlds on stage. Also theoretically the tension between onstage and offstage spaces, between what is actually present and what it is supposed to represent, has generated a range of spatial distinctions, such as perceived versus conceived space, presentational versus fictional space, scenic versus dramatic space and so on. Gay McAuley provides an insightful overview of those terms in *Space in Performance* (1999: 17–23), before presenting her own taxonomy; I fully agree with her that any attempt to orderly categorize all those spaces is to enter a 'terminological minefield' (17).

For scenographers, these spatial distinctions encompass much more than words or elements of a taxonomy. Their way of dealing with connections and transitions between those spaces conveys much of their understanding of theatre and of the aesthetic registers they employ. If for instance the transition between the stage and the theatre space surrounding the stage is obscured, this suggests that the world on stage continues beyond the proscenium arch – or the wings, walls, doors or whatever spatial border is present. As an audience, we are to imagine this 'world beyond', and we need to tap into the register of illusionary or dramatic space. If, by contrast, the distinction between the stage and theatre space is exposed, the design reveals an understanding of the theatre as a place where we *construct* worlds, where we stage illusions or create spaces of concentrated attention, and where we use machinery, conventions, light and sound, or any other means of the theatre, to do so. *L'Effet de Serge* explicitly chooses the latter option, partially because the set is clearly visible as a set: the walls end in mid-air, there is no ceiling, it is an autonomous object on a stage.

These traditions and distinctions help to show that while the cosmonaut guides us through the scenography, he meanwhile puts this scenography to work, by organizing our focus, raising attention, and creating an awareness of the vital role of creation and imagination that is at work, and that is 'our work', as an audience. Via this tour, Quesne subtly hints at the practical aspects of theatre making as well, an equally vital aspect that scenographers (have to) deal with. By revealing that the carpet is not glued to the floor, for instance – and playing with this – he points out the set's practical and technical requirements. As a touring show, this set needs to be built up and disassembled effectively; the set, including the carpet, has to fit in a touring truck. Quesne often refers to the practice of theatre making, evidenced, for example, by the reuse and reappearance of objects and other performance elements, subtly pointing to theatre's intrinsic relation with repetition (see Carlson 2001), and also to working with limited budgets (Déchery 2011). Equally typical is that this reuse becomes subject to play, creating a 'coherent and largely self-referential theatrical system' (Déchery 2011: 129). The cosmonaut, for example, is a figure that already appeared in *L'après Nature* (2006), and *L'Effet de Serge* ends with showing the first scene of the next show, *La Mélancolie des Dragons* (2008).

All in all, the opening scene is an exposé of the many spatial, aesthetic, practical and theoretical registers of scenographic thinking. Through these registers, the scene constantly cuts across the staging of illusions and the reality of the stage. Playing with these gradations of reality, *L'Effet de Serge* provides a counter-argument to rather dualistic approaches to the contemporary stage, like Hans-Thies Lehmann's postdramatic theatre (2006) or Erika Fischer-Lichte's approach to performance (2008), which both emphasize the non-illusionary, non-representational character of contemporary theatre and performance. Instead, the performance lucidly uses the conventions of dramatic theatre while constantly referring to the theatre as a staged event.

In accordance with the cosmonaut's introduction, the 'real' Serge continues the show (played by the same actor, Gaëtan Vourc'h). Each Sunday evening, Serge's living room changes into a little theatre, where he presents miniature performances with titles such as

'Rolling Effect On a Music by Händel' or 'Laser Effect On a Music by John Cage', while further taking us along in exploring scenography's toolbox.

Scenographic Analysis

There is a range of methodologies available to analyse in what or which space(s) we are. If interested in how spaces refer to specific places, how they conjure up memories, symbolic meaning or cultural connotations, or point to societal or political functions of space, we might opt for a semiotic perspective. We could adopt a phenomenological perspective if interested in exploring how staged space appeals to the senses; how the spatial and material conditions of performance affect the way we perceive a performance (cf. McKinney and Butterworth 2009: 151–70). Scenography arranges all this through the careful selection and arrangement of materials, which could be another focal point of the analysis. Here, the discourse on 'new materialism' is a valuable frame of reference, which emphasizes the vitality and agential capacity of matter and increasingly is recognized as highly relevant for scenography (McKinney and Palmer 2017; Schweizer and Zerdy 2014). As suggested above, scenography also involves aspects that could be studied through general theatre theories and concepts, such as staging and framing, spectacle and spectatorship.

This brief inventory suggests that scenography operates at the junction of the many tools and strategies with which theatre is made, as it deals with space, time, bodies, materials, narratives, media and technology, with conventions and traditions, with meaning, sensations and experience. Scenography thinks through the relating of these components, and it is specifically this relationality through which performance design 'works'. It seems more appropriate then, to not exclusively focus on either semiotic, phenomenological or material approaches but to join these perspectives in a methodology that responds to scenography's kaleidoscopic qualities. As a starting point for such a scenographic analysis, I take the inventory by Joslin McKinney and Scott Palmer in *Scenography Expanded*, where they present relationality, affectivity and materiality as core components of (expanded) scenography. Although *L'Effet de Serge* stays much closer to theatre in comparison to expanded forms of scenography, the expansion of a phenomenon also requires the articulation of its specific characteristics, which is why I think these components are relevant in any scenographic analysis – see also McKinney and Palmer's discussion of Rosalind Krauss's take on expanded sculpture (2017: 3–4). In the discussion below, I will add temporality as a fourth component and ultimately, address the issue of staging, which I think cannot be avoided in any scenographic analysis.

Relationality: For McKinney and Palmer, the component of relationality, firstly, entails that scenography is involved with creating and facilitating spaces of encounter. Relationality has a strong, although not exclusive, connection with spectatorship, as scenography plays a crucial role in 'shaping the interface between the performance and the audience' (2017: 5). In contemporary work, for instance in immersive, site-specific or ambulatory performances, these encounters could also involve other spectators, or specific sites, environments or social structures (8). McKinney and Palmer mention Rimini Protokoll's *Situation Rooms* as an example, a performance installation which places the spectators literally within the webbed actions of international arms trade. Wandering through several interrelated rooms, they step into the footsteps of, for instance, a weapons factory worker, a child soldier, a tradesman or a war journalist. This example exposes scenography as engaged in situating and positioning spectators, and with shifting viewing positions (9). In a scenographic analysis, we might ask questions such as:

- how does scenography shape and facilitate modes of encounter?
- how is spectatorship implicated in performance design and what are characteristics of scenography-as-interface?
- how are spectators addressed, situated and positioned by scenography?

Contrary to *Situation Rooms*, *L'Effet de Serge* clearly separates the stage and the auditorium. Quesne always opts for this frontality, regarding the theatre as a place for observation (Lavery 2013: 267). Interestingly, this is reflected in the company's name, Vivarium Studio. A vivarium refers to 'an enclosed space where the behaviour of organisms in their environment is observed through a glass wall for the purposes of scientific research' (267). In his vivarium, life is put under a microscope, inviting the audience 'to act as entomologists' (Quesne in Déchery 2011: 128). This also pertains to the moments when Serge presents his effects to an audience of friends. Each time the show comes to an end, they look slightly puzzled, after which they engage in an attempt to reflect on what they have seen. The seriousness of their response humorously contrasts with the small scale of the effects, and these scenes seem to expose and (gently) mock the arts discourse that sometimes overshadows the artwork itself. These Sunday evenings activate a typical theatre convention to which relationality is key: the play-within-the-play. An audience looks at a stage upon which another audience looks at something presented. Due to this duplication, the play-within-the play is also an instance of meta-theatre, a self-referential act in which the theatre exposes and reflects on itself.

Affectivity: As a second component, McKinney and Palmer focus on affectivity, since scenography often addresses all the senses, rather than employing only a scopic register. Scenography tends to communicate via sensorial experience and to generate an understanding of performance that is 'founded in sensual, emotional and aesthetic

Fig. 7.3 Serge presents one of his effects to invited audience, in *L'Effet de Serge*. Courtesy Vivarium Studio. Photo: Martin Argyroglo.

responses on the part of the viewer' (2017: 11). To provide two explicit examples of this, in a Dutch staging of *Macbeth* (Noord Nederlands Toneel [NNT], director Ola Mafaalani 2001), huge blocks of ice were dangling about one metre above the heads of the performers, like grim fore-bearers of the dark events to come. They gradually melted over the course of the performance, literally creating an icy and damp atmosphere. In *Molière* (Schaubühne Berlin, director Luk Perceval 2007), the German scenographer Katrin Brack let it snow for five hours, which created a dizzying and hallucinating effect, an 'LSD for the eyes' (McKinney and McKechnie 2016: 134). These affective components therefore instigate questions such as:

- in what ways does scenography address the senses?
- how do these affective components of spectatorship provide an entry into the work?
- how do sensorial responses reflect or impact our understanding of the work?

L'Effet de Serge reflects this approach to scenography, since the effects explicitly work with flashing light, enhanced by smoke, or spiralling laser-beams that respond to the rhythm of the accompanying music score. Meanwhile, the set addresses the senses in a subtler way. We can feel the height and depth of the living room, and also the cheapness of the materials with which the set is built. The size of the room corresponds to the measurements of relatively cheap social housing apartments, with low ceilings as indicators of an economic use of space. In Serge's living room, nothing is extraordinary, except for the purple carpet. The window in the back wall is cast in white synthetic fibre, the walls and the door to the hall are grey. If it signals anything, it is averageness. This is a very ordinary house – with an extraordinary tenant.

Materiality: Through the descriptions of materials, we arrive at McKinney and Palmer's third component. They describe materiality as the 'properties and capacities of things, places, bodies and the ways they interact and impact on our experience and understanding of performance and of the world more generally' (2017: 9). They, too, mention the relevance of new materialist theories for exploring the agential capacity of things, stuff, bodies and structures and, referring to Jane Bennett, suggest regarding matter and technologies as 'actors alongside and within us' (McKinney and Palmer 2017: 12). Materials change due to the conditions of the stage (think of the melting ice-blocks in *Macbeth*) and in turn, they set the parameters for action (like the snow in *Molière*). Materiality, therefore, takes shape *in* the work of performance. Katherine Hayles – also a new materialist thinker – observes that materiality 'cannot be specified in advance, as if it pre-existed the specificity of the work' and instead is an 'emergent property' that takes shape through multiple processes of action and response (Hayles 2002: 32–3). When analysing materiality, we might ask:

- what is the state and status of matter and materials; (how) do they show traces of use or processes of manufacturing, manipulation and fabrication?
- what (emergent or transformative) properties and capacities come to the fore?
- how do these instances of materiality inform our understanding of how materials, bodies and environments are implicated in one another?

In *L'Effet de Serge*, we see a human being who lives alone but is not alone at all. His habitat is one in which trivial stuff and things are equally important (see also Allen 2013).

The materials are handled attentively and, as we have seen, they also become objects of research. The carpet, for instance, is a sign of domesticity but also functions to cover the floor and at times, Serge. The carpet supports lying down, it is used to play with hiding and (dis)appearing (becoming a metonym for the theatre itself), it is a scenographic device for altering our perspective on the stage and the practice of theatre making.

Temporality: While elaborating on relationality, affectivity and materiality, McKinney and Palmer regularly refer to the performance as a processual event (2017: 9–10), an important aspect of *temporality*. There is, however, more to say on scenography's temporal aspects, since spaces always unfold and materialize in time, and change over time. Scenographic space often functions as a script or scenario for potential action. Spaces are deeply procedural, they generate behaviour and define how one executes procedures, procedures that could be as simple as opening a door. In its dealing with time, scenography also thinks time conceptually. In Rimini Protokoll's *Situation Rooms*, the interconnectedness of spaces emphasizes the experience of simultaneity. *Macbeth*'s dripping ice-blocks reveal a progressive time-concept, leading to an unavoidable end, with Macbeth and Lady Macbeth bathing in blood. The snow in *Molière* creates a sense of disorientation and timelessness. To analyse scenography in view of temporality, we might ask questions such as:

- in what ways does the performance space change over time; are there any remarkable transformations; does the space show traces of use?
- how does scenography function as a script or a scenario; how does it provide instructions (or restrictions) for action?
- how does time behave, in this specific space or (fictional) universe?

In *L'Effet de Serge*, time works a bit differently than in the previous examples. Serge's pace of walking or moving about the room is a little slower than our everyday pace, as though time has slowed down in this particular living room – implicitly critiquing the hectic speed and dynamism of our current 24/7 society, a kind of resistance which also marks Quesne's practice generally (Déchery 2011: 122–4). The space itself is not subjected to transformation, yet gradually, the world on stage becomes larger. In the opening sequence, we encountered the set and some offstage spaces. Later on, along with Serge's friends, the local context renders itself present. On one Sunday evening, some visitors arrive on stage rather spectacularly by car. This expands our awareness beyond the backstage and the theatre building, as Chloé Déchery remarks of that moment, 'it seems as if reality, in all its quotidian beauty, is intruding into the theatre space itself' (2011: 128). By means of these gradations, the attention shifts, moving from the set and the stage, to the theatre, to the city. This conjures up a worthwhile remark by Marianne van Kerkhoven: 'the theatre is sited in the city, the city is sited in the world, and the walls are made of skin – they are porous, they breathe' (Van Kerkhoven 2002: 137; my translation).

Relationality, affectivity, materiality, temporality: these vital components of performance space provide us with insight into scenography's *staging* strategies. Through these components, scenography sets the parameters for action and creates the conditions through which meaning and experience can emerge. *L'Effet de Serge* constantly and self-referentially refers to itself as an act of staging: by showing us around on the set, by playing with conventions and traditions of theatre making, by creating miniature performances, *L'Effet de Serge* reveals itself as an event that is artificially constructed, a process that is constantly in the making, and uses all the tools and means of theatre to organize the attention of the audience.

Scenography, Ecology, Dramaturgy

So far, I have pointed out how *L'Effet de Serge* constantly refers to itself as a work of scenography and, by putting scenography 'to work', reveals itself as an act of scenographic thinking. There are other approaches that could help to expose how scenography thinks. Two of them will be briefly discussed here, connected to scenography's close affinity with, firstly, ecology, and secondly, dramaturgy.

Scenography can be regarded as a mode of thinking that is fundamentally *ecological*, since it always deals with the entanglements of objects, humans and environments. To grasp some implications of this in relation to *L'Effet de Serge*, let's return to our central question: in what or which space(s) are we? The word 'ecology' combines the Greek oikos (the home) and logos (science) (Lavery 2013: 267). *L'Effet de Serge* takes this quite literally, since the performance could as well be regarded as a study of domesticity. We see Serge in his habitat, watching TV, playing with ping-pong balls, eating crisps, or suffering a nosebleed. Instead of providing insight into a human's psychology, Quesne's vivarium presents the human as species, surrounded by and interacting with things and objects that are equally components of this habitat. It is precisely this awareness that 'everything is connected' that, according to Carl Lavery, forms the basis for Quesne's ecological thinking (271). This sensitivity inspires many of Quesne's projects, including his *Make It Work/Theatre of Negotiations* (2015) collaboration with Bruno Latour, a simulation of a climate conference where non-human species were equally represented at the negotiation tables. *L'Effet de Serge* is actually a pun on *l'effet de serre*, the French term for the greenhouse effect (Lavery 2013: 265; Déchery 2011: 129). In an illuminating essay on Quesne's 'environmental politics', Lavery observes that Quesne's artistic principles are based on bricolage, on 'piecing things together' and recycling, offering a biocentric rather than a human-centred world view (270–1). In *L'Effet de Serge*, the cosmonaut, the car and even the window are recycled elements, and we see how Serge creates effects by reusing discarded materials.

Lavery's approach to ecology reflects back on scenography, this time related to a remarkable source: the writings of the seventeenth-century philosopher Leibniz. Leibniz used scenography as a term to describe the inherent relationality of how we make sense of the world: our viewing (and therefore understanding) of the world is always dependent on the place from which we view it. Thea Brejzek remarks that 'Leibniz developed a startlingly modern notion of space as possessing no substantial reality but rather presenting the "order of the *togetherness*," defined by the relations of objects (bodies) in space at a particular time, against Newton's dominant notion of space as absolute and mechanistic' (Brejzek 2015: 22; my emphasis). Leibniz's relational and relative world view looks rather familiar for us, yet in the seventeenth century, it was not that obvious, and even politically precarious. Therefore, it is helpful to know and also to complete the picture, that Leibniz contrasts the many perspectives of man-in-the-world with the all-encompassing view from God above (Brejzek 2015: 22–3).

Leibniz's understanding of scenography points to the intrinsic connection between scenography, perspective and spectatorship and, consequently, between scenography and *dramaturgy*, my second point of enquiry. Scenography and dramaturgy are deeply entangled practices of theatre making, both concerned with how a performance communicates with an audience. They are both modes of making-thinking, relying on the ongoing exchange between creation, observation and analysis. Dramaturgy is arguably a 'slippery term' (Van Kerkhoven quoted in Turner and Behrndt 2008: 17), yet put concisely, dramaturgy involves both the reflexive component in any theatre-making process and the strategies employed to 'piece together' a performance, strategies which mount specific arguments, even if they are obscure(d). I regard dramaturgy as an act of composition, in which at least three compositional layers can be distinguished, concerned respectively with the modes of structuring a performance – for example its specific logic of assembly, creating the performance's internal 'fabric' (Turner and Behrndt 2008: 3) – with audience address (Bleeker 2008), and with the many ways in which a performance relates to a wider cultural, socioeconomic, artistic or political context.

As we have seen, scenography thinks through all these compositional layers as well. What then, would be the difference? Without striving for clear-cut distinctions, a possible answer could be that scenographic reflexivity is often instigated by its attachment to the mundane – for example the concrete, material and occasionally trivial details of our life-world – whereas dramaturgical reflection seems primarily anchored in the societal, artistic and/or discursive context of a work. These 'docking ports' are of course not mutually exclusive, and provide an entrance into the same water. Yet it is a dynamic that may influence performance analysis: in a scenographic analysis, I could start with the carpet and then zoom out towards the living room, into conventions of the dramatic stage or to Quesne's analysis of domesticity. In a dramaturgical analysis, I would likely start with considering how the handling of the carpet aligns with related compositional choices, in order to find out which logic of organization undergirds the performance's fabric – an element that would help to recognize the performance's strategies of transparency and self-reflexivity, or to connect the logic of bricolage to that of ecology.

Thinking Scenography

In what or which space are we, in *L'Effet de Serge*? We are in a living room, which has come to mean a space of everydayness, mundaneness and triviality. At the same time, we are in the theatre, a space of artificiality, where a range of tools and tricks are used to manage the audience's attention. Precisely at their junction, we can locate scenographic thinking – and Serge's effects. On one Sunday evening, Serge presents an empty packaging box, mounted on little wheels, that is driven across the living room by means of a remote control, with a small firework on top of it. It is truly a spectacle, in the sense that it refers to nothing other than itself. It does not signify anything yet it draws attention; on an affective level, it sparkles with joy (the joy of invention, of dancing bits of firelight) and for a brief moment we enter a material universe of rotating wheels and the lightness of the carton box.

In *L'Effet de Serge*, the adventure is not 'out there', but at home. It is the adventure of imagination and ingenuity. In Serge's habitat, a packaging box is not only a means for transporting or protecting things; one can also put it on wheels and let it wander around. The sheer endless potentiality emerging here is precisely what characterizes the virtuality of objects and spaces, to paraphrase Elisabeth Grosz, in *Architecture from the Outside*. Virtuality, in this context, does not suggest an opposition with 'reality', as occasionally implicated in terms like 'virtual reality' or 'cyberspace' (cf. Grosz 2001: 78–9). Following philosophers Gilles Deleuze and Henri Bergson, Grosz regards virtuality as the latent, not-yet realized potential of spaces, the potential inherent in any design of becoming other than that which is already actualized (Grosz 2001: 130).

A packaging box is a very mundane, trivial object, yet in this performance, it is also an engine of potentiality. The space *L'Effet de Serge* presents us with, then, is ultimately a space that is charged by (Grosz's) virtuality. Despite their total insignificance, Serge's spectacles render visible the close connection between the mundane and the virtual, which is what makes scenographic thinking, in my view, profoundly relevant, especially in light of the dawning ecological crises. Not because a packaging box is recycled but, instead, because a banal object is treated with reverence such that it raises an awareness of how we might do things otherwise. Look around you: what is the first object you see? Think what you can do with that object. Think what else or more you can do with this object. Think like Serge. Think wild. If you can do this, you can do it with (almost) any topic. If you can do this, you could do other things differently: in a relationship, in an educational system, in relation to environmental issues.

Serge's micro-spectacles thus question what is actually a spectacle? When do we regard something worth looking at? And it presents us with the option that a simple act of creation, an act of putting materials on top of each other, of combining components in an out-of-the-ordinary way – in short: doing scenography – might give us intense pleasure and put us in touch with virtuality, and *that* is what is worth giving our attention to.

Performance Details

Title: *L'Effet de Serge* (2007). Produced by Vivarium Studio. Concept, staging and design: Philippe Quesne. Cast: Gaëtan Vourc'h, Isabelle Angotti, local guests. Stage Manager: Marc Chevillon. Website: http://pica.org/artists/philippe-quesne-vivarium-studio/
For background information, see the Vivarium Prospectus, available through http://www.ontheboards.org/sites/default/files/Vivarium_Prospectus.pdf (accessed 1 October 2017)
A three-minute video impression is available on Vimeo, see https://vimeo.com/8571768 (accessed 1 October 2017)

Further Reading

Aronson's much-referenced classic, *Looking into the Abyss* (2005), is a collection of essays, each of which provides nuanced and sensitive insights into the many concerns of scenography (such as staging, spectatorship and the role of technology and theatre architecture). Baugh (2014) extensively reflects on how developments in technology have formed and changed scenography throughout history, while also attending to new media technologies and their impact on performance design. Collins and Nisbet (2010) offer an interdisciplinary collection of essays and excerpts, framed in an original way, as the sections respectively attend to experiences of seeing and theories of looking; concepts of place and space in cultural theory and philosophy; scenographic design; bodies in space; making meaning. A very helpful introduction to scenography by McKinney and Butterworth (2009) covers all the basics, including a discussion of key concepts and key figures in the history of scenography, next to many relevant reflections that support the analysis of scenographic design. McKinney and Palmer's (2017) edited volume of essays by a range of experienced scholars presents a rich and stimulating survey of the many areas scenography can expand 'into' and as such, is a valuable introduction to 'expanded scenography'.

References

Allen, Richard (2013), 'The Object Animates: Displacement and Humility in the Theatre of Philippe Quesne', *Performance Research* 18 (3): 119–25.

Aronson, Arnold (2005), *Looking into the Abyss: Essays on Scenography*, Ann Arbor: The University of Michigan Press.

Balme, Christopher B. (2008), 'Space', in Christopher B. Balme (ed.), *The Cambridge Introduction to Theatre Studies*, 47–62, Cambridge: Cambridge University Press.

Baugh, Christopher (2014), *Theatre, Performance and Technology: The Development and Transformation of Scenography*, 2nd edn, Basingstoke: Palgrave Macmillan.

Bleeker, Maaike (2008), *Visuality in the Theatre: The Locus of Looking*, Basingstoke: Palgrave Macmillan.

Bosch, Anne Karin ten, Liesbeth Groot Nibbelink, Trudi Maan and Nienke Scholts (2013), 'Thinking Scenography: Inventing a Building', *Performance Research* 18 (3): 95–105.

Brejzek, Thea (2015), 'The Scenographic (re-)turn: Figures of Surface, Space and Spectator in Theatre and Architecture Theory 1680–1980', *Theatre and Performance Design* 1 (1–2): 17–30.

Carlson, Marvin (2001), *The Haunted Stage: The Theatre as Memory Machine*, Ann Arbor: University of Michigan Press.

Collins, Jane, and Andrew Nisbet (2010), *Theatre and Performance Design: A Reader in Scenography*, London and New York: Routledge.

Déchery, Chloé (2011), 'Amateurism and the "DIY" Aesthetic: Grand Magasin and Phillipe Quesne', in Clare Finburgh and Carl Lavery (eds), *Contemporary French Theatre and Performance*, 122–33, Basingstoke: Palgrave Macmillan.

Fischer-Lichte, Erika ([2004] 2008), *The Transformative Power of Performance: A New Aesthetics*, trans. S. I. Jain, London: Routledge.

Grosz, Elizabeth (2001), *Architecture from the Outside: Essays on Virtual and Real Space*, Cambridge, MA: MIT Press.

Hayles, Katherine (2002), *Writing Machines*, Cambridge, MA: MIT Press.

Kerkhoven, Marianne van (1992), 'De geschreven ruimte / The Written Space', *Theaterschrift* (2): 7–33.

Kerkhoven, Marianne van ([1994] 2002), 'Het theater ligt in de stad en de stad ligt in de wereld en de wanden zijn van huid', in *Van het kijken en van het schrijven*, 137–43, Leuven: Van Halewyck.

Lavery, Carl (2013), 'The Ecology of the Image: The Environmental Politics of Philippe Quesne and Vivarium Studio', *French Cultural Studies* 24 (3): 264–78.

Lehmann, Hans-Thies ([1999] 2006), *Postdramatic Theatre*, trans. K. Jürs-Munby, London: Routledge.

Lotker, Sodja, and Richard Gough, eds (2013), 'On Scenography', special issue of *Performance Research* 18 (3).

McAuley, Gay (1999), *Space in Performance: Making Meaning in the Theatre*, Ann Arbor: The University of Michigan Press.

McKinney, Joslin, and Philip Butterworth (2009), *The Cambridge Introduction to Scenography*, Cambridge: Cambridge University Press.

McKinney, Joslin, and Kara McKechnie (2016), 'Interview with Katrin Brack', *Theatre and Performance Design* 2 (1–2): 127–35.

McKinney, Joslin, and Scott Palmer, eds (2017), *Scenography Expanded: An Introduction to Contemporary Performance Design*, London and New York: Bloomsbury Methuen Drama.

Schweitzer, Marlis, and Joanne Zerdy, eds (2014), *Performing Objects & Theatrical Things*, Basingstoke: Palgrave Macmillan.

Turner, Cathy, and Synne Behrndt (2008), *Dramaturgy and Performance*, Basingstoke: Palgrave Macmillan.

8   How Does Theatre Think Through Things?

MIKE PEARSON

What are theatre's 'things', and what are the properties of these 'properties'? What do these things do? What do we do with them? What do they mean to mean? What do we take them to mean? And how might we account for them? In addressing these questions, this chapter makes a series of observations that from one aspect offer critical approaches, and from another are intended to act as creative stimuli. It introduces a number of metaphors (similes) to illuminate theatre's role of, and relationships with, things that are drawn from other fields, including human geography, anthropology and archaeology. The chapter's overall concern is with how we might conceive critical and creative approaches to postdramatic, site-specific, non-verbal performance works that 'acknowledge the varied qualities always possessed by things, and thus the radical differences they make to the world – both among themselves and to humans' (Olsen et al. 2012: 12); and that therefore challenge conceptions of action and agency in the theatre as solely human properties. Examples are drawn from my own performance practice with Welsh company Brith Gof (*Gododdin*, 1988–9) and National Theatre Wales (*Iliad*, 2015).

The Material Substance of Performance

Let's presume

... that the material substance of performance includes not only props, costumes and scenery, but also architectures and technologies: a concatenation of all that is of the *fixed* (the playhouse or site; its plumbed-in mechanisms); the *semi-fixed* (the scenography; its apparatuses) and the *portable* (objects; accoutrements) – apparent, germane and effective, in differing ways, to varying degrees and extents, for both performers and spectators;

... that these things – independently and in combination – serve *representational*, *decorative*, *functional*, *fictive* and/or *cognitive* purposes, and that these purposes may shift and blur from moment to moment;

... that conventionally – singly and in association – they help to establish location, social situation, historical period and generic style, conspiring dramatic context – imitative or imaginary; that – as insignia, personal effects, appurtenances – they aid the identification of the characters, their gender, status, class and type;

... that they assist performance to fulfil its objectives: advancing the drama through changes of scene; occasioning incidents, precipitating interactions, shaping and transforming connections; acting as the loci around which activity is organized; serving as tokens of exchange, actual and symbolic; and that, in this, they possess a significance beyond their monetary worth;

... that they are instrumentalized by performers, made to do and mean what they intend; and that they have their own attractions, intimate and spectacular;

... that the composition of performance may include things specially made – *fabricated* – and those appropriated from everyday life – *found*; that if fabricated, they may be in different materials and to different dimensions from their everyday equivalents. Such things are conceived, designed and constructed according to a governing artistic or stylistic concept, tradition or presentational milieu. Established conventions may prescribe a proactive strategy, or act as proscriptions in setting parameters – recommending, for instance, the range of constituents and techniques of making to be used, and the configurations and hierarchies of scenic arrangement. On the Japanese *Noh* theatre stage, for example, the schematic *tsukurimono* ('built things') are reduced to a simple bamboo frame – little more than an outline or blueprint – of hut, boat, carriage, well ... (for documentation, refer to the online Global Performing Arts Database [GloPAD] 1998–2006); they are temporary, carried on and off as called for, merely hinting at their full form. Although they condition choreography around them and may even be entered, they remain insubstantial, ghostly and unable to withstand weight or force, their actuality elucidated through the words of the narrator;

... that the shape of the playhouse and the demand for visibility may condition the form and scale of the objects and obviate the need for mimetic accuracy – the illusion of three-dimensional space by two-dimensional means in a three-dimensional space, as in creating false perspective in *trompe l'oeil*; that theatre's byelaws, codified as traditional practices, may limit the types of object included; and that genre or stylistic sub-code, or the idiolect of a particular company or director, may set further conditions of arrangement;

... that things may be works of pure invention or of fantasy. Antonin Artaud imagines 'thirty-foot-high effigies of King Lear's beard in the storm' while stipulating 'no décor' and asserting that 'all objects requiring a stereotyped physical representation will be discarded or disguised' (1970: 69);

... that if found, things may be chosen for their inherent or associative qualities: their constitution and appearance; their evocative potency or powers of cultural resonance. Bertolt Brecht describes actress Helene Weigel selecting the props to accompany her characters across the stage for their 'age, function and beauty' (1987: 427). Such things – relics of former and lost lives, redolent of other times and places; 'crystallizations of histories, projections into the future, powerful forbears of that which is to become and painful reminders of that which has been' (Harvey et al. 2014: 10) – bring with them their biographies, their stories; rendering performance multi-temporal and haunted by that which transcends mere practicality;

... that they may also be chosen for fit, feel, balance, weight and dynamism in manipulation, for their capacity to enhance the performer's efficacy; or for the opposite, in requiring corporeal adjustment: ill-fitting shoes will affect gait, deportment and stability. Such things are thus *double*: beside what they signify, they are the tools of the trade of the performer, akin to a survival 'kit' in an unfamiliar domain. They become *aides-mémoire*, mnemonics, companions, talismans, fetishes even – imbued with personal significance:

a tangible reminder of hours of rehearsal, enshrining purpose, providing orientation through familiarity;

... that things may be present by *imposition*: as a form of project design that attends to a particular aspiration in a conceptualized world complete in all its parts; applying expertise and authorial vision 'with regard to intention, affect and effect' (Shanks 2012: 70); that things may also occur through *accumulation*: through experiment or 'trial and error' in a gradual process of introduction, testing and incorporation; or in a form of *bricolage*, as ad-hoc solutions to the question at hand; aiding semantic or practical coherence, or conspiring the contrary; that such gathering involves not only *selection* but also *rejection* and *omission*; and that this is comparable – in the first of several metaphors – to the geological process of *brecciation* (Bartolini 2014): the rolling together or conglomeration of items from disparate sources within a solid matrix, into a *stratum* of '*forms and substances, codes and milieus*' (Deleuze and Guattari 1988: 502; emphasis in original);

... that the principles of ordering may include unusual and uncanny elisions, oppositions, conflicts and discontinuities – in procedures of overlapping and simultaneous *hypotaxis* and slammed-together *katachresis* (Pearson and Shanks 2001: 25) – as much as logical arrangement and articulation; and that herein lie opportunities for the generation of dramatic content, in frictions and amalgamations between things and things, as well as between performers and things;

... that performance need not be discrete: it can include objects ranging from appropriated utilitarian tools, such as ladders, to independent works of art, such as David Hockney's opera designs; and that the inclusion of that which is truly of the everyday world – animals, vehicles, industrial equipment, medical paraphernalia – may cause surprise or shock, confounding the expectations of spectators, upsetting customary attitudes to critical reception, interpretation and evaluation;

... that the admixture of literalness and fabrication can produce dramatic richness; and that the *ironic* appearance of the detritus of past theatre genres in a contemporary context – cardboard backdrops and pantomime horses in the postdramatic practices of British theatre company Forced Entertainment – can, for the spectator, cause both delight, and a readjustment of faculties in pondering what usually gets in here, what is typically allowable or excluded, and why;

... that, whatever their origin, performance – in the words of semiotician Keir Elam – 'radically transforms all objects and bodies defined within it, bestowing upon them an overriding signifying power which they lack – or which at least is less evident – in their normal social function', and that they become freighted, acquiring 'special features, qualities and attributes that they do not have in real life' (1980: 5);

... that as soon as spectators enter the theatrical space they understand that they must take the things they perceive for present substitutes for an absent world. However prosaic or banal, everything is assumed to be present on purpose. Indeed, spectators will search for, and generate, meaning in everything they see. As Elam suggests: 'If every material aspect of the performance is capable of semanticization, there can (in theory) be little 'redundancy' in theatrical communication' (Elam 1980: 26);

... that things are suggestive, that they *denote*, that they intend to mean, though their full apprehension may require specific and informed cultural competence on the spectators' part; *that* they also *connote*, evoking second-order meanings in 'a parasitic semantic function' (Elam 1980: 7), interpreted according to the perceptions, expectations, experience, assumptions and values of spectators; that any object – whether typical, atypical, exemplary or even a replica of its type – once isolated in performance comes to stand for the class of objects of which it is a member: redolent of similar objects, similar occasions; of other times and other places; working with, and on, memory; that 'The only indispensable requirement that is made of the stage sign-vehicle is that it successfully stands for its intended signified' (Elam 1980: 6) – even a simple wooden pallet can become life raft, podium, cage, stretcher; that certain things may be included specifically for their semiotic versatility, their *polysemic* capacity – Pontius Pilate lurks in the shadow of the surgeon washing his hands ... ;

... that things may transform, in both their usage and in their intimations, through the activities and applications of performers; that things are semiotically unstable, liable to slip their ascription, fungible. The 'poor theatre' of Jerzy Grotowski is reliant upon the mutability and multivalency of a limited and fixed repertoire of objects which 'must be sufficient to handle any of the play's situations'. 'Each object must contribute not to the meaning but to the dynamics of the play; its value resides in its various uses' (Grotowski 1969: 75). Each object has multiple applications, while carrying forward traces of its previous guises: in Grotowski's *Akropolis*, a bathtub becomes an altar and a nuptial bed, while 'representing all the bathtubs in which human bodies were processed for the making of soap and leather' (75). Through recurrent reuse, misuse and repositioning, the repertoire fosters dense, complex and contradictory allegories, anachronisms and ambiguities;

... that the semiotic fraction of performance is only partly controllable: 'The production of meaning on stage is too rich and fluid to be accounted for in terms of discrete objects and their representational roles' (Elam 1980: 20); that as 'a regime of signs' (Deleuze and Guattari 1988: 504) performance is unremittingly equivocal – denotative and connotative meanings jostling to inform both creative intent and its reception;

... that performance constitutes a 'special world', a set of contrived circumstances – set aside, parenthetical, bracketed off from the quotidian; a mode of cultural production, a sensorium, a utopia, a heterotopia, in which the real sites in a culture are 'simultaneously represented, contested and inverted' (Foucault 1986: 24); internally coherent around its own compositional principles and *modi operandi*;

... that performance – second metaphor – is a *heterogeneous assemblage*: according to political theorist Jane Bennett, assemblages are 'living throbbing confederations' (2010: 23). Performance draws sundry objects together into extra-daily juxtapositions and contingent taxonomies in which like can stand adjacent to unlike in new, extra-daily and even inverted correlations. Here, diverse things without natural affinities of origin, provenance and type are gathered in arrays found only in this parenthetical fragment of space/time; here, the placement, ratios and combinations of objects are governed by operational and aesthetic criteria; here, found objects and their replicas can coexist; here, familiar objects may be constructed to startling scales and gather in disquieting numbers; here may be found only red things, or one thousand spoons, or five thousand cinder blocks;

... that performance is, however, fundamentally *metonymic* or *synechdochic*, a few objects evoking a whole as the complexity, density and messiness of the everyday vernacular would appear as chaos.

Let's accept

... that in performance the semiotic attributes of things are invariably the focus of critical appraisal. Hence, let's propose alternative optics in which things are taken to possess unique properties, potentialities and propensities for engendering sensational impacts, visceral and emotional, as well as perceptual; in which the performative acts indicate, foreground and make evident such characteristics; and in which performers become intimately involved and bound up with objects and materials, as co-creators of dramatic substance.

Let's venture

... that performance can include and recontextualize things unexpectedly drawn out of their customary milieu: displacements of found and fabricated in illogical ordering, with excessive repetitions, subversions of generic codes and unconventional animations, as when the scenery becomes disconcertingly mobile;

... that the range of things and their arrangement may, by intention and design, necessitate and occasion engagements between body and object that are dramatic in their consequences; that they may purposefully upset everyday routines of engagement; that they are inciting, that they make things happen;

... that the dramaturgy of performance may conspire productive encounters, collisions and syntheses between performers and things, and things and things, as well as between performers and performers;

... that whatever the level of verisimilitude – in a mode usually regarded as illusory and fictive – performance is for the performers a sensate field of real endeavours and experiences in which they are 'perpetually mixed with things' (Webmoor 2007: 573).

As an aside: let's regard site-specific performance as a distinct category in which the boundary markers of the auditorium – framing, conventions of apprehension – disappear, upsetting the spectator's 'cognitive hold' (Elam 1980: 58); as an overlaying and interpenetration of the *found* (site) and the *emplaced* (performance); as the latest occupation of a location where other occupations – their architectures, traces and histories – are still apparent and cognitively active; as the coexistence of two basic sets of architectures and narratives: those of the extant building, that which is *at* site – architecture, fixtures, fittings – and those of the constructed scenography, that which is brought *to* site. Building and scenography might have quite distinct origins, might ignore each other's presence, and even appear paradoxical: they are coexistent but not necessarily congruent, though both are always evident for spectators.

Cliff McLucas's design for Brith Gof's site-specific show *Gododdin* was as large as the abandoned factory space in which it was performed, reaching its walls, though on a different orientation to the building's ground plan (see Pearson and Shanks 2001: 102–8). It comprised a formal arrangement of hundreds of tons of sand, dozens of trees and wrecked cars, and thousands of gallons of water, which gradually flooded the performing area. The non-pristine nature, lack of seemliness and particular atmosphere of the space allowed and necessitated the use of resources, techniques, materials and phenomena, unusual, undesirable or dangerous in the auditorium: water and electricity; objects/things not conventionally theatrical – fire, smoke, machinery, animals; wind, rain, snow, excessive light drawn into unlikely configurations, into disturbing recontextualizations, mobilized in contrary narratives and given to abrupt changes. The environment of performance here was active and the conditions – the *ecology* of surface, climate, illumination and temperature – by turn much better or much worse for performers than in everyday life.

Let's suppose

… that the characteristics of the site – its area, height, ground plan, ambience – inform and influence scenographic arrangements; that these may be acknowledged and integrated per se within the dramaturgy, strategically distributed and deployed by prior intent to precipitate creative interactions, with implications for the activities of the performers and practices applied; that this transitory occupation of the 'real' might allow the suspension and transgression of the prescribed practices and by-laws of the auditorium, and may necessitate the substitution and enactment of particular techniques in place of stage illusion and theatrical gesture in order to address and take advantage of the circumstances at site; that the range of 'things' in performance might include the immaterial, the intangible, the ephemeral in the shape of environmental phenomena and technical effects; and even audiences as fundaments.

Iliad

They hurl white plastic chairs, the kind that armies take to the desert – light, stackable, indestructible – against the wall, as many of the 200 available as possible, for ten minutes, in an urgent outburst of energy as the soundtrack swells – an action that might be a furious attack on the city of Troy, or a desperate strengthening of its defences, or both. Or are they reduced to such extremes as the words for the state of affairs are exhausted?

They are the four 'constructors' in Mike Pearson and Mike Brookes's staging of Christopher Logue's poetic rendering of Homer's *Iliad* for National Theatre Wales, an eight-hour production in four sections, shown in September 2015 at the Ffwrnes Theatre in Llanelli, Wales. In Mike Brookes's scenography, the floor of both stage and auditorium were tiled with sheets of medium-density fibreboard (MDF) to create a single unified space. The text was delivered and animated by six narrators at ten microphones that were hanging at fixed points; and it was spoken; as descriptions of people/places/atmospheres; as reportage; as direct address to the audience; as interjections and asides; in character; as voice-overs; as stage directions. In parallel, the constructors manhandled, shifted, deployed, reconfigured, manipulated and modelled a repertoire of objects and materials that included the chairs, 250 rubber car tyres, ten loose MDF sheets, lengths of timber and rolls of adhesive tape. They were erecting, assembling and deconstructing makeshift structures, settings and locales that were at times used and occupied by the narrators, at other times analogous to or redolent of images in the narrative, without ever directly illustrating it. In a continuous series of task-based activities independent of, but complementary to, the text, the constructors resembled army engineers, set-builders, film extras. Orientated by marks on the floor, they created platforms, daises and runways; barricades and palisades; ship-like forms and machinic tripods; beachhead encampments and conclaves. They rolled tyres; they pushed rows of chairs into mounds resembling a dune landscape; they hoisted bound clusters of chairs on the tripods, creating clouds or skeletal trees; and they shepherded and reorganized

Fig. 8.1 Constructors. National Theatre Wales production of Christopher Logue's adaptation of Homer's *Iliad,* Ffwrnes Theatre, Llanelli, Wales 2015. Photo: Simon Banham.

the audience into new configurations while doing so. All materials were in plain view from the outset, upsetting the familiar use of the venue and confounding spectators' expectations. As the audience entered for the first section, *Kings*, the tyres were already heaped in a single sweeping curve reminiscent of a decayed ship, with the chairs stacked in unassigned piles. At all times, spectators were free to take a chair and sit in any position of their choice, perforce becoming a scenic component.

It was the nature of things that obliged the constructors to roll, to throw, to build, to hoist in particular ways, according to their shape, mass, constitution; causing the performers – tactically – to pay attention, to respond, to modify, to compensate. A choreography developed in appreciation of the properties of properties: of their iconic and suggestive qualities; and of their intractability and unruliness: of the wobbling of tyres in motion; of the instability of heaped chairs. … A scenography in flux, ever-changing in a volatile dramatic situation, created and reconfigured by a group of experienced performers, going about their business, using mundane materials in unexpected ways, making space for their activities. At times, the constructors were barely perceptible in the onrush of text; at others, they engaged in actions that brought the full implications of the words into focus, through their skilful works of construction and energetic activities, adding kinetic impetus to weighty verbal passages, heightening the dynamic trajectory. Seeking affordance, tackling ergonomic problems, in a landscape in which they became experienced dwellers.

A Methodology of all Things

Let's conjecture

… that, after philosopher Bruno Latour, things – non-human objects and environmental effects – have *agency*, serving as actants, as sources of activity; that they possess distinct powers and capacities, such as effectivity, efficacy, volition, causality; that they can do things, make a difference, alter the course of events (see Bennett 2010: viii); and that their instability and unruliness may require compensatory 'fixing solutions' (Hodder 2012: 207);

... that things provide, in psychologist James J. Gibson's formulation, *affordance*: 'The medium, substances, surfaces, objects, places and other animals have affordances for a given animal. They offer benefit or injury, life or death' (1997: 143). According to Gibson: 'The *affordances* of the environment are what it *offers* the animal, what it provides or furnishes, either for good or ill' (127). He further suggests: 'Surfaces afford posture, locomotion, collision, manipulation, and in general behaviour'; they are also 'climb-on-able or fall-off-able or get underneath-able relative to the animal' (137; 128). While scenic materials might be expected to facilitate choreographies, their positioning may equally provide obstacles and create barriers to movement, upsetting corporeal equilibrium, occasioning dramatic unbalancing. In performative encounters with designed layouts, a rich and complex set of interactions emerges in which the fundamentals are the characteristics of the things: in positing constraints and trials that both afford and require adjusted practices to address, accommodate and animate them and to fill shortfalls, and leading to demonstrations of surprising, extra-daily virtuosity;

... that the contracts – body to scene, body to object, body to body – and the experiences they conspire may involve *modifications*. The performer's relation to the *mise-en-scène* is both sensual and *ergonomic*. It may indeed be, as suggested above, that the constructed environment of performance is active and the ecology of this special world – the affordances it offers – is much better or much worse than that of everyday life. It may greatly increase or ameliorate *ergonomic* challenges for the performer – hindering and assisting performative execution – and these may change instantly, oscillating between *acceptable*, *unacceptable* and *optimal*. We might assume that theatre tends towards a perfecting of conditions to support effective expression. The polished, *hinoki* wood floor of the *Noh* stage allows the ethereal, gliding, travelling motion of the performer, though such is their symbiotic bond that it would be difficult to assess which came first, floor or movement. But the performance conditions may also extend, limit or compromise four vectors of the performer's application: *clearance*: the headroom and legroom of the body ellipse; *reach*: the volume of the workspace envelope; *posture*: the nature and number of connections of body to work space; and *strength*: the acceptable percentage of maximal strength in output or endurance. They may restrict kinesic, proxemic and haptic abilities, capacities and potentials through increases in hazard, body stress, demand (energy expenditure) and overload (exhaustion). They can do so by the closure or limitation of sensory channels – as with blindfolding; by the invasion of that personal space which is reserved for more or less exclusive use by the self; by the arrangement of barriers within the setting. They may cause duress through increasing duration and limiting the potential adjustment of posture and reach. Environmental factors may include noise which induces annoyance during thinking and communicating; illumination with alterations in brightness, reflection and shadow; modulations in the temperature of air and surfaces, air velocity and relative humidity, the effects of which may, or may not, be mediated by clothing; vibration of whole body or hand-arm through shocks and jolts and the toxicity of liquids, gases, vapours, dusts and solids. Performance might be a difficult, risky place to work, though all here need not be traumatic; the performer is not solely acted upon but remains an actor nonetheless;

... that if ergonomics concerns the application of information about human physicality and behaviour to the problems of design, then the dramaturgy and choreography of performance may be constituted, at least in part, as its performers seeking, dealing with, and confounding, ergonomic problems and capitalizing on opportunities for affordance;

... that performance – third metaphor – constitutes a *chaîne opératoire*: in the words of archaeologist Ian Hodder, 'made up of bodily movements that incorporate both reflective knowledge (*connaissance*) and practical skills (*savoir faire*). It also includes the sequences by which materials, tools, and sources of energy are involved in the transformation of matter' (2012: 53). Within this *chaîne opératoire* the 'performance characteristics' are the 'capabilities, skills, or competences that material culture and people must have to perform their functions' (54);

... that performers in their empathetic actions demonstrate material realities, and enhance iconic and indexical reverberations and symbolic potency; and that performance is a milieu where performers enact 'a creative materiality with incipient tendencies and propensities' (Bennett 2010: 56). On display are their methods and organization of effort, their responses through improvisation, informed by previous experience, and their use of tools both created specially and ad-hoc as prosthetic extensions;

... that the 'regime of signs' also includes the *symptoms* of the performers in their endeavours: the consequences of extra-daily application, resilience and endurance, revealing human potentialities, abilities and qualities; that the labour of the performer – fourth metaphor – bears resemblance to the labour of the peasant described by writer John Berger as 'a way of being *fully at home in effort*' (Berger 2013: 41); essentially, after Yi-Fu Tuan (1974), as *topophilic* – a matter of intimacy and dependence, in an affinity as much *haptic* (close-up) as *optic* (distanced);

... that it is in corporeal engagements and re-engagements between body and environment – in the clash between energetic activities and both malleable and intractable matters – where dramatic effects are forged, in a mutual dependency, investment and entrapment where outcomes may be contingent; that expression is *mediated* by location, surface, area, volume, climate, light, ambience, by hardness, texture, acoustic, by levels of flexibility, resistance, accommodation in substances; that performance may involve improvised responses to an environment – albeit one of limited resources – as much as planned choreographies; and that, despite difficulties, the trained performer employs *rhetorics* – aesthetic ways of going on – in the *articulation* of actions: using more or less time and energy than would be applied in the everyday completion of a similar action, and using tension, exaggeration, repetition, distortion, reversal ...;

... and that it is in this *expressive quotient* that performance is revealed.

Let's posit

... that – fifth metaphor – performance is akin to a provisional *landscape*, understood as ground rather than background and regarded, after geographer Denis Cosgrove, as a gathering of 'nature, culture and imagination within a spatial manifold' (2004: 69). Landscape has no pre-existing form here that is then inscribed with human activity. Both 'being' and environment are mutually emergent, 'continuously coming into being through the combined action of human and non-human agencies' (Ingold 2000: 155). Just as landscapes are constructed out of the imbricated actions and experiences of people, so people are constructed in and dispersed through their habituated landscape. There is no privilege of origin: a place owes its character not only to the experiences it affords (as sights, sounds, etc.) but also to what is done there in social and cultural practices: landscape for the 'essential insiders' – herein performers – as 'a dimension of existence, collectively produced, lived and maintained' (Cosgrove 1998: 19). After philosopher Jean-Luc Nancy, landscape is '... a matter of *holding* (I hold it, it holds me, it holds together) and *pertinence* (It corresponds, it responds, it makes sense at the very least as a resonance)' (2005: 53). Or – sixth metaphor – after Ingold, performance is akin to a *taskscape*: 'an ensemble of tasks'; with a *task* being a practical operation carried out by a skilled agent in an environment that only gets meaning from its position within 'an array of related activities' (2000: 195). Landscape in embodied form as a network of places, as nodes in a choreography linked together in the itineraries of the inhabitants – herein performers. And rehearsal involves processes of acclimatization and habituation, of developing ways of going on, of coping, with an acute attention to the business of *dwelling* in the special world.

Performance then

... as a 'locatory matrix *for* things', 'a *substantive* place-of-occupation' (Casey 1998: 34);

... as a sequence of objectives and activities to be undertaken – under rule-based conditions albeit those specific only to a specific event – at a series of places across a terrain of locales;

... as successive, evanescent moments in the journeys of performers;

... as 'hybrid knots' of people and things, in mutually transforming relations of varying intensities;

... as a topography where things are differentiated and highlighted; but as an uneven topography 'because some of the points at which the various affects and bodies cross paths are more heavily trafficked than others, and so power is not distributed equally across its surface' (Bennett 2010: 23).

Emancipating things

If the conventional imperative of drama is to reflect upon the human condition, how may we then conceive critical approaches that deflect emphasis from 'the tyranny of subject' (Miller 2005: 36) towards an emancipation of things?

... through – seventh metaphor – envisaging a flat ontology or *symmetry* – an analytical levelling of performers and things – that recognizes the things as present in their own right and capable of making effects because of their own assets; that acknowledges that things are '*irreducible to our representations of them*' (Olsen et al. 2012: 13; emphasis in the original); and that affords no particular primacy to any particular component, stressing rather flows of interplay;

... through reconsidering the vibrancy and vitality of the things themselves in that they have the disposition 'not only to impede or block the will and designs of humans but also to act as agents or forces with trajectories, propensities, or tenancies of their own' (Bennett

2010: viii) – metamorphosing, accumulating, collapsing; that their properties may have unforeseen and spectacular outcomes; that they are not inert and, set in motion, may be disorderly and disruptive; that they persist over varying trajectories of time; and that they do things when we're not looking, such as tending towards entropy;

... through – eighth metaphor – characterizing performance, after Hodder, as an *entanglement* of humans and non-humans, of 'material and technical as well as immaterial, symbolic and conceptual components' (2012: 113), tied together in webs or networks of mutual and contingent restraints and reliances: 'the dialectic of dependence and dependency' ... 'that create potentials, further investments and entrapments' (89);

... through proposing that dramaturgy may be conceived as the sequencing and orchestration of conjunctions, attachments, intensifications, ruptures, partings and transitions, in pre-planned and improvised entanglements – thick and thin – of people and things;

...through – ninth metaphor – regarding performance, after philosophers Gilles Deleuze and Félix Guattari, as both 'a *machinic assemblage* of bodies, of actions and passions, an intermingling of bodies reacting to one another', and as 'a *collective assemblage of enunciation*, of acts and statements, of incorporeal transformations attributed to bodies' (1988: 88; emphasis in the original). Following Deleuze and Guattari, performance may be considered as a *territory* of 'decoded fragments of all kinds, which are borrowed from the milieus but then assume the value of "properties"' (503). They state: 'Continuum of intensities, combined emission of particles or sign-particles, conjunction of deterritorialized flows: these are the three factors proper to the plane of consistency' (344). Deleuze and Guattari also speak of 'a *fuzzy aggregate*', '*defined only by a degree of consistency that makes it possible to distinguish the disparate elements constituting that aggregate (discernibility)*' (344; emphasis in the original).

Let's allow

... that in the realm of performance, things have a certain independence and generative potentiality, producing effects, making things happen;

... that human and non-human actants, including the unintended and the abject (e.g. dirt or disorder) are assembled and co-present and equally likely to conspire mutually resonant repercussions;

... that performance reconfigures 'the division between the material and the immaterial as an indistinguishable whole' (González-Ruibal 2006: 119); and

... that performers become another order of 'vital materialities' (Bennett 2010: 21) in a horizontal field of connections and of distributed agency.

Let's suppose then

... that performance corresponds to Tim Ingold's 'ocean of materials': 'a flux in which materials of the most diverse kinds – through processes of admixture and distillation, of coagulation and dispersal, and of evaporation and precipitation – undergo continual generation and transformation' (Ingold 2007: 7); and that any distinction drawn between people and things is ontologically arbitrary; that performance functions not as 'the scenario of

Fig. 8.2 Narrator. National Theatre Wales production of Christopher Logue's adaptation of Homer's *Iliad,* Ffwrnes Theatre, Llanelli, Wales 2015. Photo: Simon Banham.

transactions between people, but a collective of people, things, animals and materializations of their manifold transactions' (González-Ruibal 2006: 120).

But where to begin and end in assessing the pertinence of things? As anthropologist Daniel Miller asks: 'Is an ephemeral object, a moment in a streaming video, a thing? ... Is a dream, a city, a sensation, a derivative, an ideology, a landscape, a decay, a kiss?' (2005: 7). As Gilles Deleuze and Félix Guattari observe: 'the essential thing is no longer forms and matters, or themes, but forces, densities, intensities' (1988: 343). And as Ian Hodder opines: 'entanglements and affordances and functions are always tied to abstractions (ideas, thoughts, words, feelings and senses)' (2012:120).

In an 'analytical levelling', in 'a reconfiguration of how relationship between humans and things are characterized' (Webmoor 2007: 563), we might attend to performance – tenth metaphor – through *pragmatology*, 'a thing-centric discipline' (Holbraad 2014: 235) with 'pragmata', so archaeologist Michael Shanks suggests, not only as things, 'but also "deeds", "acts" (things done), "doings", "circumstances" (encounters), "contested matters", "duties", or "obligations". The verb at the root of pragmata is *prattein* – to act in the material world, engaged with things' (2012: 69).

Reckoning with Things

In accounts of performance, we must surely determine and take cognisance of all that is operating at any one time: the interactions of all components, both entities and conventions; climate, environment, actions, intentionalities, misfires; the ramifications of the constituents and elements of site for the conceptualization, design and presentation of the work; how scenic design itself conspires conditions, both benign and adverse. 'The task becomes to identify the contours of the swarm and the kind of relations that obtain between its bits' (Bennett 2010: 31). Or, in the words of anthropologist Martin Holbraad, the task is to entangle a thing 'heuristically, with all that the people concerned with it say and do around it' (2011: 15). 'At issue, to coin another phrase, are a thing's conceptual affordances', Holbraad proposes (15) – performance may thus be considered an 'economy of their (i.e. the materials and their properties) conceptual transformations: how their material characteristics can dictate particular forms for their conceptualization' (18).

Now consider what any of that might mean for the *lifeways* of performers, those who work, dwell and survive in such regions and climes. As they both *mark* and are *marked* – 'Muscles and scars bear witness to the physical intimacy of the contact' (Tuan 1974: 97) – the challenge may be to appreciate the 'concussiveness and the largesse of that interaction between the material creature and the material world' (Scarry 1983: 96). Concluding, we might say that to fully elucidate what happened, any description of performance requires as much said about the site – its architecture, its atmospheres, its history – and the emplaced scenography – its surfaces, substances, objects, locales – as about the themes and dramaturgy; and as much said about the specifics of a place, about the temporalities evident, about performance as landscape, taskscape, eco-system.

It is a cliché of archaeology that any non-utilitarian artefact of obscure function is attributed to ritual. Ritual becomes the classificatory repository for all that is slightly beyond archaeology's purview – beliefs, ludic activities, purposeless pursuits; a discipline that struggles to escape the beating jungle drums and the blood-dripping symmetrical dances of popular anthropological imaginings. Contemporary performance might recommend a form of *experimental archaeology*, helping to understand the genesis and organization of the plethora of possible attitudes to and practices of things under special aesthetic conditions; demonstrating how they precipitate activity. Revealing, that is, how things make things happen.

Performance Details

Iliad, a theatrical staging of Christopher Logue's *War Music; an account of Homer's Iliad* (1959–2011). Presented by National Theatre Wales, in association with and at Ffwrnes Theatre, Llanelli, Wales, 21 September–3 October 2015. Directors: Mike Pearson and Mike Brookes.

Further Reading

Fiona Candlin and Raiford Guins's *The Object Reader* (2009) gives a useful overview of foundational theoretical writing on objects. *Performance Research*'s issue 'On Objects' (2010) offers a number of theoretical and practical considerations of objects in and as performance. Daniel Miller's *The Comfort of Things* (2008) is his most accessible account of the relationship between people and their possessions, while artist André Stitt's *Substance: Residues, Drawings & Partial Objects 1976–2008* (2008) illustrates his long-term inclusion and examination of everyday objects in performance contexts. And Philip Howes and Zoe Laughlin's *Material Matters: New Materials in Design* (2012) discusses the properties of new materials and, by implication, their potential role in performance.

References

Artaud, Antonin (1970), *The Theatre and its Double*, trans. V. Corti, London: Calder & Boyars.

Bartolini, Nadia (2014), 'Critical Urban Heritage: From Palimpsest to Brecciation', *International Journal of Heritage Studies*, 20 (5): 519–33.

Bennett, Jane (2010), *Vibrant Matter: A Political Ecology of Things*, Durham, USA: Duke University Press.

Berger, John (2013), *Understanding a Photography*, London: Penguin.

Brecht, Bertolt (1987), *Poems 1913–1956*, ed. John Willett and Ralph Manheim, London: Methuen.

Candlin, Fiona, and Raiford Guins, eds (2009), *The Object Reader*, London and New York: Routledge.

Casey, Edward (1998), *The Fate of Place*, Berkeley: University of California Press.

Clark, Laurie Beth, Richard Gough and Daniel Watt, eds (2010), 'On Objects', *Performance Research* 12 (4).

Cosgrove, Denis (1998), *Social Formation and Symbolic Landscape*, Madison: University of Wisconsin Press.

Cosgrove, Denis (2004), 'Landscape and Landschaft', *German Historical Institute Bulletin*, 35: 57–71.

Deleuze, Gilles, and Félix Guattari (1988), *A Thousand Plateaus*, trans. B. Massumi, London: The Athone Press.

Elam, Keir (1980), *The Semiotics of Theatre and Drama*, Routledge: London.

Foucault, Michel (1986), 'Of Other Places', *Diacritics*, 16: 22–7.

Gibson, James J. (1997), *The Ecological Approach to Visual Perception*, Boston: Houghton Mifflin.

GloPAD (Global Performing Arts Database) (1998–2006). Available online: http://www.glopad.org/pi/en/series.php?seriesid=91 (accessed 4 December 2017).

González-Ruibal, Alfredo (2006), 'The Past is Tomorrow. Towards an Archaeology of the Vanishing Present', *Norwegian Archaeological Review*, 39 (2): 110–25.

Grotowski, Jerzy (1969), *Towards a Poor Theatre*, London: Methuen.

Harvey, Penny P. et al., eds (2014), *Objects and Materials, A Routledge Companion*, London: Routledge.

Hodder, Ian (2012), *Entangled. An Archaeology of the Relationships between Humans and Things*, Chichester: Wiley-Blackwell.

Holbraad, Martin (2011), 'Can the Thing Speak?', *Open Anthropology Cooperative Press Working Papers Series* 7. Available online: www.openanthcoop.net/press (accessed 4 December 2017).

Holbraad, Martin (2014), 'How Things Can Unsettle', in Penny Harvey et al. (eds), *Objects and Materials: A Routledge Companion*, 228–37, Abingdon: Routledge.

Howes, Philip, and Zoe Laughlin (2012), *Material Matters: New Materials in Design*, London: Black Dog Publishing.

Ingold, Tim (2000), *The Perception of the Environment*, London: Routledge.

Ingold Tim (2007), 'Materials Against Materiality', *Archaeological Dialogues*, 24 (1): 1–16.

Miller, Daniel, ed. (2005), *Materiality*, Durham, USA: Duke University Press.

Miller, Daniel (2008), *The Comfort of Things*, Cambridge: Polity.

Nancy, Jean-Luc (2005), *The Ground of the Image*, trans. J. Fort, New York: Fordham University Press.

Olsen, Bjørnar, Michel Shanks, Timothy Webmoor and Christopher Witmore (2012), *Archaeology. A Discipline of Things*, Berkeley: University of California Press.

Pearson, Mike, and Michael Shanks (2001), *Theatre/Archaeology*, London: Routledge.

Scarry, Elaine (1983) 'Work and the Body in Hardy and Other Nineteenth-Century Novelists', *Representations* 3 (Summer): 90–123.

Shanks, Michael (2012), *'Let me Tell You About Hadrian's Wall…' Heritage, Performance, Design*, Amsterdam: Reinwardt Academy/Amsterdam School of the Arts.

Stitt, André (2008), *Substance: Residues, Drawings & Partial Objects 1976–2008*, exhibition catalogue. Exeter: Spacex.

Tuan, Yi-Fu (1974), *Topophilia: A Study of Environmental Perception, Attitudes and Values*, Englewood Cliffs: Prentice Hall.

Webmoor, Timothy (2007), 'What About "One More Turn After the Social" in Archaeological Reasoning. Taking Things Seriously', *World Archaeology* 39 (4): 563–78.

9 How Does Theatre Think Through Incorporating Media?

STEVE DIXON

This chapter asks the question, 'how does theatre think through incorporating media?' so as to investigate the multifarious ways that film, video or digital projections are used in stage productions, and the vast range of ideas, meanings and effects that are created. As we will see in case studies of practitioners including Robert Lepage, Katie Mitchell, The Wooster Group and The Builders Association, there are myriad ways in which theatre thinks through, investigates and experiments with the potent conjunction of live performance and recorded media.

The inclusion and incorporation of moving image projections on stage significantly expands the vocabulary of theatre, adding another element or a dual 'text' that opens a complex dialogue with the live action. This dynamic interaction between the two texts of live stage events and projected imagery can beget numerous dramaturgical, psychological and semiotic effects. It should therefore be noted from the outset that theatre does not 'think through media' in any one specific way, but rather explores and makes use of its unique form in many divergent ways. In doing so, it offers audiences a new type of theatre that, first and foremost, plays with potent juxtapositions and metamorphoses of time, space, bodies and meanings.

Most theatre practitioners 'think through media' by exploring, highlighting, parodying or critiquing media's distinct *difference from theatre*. But others seek to conjoin rather than separate the two forms – thinking through media in terms of its potential *fusion with theatre*, including using modern projection technologies to further ancient theatrical traditions of conjuring an artful illusion of another world, or reality, on stage.

Multimedia theatre – a generic term I use here to describe any stage production that incorporates film, video or digital projections – is over a hundred years old. 'Magic Lantern' projectors beamed coloured slides with animated effects onto stages in the nineteenth century, and a cabaret in Germany in 1909 is the first known incidence of movie film being projected onto a backcloth during a live performance. In 1914, Winsor McCay toured his one-man show *Gertie the Dinosaur* around the United States, delighting audiences by successfully commanding a projected animation drawing of a dinosaur to sit up, roll over and perform tricks. McCay's live action was beautifully timed so as to convey the illusion that the pre-recorded dinosaur animation was responding spontaneously and in real time to the stage events – firstly smiling at and obeying her trainer, then later crying, disobeying and snapping angrily at him.

The climax was greeted with cheers as the live McCay walked behind and apparently 'into' the screen. In precisely the same position that he disappeared, he suddenly reappeared on screen in the same scale as an animated figure, who strode up to Gertie, jumped onto her back and rode off into the sunset. It was the first example of a show attempting to convey the sense of a *fusion* of media and theatre referred to above. This stage-to-screen crossover effect has since been repeated often and in increasingly convincing ways, as theatre practitioners have sought ever more intricate effects and illusions of where the stage and screen appear to merge and synthesize.

In the 1920s, theatre makers such as Frederick Kiesler and Erwin Piscator constructed spectacular theatre productions using multiple projectors that screened film footage onto giant sets. For Piscator's *Hoppla Wir Leben!* (*Hoppla, We're Alive!,* 1927), six separate rooms were contained within a vertical scaffolding structure at either side of a huge central projection screen which showed documentary footage of political rallies and revolutions, boxing matches, dancing girls and decadent parties, as well as specially shot sequences including 'news reports' which advanced the play's plot. The six rooms had individual back-projections to conjure and progressively change the scenic settings – from offices and living rooms to hotels and prison cells.

In the 1940s, American theatre designer Robert Edmund Jones advanced the cause of multimedia theatre with influential books and lecture tours presenting a bold and evangelical vision of what he called 'the theatre of the future'. Combining film projection and theatre, he said, created an entirely new art form with endless possibilities, that can reveal the very soul of the play's characters by expressing (on screen) their subconscious hopes, fears and dreams:

> On the stage: their outer life; on the screen: their inner life. The stage used objectively, the screen used subjectively, in a kind of dramatic counterpoint. Not motive as it is revealed in action, but action *and motive* simultaneously revealed to us. The simultaneous expression of the two sides of our nature is an exact parallel to our life process. We are living in two worlds at the same time – an outer world of actuality and an inner world of vision. (Jones 1992: 77)

Subsequently, multimedia theatre developed with inventive directors, including Joseph Svoboda in the 1950s, Robert Whitman in the 1960s (when video first began to replace film as the major projection medium) and Geoff Moore in the 1970s. In the 1980s, groups such as The Wooster Group (directed by Elizabeth LeCompte) pioneered new approaches to multimedia theatre, and since the 1990s, the 'digital revolution' has prompted an explosion of new projection ideas and forms, including responsive and interactive stages in the work of groups such as The Builders Association and Ex Machina (directed by Robert Lepage). Mainstream theatre also increasingly embraced the form to bring projections to the forefront of shows on New York's Broadway and in London's West End.

The Pleasures and Perils of Multimedia Theatre

Yet, while audiences have become increasingly accustomed to such practice, it is important to note that for many people still, live theatre and media projections remain uneasy 'bedfellows' and throughout the history of multimedia theatre, there has been fierce resistance from theatre makers, academics and critics. This is because the two forms are seen as alien and too distinctly different in their 'ontologies' (essential natures) – most notably because one is live, in the moment, ephemeral and three-dimensional while the other is dead, in the past, recorded and two-dimensional.

Interestingly, as theatre academic Allardyce Nicoll argued in his 1936 book *Film and Theatre*, they also have inherent differences in terms of their types of dramatic representation and their different senses of 'truth'. Theatre is characterized by artifice, pretence and artificiality, he says, and 'dramatic illusion is never ... the illusion of reality; it is always imaginative illusion' (1936: 166), whereas film seems to enshrine the idea of 'truth' and authenticity. Even though we may know that the idea that 'the camera cannot lie' is a myth, 'in our heart of hearts we credit the truth of the statement ... What we have witnessed on the screen becomes the "real" for us' (167; 171). When multimedia theatre reached a highpoint of development and experimentation in the 1960s, a fiery debate raged, as Susan Sontag summarized:

> The big question is whether there is an unbridgeable division, even opposition, between the two arts. Is there something genuinely 'theatrical', different in kind from what is genuinely 'cinematic'? Almost all opinion holds that there is. A commonplace of discussion has it that film and theatre are distinct and even antithetical arts, each giving rise to its own standards of judgment and canons of form. (Sontag 1966: 24)

Around the same time, one of the most influential theatre directors of the twentieth century, Jerzy Grotowski, openly denounced media projections, equating them with cheap and futile theatrical attempts to compete with cinema. He dubbed them 'hybrid spectacles, conglomerates without back-bone or integrity ... [a] "Rich Theatre" – rich in flaws' (Grotowski 1968: 19) and called instead for a 'poor theatre' that retained the purity and humility of the live form. Today, despite over a hundred-year history of media's incorporation on stage, many leading theatre critics remain sceptical of its value, including *The Guardian*'s Lyn Gardner:

> when theatre has tried to incorporate film and video into live performance it often gets it horribly wrong ... multimedia is a word I've come to dread in the theatre. ... too often video in the theatre is a mere distraction, like trying to hold an intimate conversation in a room where the television is blaring loudly. Your eye is always drawn to the screen rather than to the person talking and everything else swims in and out of focus. (Gardner 2006)

Philip Auslander's book *Liveness* (1999) examines the changing concept of 'liveness' in a mediatized society, and argues that nowadays their ontologies seem less different or distinct than they used to. Since media is such an integral part of modern life, we hardly perceive a difference, he says: 'all performance modes, live or mediatized, are now equal; none is perceived as auratic or authentic' (1999: 50). He takes this further, suggesting that since digital media has become culturally dominant over the live, when we watch multimedia theatre we invariably pay more attention to the screen actors than the flesh-and-blood ones. Others have challenged this viewpoint, suggesting that a live actor will always have more 'presence' than a projected one, or that it is more the nature of the performer's activity that will command an audience's interest, and thus it is *content*, rather than *container* that defines presence.

The Chameleons Group

The Chameleons Group, a performance-as-research theatre company that I direct, pays particular attention to this notion of presence, and 'thinks through media' with specific reference to how to equalize the relative power and 'presences' of live performers and their projected 'doubles' (see Figure 9.1). A key technique in this is to enhance the sense of 'liveness' of the pre-recorded screen performer. The group acknowledges the ontological differences between actors on stage and screen, but nonetheless seeks to create a fusion or symbiosis between them. But the group takes a different perspective to Auslander's in 'thinking through incorporating media', recognizing that while projected screen characters may indeed be seductive in arresting audience attention, they also tend to be very 'flat' in comparison to live performers, not only in their two-dimensionality, but also in their performance energy. While there may be some truth to Auslander's contention that screen performers tend to dominate live ones, due to their larger scale and the allure of their electronic *presence*, nonetheless their *performances* may not hit the same mark.

Doubles are a central part of *Chameleons 4: The Doors of Serenity* (2002), and in one scene the Paranoid Cyborg character conducts a schizophrenic conversation with two of his alter egos (pre-recorded and played by the same actor) who appear in the same shot on screen behind him – a visionary mystic, and a nihilistic cynic. In attempting to create the illusion that all three characters are 'live' and the conversation is real and spontaneous, precise timing and extensive rehearsal of the dialogue is crucial. But so too is the particular energy and intensity of the two alter ego screen characters' performances, so that each of the three embodiments (one live, two video-recorded) appear equally vibrant, energized and 'alive'.

Actors know that levels of attention and adrenalin are all greatly heightened when performing on stage in front of a live audience, but are quite different when shooting a movie. In the latter, the actor's level of concentration and focus may be comparable, but due to the different conventions of screen acting as well as the environmental context (with no audience, lots of waiting between shots, and the knowledge the actor can fail many times and just re-take), the body is inevitably more relaxed, and the actor's mental energy tends to be calmer and more internally focused. To try to reverse this, the group therefore uses acting and directing techniques to inject a heightened sense of tension, vulnerability, danger and adrenalin when pre-recording the screen sequences, in order to prompt a comparable psychophysical energy that emulates theatrical liveness:

> These methods are employed so that when the live actor meets the supposed 'absence' and the 'past tense' of her projected double, the doppelgänger can assert itself as doubly 'present', both in time and space, and in terms of equal theatrical presence. As the flesh-and-blood actor meets her virtual self, the physical 'absence' of the digital body becomes a palpable presence, and past (the time when the video image was recorded) becomes present (in theatrical time and space). (Dixon 2012: 50)

In The Chameleons Group's one-man theatrical reworking of T. S. Eliot's poem *The Waste Land* (2013), I play the narrator and several different characters on stage, while a succession of the poem's other characters (played by other actors) appear on screen to talk and interact with me, including a clairvoyant, a murderous sailor, a woman in a straightjacket, and Cleopatra. Thinking through this incorporation of media, my strategy is both conceptual and pragmatic. Pre-recording the other actors and projecting them, often in huge close-up, behind the stage protagonist who exists in what Eliot calls the 'unreal city' of London, adds to the growing sense of claustrophobia, isolation, paranoia and madness within the text.

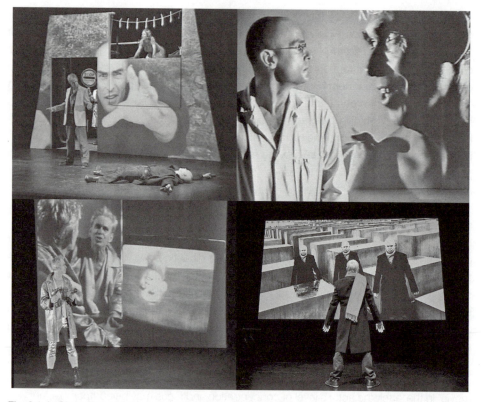

Fig. 9.1 In Chameleons Group productions, the author, Steve Dixon, interacts with other characters (top images) and with multiple *doppelgänger* doubles of himself on screen (bottom images). Clockwise from top left: *In Dreamtime*, 1996; *Net Congestion*, 2000; *T. S. Eliot's The Waste Land*, 2013; and *The Doors of Serenity*, 2002.

At the same time, it has enabled me to very easily tour the show in Asia, the United States and South America at minimal cost, travelling alone with only a costume and a thumb drive of the video with its embedded music and soundtrack (by Joyce Beetuan Koh). The core component of theatre, the ensemble of actors, has been shrunk to fit in my pocket, becoming a dehydrated part of a portable plug-and-play performance that can be forever reanimated in an instant using a simple projector and screen, when they become stars of an 'expanded cinema' performance.

How Do Theatre Makers Think Through Incorporating Media?

As an investigative methodology, I have set myself the task of attempting to categorize the primary reasons theatre artists over the decades have used media projections, the methods and strategies they undertake, and the different types of effect they elicit. Precisely how do media projections operate in relation to live theatre? How do they illuminate or complicate meanings for audiences, and what different aesthetic, semiotic, psychological, somatic and dramaturgical effects can they create? In attempting to answer these questions, I will go on to propose a type of taxonomy of multimedia theatre. This defines five principal categories of effects that are elicited through different approaches to incorporating media in theatre.

Phaedra Bell (2000) suggests that when media is projected onto a theatre stage, it operates in one of three ways in relation to the live actors and action. She lists them hierarchically, and notes that they are dependent on how dramatically or subtly the media is incorporated, its specific content and its level of prominence and impact in relation to the overall drama and stage aesthetic. Where the media is a dominant force, she calls it the *primary* medium; where it is more incidental or decorative it is the *secondary* medium; and where there is an equivalent balance between the relative importance of stage and projection, it is a *dialogic* medium.

Examples of projections being the *primary* medium include performance ensemble Gob Squad's *Kitchen (You Never Had it So Good)* (2008), an intoxicatingly chaotic retelling of the story of the countercultural 1960s and Andy Warhol's 'Factory'. The dominance of the media is evident immediately, when audience members enter and are given a 'backstage' tour around a three-room set with various video cameras in position. When they are taken to their seats, they see three large screens at the front of the stage, which obscure the view of the sets behind. All the stage action (apart from occasional moments when the performers venture onto the forestage) – including anarchic parties and recreations of Warhol's films, such as *Sleep* (1963) with audience members recruited as the central characters – happens out of the audience view, but is relayed as live video projections onto the three screens: one for each room.

Media projections operating as a *secondary* medium are the most common manifestation, and productions employ them in myriad ways, including back-projections of rooms to represent physical locations, documentary footage (for example, shots of urban deprivation to add a sense of gritty realism), and imagery designed to enhance the atmosphere or visual aesthetics of a scene (for example, many productions have used video sequences of beautiful natural phenomena, such as speeded-up clouds or slow-motion ocean waves).

But it is within the *dialogic* mode – when the live and the mediatized operate and interact on equivalent terms, and where the audience gives equal attention to each of them – that the most acclaimed examples of multimedia theatre tend to be found, from *Gertie the Dinosaur* a century ago to The Wooster Group's *Hamlet* (directed by Elizabeth LeCompte, 2007).

Dialogues and Syntheses

In *Hamlet*, there is a continual dialogic interaction between the performers and the screen that resembles a cross between a balletic *pas de deux* and a wrestling match, as the two ontological forms, by turns, interweave gracefully and compete aggressively for audience attention. On stage are The Wooster Group actors performing Shakespeare's play with Scott Shepherd in the lead, and on screen is a film recording of John Gielgud's celebrated 1964 Broadway stage production with Richard Burton in the same title role. The task of The Wooster Group actors is to follow the lead of their film counterparts and attempt to mirror their movements and gestures in every detail (see Figure 9.2). This task is complicated by the show's video operator technicians who act as VJs, slowing down or speeding up the film footage at predetermined points, and 'scratching' the film footage to reverse, repeat and freeze it, and to replay lines of dialogue. As the camera angle changes on the film, the actors also rush around the stage moving furniture and a specially designed table (which they

Fig. 9.2 Scott Shepherd mirrors and synchronizes his actions with those of his film counterpart from the 1960s, Richard Burton, as they both portray the title role in The Wooster Group's *Hamlet*, 2007, directed by Elizabeth LeCompte. Photo: Paula Court.

elongate or retract) in order to visually align their positions in accordance with the camera perspective of the 1964 *mise en scène* shown on the screen.

It is an extraordinary 'dialogic' production where the live action attempts to precisely align and fuse itself with the film footage not only visually but also sonically, with words sometimes spoken by the live actors, sometimes by the screen ones, and sometimes they are cross-mixed live by the technicians, eerily fading in and out of one another. At other points, the images of the actors on screen also appear to fade out as their faces and bodies are treated with digital effects to render them ghostly, visually 'distressed' and partially erased, including when Hamlet contemplates suicide and asks: 'what is the quintessence of dust?'

A Taxonomy of Media Projection Effects

I will now adopt a different perspective to Phaedra Bell in analysing 'how theatre thinks through incorporating media', and propose a different type of taxonomy. I believe that there are five key defining types or categories of effect that theatre directors and companies elicit and employ. This is not to say that these are either definitive or exhaustive. Others might reasonably suggest there are more (or less) defining categories, and there are certainly differing ways to describe them. But I suggest that the following are five of the most important and impactful ways in which theatre directors think through incorporating media:

1. The Synesthetic Pleasure Principle
2. Semiotics and Politics
3. Shrinking Theatre and Expanding Cinema
4. Ghosts and Doubles
5. Metamorphosing Time and Space

1. The Synesthetic Pleasure Principle: Sigmund Freud suggested that the human 'id' is driven by a strong desire for pleasure, and when the live and the recorded are conjoined in interesting and inventive ways, for audiences there can be a delicious sense of what Freud termed 'the pleasure principle'. Although the first of my distinct categories, this idea is actually common to all five: it is a key reason directors incorporate media into productions and an overarching multimedia theatre phenomenon. The meeting of two separate and arguably 'warring' ontological forms is stimulating and pleasurable to audiences, and when creatively employed, it may also give rise to a type of *synesthetic* effect, where there is both disorientation and a heightening of the audience's senses.

Synesthesia is a condition resulting from a cross wiring of the brain's synapses that re-routes the five human senses so that, for example, sounds may be seen (e.g. as colours and shapes) and words may be tasted (e.g. 'theatre' tastes of strawberries). Gene Youngblood suggests that 'Whatever divisions may exist between the two media are not necessarily "bridged", but rather are orchestrated as harmonic opposites in an overall synaesthetic [*sic*] experience' (Youngblood 1970: 365); and Carolee Schneemann argues that juxtaposing theatre and media serves to 'dislocate, disassociate, compound, and engage our senses to allow our senses to expand into primary feelings' (cited in Youngblood 1970: 366).

There is a particular synesthetic pleasure principle in the synchronization of live human performers and recorded ones, as exemplified in The Wooster Group's *Hamlet*, and also in live actors synchronizing with animated characters, or appearing to be located amid fantastical, animated worlds, as in the work of the theatre group '1927'. The synesthetic pleasure principle of their multimedia theatre has been noted keenly by UK critics, who have variously described them as 'dazzlingly synchronized', 'funny, unsettling and unforgettable', 'groundbreaking with strokes of genius', and 'unlike anything you will have experienced before' (1927 website).

Works such as *Golem* (2014) and *The Magic Flute* (2013, with Komische Oper Berlin) hark back to the bygone era of the company's '1927' name, with animated expressionist sets redolent of the 1920 film *The Cabinet of Doctor Caligari*, and an aesthetic that evokes Buster Keaton movies, Franz Kafka novels and André Breton's first surrealist manifesto (1924). Performers in mime-style white make-up work close to the screen, sometimes standing on ledges at different heights, and appear to be entirely immersed within the black and white, animated projection imagery. They are consumed within kaleidoscopic worlds where they (seemingly) jump across rooftops, inhabit giant clocks and machines, try to control oversized barking dogs, encounter skeletons and hellfire, fly with insects and butterflies, get struck by lightning and are attacked by hoards of spiders while being trapped in their webs.

2. Semiotics and Politics: For other directors, keeping a distance and separation between the mediatized and the live allows a Brechtian *Verfremdungseffekt* to take effect. Rather than using media to 'pleasure' and draw audiences in to the spectacle and dramatic narrative, the mechanics are revealed, the artificial construction is foregrounded and the separate ontologies of stage and screen are highlighted rather than diminished, and consciously separated rather than melded. Through this 'distancing effect', the audience can more carefully, consciously and cerebrally consider and 'read' the semiotic relationships of the dual texts of stage and screen, and consider how they intersect or inform one another to convey underlying messages and meanings.

In the sophisticated and densely layered productions of The Builders Association (directed by Marianne Weems), there is a concern to engage with media for its powerful semiotic potentials. The group explores how concurrent media images can affect and change the interpretation and meaning of what is happening on stage, as well as deliver powerful socio-political messages and critiques. Perhaps ironically for one of the world's most technologically-oriented theatre groups, in works such as *SUPER VISION* (in collaboration with dbox, 2005) their political critiques often target technology itself: 'what you see are people isolated, melancholy, in various states of fragmentation. Technology is not creating communities that anyone would hope for. And this is a political message' (Zinoman 2005: 15).

The production explores surveillance and the increasingly intrusive 'dataveillance' of contemporary life; and the multiple video projections reflect this by becoming progressively more dense, intense and oppressive as the show progresses. In one scene set in an airport, Mr Shah, a Ugandan-born Indian traveller, has a nightmarish border control experience. As he is interrogated by passport officials upstage, a stream of projection images gradually build up and accumulate on a small mobile screen downstage: his signature, fingerprints, retinal scans and facial recognition data, together with his credit card details and recent transactions.

In semiotic terms, as the wholly innocent Mr Shah attempts to maintain his dignity, explain who he is and defend his travel plans, the projections convey his vulnerability and his insignificant position within a mistrustful and uncaring 'Big Brother' society. As the interrogation intensifies and he becomes increasingly beleaguered, the dataveillance becomes even more intimate and intrusive with details of his medical history, his family and even his average intake of tobacco and caffeine. As it does, the small screen immediately in front of him is almost entirely filled with the overlapping images, and Mr Shah becomes 'less of a physical presence and more of a presence defined in the body of data that accumulates around him' (cited in Kaye 2005: 569).

Foregrounding communications technologies on stage to explore its negative socio-political impacts carries on a tradition of many multimedia theatre artists such as George Coates. An innovative pioneer who was the first to bring 3D Virtual Reality projections into the theatre in the early 1990s, he maintains that 'Using technology to critique technology is no more a contradiction that it is to call the phone company to complain about the service or to use a calculator to challenge the bill. The use of a particular tool implies no endorsement of values beyond itself' (Coates 2000).

'Meaning and significance are not synonymous', wrote Michael Kirby (1966: 60), when referring to the effect a specific media projection might have in relation to the stage action, and the ways audiences might receive and interpret it. He was particularly discussing projections of an abstract or graphical nature, as well as documentary or narrative film sequences that initially appear to have no direct link or relation to the action on stage, and may thus mystify the audience. His point is that while a semiotic analysis of certain projections may be unable to unlock any clear or literal *meanings* in relation to the onstage drama, their dramatic *significance* and impact may be nonetheless profound. For example, they may excite a particular mood or atmosphere, arouse in the audience a feeling of calm or foreboding, or conjure a sense of uncertainty, suspense, mystery, humour or absurdity. These effects and feelings may actually work counter to, or be in direct contrast with, the main stage action, yet still render an overall effect that is highly dramatic, affective and compelling to the audience.

3. *Shrinking Theatre and Expanding Cinema*: Many theatre artists think through media by miniaturizing or shrinking the live theatrical components while expanding the cinematic form, thus making the projections the *primary* medium within Phaedra Bell's classifications. When actors become media projections, either by being pre-recorded or by being filmed and projected live as they work on stage, they are effectively *shrunken* by the camera lens, transported through cables and circuits, and bottled into a video file. Like a genie, they appear or reappear magically on screen at a given cue, and their performances become a new form of cinema that is *expanded* by virtue of the other scenic elements that share the stage, and the live flesh-and-blood actors who interact with the projection.

The term *Expanded Cinema* was coined by Gene Youngblood in the title of his influential 1970 book that explored the experimental film and multimedia (he called it 'intermedia') theatre of the time, and reflected on a 'synaesthetic [*sic*] cinema [that] transcends the restrictions of drama, story, and plot' (Youngblood 1970: 77), which heightens the audience's senses and 'attempts to express a total phenomenon … [our] own consciousness' (76).

The idea of using media to minutely scrutinize and miniaturize theatrical components is a hallmark of director Katie Mitchell and her video artist collaborator, Leo Warner. She has described her particular take on thinking through incorporating media as being a direct response to being bored by theatre's reliance on words and consecutive scenes, whereas real-life experiences and relationships are much more chaotic: 'I was looking for something that represented that chaos but still had all that feeling in it. And that's why we started to use video and sound, and fragmenting the stage picture and combining video output with the live construction of it' (Mitchell 2011).

In what Mitchell calls 'live cinema', her actors not only perform but take turns as live camera operators and real-time Foley sound effects technicians, to create beautiful screen sequences and tableaux in real time, which are projected on different screens on stage. In performances such as their reworking of Virginia Woolf's novel *Waves* (2006), they scuttle around with portable lights, setting up numerous mini-film sets where images, tableaux, monologues and scenes are enacted, predominantly in close-up. Exquisite and evocative images are cleverly conjured with a true eye for detail, as an antique dinner table is set lovingly, drops of blood fall poetically into water, and portable lights slowly pan across moody faces to render classic cinematic close-up shots on the giant cyclorama screen, echoing nostalgic movie genres of the past.

Thus, while the stage actions are fascinating, it is the results on screen that are most compelling, and sometimes mesmerizing. Like a theatre spotlight being gradually shut down to a pin-spot, there is intense concentration on a type of shrinking and miniaturization on stage while the arresting power of the cinema image intensifies, and its presence and impact expands.

As the live actors oscillate between being ensemble performers shooting a film and being movie actors captured within the camera's frame, they switch between the acting conventions of stage (externalized, exaggerated) and film (internalized, minimal) and between what Nicoll describes (noted earlier) as the artifice of theatre and the truth of film. A revealing documentary on the making of *Waves* emphasizes these ideas (Mitchell 2011), with actor Ben Whishaw describing how a beautiful window is created on the screen by an onstage actor holding a light behind a crude plastic sheet and some plastic flowers: 'There's constant juxtaposition of image and the artificialness of how that image is made'. Artifice, and what I call the theatrical 'shrinking' effect is also evident in Mitchell's description of how she is 'into the science of very, very, minute construction of feeling for the audience. ... So, I am artificially giving you the impression of a dreamlike emotional landscape. It's completely constructed'. Actor Paul Ready similarly reuses some of his words for emphasis when describing the liberating feeling of reducing theatre to its smallest details for the camera: 'you can focus on these tiny, tiny, tiny bits of acting', he says (all Mitchell 2011).

4. Ghosts and Doubles: We saw earlier how The Chameleons Group juxtaposes a live actor with multiple pre-recorded doubles of himself on screen in order to create the sense of a disturbed or schizophrenic character, and how The Wooster Group plays with ghosts from the past on screen (Richard Burton and most of his fellow actors from the 1964 production have since passed away). When actors on stage act opposite recordings of themselves on screen, they similarly confront a form of 'dead self' (since the recording was in the past) or ghost. In 'Screen Test of the Double', Matthew Causey suggests that when the 'double' or doppelgänger of a live actor on the stage also appears simultaneously on screen, it is a type of 'autopsy of perception' (Causey 2002: 65) that enacts the splitting of the subject (the actor) and thereby 'the subject's annihilation, its nothingness. The uncanny experience of the double is Death made material. Unavoidable. Present. Screened' (Causey 1999: 385–6).

Mary Oliver creates one-woman performances that are entirely based on a structure of her interacting with a number of different screen doubles of herself, who talk to her from separate TV monitors placed around the stage, including *Mother Tongue* (2001), in which she simultaneously plays all the members of her family. She 'thinks through incorporating media' in relation to the issue of what she terms 'screen seduction', which tends to draw the audience's attention more to her screen doppelgängers, resulting in what she calls 'an unequal relationship between the actual and virtual performer' (2008: 61). She acknowledges their separate ontologies but insists that while they 'can exist independently' this should not be 'to the exclusion of the other' and rather they should establish 'a symbiotic relationship' (65). Her method to seek to attain this is through rapid, dramatic and often comic quick-fire dialogues between her live stage character and her doubles on the screens. This strategy is designed to break the lure of the screens to ensure audience attention continually keeps returning to her stage character.

The notion of *presence* has become an important area of theatre and performance studies (for example, see Giannachi and Kaye 2011), and Oliver enacts some of this theory through a fascinating battle for presence with her recorded doubles. While some critics perceive a binary opposition between the presence of the live and the *absence* of the double (since it is 'dead', a trace of the past and not physically there), others, such as media theorist Jean Baudrillard, argue that on the contrary, media now has such a privileged and dominant presence that it dwarfs the human and has essentially replaced the real. But in relation to multimedia theatre, as demonstrated in the work of Mary Oliver and The Chameleons Group, it is perhaps more fitting to consider that that the live and the screened are simply different *types* of presences, and that their alchemical synthesis, through an eradication of their differences, remains a holy grail for a number of directors and groups.

5. *Metamorphosing Time and Space*: From the earliest days of film's inclusion in theatre, such as *Hoppla Wir Leben!* (1927) discussed earlier, media projections have been used as a scenographic tool to provide scene-setting backcloths using still or moving images in place of physical sets. In the 1990s, groups such as George Coates Performance Works and ieVR pioneered the use of Virtual Reality technologies to project 3D environments on stage, with audiences using 3D headsets or goggles.

Robert Lepage thinks through media as a way to metamorphose time and space, and to take his audience on a journey through ever-changing places, spaces and worlds. Perhaps more than any other theatre artist, Lepage has consistently employed media to explore the scenographic potentials of the stage, using both symbolic and representational imagery. He creates new types of stagescape where spaces move from the realistic to the abstract, and continually mutate. He has used different types of screens, sometimes in conjunction with moving sets, including a circular, rotating screen in *Needles and Opium* (1991), which at one point he is suspended in mid-air in front of (using a hidden flying harness). He makes a series of somersaults to simulate a fall from a tall building, whose projection lurches vertiginously upward in synchronization with his dramatic, tumbling descent.

Lepage has always been fascinated by media's scenographic potentials, and its ability to instantly segue 'from naturalism to fantasy and back again. It's that sort of imaginative fluidity that I'm striving after', he says (cited in Christiansen 2005). John O'Mahoney describes Lepage's 'chimeric ... uncanny, almost unnatural powers of visual transfiguration, as waterlogged lecture halls transform themselves into the canals of Venice, piles of old books meld into the New York city skyline, an old tumble dryer becomes a spacecraft's docking bay' (O'Mahoney 2001).

A successful film-maker, as well as an actor and theatre director, Lepage adopts a cinematic approach to projections, including using a letterbox proportioned screen in productions such as *The Far Side of the Moon* (2000). As I have discussed elsewhere, this screen:

> is utilised in conjunction with sliding mirrored panels, archival film, original video images and blackboard backdrops to seamlessly metamorphose locations from lecture theatres and elevators to airplane interiors and wardrobes. Prosaic domestic objects transform into high-tech devices, as an ironing board becomes a workout bench and then an MRI scanning table. A circular window in the set becomes pivotal to the metamorphosis of spaces and objects ... a springboard to conjure and express metaphorical links, lateral thought shifts, and hallucinatory transformations. (Dixon 2007b: 503–4)

These transformational effects not only change the scenic spaces but also simultaneously alter the sense of time. Time and space are, of course, intimately linked, and in *Far Side of the Moon* the rapid location changes also serve to fragment the sense of time. Its story of two warring twin brothers (both played by Lepage) trying to cope with the death of their mother is played out in a series of flashbacks and flash-forwards. In one scene, Lepage stares at a circular video projection of a swirling washing machine, which transforms into the twin siblings as foetuses in his mother's stomach, then mutates again to become a rocket porthole with an astronaut gazing down towards the earth.

Lepage thinks through media's incorporation so as to explicitly examine the relationship between time and space, and in *Far Side of the Moon* this extends as far as outer space in its parallel story about the Soviet-American space race, and the search for extraterrestrial intelligence (SETI) programme. The final image is unforgettable, as the earlier foetus image returns and the sense of past and present are reunited, with Lepage lying in a foetal position in the centre of the stage. Simultaneously, his image is cast up above, floating weightlessly like an astronaut on a moon walk, as his reflection in a large angled mirror combines with projections of a star-filled cosmos, placing him within the black, vast and twinkling sky of outer space.

Conclusion: Alchemical Syntheses

Multimedia theatre makers create memorable dramas and compelling aesthetic effects when conjoining or attempting to fuse two different ontological forms. For Susan Sontag, they explore and pursue 'the intensification of what each art distinctly is' in order to 'seek a vast behavioural magma or synaesthesis [sic] ... to support a perennial modern quest – the quest for the definitive artform' (Sontag 1966: 24). In conjoining theatre and media, they intensify and highlight the essences of each of their distinct forms, and play within the liminal space that separates them. Like chemists or alchemists, they seek both to eradicate their distinctions and dissolve their boundaries, as well as to investigate the potent interplays and dialectical tensions between them that we have identified:

Stage	Screen
Text	Subtext
Conscious	Subconscious
Artifice	Truth
Alive	Dead (but reincarnated)
Present	Past (but reanimated)
Presence	A different presence (*not* absence)

Theatre artists think through media in differing ways so as to elicit and excite pleasurable and synesthetic effects: synchronizing live actors with dead ones and their own ghostly doubles; conveying complex ideas, meanings and political messages; shrinking the stage so as to mediatize and expand it vividly on screen; and staging spectacular spatial and temporal metamorphoses. Katie Mitchell has discussed how 'These new tools enable us to jump effortlessly and speedily between different people, times, events and places' (Mitchell 2011); and 1960s multimedia theatre pioneer Josef Svoboda describes what he calls a 'psycho-plastic space' where both the physical and the screen objects and actors 'acquire new relationships and significance, a new and different reality' (cited in Burian 1971: 81).

While the entire practice of multimedia theatre may long remain a contested territory, forever struggling with complex ontological debates, Marshall McLuhan's influential ideas in *Understanding Media: The Extensions of Man* (1964) may nonetheless perennially hold true:

> The hybrid or the meeting of two media is a moment of truth and revelation from which new form is born. ... The moment of the meeting of media is a moment of freedom and release from the ordinary trance and numbness imposed on them by our senses. (McLuhan 1964: 55)

Performance Details

Chameleons 4: The Doors of Serenity by theatre group The Chameleons Group. Devised by the company. Direction: Steve Dixon. Performers: Steve Dixon, Anna Fenemore, Wendy Reed, Barry Woods. Performances: 14-venue European tour, including HOMO ALIBI 3.0 Festival, Riga, Latvia, and the Universities of Hull, Goldsmiths, and Dartington College of Arts, UK. September and October 2002. https://youtu.be/zvP4xky5Ar0

Further Reading

Dixon's *Digital Performance: A History of New Media in Theater, Dance, Performance Art and Installation* (2007a) provides a comprehensive overview of the history of multimedia theatre and performance and summarizes the key issues and theoretical debates. Causey's *Theatre and Performance in Digital Culture: From Simulation to Embeddedness* (2006) offers an in-depth theoretical examination of how incorporating media changes the nature of theatrical productions. Another helpful introduction to the subject, with many case studies, is *Multimedia Performance* (2012) by Klich and Scheer. *Liveness: Performance in a Mediatized Culture* (1999) by Auslander is an influential polemic on the changing nature of liveness in performance and culture. Robert Edmond Jones's series of important lectures, delivered between 1941 and 1952, in which he enthused about 'a wholly new theatrical art' and explored its psychological effects on audiences, was published in 1992 as *Towards a New Theatre*.

References

1927 (2017), '1927' website. Available online: http://www.19-27.co.uk (accessed 1 June 2017).

Auslander, Phillip (1999), *Liveness: Performance in a Mediatized Culture*, London: Routledge.

Bell, Phaedra (2000), 'Dialogic Media Production and Inter-media Exchange', *Journal of Dramatic Theory and Criticism*, 14 (2): 41–55.

Burian, Jarka (1971), *The Scenography of Josef Svoboda*, Middletown, CT: Wesleyan University Press.

Causey, Matthew (1999), 'Screen Test of the Double: The Uncanny Performer in the Space of Technology', *Theatre Journal*, 51 (4): 383–94.

Causey, Matthew (2002), 'The Aesthetics of Disappearance and the Politics of Visibility in the Performance of Technology', *Gramma*, 10: 59–72.

Causey, Matthew (2006), *Theatre and Performance in Digital Culture: From Simulation to Embeddedness*, London: Routledge.

Coates, George (2000), 'Blind Messengers', Database entry, *Digital Performance Archive*. Originally at: http://art.ntu.ac.uk/dpa (accessed 25 August 2005, no longer available).

Christiansen, Rupert (2005) 'Theatre's Most Dazzling Sorcerer', *Daily Telegraph*, 23 April.

Dixon, Steve (2007a), *Digital Performance: A History of New Media in Theater, Dance, Performance Art and Installation*, Cambridge, MA: MIT Press.

Dixon, Steve (2007b), 'Space, Metamorphosis and Extratemporality in the Theatre of Robert Lepage', *Contemporary Theatre Review*, 17 (4): 499–515.

Dixon, Steve (2012), 'Researching Digital Performance: Virtual Practices', in Baz Kershaw and Helen Nicholson (eds), *Research Methods in Theatre and Performance*, 41–62, Edinburgh: Edinburgh University Press.

Gardner, Lyn (2006), 'Waves Sets a High-water Mark for Multimedia Theatre', *The Guardian*, 14 December. Available online: https://www.theguardian.com/stage/theatreblog/2006/dec/04/wavessetsahighwatermarkfo (accessed 15 April 2017).

Giannachi, Gabriella, and Nick Kaye (2011), *Performing Presence: Between the Live and the Simulated*, Manchester, UK: Manchester University Press.

Grotowski, Jerzy (1968), *Towards a Poor Theatre*, London: Methuen.

Jones, Robert Edmond (1992), *Towards a New Theatre: The Lectures of Robert Edmond Jones*, ed. Delbert Unruh, New York: Limelight Editions. (Lectures first delivered 1941–52.)

Kaye, Nick (2005), 'Screening Presence: The Builders Association and dbox, SUPER VISION (2005)', *Contemporary Theatre Review*, 17 (4): 555–75.

Klich, Rosemary, and Edward Scheer (2012), *Multimedia Performance*, Basingstoke: Palgrave Macmillan.

Kirby, Michael (1966), 'Film in the New Theatre', *TDR: The Tulane Drama Review*, 11 (1): 49–61.

Mitchell, Katie (2011), 'Katie Mitchell on Directing Multimedia Productions', National Theatre Discover, 6 May. Available online: https://www.youtube.com/watch?v=rAij9r9RvF0 (accessed 20 May 2017).

McLuhan, Marshall (1964) *Understanding Media: The Extensions of* Man, London: Routledge and Kegan Paul.

Nicoll, Allardyce (1936), *Film and Theatre*, New York: Thomas Y. Crowell Company.

Oliver, Mary (2008), 'The Emancipating Possibilities of Performing with Cartoons', *International Journal of Performance Arts and Digital Media*, 4 (1): 59–67.

O'Mahoney, John (2001), 'Aerial Views', *The Guardian*, 23 June. Available online: http://www.guardian.co.uk/saturday_review/story/0,3605,510950,00.html (accessed 30 June 2001).

Sontag, Susan (1966), 'Film and Theatre', *TDR: The Tulane Drama Review*, 11 (1): 24–37.

Youngblood, Gene (1970), *Expanded Cinema*, New York: P. Dutton & Co., Inc.

Zinoman, Jason (2005), 'THEATER; All the World's A New Technology Incubator', *New York Times*, November 20.

10 How Does the Trained Body Think?

BRODERICK D. V. CHOW

In 2005, I moved to London, England, from my hometown of Vancouver, Canada, where I'd lived all my life. I was two years out of university, and I had a newly printed Canadian Actor's Equity Card in my pocket, and a supporting lead as Thuy in *Miss Saigon* on my CV. The plan was to take a year in London to 'train', after which I'd return to Vancouver and resume my career as an actor. This is what I nervously explained to my agent, a tiny but fearsome former model named Brenda Wong, while sitting in her brightly sunlit Gastown office.

> 'Can you maybe not send me out for anything, for a bit?'
> 'How long?' she asked.
> 'Um … a year? I'm going to do a Masters in London.'
> 'Why?'
> 'Well, you know, to *train*. To work on my craft.'
> 'Oh honey', she replied. 'OK. You go do that, and you come back even better and you make us more money. It'll be good for your resume. Shame, I was going to send you out *for Battlestar*.'

More than a dozen years later and I'm still here. Sorry, Brenda. Why did I say I was going to 'train'? Why didn't I say I was *studying* theatre? Perhaps saying 'training' was unconscious. I thought it was impressive how biographies for actors in the UK always began with: 'Training: RADA'; 'Training: Mountview'. For me, London was the centre of theatre training. Training there would be an apprenticeship in a craft with an ancient history, like learning to make leather wallets. But by telling people I was training, rather than studying, I was unconsciously confirming a subtle system of value that divides the 'trained' body from the 'studying' mind. 'Training' and 'studying' do signify different things. We train horses, dogs and actors, but we study English, History and Biology. To be trained is to be an object of a verb. To study is to be the subject. Training suggests *following* and to be 'in training' suggests a process. The French preposition *en train de* means exactly this: in the process of something. In this sense, training means following an existing practice, which explains the tendency of actors to speak about their 'craft', rather than their 'art'. Etymologically, 'study' derives from the Latin for 'zeal; painstaking application'. But today, it seems to imply distance from the 'dead' object. Scientists study things, mainly dead things, and at university I studied literature, mostly dead guys (also rich, white and English). I did not want to kill the vital, living, breathing theatre I loved by studying it. I'm reminded here of that overused and mangled quotation attributed to E. B. White: 'analysing humour is like dissecting a frog. Few people are interested and the frog dies of it.' (How ironic that my PhD should be in humour studies.) The division between training and study relates to the way, in the UK especially, theatre and performance in educational institutions is divided between the conservatoire or drama school where actors are trained, and the university BA degree where theatre is studied. Conservatoire training is celebrated as more practical or hands-on than the intellectual study of theatre that takes place in university degree schemes. In Vancouver, I trained at a now-shuttered independent acting school called the Lyric School of Acting, based on the Neighborhood Playhouse model of Sanford Meisner. In many of my American-method inflected scene study classes, I was told to 'get out of my head'. Thinking, it seemed, was the opposite of *acting*. In essence, my training trained me *not* to think.

This value system is so normalized we can overlook how it *devalues* the idea of the trained body, which, associated with physical skill and somatic responsiveness, is supposed to be an unthinking body. As I said before: horses, dogs and actors. The people who do the thinking in the theatre – writers, directors, designers – are associated with authorship and creativity. Thus, the Cartesian dualism between the trained body and the thinking mind enforces a hierarchy of practice. This isn't only true for actors. Take, for example, dance scholar Susan Leigh Foster's description of the 'hired' body, a body drilled and trained to 'make a living at dancing'. 'The hired body', she writes, 'built at a great distance from the self, reduces it to a pragmatic merchant of movement proffering whatever look appeals at the moment' (Foster 1997: 256). Foster argues that training *constructs* the body, in the image of another, *ideal* body, in this case one assumed to be neutral, adaptable and for hire. Through training and drill, she writes, 'the images used to describe the body and its actions *become* the body' (Foster 1997: 239). While in other areas of her work Foster indeed conceptualizes a kind of bodily thinking, the 'hired' body, trained and constructed in relation to an industry standard, seems to be a vehicle for others' creative action, rather than its own.

As Mark Evans, writing on actors' movement training, argues, the body trained to be neutral and 'ready for work' is also a 'body shaped by cultural history and the cultural economics of the "natural" body' (Evans 2009: 69). This resonates with a social constructivist theory of the body in which the body and the self submit to culturally determined scripts. This theory of cultural conditioning can be traced back to French philosopher Michel Foucault, who suggests that the body is constructed by social 'discourses', because it takes on meaning through shared signs and norms that regulate its behaviour (1980). Foucault's concern was how power operates, and his historical research uncovered a shift in the late eighteenth century. As Turner summarizes, power 'found a new object of exploration and control – the human body itself. The spread of scientific and techno-rational procedures, having gained a foothold in technology and consciousness, latched onto a new terrain, the body of individuals and the body of populations' (1996: 161). Part of this modern control of the body was the spread of 'disciplinary' practices. Foucault writes: 'Discipline "makes" individuals; it is the specific technique of a power that regards individuals both as objects and as instruments of its exercise' (Foucault 1977: 170). Exercised in practices like 'gymnastics, exercises [and] muscle building', discipline turns the individual's gaze onto him or herself, which means that power could act even more effectively through self-surveillance rather than outside punishment (Foucault 1980: 56). In other words, according to Foucault, the trained body is a controlled one.

Scholars influenced by Foucault's paradigm-shifting analysis of power have applied it directly to the critique of training regimes. For example, Cole, Giardina and Andrews write that 'sport ... is a good example of how power operates without coercive forces: individuals who recognize the necessity of their own discipline freely submit to governing techniques' (2004: 214). Markula and Pringle, writing on the related discipline of physical fitness, note that 'by imposing a regime of physical fitness on a population, it is possible to govern individual bodies' (2006: 70). And Evans, writing more specifically about movement training for actors, says:

> In a very straightforward sense, clearly the function and purpose of movement training for actors is to 'produce' the body of an actor. Power shows itself through its inscription of knowledges on the actor's body; inscriptions which are not often noticed or considered. (Evans 2009: 120)

The common thread here is that training enables a kind of *self-government*, a way of unconsciously accepting the norms, values and practices of power. Certainly, we can see how this might work in practice. Training – be it for ballet or bodybuilding – compels you to return to the same place, day after day, performing the same exercises, and to evaluate your progress. It also changes you by altering your body in terms of strength, flexibility, power or speed, and so changes your orientation and disposition in everyday life – what Pierre Bourdieu calls a person's *habitus*, or embodied norms and tendencies, 'which organise... practices and the perception of practices' (Bourdieu 1984: 170).

However, anybody who has ever trained in a physical practice knows that this is hardly the whole story. When I first read Foucault's *Discipline and Punish*, I thought his model of the way power operates through the body made sense intellectually, and yet, something in my body, my *trained* body – arms and legs that lift weights and dance, fingers that play the piano, a vocal instrument that speaks and sings – kicked back. Perhaps this disquiet in my body was the first sign that the trained body isn't so unthinking after all. As Evans suggests, training embodies social and institutional values but also offers a potential process for interrogating them. This is because the trained, 'docile' body (Foucault 1977: 135–69) does not *replace* the untrained, uninscribed, unruly body, but exists in dialectic with it. Drawing on the work of feminist theorist Elizabeth Grosz, Evans writes that 'the "pre-inscriptive" body may, in this way, only be knowable through the ways in which it becomes inscribed' (2009: 144). In other words, the idea of a natural, untrained body is only produced by the process of training, and training itself becomes a way of knowing the body – or, *thinking through the body.*

In this chapter, I intend to pick up on the assertion that the trained body thinks. I ask *how does the trained body think?* And what we can learn by thinking through training? In contrast to Evans's research, which focuses on expressive forms of movement, I am interested in forms of physical training that might initially seem quite rigid and codified. Thus, my first example is a performance form that represents sport (professional wrestling, or pro wrestling) and my second is a legitimate sport with a strongly theatrical heritage (Olympic weightlifting). Firstly, I discuss an ethnographic investigation of a professional wrestling school undertaken in 2011–12 to shed light on the concept of *embodied knowledge.* I suggest that the specific techniques and gestures of professional wrestling, seen in relation to their historical, social and economic context(s), 'think through' a form of embodied politics that relies on cooperation and empathy. Next, I use my practice as a weightlifter, ongoing since 2014, to explore in detail how embodied experience puts pressure on social conditioning and thus how training itself might be a form of creative thought, by producing the conditions for new gestures and practices. Finally, I will offer some practical suggestions about how to approach research through physical training, drawing on the methods and practices of critical ethnography and auto-ethnography.

Professional Wrestling and Embodied Knowledge

If, as I have proposed, the trained body *thinks*, what is the nature of this thinking? As I suggested in the opening anecdote of this chapter, theatre and performance pedagogy often separates training-as-doing from study-as-knowing. It follows, then, that if training, indeed *thinks*, then it must produce knowledge of something, specifically, an *embodied knowledge*. How do we define a slippery concept like embodied knowledge? Ben Spatz (2015), following vital work by Marcel Mauss, Michel Foucault, Nick Crossley and others, argues that '*Embodied practice is epistemic.* It is structured by and productive of knowledge. Accordingly, an epistemological account of embodied practice is one according to which such practice actively encounters and *comes to know* reality through technique, rather than simply producing or constructing it' (2015: 43).

In other words, technique is how we come to know the world, and it develops dialectically with the changing world. Technique is continually developing, which 'demands new mappings and understandings of the body' (Spatz 2015: 43). Furthermore, I would argue that because technique exists dialectically with lived, material reality, which includes social, economic, political and historical contexts, technique and, by extension, embodied knowledge is always in some ways embodied *political* knowledge, as it always concerns the positioning of the lived, corporeal body within the contexts above.

When I set out to research professional wrestling training, I was influenced by French sociologist Loïc Wacquant's exploration of the boxer's embodied knowledge, published as *Body & Soul: Notebooks of an Apprentice Boxer* (2004), which has become a classic of auto-ethnographic writing. While pursuing research on the lives of African American Chicagoans below the poverty line in the South Side 'ghetto', Wacquant enrolled at the Woodlawn Boys Club, a boxing gym on Chicago's South Side, a poor black neighbourhood that literally shares a border with the private, wealthy university. Rather than a traditional ethnography describing the lives of his informants, training at the gym affords Wacquant a different perspective, describing the 'embodied practical reason' of boxing (Wacquant 2006: 98). Boxing, he writes, 'reveals itself to be a sort of "savage science", an eminently social and quasi-scientific practice, even as it might seem to involve only those individuals who risk their bodies in the ring in a singular confrontation that appears rough and unbridled' (Wacquant 2006: 149). This savage science 'invites [Wacquant] to move beyond the traditional distinctions between body and mind, instinct and idea, the individual and the institution' (149). Wacquant was no slouch: he trained nearly every day, competed, and at one point even considered quitting his well-paid professorial position to take up boxing full-time.

In 2011, I began training at a professional wrestling gym in East London, though my circumstances were rather different to Wacquant's. While Wacquant used the site of the gym to learn about the social cosmos of Woodlawn, I wanted to go deeper into the embodied technique of professional wrestling. From my first training session, the techniques of professional wrestling surprised and fascinated me (Chow 2014). A good illustration of this is the 'lock-up'. This is the most common starting position in wrestling matches, where the left hand grasps the back of the partner/opponent's neck and the right drapes over the partner's bicep. The hold communicates a struggle for dominance to the audience. I found the move itself easy to learn. With a background as an actor and musical theatre performer, I had no trouble manipulating my body into particular shapes and forms. Yet what needed to be trained was the *dynamic* of the movement. The particular dynamic of nearly all pro wrestling technique is called 'working loose'. This involves a light touch and flexibility that enables wrestlers to respond to each other in an improvisatory fashion. It was only after I trained with the head coach of the wrestling school that I learnt this quality. As I wrote in my article on the subject:

> The quality of touch surprises me with its lightness. ... With a true professional wrestler, there is no bearing down or test of strength. All the exertion and muscular strain turns out to be a 'sell', a fake or con. The struggle is perceived not because it is 'real', but because it is communicated to the audience. (Chow 2014: 73)

The dynamic of working loose illustrates the unique logic of professional wrestling, its embodied knowledge. I wrote: 'I began to read past wrestling's spectacular surface and became cognizant of issues connected to corporeality: its status as a form of shared theatrical labour that allows for participants to model and practice a political principle of friendship, regardless of difference' (Chow 2014: 73). By training in the form, wrestling became less about what it said to the audience than what its technique spoke to those who practised it – it spoke to us because it was a form of cooperation, trust, physical empathy and care.

Through training, I became more and more invested in this physical logic and found myself (despite physical exhaustion and sometimes injury) looking forward to those moments of co-operative improvisation where I could 'work' with another person intuitively. Often, I might not even know the other person's name, yet if they had some experience in the form, we were able to communicate. I also enjoyed watching how the very experienced members of the school, that is those who performed professionally, thought through the body. Using their embodied knowledge of technique alone, they could create an exciting performance with a consistent narrative and logic, spontaneously. Though professional wrestling is often thought of as 'fight choreography', it is in fact a complex form of improvisation. Furthermore, I admired the complex embodied negotiation of risk and trust that experienced, trained wrestlers could call upon. On one occasion, I watched G. B., the head coach, take a 'hurricanrana' from a student, a move that involves throwing the opponent by the head, in a turning motion, with one's legs. The trust and care between the wrestlers was impressive in the context of the risk involved in this movement.

While I cannot elaborate every aspect of my research on wrestling here, I argue that the contemporary pro wrestling technique is a form of co-operative embodied politics that developed in response to the seizing of power away from the wrestler by the promoter. Since antiquity, wrestling has been a popular spectacle, with some variant arising in nearly every continent. However, by the Second World War, wrestling spectacles became big business. Promoters discovered that by determining the outcome of the match in advance, they could semi-stage their bouts and satisfy the public hunger for spectacular moves. 'Fixing' wrestling also affected wrestlers' lives by incentivizing physically dangerous moves (leaps and falls or 'bumps'), overtraining and steroid abuse to achieve superhero-type physiques, and creating an economy in which the wrestler is in the most precarious position of all. By training in professional wrestling, learning the moves, wrestling with many different people, I began to see that professional wrestling is a politically-charged affective and sensual physical practice that, above all, seeks pleasure in working together. I found that the 'work' of pro wrestling creates a different type of value – an ethics or politics of openness, friendship and trust – that exists largely outside of strictly economic terms. In other words, because professional wrestling *presents* a simulacrum of violent combat, economic pressures force promoters to demand ever more complex and risky/violent moves, and as a result, wrestlers more and more need to communicate and care for each other in the ring, through their bodies.

This embodied knowledge is political, and specifically, it is a politics of *friendship*. Wrestling is a shared physical language that can operate regardless of one's identity. Wrestlers from around the world can 'work' together, even if they do not share a verbal language. I was particularly struck by the way that, in training, my body was able to communicate with and respond to the bodies of people who were otherwise strangers. In this way, perhaps wrestling is an embodiment of Jacques Derrida's definition of the politics of friendship: 'Let us say yes *to who or what turns up*, before any determination, before any anticipation, before any *identification*' (Derrida 2000: 77). This changed my view of the theatrical form of professional wrestling, which is quite rightly maligned for its often racist, sexist or homophobic content. Seeing past what is represented, I summarized, 'one might therefore read the history of wrestling not as a compendium of the most offensive stereotypes ... but rather as a place where the marginal, the excluded, and the immigrant have found friendship with others through a shared practice' (Chow 2014: 83).

After my ethnographic research on professional wrestling was 'done', and the articles written and submitted, I found that while I intellectually knew I should move on, my body was not yet ready to let go of my training. I began taking the movement vocabulary of professional wrestling into the studio with my collaborator, Tom Wells. I began teaching what I had learnt to Tom, and together we continued to train. Outside the context of the wrestling gym, my training began to produce new meanings and resonances. We explored the synergies between professional wrestling and Contact Improvisation (as well as the embodied politics of each form), creating a unique physical vocabulary. Inspired by the focus on work and labour in professional wrestling we created a dance-theatre piece entitled *Work Songs* set in a modern financial office (Chow and Wells 2013). The piece highlighted the deliberate conflict between the immaterial nature of financial labour (digital numbers on screens) and the material labour of the performing bodies on stage. The addition of new 'theatrical' elements, where actual wrestling moves and holds were embedded within a contemporary dance/Contact Improvisation vocabulary, highlighted aspects of the form I was perhaps unaware of when training in it, such as emotional investment and the experience of time.

Training in wrestling, therefore, was precisely *not* a process where I was drilled into becoming an unthinking and docile body, but one where I came to a new embodied knowledge of the politics of friendship. Wrestling training also enabled a new line of thought in my creative practice. In other words, training *thinks*, creatively, and through the body. In the following section, I will further explore the thinking trained body through my ongoing practice of Olympic Weightlifting.

Weightlifting, Agency and Thinking the Material World

As trained and built bodies are so often considered unthinking, dominated and docile, the example of weightlifting provides a fertile ground to illustrate an investigative methodology that finds agency in gesture, movement and kinaesthetic experience. The practice of fitness has been read as a disciplinary apparatus from multiple perspectives. Historians of physical culture (Budd 1997; Zweiniger-Bargielowska 2010; Jacobs 2011; Tumblety 2012) have primarily focused on the way the discipline was instrumentalized as a tool of the state. Fitness, it is proposed, functions as a 'panoptic' apparatus that enabled personal self-management. For example, Michael Anton Budd suggests that the reader's letters and photographs sent to magazines such as *Sandow's Magazine* and *Physical Culture* opened the letter writer's body to an external gaze, but since the writer could not be sure where the gaze was coming from, like the prisoner in Jeremy Bentham's panopticon, it enforced self-discipline. In sociology, similar perspectives have been applied to practices of fitness and bodybuilding (Maguire 2008; Sassatelli 2010). As Mansfield and McGinn write: 'Foucault's model of the panopticon and what we might call a model of "urban disciplining" can be used to elaborate a contemporary testing of the body in the gym. ... Both dieting and bodybuilding are seen as powerful panoptic technologies producing self monitoring "docile" bodies' (1993: 53). In summary, fitness and physical culture practices are conceived of as a means of training compliant, productive citizens. While these theories are helpful in understanding the role of fitness in circulating certain ideologies (it is certainly true that the ideal of the productive, successful individual in Western society is one who keeps fit), they overlook what embodied or phenomenological experience can tell us.

In September 2014, I find myself Googling 'Olympic Weightlifting Clubs London'. Ostensibly, this is in service of my current research, but this is not my only reason. I have never enjoyed team sports, but I've always enjoyed training and the environment of gyms and am craving a new challenge. Coincidentally, my search returns 'Brunel Weightlifting', a British Weightlifting affiliated club based in the Indoor Athletic Centre (IAC) at Brunel University London. I email the head coach, Mike Pearman, and he invites me to drop by one afternoon. When I get to the IAC, Coach Pearman is there already, doing some presses and squats with light weights on the bar. He is in his seventies (born 1941), and solid through the trunk. I introduce myself and he tells me about the club and his lifters. 'And sometimes I do a bit myself, for my sins', he says. 'Get your kit on and I'll take a look at you.' He asks how old I am. '32', I say. 'I was retired at 32, you know. Just from your age, you know, you'll never snatch bodyweight.' Despite that un-encouraging beginning we run some positions. My mobility surprises him: 'Most men your age can't keep their arms above their head like that in a full squat. You keep at it, you *will* snatch bodyweight.'

Two days later I meet Kristian, one of the team, who will become my coach and friend. Kristian is training himself, but he takes me through the basics, sharing the platform. I perform a snatch for the first time, with the empty bar, and a clean and jerk with maybe 40 kg. Kristian is hitting snatches on 90, or 100. Lewis and Andy, two of the other competitive lifters, are lifting even more. Yet the atmosphere is unintimidating. It's the lifts themselves that scare me. Both involve a kind of magic against gravity.

The first phase ('pull') uses brute strength to get the bar off the ground. In the second, the lifter shrugs and extends through the legs and back to push the bar into the air with the hips. There is a moment when the bar is weightless in the air, and in that fraction of a second, you must dive under the bar to 'catch it'. And then you have to stand up. The movement is so complex, the attrition rate for weightlifting is extremely high: 'Most guys never come back after the first session', Kristian says. Several years later, weightlifting is a defining part of my identity. Training four times a week, on average for nearly two hours, I effectively spend an entire day each week picking things up and putting them down. I have lifted at clubs in London, Newcastle, Vancouver, Montréal, Minneapolis, Austin, Hamburg and New York City, sometimes playing hooky from academic conferences to do so. I have shared platforms with students, Broadway actors and professors of political philosophy. I have sometimes eaten two dinners in an evening and gone to bed hungry.

Above all, I have found what the anthropologists Jean Lave and Etienne Wenger (1991) call a 'community of practice', that is, a community defined not according to identity but affiliated by participation in a craft. I lift with people whom I know little else about (sometimes not even their names), yet there is an intimacy to this relation (as with professional wrestling) that comes with sharing embodied knowledge. Observing my own body's adaptations to the rigours and demands of the practice has in some ways produced a greater sense of embodied agency.

Yet, how does a practice with a very small repertoire of movements produce 'agency'? After all, mastering the difficult gestures of weightlifting would seem to reveal the success of discipline's hold on the body. However, mastery must be understood dialectically with the unruliness of the body produced by training. In my field notes, I record instances of overcoming and conquering the bar, but there are also copious instances in which my body seems to escape my control. It requires constant maintenance – twice-daily sessions of stretching and foam rolling to ward off back pain and stiffness. There are complaints and injury – not being able to lift a weight that was easy the previous day, a slight tightness in the calf that defeats me. 'Don't worry about it,' Kristian tells me when a light weight seems to be impossible during my warm up, 'it could be anything. It'll feel different every day'. This experience of the unruly and unmastered body, experienced synchronously with cultivating the body, 'speaks back' to the social conditioning produced by training.

In her book, *Agency and Embodiment*, the theorist Carrie Noland suggests that 'kinaesthetic experience, produced by acts of embodied gesturing, places pressure on the conditioning a body receives, encouraging variations in performance that account for larger innovations in cultural practice that cannot otherwise be explained' (Noland 2009: 2–3). Therefore, while training inscribes patterns of movement onto the body, it also enables the embodied subject to *re-experience* these patterns of movement. Noland concludes that perhaps 'it is only through repetition, and not acquisition, that we gain the experience to separate momentarily from our social roles' (194). Discussing Judith Butler's concept of gender as an accumulation of performances, she asks: 'what if in performing the curtsy the subject felt not only "feminine" but also sore? What if the socially established meaning of the act were overwhelmed, at least momentarily, by the somatic experiences of pressure, friction, and pain? What if, in other words, the body spoke back?' (194). When participating in the vital and dynamic practice of weightlifting, I am constantly reminded of Noland's phenomenological methodology (which itself draws on the works of Marcel Mauss, Maurice Merleau-Ponty and André Leroi-Gourhan, among others). The lived experience of repetition, in training, while building towards what might be thought of as uniformity – the ability to consistently repeat a movement – actually produces *difference* and *variation*, since kinaesthetic experience is rarely uniform day to day, moment to moment, body to body.

This, I think, is how the trained body 'thinks': it encounters technique, in a particular place, on a particular day, with other particular bodies, and in this singular encounter (or *performance*) there is a multiplicity of meaning – the body works against its ingrained techniques and habitus, producing its own frictions, the navigation of which produces for me a feeling of physical agency. While the actual movement of the snatch or clean and jerk never varies, the performance of the script indeed does, through variations in inflection, attitude, excess, force and dynamics. Training with the Brunel Weightlifting Club after one very long Thursday afternoon, I begin missing lifts, feeling the weight as much heavier than the previous training session. Mike, the head coach, tells me: 'Be more *adventurous* with your snatch. Don't worry about getting it right. You're not a beginner anymore, you can afford to be a bit more daring.' So, I *dare*. I get the lift. What has changed? An inflection, an attitude? Perhaps a form of embodied agency catalysed by the experience of friction.

If the object of embodied thought for professional wrestling is the politics of bodies working together in empathy and friendship, what weightlifting 'thinks about' is the relationship between the subject and the material world. After all, weightlifting is basically about lifting things up and putting them back down, and, in doing so, lifters develop an interesting relationship to the things of weightlifting: barbells and plates. Several schools of thought, such as Object Oriented Ontology (OOO) or Bruno Latour's 'actor-network theory', posit an equality between subject and object. Objects, like people, perform or act. Weightlifting, more so than many other sports, evidences the object's agency. The central props in the performance, the bars and plates, are 'scriptive' in the sense used by Robin Bernstein: they demand or encourage performances (Bernstein 2009: 69). But the very nature of these objects – their mass and weight – means that they always threaten to reassert their 'thingness'. The philosopher Martin Heidegger distinguishes between 'objects' and 'things'; an object is a thing that has a function or socially determined value; whereas things are objects that become more 'present' to us through their breakdown or misuse. Bars or plates are objects whose social value *is* their thingness; in other words, we use them because they threaten to defeat us.

Mastering a lift feels like fluently working *with* the world. Failure makes the world present again. After a difficult session in February 2015, I wrote:

> I missed one clean then made the second, only to jerk up and hit myself in the face with the bar while doing it. I wasn't hurt, but I was shocked. I was using all my force to jerk the bar upwards and the millisecond it collided with my chin it was almost as if I was thrown back into myself. (Field notes, 4 February 2015)

In other words, whereas training in wrestling makes me think about my relationship to other bodies, training in weightlifting makes me think about my relationship to the material world; my own presence and being.

Researching Training: Critical and Creative Challenges

In the two examples given, I have established that the trained body thinks, or, more practically, that (physical) training produces embodied knowledge. To conclude this chapter, I want to outline some critical and creative challenges that one might face when researching training.

Ethnography and ethics: The most practical method of researching training is through 'ethnography', a methodology most commonly associated with anthropology and sociology that attempts to describe a people or a way of life. Ethnography is also an ethical and theoretical minefield. After all, the first ethnographies were made during Empire, via armchair analysis of travel writing and colonial documents, in order to understand and study the 'native' population. Ethnography still carries that whiff of academic colonialism. However, beginning with Bronisław Malinowski (a pioneer of fieldwork-based ethnography), anthropologists have wrestled with these questions of self and other. For example, Clifford Geertz acknowledges that the ethnographer is part of the process. In his essay on 'thick description', he describes a hypothetical series of winks, each with its own separate intention and motivation (Geertz 1973: 5–7). This highly theatrical example demonstrates that the same bodily action signifies in three different ways according to a cultural script. Therefore, the fieldworker must learn to interpret a phenomenon (even a tiny bodily gesture such as a wink) according to the 'native' frame of reference, rather than her own.

This is what is called the 'ontological turn' in anthropology. According to Liana Chua, the ontological turn seeks to 'apprehend ethnographic phenomena, however bizarre or counterintuitive, on their own (ontic) terms' (Chua 2015: 643). In other words, the ethnographer's job is to acknowledge the inadequacy of his/her own concepts in making sense of the lives of others. However, as Chua argues, this is also ethically problematic, since in attempting to privilege the native experience or voice, the ethnographer can actually ignore the understanding that can come from her relations, friendships and affiliations with her subjects. More importantly, it might arrest the understanding that comes with being transformed by these relations (Chua 2015: 645). Chua instead proposes a relational model of anthropology, which she calls co-presence, similar to what Dwight Conquergood calls 'co-performative witnessing', defined as being 'radically engaged and committed, body-to-body, in the field … a politics of the body deeply in action with Others' (Madison 2007: 826). This relational model of ethnography, for me, is most helpful in navigating the ethical pitfalls of ethnography when researching training. By focusing so strongly on bodies together in shared time, engaging in shared activities, it is also quite close to the experience of the theatre event. In this mode of fieldwork, ethnography becomes a process of what might be called 'deep getting stuck in', involving oneself with a practice, a community, a place, with all attendant transformations that arise from it.

Self-reflection and objectivity: Researching embodied knowledge involves a strong degree of self-reflection, which brings with it questions of objectivity. How do I know that my reading of professional wrestling as an embodied politics of friendship is shared by anyone else? What if other weightlifters do not think of bars and plates as things to be reckoned with? How do we deal with the subjectivity of the researcher? One solution to the problem of the self-reflection and objectivity is to 'triangulate' your research. Indeed, this is what I have done in both my projects, and it simply means that the researcher compares his/her own interpretation of the experience against the experience of others (in the form of reflections gathered through interviews, for example) and the conceptualizations of other scholars (for example, in published research). For my project on wrestling, I kept detailed field notes and wrote up my own self-reflections on my embodied experience, but also conducted a number of recorded but unstructured interviews with other wrestlers. I compared these interpretations to other research on professional wrestling from performance studies, history, and media and cultural studies.

Documentation and 'field notes': Field notes are the ethnographer's stock in trade, forming the 'data' that is then coded and interpreted in their finished publications. But traditional written field notes, which describe experience, are often quite inadequate for capturing the embodied and visceral experiences of physical training. Furthermore, since training is quite a repetitive process, it can sometimes seem like the researcher is describing the same scene over and over again. Here, I think creative tools are valuable. Video is useful in capturing intense moments of training, and the process of editing can be a way of reflecting upon and interpreting experience. The techniques that you have trained in can also be experimented with and explored in new ways via creative studio work (as in my project *Work Songs*). Digital technologies and social media provide a useful means of capturing experiences in the moment; in my current project, I use the platform Instagram extensively to document moments of training. By tagging the videos and images, I participate in a digital culture of other weightlifters who do the same, so my ethnographic project is simultaneously a form of 'digital ethnography'.

Conclusion: Making Thinking

When I trained as an actor, I worked on a scene from John Patrick Shanley's strange and brutal comic-drama about family dysfunction, *Beggars in the House of Plenty.* I played Johnny, a young writer, who, in the play's fantastical final scene, encounters his violent and abusive father (known as 'Pop') as a kind of demon. My friend Giles (who was a year younger than me) played Pop. We struggled with the difficult dialogue ('I look like the Bronx inside. I could vomit up a burning car'), the blunt declarations of emotion ('We could have loved each other'). The scene fell flat again and again; we had no idea what we were doing on stage. We retreated to cod-psychology. This was so Freudian, wasn't it? We played it like fathers and sons we'd seen in movies, we thought about motivations and objectives and Stanislavski, but again and again our teacher, Nancy, would shout 'get out of your head!'. One night, nearing the day we were to present the scene, we are yet again in the middle of a flat and awkward run. When I speak my line – 'I'll never think of you without being shocked by your lovelessness' – Giles does something he never has before. He hugs me. And then, with a kind of smug, patronizing smile befitting the character of Pop, he pats my cheek. In an instant, I reach out and slap him across the face – not hard, but hard enough to demand a reaction. Giles starts grinning and so do I, and we start roughhousing on the studio floor, again, not really violent, but not controlled, either. Nancy lets it go on for a second and then says – 'From there! Say your lines!'. We finish the scene, breathing heavily, and for the first time letting go of the false characterizations (no more fake teenager or puffed-up fifty-something). 'OK', Nancy says, when we finish, 'we can start working from here.'

I'm not going to pretend the scene was any good when we performed it a few weeks later. We still had no idea how to work with the text. But it was transformed. The wrestling became a warm up for us before we ran the scene, and through this embodied practice we built a trust and physical responsiveness to the other that carried into how we worked together on stage. This is what Nancy meant when she said, 'get out of your head' – the familiar dictum of acting teachers does not mean 'don't think', but rather, 'think through the body'. The embodied practice became a way of thinking through a difficult piece of dramatic writing, but it was also a way of thinking a relation, a friendship, a politics of working with the other that I only became fully cognizant of when training, over nearly ten years later, in professional wrestling.

My aim in this chapter has been to challenge the idea that the trained and drilled body responds automatically and unthinkingly. As I have argued, training is a way of thinking about the world, whether that is other bodies or material things. Although my examples, wrestling and weightlifting, have been drawn from outside the field of what we might typically consider 'theatre and performance', I encourage the reader to apply this framing to more established forms of training within the theatre industry. By reframing theatre training such as acting, voice or movement as ways of thinking, we might encourage a shift towards reconceptualizing them as forms of creative or even critical thinking. Acting might be a way of thinking through social situations and power relations; voice might be an embodied way of thinking critically about gender and its performance; and movement could be a way of creatively challenging colonizing gestures and choreographies. In this way, the thinking trained body might overcome some unhelpful binaries in theatre and performance studies: training and study, conservatoire and university, practice and theory.

Further Reading

Spatz (2015) is an excellent resource for researcher-practitioners, practitioner-researchers, artist-scholars or any other articulation of those self-reflexively engaging with practice and research (PaR). The book offers an epistemology of embodied technique *as* knowledge, and contributes to the discussion of practice-as-research in the university (while remaining critical of how PaR has been conceptualized thus far). Noland (2009), a scholar of French Modernist poetry, might be an unlikely figure to write about gesture, but as a former dancer and practitioner of yoga, she brings her knowledge of embodied technique to her readings of the philosophy of movement and the body. The book concerns how bodies make meaning, and importantly to anyone studying training, she suggests that repetition can be the impetus for difference.

References

Bernstein, Robin (2009), 'Dancing with Things: Material Culture and the Performance of Race', *Social Text*, 101, 27: (4), 67–94.
Bourdieu, Pierre (1984), *Distinction: A Social Critique of the Judgement of Taste*, Cambridge: Harvard University Press.
Budd, Michael Anton (1997), *The Sculpture Machine: Physical Culture and Body Politics in the Age of Empire*, New York: New York University Press.

Chow, Broderick, and Tom Wells (2013), *Work Songs*, available online: https://vimeo.com/59583569 (accessed 30 November 2017).

Chow, Broderick D. V. (2014), 'Work and Shoot: Professional Wrestling and Embodied Politics', *TDR/The Drama Review*, 58 (2): 72–86.

Chua, Liana (2015), 'Troubled Landscapes, Troubling Anthropology: Co-presence, Necessity, and the Making of Ethnographic Knowledge', *Journal of the Royal Anthropological Institute*, 21, 641–59.

Cole, C. L., Giardina, Michael and David L. Andrews (2004), 'Michel Foucault: Studies of Power and Sport', in Richard Giulianotti (ed.), *Sport and Modern Social Theorists*, 207–23, Basingstoke: Palgrave Macmillan.

Derrida, Jacques, and Anne Dufourmantelle (2000), *Of Hospitality*, trans. R. Bowlby, Stanford: Stanford University Press.

Evans, Mark (2009), *Movement Training for the Modern Actor*, London: Routledge.

Foster, Susan Leigh (1997), 'Dancing Bodies', in Jane C. Desmond (ed.), *Meaning in Motion: New Cultural Studies of Dance*, 235–69, Durham and London: Duke University Press.

Foucault, Michel (1977), *Discipline and Punish: The Birth of the Prison*, New York: Vintage Books.

Foucault, Michel (1980), *Power/Knowledge: Selected Interviews and Other Writings*, New York: Random House.

Geertz, Clifford (1973), *The Interpretation of Cultures*, New York: Basic Books.

Jacobs, Wilson Chacko (2011), *Working Out Egypt: Effendi Masculinity and Subject Formation in Colonial Modernity, 1870–1940*, Durham: Duke University Press.

Lave, Jean, and Etienne Wenger (1991), *Situated Learning*, Cambridge: Cambridge University Press.

Madison, D. Soyini (2007), 'Co-performative Witnessing', *Cultural Studies*, 21 (6): 826–31.

Maguire, Jennifer Smith (2008), *Fit for Consumption: Sociology and the Business of Fitness*, London: Routledge.

Mansfield, Alan, and Barb McGinn (1993), 'Pumping Irony: The Muscular and the Feminine', in Sue Scott and David Morgan (eds), *Body Matters: Essays on the Sociology of the Body*, 49–68, London: The Falmer Press.

Markula, Pirkko, and Richard Pringle (2006), *Foucault, Sport and Exercise: Power, Knowledge and Transforming the Self*, London: Routledge.

Noland, Carrie (2009), *Agency and Embodiment*, Cambridge: Harvard University Press.

Sassatelli, Roberta (2010), *Fitness Culture: Gyms and the Commercialisation of Discipline and Fun*, Basingstoke: Palgrave Macmillan.

Spatz, Ben (2015), *What a Body Can Do: Technique as Knowledge, Practice as Research*, London: Routledge.

Tumblety, Joan (2012), *Remaking the Male Body: Masculinity and the Uses of Physical Culture in Interwar and Vichy France*, Oxford: Oxford University Press.

Wacquant, Loïc (2006), *Body and Soul: Notebooks of an Apprentice Boxer*, Oxford: Oxford University Press.

Zweiniger-Bargielowska, Ina (2010), *Managing the Body: Beauty, Health, and Fitness in Britain, 1880–1939*, Oxford: Oxford University Press.

11 How Does Theatre Think Through Work?

THERON SCHMIDT

So, you want to work in theatre. But what kind of 'work' is this? The task of the actor has long been a subject of scepticism, and often scorn, accused of being not real work: either it is 'not real', in that it is only pretending or simulation, or it is 'not work', in that it is merely the pursuit of pleasure. Plato, for example, famously banned actors from his ideal Republic, on the grounds that their mimetic talents perpetuated false knowledge and appealed to base emotions; and several centuries later, Jean-Jacques Rousseau similarly saw no place for theatre in the modern state, likening it to a prostitution of the self: 'What is the profession of the actor? It is a trade in which he performs for money, submits himself to the disgrace and the affronts that others buy the right to give him, and puts his person publicly on sale' ([1758] 1960: 79). Such an 'antitheatrical prejudice', as Jonas Barish (1981) has exhaustively catalogued it, persists to the present in the ridiculed caricature of the theatrical 'luvvie': histrionic, self-indulgent and parasitical on public funds.

Explicitly or implicitly working against these negative views, theatre innovators in the Western tradition have often sought to legitimate the theatre as serious work. For example, in developing his 'biomechanical' principles for the efficient use of the actor's body, Vsevolod Meyerhold took inspiration from Taylorism, the scientific management of the factory assembly line (see Gordon 1974); and Antonin Artaud described the actor as a 'heart athlete' who must work unrelentingly to develop what he called an 'affective musculature' ([1935] 1993: 94). Most influentially, Konstantin Stanislavski designed his 'system' for acting to counteract the histrionic excesses of melodramatic acting and bring consistency and repeatability to performances: 'an actor of our type is obliged to work so much more than others', he wrote (Stanislavski [1936] 1980: 16). Stanislavski's system has informed subsequent 'methods' from teachers such as Eric Meisner, Lee Strasberg and Stella Adler, who developed exercises for acting as a systematic and rigorous labour. In turn, their followers have cast this work as 'craft', a term that has been popularized in the titles of innumerable acting programmes and manuals, and echoed in the words of any aspiring actor who has learnt to refer to their vocation as 'working on my craft'. Thinking of theatre as work helps to distance it from its association with pretence, falsehood and self-indulgence, and instead shape it as a form of self-discipline, self-management and professional training (see Chow 2013).

But in thinking through its own work, theatre can also help us to think through how work is understood and valued in culture more broadly. In this chapter, I will focus on two moments in which theatre seems to have been particularly interested in its relationship to work, and in which, by turn, we can track the changing nature of work itself. In the 1960s and 1970s, performance artists turned to 'task-like' or 'work-like' performance as a way to bring everyday reality to the theatrical event – and, by extension, to remedy the way in which wider culture was perceived as increasingly detached and 'theatricalized'. Here, the apparent 'realness' and 'authenticity' of work-like performance is positioned in contrast to the increasing alienation and disembodiment of everyday life. But in subsequent decades, the nature of work itself has undergone a gradual but irreversible shift, such that its paradigmatic figure is no longer the factory worker (or the craftsperson), but instead the service provider, who is a kind of 'emotional labourer' whose work is very similar to that of the actor. Here again, new forms of theatre, such as immersive and one-to-one theatre, emerge as a challenge to the theatricality of everyday life. I will explore these themes through a comparison of how two artists from very different periods, Yvonne Rainer in the 1960s and Adrian Howells in the 2000s, used their creative practice to think through questions of work, alienation and everyday life.

Yvonne Rainer and Task-Based Performance

Guy Debord's 1967 diagnosis of 'the society of the spectacle' presented a scathing diagnosis of contemporary culture at that time, and one that continues to resonate to the present day. Debord argued that we live in a culture mediated by the logic of the spectacle, which has taken the place of true relations between people and which has become so thoroughly naturalized that we only recognize our desires when they are presented to us as images: 'All that once was directly lived has become mere representation', Debord writes ([1967] 1994: 12). His critique of spectacle is a critique of a society that has become theatricalized ('*spectacle*' is the French term for theatre), in which our everyday experience has become a proliferation of simulation and 'pseudo-events' (114). What remedy might be offered by artistic practices? Can the artistic sphere be constituted as an oppositional space in which unmediated experience might be possible? To do so would require artists to overcome the mediation of theatre itself – something Debord had suggested a decade previously in founding the Situationist International, advocating the proliferation of the 'situations' from which this movement derived its name: 'The construction of situations begins on the other side of the modern collapse of the idea of the theater' ([1957] 2002: 47).

It's in this context that the idea of 'work' comes to be of interest within theatre and performance practices. Various artists during this period experimented with physical tasks as a way of circumventing the 'pretence' of theatre, and its mimetic distance from 'real' experience, through the literal (rather than representational) execution of tasks and actions. Allan Kaprow's 'Happenings', for example, which gained prominence following his *18 Happenings in 6 Parts* (1959), sought to explore what Kaprow would later describe as 'lifelike art' as opposed to 'artlike art'. 'The line between the Happening and daily life should be kept as fluid and perhaps indistinct as possible', Kaprow argued, and he orchestrated and championed events that shared a set of features that blurred these boundaries: they were not dependent upon designated places (such as theatres); they were continuous with activities of life itself; they involved unrehearsed actions executed by non-performers; and they sought to avoid representation in favour of simply 'doing' (Kaprow [1966] 2003: 62–4). Happenings tested a form of performance that can be distinguished from 'acting', as Michael Kirby (1972: 3) observed at the time: 'Acting means to feign, to simulate, to represent, to impersonate,' he writes; however, '[a]s Happenings demonstrated, not all performing is acting'. More recently, Carol Martin has described these forms of non-representational performance in relation to the emergence of what she calls the 'theatre of the real': 'Kaprow and those influenced by him made performances not by acting, but by performing a series of tasks, nontransformational scores of movement, gesture, and voice' (2013: 27).

The form of the task-based performance was useful not only to develop forms of performance distinct from representational acting, but also as a way of opposing the alienation of everyday life by reconnecting the physical body with its material environment. Inspired by George Brecht, the Fluxus International movement proliferated the form of the 'event score': open-ended instructions whose literal functionality resists interpretation or meaning: '250 nails are hammered', 'Keep walking intently', or 'Hit a wall with your head', to pick a few one-line examples from scores by Tomas Schmit, Takehisa Kosugi and Yoko Ono (Friedman et al. 2002: 91, 74, 86). As Hannah Higgins observes, these scores encouraged an attention to one's cultural and physical surroundings: 'Far from being cynical and alienating', Higgins writes, 'the Fluxus experience, in its matter-of-factness, situates people radically within their corporeal, sensory worlds' (2002: 67). They are 'emancipatory', Higgins argues, 'not because they construct political ideologies but rather because they provide contexts ... for primary experiences' (58). Another pioneer of task-based performance was dance-maker Anna Halprin, who used repetitive physical tasks, such as sweeping the floor over and over, and responsive scores as a way of exploring the capacities of the performer's physical body in relation to her environment (see Worth and Poynor 2004). 'In doing these tasks we were not playing roles or creating moods; we simply did something', Halprin recollected (Rainer [1965] 1995: 143).

Directly influenced by Halprin and Kaprow, the dance work made by Yvonne Rainer in the 1960s can be located within this approach to task-based performance – although as I will describe, it also departs from it in interesting ways. In her 1965 *Parts of Some Sextets*, for example, Rainer asked dancers to interact with unwieldy mattresses, such that the sheer effort required to manipulate their bulky, awkward materiality prohibited embellishment or pretence on the part of the performers. Writing at the time, Rainer described this work in similar terms as Halprin above: 'undynamic movement, no rhythm, no emphasis, no tension, no relaxation. You just *do* it, with the coordination of a pro and the non definition of an amateur' (1965: 170). Such a work is consistent with what Carrie Lambert-Beatty has described as a kind of 'literal, physical *thereness*', with which dance from this period is associated (2008: 4). This association is thanks in no small part to an afterthought Rainer appended to her written reflections on *Parts of Some Sextets*, which subsequently has been celebrated under the name (given to it by others) of the 'No Manifesto':

> NO to spectacle no to virtuosity no to transformations and magic and make-believe no to the glamour and transcendence of the star image no to the heroic no to the anti-heroic no to trash imagery no to involvement of performer or spectator no to style no to camp no to seduction of spectator by the wiles of the performer no to eccentricity no to moving or being moved. (Rainer 1965: 178)

It's not hard to see this as an attack on the alienation and mediation of spectacle, easily placed next to Debord's critique of the 'society of the spectacle' that would be articulated two years later. Rainer herself made this connection between the 'spectacle' of the theatre and the spectacularization of culture in the programme notes for her next performance piece, *The Mind is a Muscle* ([1968] 1974), in which she describes her own 'horror and disbelief upon seeing a Vietnamese shot dead on TV – not at the sight of death, however, but at the fact that the TV can be shut off afterwards as after a bad Western'. The performance event is situated in opposition to this state of affairs, foregrounding the physicality and co-presence of the performer: 'My body remains the enduring reality.'

And yet, there is an important difference between the resistance to spectacle advocated by someone like Kaprow, in which the lines between art and life are blurred, and the approach taken by Rainer, who continues to make dance that exists to be watched by an audience (and who later moves into filmmaking). In this way, Rainer can be seen as using spectacle to engage with spectacle; or, to take the terms of this collection, using spectacle to *think through spectacle*. As Elise Archias argues, 'Rainer's performance practice "worked through" questions of spectacle by resembling the forms and structures of life in spectacle culture' (2016: 23). This 'working through' of spectacle is epitomized in one of Rainer's most influential works, *Trio A*, which premiered as a work-in-progress in 1966 and was presented in 1968 as the central element of *The Mind is a Muscle*. In a reflective analysis written during the time of the work's making, Rainer argues that traditional dance operates in the field of the production of images, which, as with Debord, is a field of alienation from which Rainer wishes to withdraw. For Rainer, the challenge to avoid this spectacular dance was, as with her so-called 'No Manifesto', one of negation: how do you create a dance that is without climax? What would dance be if it did not have moments of virtuosity, of extremity, of seduction?

In order to explain the effect that she was after, Rainer presented an extended comparison with minimalist sculpture of the period, which, through its use of unadorned materials and relatively simple shapes and surfaces, emphasized the 'literal, physical *thereness*' of the object (to recall Lambert-Beatty's phrase earlier). For example, if minimalist sculpture sought to eliminate or minimize 'texture', 'figure reference' and 'illusionism', then in her dance, Rainer sought to eliminate, respectively, 'variation and dynamics', 'character' and 'performance' ([1966] 1968). And where minimal sculpture emphasizes 'nonreferential forms' and 'literalness', Rainer would substitute 'neutral performance' and 'task or tasklike activity' (263). In the body of her essay, she explains her interest in 'task' as oriented towards the achievement of 'movement-as-object' (269), and her use of repetition is intended to 'objectify' movement, to 'make it more objectlike' (271). Rainer writes:

> the 'problem' of performance was dealt with by never permitting the performers to confront the audience. Either the gaze was averted or the head was engaged in movement. The desired effect was a worklike rather than exhibitionlike presentation. (271)

The resulting work, *Trio A*, although only about four-and-a-half minutes long, has gone on to be Rainer's 'most reproduced and reproducible dance' (Lambert-Beatty 2008: 159), a 'signature work' that has influenced generations of performance makers with its matter-of-fact sequence of continuous movement: arms circling, head rolling and the body twisting, crouching, balancing and rolling on the floor, each action morphing into the next without any apparent motif or choreographic structure. (A short excerpt from a 1978 film is available online; see Rainer et al. 1978.)

Pat Catterson, who would later dance *Trio A* in some of its iterations, described her initial response to seeing Rainer perform by comparing it to other kinds of labour:

> It was like watching the ease, calm attention to detail, elegance, efficiency, and flow of someone doing anything in life that is practiced and familiar. It was like seeing my

mother make a bed, or a cobbler fix a pair of shoes, or a store clerk ring up and bag your groceries, or someone fold her laundry and noting the beauty of that doing, that performing. (2009: 4)

Here, then, in Rainer's 'task or tasklike activity' and 'worklike rather than exhibitionlike presentation', is a resonance with the 'series of tasks' and 'nontransformational scores' of Kaprow and his contemporaries. However, there's an important difference in what Rainer is doing: her performance may be *like* making a bed, or folding laundry, but it is not the same kind of task as these. Whereas Happenings and Fluxus scores might incorporate everyday actions into performance, *Trio A* takes the same 'tasklike' aesthetic but applies it to a very specific kind of labour: dance. It is not 'on the other side' of theatre (as in Debord's description) – not turning the theatre into some other kind of event – but very much remains a piece of displayed performance, aware of being watched. Rather than an art that disappears into life – 'the sublation of art in the praxis of life', as Peter Bürger ([1974] 1984: 51) described the goal of the historic avant-garde – here the everyday is absorbed completely into the 'work' of art – the sublation of life into the praxis of art.

The work of Rainer and her contemporaries has been described as 'pedestrian movement' (see Banes 1987), in that none of the individual actions appear to require any particular virtuosic skill and could theoretically be performed by anyone; but its precise sequence of continuous momentum, never resolving into a single image, is deceptively challenging to achieve, as scholar (and self-described non-dancer) Julia Bryan-Wilson found when she joined a class being taught *Trio A* by Rainer herself:

it turns out that most of our received ideas about this dance are slightly misleading; it is not full of 'everyday' actions (for instance, it includes a free handstand in the middle of the room, and balance *en demi pointe* while wearing tennis shoes). Rather, it is exhausting, it is strenuous, it is very physically challenging, and Rainer has incredibly precise ideas about the ways the body needs to configure itself, where exactly the gaze should land, how even the fingers should be positioned. (2012: 59)

In her writing, Rainer is aware of the contradictions in her work – indeed, the contradictions in its very work-like-ness. Though she aspired to a 'worklike' rather than 'exhibitionlike' presentation, she recognizes that the performance is nonetheless an orchestrated display: although this work is different from previous dance in that any 'body' can do it, it is not the case that the performers are simply 'being themselves'. In the same piece of writing, she acknowledges the artifice within her method: 'I have exposed a type of effort where it has been traditionally concealed and have concealed phrasing where it has been traditionally displayed' (Rainer [1966] 1968: 271).

In this way, Rainer created what Catherine Wood has described as 'theatre with a "process" look', a carefully constructed aesthetic that stages the work of making theatre itself (2007: 20). Such a look can be seen in subsequent iterations of contemporary theatre that work to avoid mimetic representation in favour of showing the work of performance itself: think of the self-reflexive commentary of Forced Entertainment, evident even in the titles of such productions as *Showtime* (1996) or *Dirty Work* (1998); or the use of processual tasks in The Wooster Group (see Auslander 1985; Quick 2007); or the incorporation of pedestrian movement and re-enactment in Goat Island, who cite Rainer as a direct influence (see Bottoms and Goulish 2007: 69–70); or performance works such as Quarantine's *Entitled*, in which the work of the stagehands and production team are visible (see Schmidt 2013). In this lineage of post-1960s performance the labour of mimesis is made explicit.

Adrian Howells and Affective Labour

We have seen how artists in the 1960s and 1970s sought to use work and work-like action as a way to overcome the problem of representation and imitation – the 'problem of "performance"', as Rainer put it. I have argued that Rainer's *Trio A* presents a distinctive form of engagement with the idea of work, using the theatrical event as a site to work through issues of spectacle and theatricality more broadly. However, in the following decades, the nature of work itself has changed, and with it the potential relationship of theatre practices to wider economies. Such a change was tracked in the 1980s by an in-depth sociological study of the training and workplace behaviour of airline flight attendants, conducted by Arlie Hochschild in her influential work, *The Managed Heart: Commercialization of Human Feeling* ([1983] 2003). Hochschild noted that the tasks of the airline steward included not only physical and mental tasks, but something additional, which Hochschild would call 'emotional labour', and which was different from the demands on traditional workers – for example, a boy in a factory that manufactures wallpaper:

> In the case of the flight attendant, the emotional style of offering the service *is part of the service itself*, in a way that loving or hating wallpaper is not a part of producing wallpaper. Seeming to 'love the job' becomes part of the job; and actually trying to love it, and to enjoy the customers, helps the worker in this effort. (5–6)

As Hochschild observed, this work is double in its nature: in order to produce a desired emotional quality in customers – 'the sense of being cared for in a convivial and safe place', in the case of the flight attendant – the worker must also learn to regulate his or her own emotions (6–7). Although Hochschild does not refer explicitly to Marx, her observations recall Marx's influential analysis of alienation, which describes how, under capitalism, one becomes alienated from one's labour (and one's own life-activity) as a result of having to sell it as a commodity. In the case of the boy in the wallpaper factory, she notes that the boy's arm becomes part of the apparatus itself. By extension, Hochschild asks, what happens 'when the managing of emotions comes to be sold as labor?' (19) – and her analysis goes on to describe the negative effects of estrangement from one's own emotions, and indeed the sense in which, once we are selling them to others, we might no longer be able even to call them our 'own' emotions.

Hochschild's observations about the capacity to separate emotions from autonomous experience – to manufacture them, buy them and sell them – anticipated what has subsequently been theorized as 'affect'. This concept calls attention to our emotional and sensory experiences as significant elements of our everyday experiences of self, but also notes the ways in which those experiences are produced by (and productive within) flows and networks that exceed the autonomous self; they are 'visceral forces beneath, alongside, or generally *other than* conscious knowing' (Seigworth and Gregg 2010: 1). Hochschild's analysis of 'emotional labour' also anticipated what has more recently been characterized as 'affective labour' or (more broadly) 'immaterial labour', as in these definitions from Michael

Hardt and Antonio Negri: 'labour that produces an immaterial good, such as a service, a cultural product, knowledge, or communication', and which is 'involved in communication, cooperation, and the production and reproduction of affects' (2000: 290, 53). This shift in what constitutes work, flagged by Hochschild within specific service industries, now extends across most of contemporary economies to the extent that we hardly even notice it: it's not just flight attendants who have to 'love their job', but all of us who are expected to invest emotionally and affectively in our work, not only in order to do our job better, but to do our job at all.

The idea of the manufacture and circulation of relationships and feelings, and indeed the idea that such production might disappear and become invisible, is of course a familiar way of thinking about the theatre, particularly in the theatrical tradition that foregrounds psychologically realistic characters or behaviours, where 'good' acting is that in which we don't see the effort involved. Erin Hurley makes this connection explicit in her description of the 'feeling-labour' of theatre: 'the work theatre does in making, managing and moving feeling in all its types (affect, emotions, moods, sensations) in a publicly observable display that is sold to an audience for a wage' (2010: 9). And conversely, it should be little surprise that performance is evoked as a metaphor to describe this immaterial, affective labour. For example, Paolo Virno describes the proliferation of what he calls 'virtuosic labour', by which he means:

> an activity which finds its own fulfilment (that is, its own purpose) in itself, without objectifying itself into an end product, without settling into a 'finished product,' or into an object which would survive the performance. Secondly, it is an activity which requires the presence of others, which exists only in the presence of an audience. (2004: 52)

Given these synergies between wider economies and theatre practices, what critical or imaginative role might theatre and performance play? In what ways might contemporary artists echo Rainer in saying 'no to virtuosity', and also 'no to virtuosic labour'? As Nicholas Ridout suggests: 'precisely because it is a part, rather than a reflection, of this [service] economy, it becomes possible for performance to enact some kind of critique of its procedures' (2009: 128). If work looks more and more like performance, then performance, paradoxically, might be a place to interrogate, amplify and repurpose these tendencies – the manufacture of affect, the production and commodification of emotion, and the on-demand fabrication of relationality.

As described above, Erin Hurley argues that the production of emotion has been central to the function of theatre across its history: 'theatre exists to perform crucial and necessary feeling-labour' (2010: 38). Such a correlation spans historical periods and theatrical conventions. Nevertheless, recent trends have accentuated the relational and affective dimensions of performance by leaving behind the theatrical auditorium in favour of such configurations as site-specific, immersive and one-to-one performance. For Rachel Zerihan and Maria Chatzichristodoulou this tendency corresponds to an increasing feeling of isolation and disconnection – itself an affective production symptomatic of the times:

> Immersing oneself in an arresting, engaging, provocative encounter, where even the form (appears to) promise attention and presence can, momentarily, buffer sensed isolation and disparity. The potential of this opportunity enables a shared desire to connect, engage and discover an other, elucidating a critical opportunity offered through the ephemeral liveness of live art: its aptitude for delivering relational experiences. (2012: 5)

There are echoes here with the 1960s: just as the emergence of 'situations', Happenings, and task-based performance can be placed in relation to the alienating effects of mass television and the 'society of the spectacle', so can the desire for 'liveness' and 'relational experiences' be placed in relation to the pervasive effects of online culture and the increasing commodification of emotion in affective labour. This relationship is an ambivalent one: it is possible to conceive immersive and one-to-one forms of performance in opposition to the commodification of feeling, but one could also see their popularity as merely one more symptom of the service economy. As I argued in relation to Yvonne Rainer, one aspect of the *work* of the artist, then, is to negotiate the relationship between art and the theatricalization of everyday life, which I will think through in relation to the artist Adrian Howells.

Howells was a UK performance maker who began his career at Glasgow's Citizens Theatre and later performed with Nigel Charnock's dance and physical theatre company (for a full survey of Howells's life and career, see Heddon and Johnson 2016). But from 2003 to his death in 2014, he focused on interactive experiences, and has been described as 'a trail blazer in the field of intimate performance practice' (Heddon 2014: 418). In interviews, Howells described this transition as one motivated by a desire to achieve a greater level of intimacy and connection than could be had in a traditional theatre set-up: 'how do you have an intimate relationship with 700 people at the same time? So I thought, what if we just chuck the 699 other people out of the room, and try to focus on one person at a time' (Johnson 2013: 179). But he also described this move as a response to the demands of what we might recognize as the 'feeling-labour' of performing:

> I was both exhausted and exasperated by the audience always wanting me to give more of myself (and I always thought I HAD to meet their demand, as some kind of duty or penance or simply for the attention!), and where I was often required to be totally self-lacerating and exposing and to wash my dreadful dirty laundry to large audiences who were never waiting for me at the stage door to see if I was alright, or if I needed company or affection, or help in stitching myself back up! (Howells quoted in Zerihan 2009: 34)

Taking literally the metaphor of exposing his 'dirty laundry', Howells began his movement into one-to-one performance with *Adrienne's Dirty Laundry Experience* (2003), based around his quasi-drag persona of Adrienne, in which participants would arrive with a bag of dirty laundry and talk with Adrienne over tea while their clothes were washed.

Over the next decade, Howells would continue to develop intimate experiences, typically using the form of a one-to-one encounter. His work in this area coincided with the expansion of similar forms described above; but, as Dominic Johnson notes, the tendency for these one-to-one encounters is to contain them within a relatively brief duration – say, 5–10 minutes – whereas one of Howells's innovations was to extend the form to durations that might match those of staged theatre productions (2013: 174). Howells's ability to explore extended durations was partly enabled by gaining support for his work outside market economies, in the form of public funding from the UK Arts and Humanities Research Council on a three-year project as Creative Fellow. Over the course of this development, Deirdre Heddon notes that Howells's interest shifted away from autobiographical, confessional forms in which Howells was the main protagonist; gradually abandoning the 'drag performance mask' of Adrienne, and eventually even giving up talking altogether in favour of silent experiences (Heddon and Howells 2011: 2).

For example, *Held* (2006) consisted of three stages of interaction that encapsulated this trajectory towards silence and intimacy: participants would first hold hands with Howells across a kitchen table—while Howells engaged them in a conversation about hand-holding; then would move to sitting side-by-side on a sofa while listening to music selected by the participant; and finally would lie in a bed while being 'spooned' by Howells for up to half an hour, usually in silence. In this way, not only the body of the participant is held, but silence as well: 'In a noisy culture like mine', Howells commented, 'silence rings out loudly, offering another place to "be" or to become: to reflect, to imagine, to project, to re-connect – with self and others and other selves – through the unique relationship of a quiet, considered, one-to-one encounter' (Heddon and Howells 2011: 12).

Elsewhere, Howells argues passionately for the need for these kinds of connections, critiquing the alienation of contemporary culture in a way that recalls Kaprow and Debord in its fervour:

> I also want to offer here a passionately held belief that the more isolatry and disconnected our experience of life becomes – and our alienation and isolation from other human beings – and in my opinion, this is in direct correlation to an overwhelmingly speedy advancement in technology and the proliferation of synthetic experience and instant gratification, that people are in real need of nourishing, intimate, person-to-person, eye-to-eye, flesh-on-flesh experiences and exchanges. AND NOTHING ELSE CAN BE A SUBSTITUTE FOR THIS! (Zerihan 2009: 36)

Having attended a foot-washing ceremony in a Christian religious context, in which the gesture of washing was highly suggestive seemed perfunctory to him, Howells decided to develop a performance work that would develop this gesture into an act of generosity. In *Foot Washing for the Sole* (2008), Howells wrote, he 'simply' 'washed, dried, anointed with oils, massaged, and kissed the participant's feet' (Howells 2012: 131). But there is nothing simple about this; as Helen Iball (2016) observes, it is a carefully negotiated encounter, during which Howells is constantly sensitive to the changing relationship between the two bodies: a care and preparation in the ritual action that includes attention to breathing, eye contact and constant checking-in through verbal and non-verbal communication. It is rigorous, careful and challenging work. We might describe this as task-based performance for the affective economy.

Howells shares some affinity with the task-based performance of the 1960s, in that the 'realness' of the work being done seeks to avoid the 'merely representational' critique of theatre: 'I am proud to be identified with a group of people who might be working to achieve the real rather than artifice, pretence, and fakery', he said in an interview with Dominic Johnson (2013: 182). But what is it that differentiates this 'artistic' labour from the general conditions of work within a service economy? This is something Johnson asked Howells regarding 'the difference between, say, participating in *Foot Washing for the Sole* and receiving a pedicure on the high street', and Johnson suggests that it has to do with what he calls 'the aesthetic engineering of the situation'. Howells agrees, noting the importance of taking care in the selection of materials, the organization of the space and the framing of the event: 'I'm really careful about colours, proximity and the space around things, lighting, temperature, and the way objects and arrangements might be read' (Johnson 2013: 186). That is, while some of the work may be indistinguishable from service economies, there is additional, theatrical work being done here: specific details of choice and attitude, as well as consideration of staging and production.

Rather than oppose 'real' and 'synthetic' experiences, we might follow Adam Alston's analysis of immersive performances, which he usefully likens to 'experience machines', through paying attention to the 'mechanics of affect production' (2016: 44). As Alston points out, just because an affect is constructed does not make it simply 'false': 'there is no such thing as an unreal affect', he emphasizes (58). Instead, the theatrical event, in its very ambivalence, can make visible the otherwise implicit negotiations and conditions on such production. Howells recounts an encounter with an elderly woman in Munich, who, despite the work being clearly described in the title and publicity, was surprised by having to remove her shoes and socks.

> She said 'No, no, no, I don't want to do this performance', which was fine, and I encouraged her to go back to the box office and ask them to refund her ticket. She stayed, and asked, 'But is this art?' I explained that I didn't know, and that I hoped it was, but that I could definitely claim that it was an experience. She sat there for more time, and eventually said, 'I will do your "experience"', as though she was doing me a great favour. (Johnson 2013: 185)

The work that makes this *theatre*, then, is work undertaken by *both* parties in the manufacture of a relationship. Writing about his experience of *Foot Washing for the Sole*, Fintan Walsh reflects, 'we are not just here to see, think, and freely feel, but to work affectively. If we do not engage in this labour, the performance won't happen' (2014: 59).

At first glance, Howells's approach, in which connection and intimacy are all, seems diametrically opposed to Yvonne Rainer's mode of work-like performance, in which the performer withdraws her gaze from the audience and is absorbed in her task. And yet both positions represent different ways of using 'work' to intervene within a broader cultural condition of alienation, and also to intervene within the condition of theatrical encounter itself: Lambert-Beatty calls Rainer 'a sculptor of spectatorship' (2008: 9), and in Howells's comments we can see how carefully he crafted the conditions of participation within his works. One of the ways that the work of theatre can distinguish itself from the economies within which it is located, then, is that the conditions of the work might themselves become part of the work as material that the artist can shape: carefully, with attention to detail, and in constant negotiation with the spectator about the role that she or he is being given to play.

In the 1960s, theatre explored ways of becoming more work-like in order to overcome or confront its own theatricality. But since that time, work itself has become more theatre-like. While I have focused here on critical accounts of 'affective labour' that warn of the adverse effects of the commodification of feeling, not all commentators have been so negative. In 1999, B. Joseph Pine and James H. Gilmore popularized the idea of the 'experience economy' and urged all companies and entrepreneurs to embrace this shift in emphasis from material product to immaterial experience, and they did so through extensive (if reductive) use of the metaphor of the theatre. Their influential book *The Experience Economy* ([1999] 2011) was originally subtitled, 'Work is Theatre & Every Business a Stage', and included chapters with such theatre-based titles as 'Setting the Stage', 'The Show Must Go On', 'Get Your Act Together', and so on, concluding with 'Finding Your Role in the World'. In many ways, then, those of you setting out to work in the theatre are not so different from any other kind of worker. What distinguishes your work from others is not so much that one kind is more 'real' than the other, but that your workplace is one where different ideas of 'work' can be 'worked through'… if that's the task you want to set yourself.

Performance Details

Yvonne Rainer's *Trio A* was first presented as part of *The Mind is a Muscle, Part 1* (Judson Memorial Church, New York, 10 January 1966), and subsequently as part of *The Mind is a Muscle* (Anderson Theatre, New York, 11, 14, 15 April 1968).

Adrian Howells's *Foot Washing for the Sole* was performed in various locations internationally, including in the UK, Ireland, Israel, Singapore, Germany, Japan and Canada (2008–12).

Further Reading

In his short provocation 'An Actor Manages: On Acting and Immaterial Labour' (2013), Broderick Chow gives an excellent overview of the parallels between actor training and contemporary forms of labour, such as working in a call centre—which, as he ruefully notes, is often the 'real' job of many actors seeking employment. Catherine Wood's *Yvonne Rainer: The Mind is a Muscle* (2007) provides historical and critical context for Rainer's most celebrated work and offers outstanding analysis of its ongoing significance. Rainer's own writing on her process in 'A Quasi Survey of Some "Minimalist" Tendencies in the Quantitatively Minimal Dance Activity Midst the Plethora, or An Analysis of *Trio A*' ([1966] 1968) sets up a stimulating analogy between minimalist sculpture of the 1960s and the dance she was making, and reveals a remarkably frank reflection on the behind-the-scenes effort required to achieve the 'look' she was trying to achieve. Rachel Zerihan (2009) is one of the first scholars to track the emergence of one-to-one performance. Her *Live Art Development Agency Study Room Guide on One to One Performance* is an introduction to the form, and includes contributions from sixteen artists who work in that way, including Adrian Howells. Deirdre Heddon and Dominic Johnson's *It's All Allowed: The Performances of Adrian Howells* (2016) is a beautifully assembled, posthumous collection that compiles images, essays and reflections on Howells's work and legacy.

References

Alston, Adam (2016), *Beyond Immersive Theatre: Aesthetics, Politics and Productive Participation*, Basingstoke: Palgrave Macmillan.

Archias, Elise (2016), *The Concrete Body: Yvonne Rainer, Carolee Schneemann, Vito Acconci*, New Haven and London: Yale University Press.

Artaud, Antonin ([1935] 1993), 'An Affective Athleticism', in Antonin Artaud, *The Theatre and Its Double*, trans. V. Corti, 88–95, London: Calder.

Auslander, Philip (1985), 'Task and Vision: Willem Dafoe in *L. S. D.*', *The Drama Review* 29 (2): 94–8.

Banes, Sally (1987), *Terpsichore in Sneakers: Post-Modern Dance*, Middletown, CT: Wesleyan University Press.

Barish, Jonas (1981), *The Antitheatrical Prejudice*, Berkeley: University of California Press.

Bottoms, Stephen, and Matthew Goulish (eds) (2007), *Small Acts of Repair: Performance, Ecology, and Goat Island*, New York and London: Routledge.

Bryan-Wilson, Julia (2012), 'Practicing *Trio A*', *October* 140: 54–74.

Bürger, Peter ([1974] 1984), *Theory of the Avant-Garde*, trans. M. Shaw, Minneapolis: University of Minnesota Press.

Catterson, Pat (2009), 'I Promised Myself I Would Never Let It Leave My Body's Memory', *Dance Research Journal* 41 (2): 3–11.

Chatzichristodoulou, Maria, and Rachel Zerihan, eds (2012), *Intimacy Across Visceral and Digital Performance*, Basingstoke: Palgrave Macmillan.

Chow, Broderick (2013), 'An Actor Manages: On Acting and Immaterial Labour', *New Left Project*, 29 January. Available online: http://www.newleftproject.org/index.php/site/article_comments/an_actor_manages_on_acting_and_immaterial_labour> (accessed 1 October 2017).

Debord, Guy ([1957] 2002), 'Report on the Construction of Situations and on the Terms of Organization and Action of the International Situationist Tendency', trans. T. McDonough, in T. McDonough (ed.), *Guy Debord and the Situationist International: Texts and Documents*, 29–50, Cambridge, MA, and London: MIT Press.

Debord, Guy ([1967] 1994), *The Society of the Spectacle*, trans. D. Nicholson-Smith, New York: Zone Books.

Friedman, Ken, Owen Smith and Lauren Sawchyn, eds (2002), *The Fluxus Performance Workbook*. 40th anniversary edn, Performance Research e-publication. Available online: https://monoskop.org/File:Friedman_Smith_Sawchyn_eds_The_Fluxus_Performance_Workbook.pdf (accessed 1 October 2017).

Gordon, Mel (1974), 'Meyerhold's Biomechanics', *The Drama Review* 18 (3): 73.

Hardt, Michael, and Antonio Negri (2000), *Empire*, Cambridge, MA, and London: Harvard University Press.

Heddon, Deirdre (2014), 'In Memoriam: Adrian Howells (9 April 1962–16 March 2014)', *Contemporary Theatre Review* 24 (3): 418–20.

Heddon, Deirdre, and Adrian Howells (2011), 'From Talking to Silence: A Confessional Journey', *PAJ: A Journal of Performance and Art* 33 (1): 1–12.

Heddon, Deirdre, and Dominic Johnson, eds (2016), *It's All Allowed: The Performances of Adrian Howells*, London and Chicago: Live Art Development Agency and Intellect Books.

Higgins, Hannah (2002), *Fluxus Experience*, Berkeley: University of California Press.

Hochschild, Arlie ([1983] 2003), *The Managed Heart: Commercialization of Human Feeling*, Twentieth Anniversary edn, Berkeley: University of California Press.

Howells, Adrian (2012), 'Foot Washing for the Sole', *Performance Research* 17 (2): 128–31.

Hurley, Erin (2010), *Theatre & Feeling*, Basingstoke: Palgrave Macmillan.

Iball, Helen (2016), 'Towards an Ethics of Intimate Audiences', in D. Heddon and D. Johnson (eds), *It's All Allowed: The Performances of Adrian Howells*, 190–203, London and Chicago: Live Art Development Agency and Intellect Books.

Johnson, Dominic (2013), 'The Kindness of Strangers: An Interview with Adrian Howells', *Performing Ethos* 3 (2): 173–90.

Kaprow, Allan (2003), *Essays on the Blurring of Art and Life*, ed. Jeff Kelley, expanded ed., Berkeley: University of California Press.

Kirby, Michael (1972), 'On Acting and Not-Acting', *The Drama Review: TDR* 16 (1): 3–15.

Lambert-Beatty, Carrie (2008), *Being Watched: Yvonne Rainer and the 1960s*, Cambridge, MA and London: October Books/MIT Press.

Martin, Carol (2013), *Theatre of the Real*, Basingstoke: Palgrave Macmillan.

Pine, B. Joseph, and James H. Gilmore ([1999] 2011), *The Experience Economy*, updated edn, Boston: Harvard Business Review Press.

Plato ([380BC] 1974), *The Republic*, trans. D. Lee, 2nd edition, New York: Penguin.

Quick, Andrew (2007), *The Wooster Group Work Book*, New York and London: Routledge.

Rainer, Yvonne (1965), 'Some Retrospective Notes on a Dance for 10 People and 12 Mattresses Called "Parts of Some Sextets" Performed at the Wadsworth Atheneum, Hartford, Connecticut, and Judson Memorial Church, New York, in March 1965', *Tulane Drama Review* 10 (2): 168–78.

Rainer, Yvonne ([1966] 1968), 'A Quasi Survey of Some "Minimalist" Tendencies in the Quantitatively Minimal Dance Activity Midst the Plethora, or An Analysis of *Trio A*', in G. Battcock (ed.), *Minimal Art: A Critical Anthology*, 263–73, New York: Dutton.

Rainer, Yvonne ([1968] 1974), '"Statement" from The Mind Is a Muscle, Anderson Theater, New York (April 1968)', in Yvonne Rainer, *Work 1961–73*, 70–1, Halifax: Press of the Nova Scotia College of Art and Design.

Rainer, Yvonne ([1965] 1995), 'Yvonne Rainer Interviews Anna Halprin', in M. R. Sandford (ed.), *Happenings and Other Acts*, 137–59, New York and London: Routledge.

Rainer, Yvonne, Robert Alexander and Sally Banes (1978), *Trio A* [excerpt]. Available online: http://www.vdb.org/titles/trio (accessed 26 December 2016).

Ridout, Nicholas (2009), 'Performance in the Service Economy: Outsourcing and Delegation', in C. Bishop and S. Tramontana (eds), *Double Agent*, 126–31, London: ICA.

Rousseau, Jean-Jacques ([1758] 1960), *Politics and the Arts: Letter to D'Alembert on the Theatre*, trans. A. Bloom, Ithaca, NY: Cornell University Press.

Schmidt, Theron (2013), 'Troublesome Professionals: On the Speculative Reality of Theatrical Labour', *Performance Research* 18 (2): 15–26.

Seigworth, Gregory J., and Melissa Gregg (2010), 'An Inventory of Shimmers', in Melissa Gregg and Gregory J. Seigworth (eds), *The Affect Theory Reader*, 1–25, Durham, NC: Duke University Press.

Stanislavski, Konstantin ([1936] 1980), *An Actor Prepares*, trans. E. R. Hapgood, London: Metheun.

Virno, Paolo (2004), *A Grammar of the Multitude: For an Analysis of Contemporary Forms of Life*, trans. I. Bertoletti, J. Cascaito and A. Casson, Los Angeles: Semiotext(e).

Walsh, Fintan (2014), 'Touching, Flirting, Whispering: Performing Intimacy in Public', *TDR/The Drama Review* 58 (4): 56–67.

Wood, Catherine (2007), *Yvonne Rainer: The Mind Is a Muscle*, London: Afterall Books.

Worth, Libby, and Helen Poynor (2004), *Anna Halprin*, Routledge Performance Practitioners, London and New York: Routledge.

Zerihan, Rachel, ed. (2009), *Live Art Development Agency Study Room Guide on One to One Performance*, London: Live Art Development Agency. Available online: http://www.thisisliveart.co.uk/resources/catalogue/rachel-zerihans-study-room-guide (accessed 1 October 2017).

Part 3 Traces

12 What Is an Intercultural Exchange?

MIGUEL ESCOBAR VARELA

Intercultural performances are commonly staged around the world and most people will encounter intercultural performance theories in the course of their undergraduate studies in theatre. These theories are helpful to tease out the intricacies of performances we might encounter but they have another more crucial application. Many people studying and doing theatre today will have intercultural experiences as part of their training, personal lives and creative work. We might go as far as to say that intercultural experiences are becoming fundamental to theatre work around the world today and that in some locations, the capacity to tackle the ethical, technical and intellectual implications of intercultural work is fundamental for a career in theatre, be it in practice or research. Travel, collaborations and training in foreign performance traditions are perhaps the primary sites through which we can think through interculturalism today. It is not just a matter of thinking *about* interculturalism in relation to these experiences. When we study and work interculturally, everyday challenges and decisions are concrete intercultural problems and the actions we decide to carry out, or refrain from doing, are modes of thinking interculturalism through practice.

In what follows, I offer a personal account of my attempts to think interculturalism over the ten-year period during which I have been working on Javanese theatre. The writings of Rustom Bharucha and Dwight Conquergood have been essential companions in this journey, both as catalysts for reflection and as guidebooks to plan projects into the future. These reflections are necessarily very personal (as are the writings of Bharucha and Conquergood), but in the concluding sections, I draw a more general sketch about the ways theory is necessary for the pressing, practical problem of thinking intercultural performance through travel.

Beginnings

After completing my bachelor's degree, I went to Indonesia to study Javanese *wayang kulit* (shadow puppetry). Originally, I was planning to spend only six months in that country. I had studied playwriting and directing in Mexico City and I wanted to develop my creative work. As an aspiring playwright, I was wary of the new playwriting in Mexico City at the time. Many writers were interested in postdramatic theatre, eschewing notions of character and plot in favour of expanding the conceptual possibilities of theatre. Although I was interested in these ideas, I found many of the performances repetitive and lacking in creativity. And I was – and always have been – someone who loves stories, old-fashioned as that may be. Therefore, one thing that particularly attracted me to the performing arts of Java was the strong emphasis on narrative material. I had serendipitously encountered Javanese *wayang kulit* and found it fascinating (Figure 12.1). I knew little about this tradition at the time, but I knew this tradition had been practised for at least one thousand years and that its narrative material is derived from two Sanskrit epics, the *Mahābhārata* and the *Rāmāyaṇam*. In these performances, the musical accompaniment is provided by a *gamelan* orchestra that consists of at least a dozen musicians, which is led by the *dalang* – the puppeteer and director of the show. I was especially fascinated by what I perceived to be the enormous creative freedom of this *dalang*, a single artist who, besides the music, is responsible for animating all the puppets and speaking all the character parts. There was something of this dictatorial control that spoke directly to my youthful creative arrogance. I had a clear and simple plan: I wanted to learn enough *wayang kulit* to be able to create one-man shows that delivered Mexican stories via Javanese puppets.

I formulated that plan before developing in-depth knowledge of *wayang kulit*, and for a while I thought my plan was going surprisingly well. I found a scholarship to study Indonesian at Gadjah Mada University, travelled to Yogyakarta and started studying *wayang kulit* with a local teacher. At the end of six months, I performed a thirty-minute show based on a Mexican legend. I commissioned a local craftsman to build custom puppets for this and collaborated with a group of international musicians from Indonesia, Australia, England and Japan who were also studying in Yogyakarta. The process was a challenging learning experience but we were all satisfied with the result. The novelty of the combination warranted substantial media attention for our performance, in spite of my poor skills as a puppeteer and my heavily accented Indonesian.

When my stay in Indonesia was over, I moved to the Netherlands with a scholarship for graduate studies. I originally planned to keep developing my Mexican *wayang* project and present it in Europe. However, while studying there, I encountered the texts of Rustom

Fig. 12.1 A performance of traditional *wayang kulit* in Yogyakarta in 2017. Photo: Miguel Escobar Varela.

Bharucha, which drastically changed my attitude to my own work. Bharucha is a theatre director, cultural critic and Professor of Theatre and Performance Studies at the Jawaharlal Nehru University in New Dehli, India. Originally from Calcutta, he went to Yale University for his postgraduate degrees and he has been involved with theatre projects as activist, dramaturg and director in the Philippines, South Africa, Brazil, the United States and the Netherlands. His many books and articles cover a wide range of topics, from oral history to political theatre in India. But perhaps his two most influential books in theatre and performance studies are *The Politics of Cultural Practice: Thinking through Theatre in an Age of Globalization* (2000) and *Theatre and the World: Performance and the Politics of Culture* (1993). It was these two texts that prompted me to ask uncomfortable questions for which I had no answers. This paralysis led to a hiatus in my performance project and, eventually, to a redefinition of my career. There were many things about Bharucha's *Theatre and the World* which impressed me. Here, I summarize those points and make a specific connection to my own work and travels in order to show how one can think interculturalism through travel and international exchanges. As mentioned earlier, this thinking through is primarily rooted in experience, but theories are fundamental to add nuance and precision to formless experiences.

Reading Bharucha in the Netherlands

The main argument of Bharucha's book is that intercultural performance is a slippery territory and that it is very easy for artists to create superficial work that reproduces dominant global inequalities. The book explores multiple facets of this issue through different writing strategies, ranging from the incisive analysis of key intercultural performances to narrative accounts of his own attempts to develop intercultural and intracultural work in India. One of the chapters is written as a letter to Jerzy Grotowski. Grotowski (1933–99) was a Polish theatre director who first achieved fame in the 1960s for his *poor theatre*, a systematic quest for the essential aspects of performance that led him to concentrate strongly on actor training. His main interest was on how theatre training can help people achieve their full potential and this led him to abandon theatrical productions in favour of other modes of work. In the early 1970s, he left the professional theatre scene and instead concentrated on a variety of *paratheatrical* events around the world, with participants from many different cultures. These events were located in outdoor, mostly natural, settings and there were no distinctions between performers and audience, although some people served as leaders. In his letter to Grotowski, Bharucha takes issue with several aspects of Grotowski's work, such as his double move in regard to theatre, where he both abandoned professional theatre work but continued to profit from the endorsement of celebrities such as Peter Brook, Eugenio Barba and André Gregory. He also questions the psychological treachery he identifies in Grotowski's paratheatrical work. More to the point of intercultural performance and its complex relations to economic inequalities is an anecdote of Grotowski's trip to Khardah to find participants for his workshop. Bharucha describes Grotowski's exercises as nonsensical. For example, Grotowski asked the participants to keep silent for three hours and then had his assistants guide the Khardah actors through their own landscape. Bharucha bluntly highlights the economic importance of these activities: 'If you had not been Grotowski, you would have been treated like a madman and probably asked to leave. But let's face it, if the actors accepted your "madness" there was something expedient in their interest. You were their first (and perhaps, only) possibility of getting abroad. You had come to Khardah not just to feel the Bengal countryside, but to select three actors who could spend time with you in Poland on the Theatre of Sources' (Bharucha 1993: 51). As a result of this workshop, three actors were selected to travel to Poland. All expenses from Mumbai to Poland were covered, but the problem was finding money for the second-class ticket to reach Mumbai by train, which prompts Bharucha to write: 'Dear Grotowski, our economic disparities are ridiculous at times, aren't they?' (52).

The reader might agree or not with Grotowski or Bharucha and my intention here is not to offer an apology for either of them. But I want to convey the shock I experienced upon reading Bharucha's words for the first time. Back then, I idolized Grotowski (I had trained in Mexico City with Jaime Soriano, who had worked for many years with Grotowski). I had unquestioningly accepted the economy of prestige that association with Grotowski had created in Mexico, not once questioning the ways in which financial differences underwrote that economy, or the anxieties and hopes of those who had been selected or rejected by Grotowski's workshops around the world. The kind of scrutiny to which Bharucha subjects Grotowski's work struck me as a radically new way of interrogating his work. With the benefit of hindsight, my previous inability to entertain that such political analysis was possible is a symptom of my naivety. But it also made me think more critically of my own place as scholar and artist in the world, about the economic and political infrastructures that supported or hampered my own international efforts. The consequences of these thoughts will become more apparent after I examine some of Bharucha's other points.

In another chapter of the book, Bharucha famously criticizes Peter Brook for his usage of the *Mahābhārata*, one of the two major Sanskrit epic poems used as narrative material in theatrical traditions across South and Southeast Asia. When Brook directed *The Mahabharata* (1985), he was already a celebrity. He originally achieved fame as an innovative director of Shakespeare's work in England, his native country. In 1970, he moved to France and founded the International Centre of Theatre Research, which focused on interdisciplinary and intercultural work, often involving collaborations with performers from all over the world. Reviewing Brook's work, Bharucha's main argument is that true intercultural dialogue is very difficult to achieve, as intercultural work is always circumscribed by economics, history and politics. In the case of Brook's *The Mahabharata*, the limitations of this dialogue manifest themselves in different ways. Brook, an Englishman, uses the *Mahābhārata* not as the rich tapestry of interspersed traditions it is in India, but mostly as raw material for the development of an international commercial product. The troubling parallels between this operation and the economic project of British colonization of India go unacknowledged in the performance. A second, but related point, is Brook's disrespect for the context of *Mahābhārata* performances in India. Brook's piece was celebrated for its long duration, but Bharucha points out that Brook's rendering is in fact 'pitifully short' given that *Mahābhārata* performances in India are often longer and they would never attempt, as Brook did, to present the epic in its entirety (Bharucha 1993: 75).

Another example Bharucha identifies of Brook's disrespect for traditions is in the meaning assigned to the performance. A bit of context on this story is necessary to understand the full implications of Bharucha's critique. The *Mahābhārata* is a complex epic narrative, with many intersecting story lines that span several generations of kings, warriors, gods and demons. The main plot is the conflict between two groups of cousins, the Pandavas and the Kauravas, over the control of a kingdom. In the Hinduist religious context, this ancient poem is considered sacred and regarded as both a historical narrative and a source of moral laws. In a section known as the *Bhagavadgītā* ('The Song of God'), one of the main Pandavas is having doubts about going to war with the Kauravas. His adviser Krishna instructs him not to worry about the consequences of his actions. In Brook's performance, this segment prompted the audience to laugh: 'If the New York audience laughed, it is not because their own ideology of capitalism and self-interest had been called into question. Krishna's statement came out of the blue without any depth of meaning or resonance. What could have been a moment of revelation was reduced to a banality' (72).

For Bharucha, this is one more in a series of flaws that show Brook's essentialist reading of the *Mahābhārata* as universal, in disregard of local exegesis: 'What is the Mahabharata without Hindu philosophy? Apart from Krishna ... Brook gives us vignettes of Ganesh, Siva, Hanuman; some bleak predictions about the end of the world; a scattering of references to dharma; and a five-minute encapsulation of the Bhagavad Gita' (74). I was unsure of the degree to which I agreed with Bharucha on this point, given that *Mahābhārata* performances in Indonesia have been ingrained into non-Hindu frames of reference for centuries. On the other hand, this point does not fully exonerate Brook – the *Mahābhārata* is different in different cultural contexts but not necessarily universal in a reductive way. Bharucha's line of questioning thus struck me as relevant to any intercultural theatre endeavour. I knew that I did not want my own intercultural performances to be faulted for such omissions and misappropriations.

Initially, I thought that my Mexican *wayang* project could easily sidestep many of the potential criticisms that could be launched against it, as I could frame it as a 'South-South' collaboration that avoided some of the inherent power structures so often found in intercultural projects where participants come from disparate economic backgrounds. However, upon closer inspection, I became aware that the mere act of *framing* my project as a South-South collaboration could easily be an empty gesture. There was a latent danger of self-exoticizing myself and my fellow Indonesian artists. A true collaboration could have to do more than just pay lip service to common Third World origins. Bharucha also notes how artists that hail from big cities in India often misappropriate traditions from places they don't fully understand: 'the clientele of "folk drama" is not the "folk," but city people who need to be reminded of their "roots and native places" from which they are irrevocably displaced' (202). Hailing from Mexico City, I saw more of myself reflected in this sentence than I would have liked.

But is there a way forward, can someone effectively navigate the treacherous land of intercultural exchange? Bharucha's advice on this is unequivocal: 'Perhaps what is most needed in any kind of intercultural work is a long-term commitment' (163). I was forced to accept that my six-month stint in Indonesia did not provide me with the kind of understanding of *wayang kulit* that would enable a deep intercultural engagement. My knowledge of technique was rudimentary and, more importantly, I did not speak a word of Javanese. Though I had acquired a working knowledge of Indonesian, which facilitated conversations with artists, I was completely unable to appreciate the linguistic aspects of *wayang kulit*, which is delivered almost entirely in Javanese.

At this point, I decided to return to Indonesia and immerse myself in the study of *wayang kulit* and Javanese. I began taking private lessons in Javanese and enrolled in a more formal *wayang kulit* course at Habirandha, the royal puppetry school attached to the Yogyakarta *Kraton* (palace). My interest in *wayang* led to a PhD that focused on *wayang kontemporer*, the modern reinterpretations of *wayang*. Focusing on these recent performances was also motivated by my engagement with intercultural theory. Like Bharucha, John Russell Brown has criticized Western interculturalists for their implicit framing of Asian (and other non-Western) traditions as timeless (Brown 1998). My PhD project aimed to tackle this problem by focusing on new developments of *wayang* that were rarely discussed or even reported in academic papers. At the time I began, most of the literature focused exclusively on classic *wayang*, with the notable examples of work by Tim Behrend (1999), Matthew Cohen (2007) and an edited volume by Jan Mrázek (2002). However, the reality of the shows I was seeing in Java demanded more extensive and sustained critical attention.

Bharucha's suggestion that only long-term commitment to a place or theatre tradition can sustain true intercultural work has had a profound effect on me. I have found additional inspiration for this mode of deep engagement in the lives and work of many people whom I've met in Indonesia. Kathryn Emerson, for instance, has dedicated twenty years to the sustained and careful study of Javanese music, language and *wayang kulit.* She often works as live translator for *wayang* shows, where she provides real-time English translation and exegesis of *wayang* conventions for international audiences. Like other translations, this is an extraordinary service to intercultural understanding of performance and these feats are particularly highlighted by the fact that Javanese *wayang* performances last six hours or more. Brown also highlights the importance of long-term commitment, praising in particular the life and work of Takahashi Yasunari (1932–2002), a renowned professor of both English literature and Japanese theatre whose life work was dedicated to contextualizing theatre across different cultures (Brown 1998: 12).

As I enter the ten-year mark of my study of *wayang*, I can only hope to continue dedicating substantial efforts to the study of this tradition. My encounter with the theories I reference above has changed how I have worked over the past decade. By providing autobiographical details and extensive references to a single author, I hope to have shown the reader a way in which one can use travel and the study of foreign art forms to think through intercultural theory. My examples are necessarily narrow in scope and I don't aim to convince anyone to follow in my exact footsteps. In the next section, I ponder what more general lessons can be drawn from intercultural theory and in what other ways might we think intercultural experiences through intercultural theory, and vice versa.

Drawing General Lessons

How would someone who is in the early stages of an intercultural journey engage with ideas such as the ones outlined here? In this section, I consider two scenarios: short-term intercultural work and long-term engagements.

Short exposures to foreign theatrical practices and short-term collaborative intercultural work can be useful, but it is important to be aware of potential pitfalls and have realistic expectations of what one can accomplish. This is, however, easier said than done. Over

Fig. 12.2 The participants of an intercultural dance workshop as part of a field trip to Indonesia in 2017. Photo: Miguel Escobar Varela.

the past five years, I have organized short study trips to Indonesia for my students at the National University of Singapore. In these trips, they learn a variety of practices (classical Javanese dance, *gamelan* music and leather puppet craftsmanship) and watch dance, theatre and puppetry performances. They also develop short collaborative performances with their peers from Gadjah Mada University (UGM) (Figure 12.2).

Immersions in Indonesia are useful in the context of courses on theatre, but it would be difficult to use this experience to create work that would count as truly intercultural. Upon returning to Singapore, I ask my students to reflect on the trip, by mode of essays and performances. But I also warn them against trying to apply what they've learnt superficially to their work. One example is Javanese dance, an artform rich in conventions. In Java, they watch a performance and learn the basics of this form. There are certain elements they could easily incorporate into their work – such as a specific movement of the hand. But these short courses can only provide a superficial introduction to the incredibly nuanced and varied aspects of classical Javanese dance in which professional performers train from childhood.

Short exposure experiences help one become sensitized to other kinds of performances. But perhaps it would be useful to resist applying this too quickly to one's own work. As Brown suggests, rather than incorporating foreign aesthetic conventions in a tokenistic fashion into our performances, we can use travel instead to develop a sensitivity to other notions of what theatre can be in other places. He terms this operation 'invisible pillage' and describes it as follows:

On the return home, the theatre explorer has many questions to ask of his or her own theatre, especially in its essential elements that involve actors and audience. By trying to answer them honestly and then putting the tentative answers to the test of practice, thanks and respect can be best given to the theatres that provoked the interrogation of practice. No pillage will have been caused if nothing tangible is transported out of the society from which a theatre's life springs and by which it is possessed. Performances that result will speak for themselves without intrusive signposting of intercultural origin if the experiments are conducted with means already available in the traveler's own theatre. (Brown 1998: 18)

Building on these suggestions, I encourage my students to explore one 'general' aspect that they found interesting while in Indonesia, rather than copying a specific convention. For example, they can choose to address 'the relationship between performers and spectators' as a theme, rather than reproduce the complex culture of connoisseurship that is essential to the enjoyment of *wayang*.

This approach to intercultural borrowings is akin to that of American film and theatre director Julie Taymor. Taymor has directed many influential films and theatre pieces, but perhaps her most famous work is the world-travelling musical, *The Lion King* (1997). A little-known fact about Taymor is that she resided in Indonesia for several years and worked in professional theatre productions, but she never consciously tried to apply the elements from Indonesia that she witnessed to her Broadway shows. Yet, some aspects of what she observed have given her productions a distinctive angle (Taymor 1979).

Another way in which a short immersion can be useful is that it can trigger someone's curiosity to learn a given performance practice more deeply. In some ways, modern-day institutions make it hard for a younger student or scholar to focus fully on a topic for years on end. Our academies and curricula are modelled on an idea of gaining breadth rather than depth. However, by that same token, international travel and possibilities for exchange and long-term residency or study programmes are easier to conduct than ever before.

Learning Languages

My main recommendation to any budding intercultural researcher or practitioner is this: study the language(s) connected to the practices that interest you. Even if you don't consider yourself to have a talent for languages or if you are uncertain about the prospect of progressing in this quest, *any* immersion in the technical vocabulary of a tradition is immensely useful. No language maps directly onto another and by learning other languages one also discovers a different kind of window into other foreign theatre traditions. An example is Javanese dance, which from a Western point of view might encompass practices that are considered distinct in Java: ritual trance dances, popular dances and classical dance. The word dance could be translated into Javanese as *dhansah*, *ngigel* (animals), *joged, beksa* and *nandhak*. *Beksa* refers to classical and highly stylized patterns whereas *nandhak* is used exclusively to denote improvised sequences (Brakel-Papenhuijzen 1995: 3). Grasping this tapestry of meanings allows us a different intuition into the social role of dance in Java.

Learning a language has immense practical benefits but there is a strong conceptual case to be made for it as well. Asian and other traditions are often studied purely as bodily techniques, separate from the narrative materials that support them and from the sociolinguistic environments in which they are developed. Brown and other intercultural critics have seen aspects of reductive orientalism in this overt emphasis on the body (Brown 1998; Yong 2004). As Lo and Gilbert suggest, 'intercultural theatre has tended to favor visual spectacle over linguistic innovation; nevertheless, there are significant language-based issues that pertain to both its processes and products' (Lo and Gilbert 2002: 46). By pursuing linguistic, musical and movement-based studies of the practices that interest us (be they modern or classical), we can help destabilize the dominant frames into which performances are narrowed down.

Finding Authentic Experiences

There is only one place where you will find a fully authentic experience of other theatrical cultures: in your head. Reading and critically assessing the history of practices is very important in order to understand how ideas of tradition and authenticity are constructed in specific places. Perhaps all theatre traditions are, in one way or another, 'constructed'. A well-known example is the *kecak* dance in Bali. This form of dance, advertised today as 'traditional', was developed between local artists and Western expatriates in the 1930s, based on the *sanghyang dedari* trance dance and music repertoire (Stepputat 2012: 48). It is currently a touristic tradition – a very common dance but one that does not appeal to locals. To complicate things further, it has re-entered local tastes by way of *kecak kreasi*, modern re-adaptations of this tradition (49). So, is *kecak* artificial or traditional, foreign or local? How long should a performance be practiced so as to be considered traditional and what kinds of connections must it have to a local performance ecosystem to be deemed local?

Another example is classical dance in Java. The dances one encounters in the Yogyakarta and Surakarta palaces today are authentic in the sense that they have been practiced for a long time, and are taught not only to professional dancers but to many people who then become spectators of the dance. However, as Diyah Larasati notes, in its current form classical dance is a hygienic depoliticized form that is the result of a specific history (Larasati 2013). It is important to remember that all performances are, to a certain extent, socially constructed over time, according to specific political and economic circumstances. The discourses that surround their pedagogy, performance, documentation and enjoyment are affected by changing practices that frame and limit what the performance practices in question can be. As Lo and Gilbert suggest, 'we should treat authenticity with caution, recognizing that it registers, and responds to, hierarchies of power. In this context, the ability to manipulate markers of authenticity becomes another measure of agency' (Lo and Gilbert 2002: 46).

Being aware of this, however, does not make it easier to escape the traps of imagined authenticity. When I was in Indonesia the first time, I went through a phase where I wanted to do everything 'in a Javanese way', but I quickly realized how ridiculous this idea was. For example, I would eat only local food at a *warung* (small roadside hawker stores) instead of at foreign chain restaurants. But most of my local friends ate at both of these places, and there is of course no such thing as a fully Javanese behaviour. This level of simplification is almost grotesquely laughable, but I've recognized subtler versions of this desire – in myself and others – numerous times. I found an appropriate vocabulary to describe these experiences in the work of Dwight Conquergood. Conquergood (1949–2004) was an ethnographer and performance scholar known for his work with the Hmong of Southeast Asia, street gangs of Chicago and refugees in Thailand and Gaza. He was Professor of Performance Studies at Northwestern University and some of his most influential pieces dealt with the ethics of ethnography. My superficial desire to be 'fully Javanese' could have been described by Conquergood as an example of 'the enthusiast's infatuation', one of the four sins or 'ethical pitfalls' of those who aim to study other cultures (Conquergood 1985: 4).

The Map and the Guidebook

In 'the enthusiast's infatuation', someone becomes completely but superficially enthralled by another performance tradition. There are three other pitfalls identified by Conquergood. An example of the second one, the 'custodian's rip-off' is that people trained in a given tradition perform it for money (or other incentives) even when violating specific prohibitions of codes within the environment that a performance comes from (Conquergood 1985: 6). The 'curator's exhibitionism' overemphasizes difference and wants to astonish rather than understand (7). This is perhaps a very common trap for travellers and ethnographers where we might overemphasize the bizarre aspects of our experiences to the delight of our audiences back home. The 'skeptic's cop-out' is the stance that sees only difference and no reason to engage, arguing that any attempt to understand another culture is futile. This stand is only possible for the members of the dominant culture and Conquergood considers this the most morally reprehensible of the pitfalls (8). The ideal is somewhere in the middle, a 'dialogical performance' that 'struggles to bring together different voices, world views, value systems, and beliefs so that they can have a conversation with one another' (9). Although Conquergood was originally thinking about performance ethnographers, his words are equally applicable to the seekers of intercultural experiences:

> Dialogical performance is a way of having intimate conversation with other people and cultures. Instead of speaking about them, one speaks to and with them. The sensuous immediacy and emphatic leap demanded by performance is an occasion for orchestrating two voices, for bringing together two sensibilities. (10)

These pointers are useful because they can be readily put to use to identify what oneself (or others) are unknowingly doing. Although any theoretical model is necessarily abstract, Conquergood's four pitfalls and the ensuing advice are easy to operationalize. They could be thought of as a guidebook for the complex territory of intercultural practice. That territory has probably been best mapped by Lo and Gilbert, who draw careful distinctions between multicultural, intercultural and postcolonial theatre. Multicultural theatre means different things in different places, and this is linked to a country's policy on multiculturalism. Small 'm' multicultural theatre features a racially mixed cast without drawing attention to their differences, or resorting to folkloric display of different art forms in discrete categories (Lo and Gilbert 2002: 33). Under big 'M' multicultural theatre they identify ghetto theatre, migrant theatre and community theatre (34). All these approaches seek to destabilize dominant narratives but don't fully interrogate cross-cultural possibilities. In contrast, postcolonial theatre performances and texts explicitly address the legacy of imperialism. This can also be divided into two categories. The first one, syncretic theatre, usually involves the 'incorporation of indigenous material into a Western dramaturgical framework', which is itself modified by the process (36). Non-syncretic theatre only uses one cultural form (usually linked to the imperial regime) to voice postcolonial concerns. Intercultural theatre, which they define as an intentional hybrid between different performance cultures, can also be divided into three categories. Transcultural theatre transcends specific theatrical codes in order to find universal aspects. Well-known examples are the works of Eugenio Barba, an Italian theatre director based in Denmark who worked as Grotowski's collaborator in the 1960s, founded the intercultural theatre company Odin Teatret and the International School of Theatre Anthropology (ISTA). Intracultural theatre denotes cultural encounters between and across specific communities within a nation state (Lo and Gilbert 2002: 38). In Lo and Gilbert's formulation, extracultural theatre 'refers to theatre exchanges that are conducted along a West-East and North-South axis'. This description captures the bulk of intercultural theatre but fails to account for possible collaborations between South-South or East-East nation states.

They suggest that these ideas improve upon previous models, such as the hourglass model first defined by Patrice Pavis, a former professor of theatre semiology who held positions in France, England and the United States. In this model, Pavis imagines intercultural theatre as an hourglass clock, with theatre conventions as grains of sand trickling down from a source culture to a target culture (Pavis and Kruger 2001). Lo and Gilbert suggest that this model is too neat as it fails to account for the 'blockage, collisions, and retroaction as sites of either intervention or resistance' (Lo and Gilbert 2002: 43). Lo and Gilbert provide a map, and Conquergood provides a guidebook. Besides granting a precise vocabulary to describe common oversimplifications and ethical pitfalls, Conquergood's writing provides readers with a charitable hermeneutics for their own journeys: you will often err on different sides of the 'ethical minefield of performance plunder' and this is fine (Conquergood 1985: 9). An intercultural project, like any intellectual or artistic endeavour worth its salt, must be a prolonged, iterative project where mistakes will be made. Time and reflexivity are of the essence for a true intercultural dialogue.

Like Conquergood, Lo and Gilbert also stress the political dimension of intercultural dialogic performances. They suggest taking a cue from feminist performances, which are political first and aesthetic later. But they also emphasize the importance of continued practice, not just critique, as a strategy to think through the complexities of intercultural performances. 'Such moral critiques, while absolutely essential to the politicizing of interculturalism, risk instigating a kind of paralysis insofar as they suggest that virtually no form of theatrical exchange can be ethical' (Lo and Gilbert 2002: 49).

One way to move away from this paralysis is to look at intercultural writing that has been developed by performers. Although it rarely reaches the abstraction of the generalizable theories we have just seen, performers describing their own experiences engage with the theories substantially while also providing accounts of how to navigate thorny ethical issues. In one example, Barry Freeman contrasts the orderly accounts of intercultural exchange with his messy experiences. He suggests that postmodern ethnography, which does not assume scientific objectivity and is always situated in specific contexts, provides a valuable tool for narrating intercultural exchange. To demonstrate this, he offers two accounts of the Prague-Toronto-Manitoulin Theatre Project (PTMTP), one that aims at pure factuality and the second one that is inspired by postmodern ethnography. He concludes with an argument for the usefulness of the latter: 'in my view, understanding how both collaboration and interculturalism operate requires an approach that celebrates the messiness of process: its multiple messages, delicate negotiations, conflicting perspectives, and accidents of creativity. The value of postmodern ethnography is that it seeks out (and is not obliged to quickly tidy) that messiness' (Freeman 2009: 65).

For all my insistence on the importance of long-term commitments to other cultures, I must confess I am still not sure of how to create truly dialogical performances and I still often suffer from the paralysis that Gilbert and Lo identify. But, as they suggest, there is also a moral imperative to try to attempt such dialogues, imperfect as they are. With this idea in mind, I have tried to perform again, after the years of moral anxiety that an excess of intercultural theory created in me.

Nowadays, I work mostly as a teacher and researcher. I have occasionally performed *wayang kulit* but I once found myself performing alongside the artists of Wayang Hip Hop, a troupe that I have written about (Escobar Varela 2014). For the troupe's anniversary, they invited me to write a song with them. This song was not an attempt to combine the complex semiotic regimes of Mexican folktales and *wayang* that I attempted years earlier, but a song about political injustices in our respective countries using the conventions of hip hop that are now globally recognizable. But perhaps that which is political about this is not its subject matter but the fact that by using hip hop as an in-between form, we have found a way to bring attention to the conditions of our own artistic traditions and not self-exoticize our origins. On a personal level, this collaboration was immensely satisfactory since it was the product of years of friendship with artists I admire. I conclude by linking my own experience to generic suggestions for those at different stages of intercultural lives and creative journeys: when you read intercultural theories, these need not only apply to the aesthetics of performances. They are not only tools to dissect and pick performance processes apart; they also provide a way to be in dialogue with your own experiences.

Further Reading

Bharucha (1993) is an extraordinary book, and required reading for anyone attempting to make performances across cultural and socioeconomic fault lines. The book combines performance analysis, history and personal narratives in a highly readable – if controversial – series of accounts, letters and histories. Pavis (1996) is a comprehensive compendium of theories of intercultural theatre, both from celebratory and critical perspectives. This book is ideal for someone wishing to learn more about the multiple theoretical perspectives on intercultural performance. Holledge and Tompkins (2000) is a comprehensive examination of contemporary intercultural performances by women around the world. Although the intersections of feminist theory and interculturalism are essential to contemporary performance, they are still rarely addressed. This book fills this gap and shows the complexities of contemporary performance. Dwight Conquergood's work has inspired many ethnographers and performance scholars. He passed away at an early age and most of his writings are scattered across different journals. Conquergood (2013) brings together his most influential contributions and addresses the ethics and methods of interculturally sensitive research and practice in performance studies.

References

Behrend, Tim (1999), 'The Millennial Esc (H) Atology of Heri Dono: "Semar Farts" First in Auckland, New Zealand', *Indonesia and the Malay World* 27 (79): 208–24.

Bharucha, Rustom (1993), *Theatre and the World: Performance and the Politics of Culture*, London and New York: Routledge.

Bharucha, Rustom (2000), *The Politics of Cultural Practice: Thinking through Theatre in an Age of Globalization*, Hanover, NH: University Press of New England.

Brakel-Papenhuijzen, Clara (1995), *Classical Javanese Dance: The Surakarta Tradition and Its Terminology* (Verhandelingen van Het Koninklijk Instituut Voor Taal-, Land- En Volkenkunde, No. 155), Leiden: KITLV Press.

Brown, John Russell (1998), 'Theatrical Pillage in Asia: Redirecting the Intercultural Traffic', *New Theatre Quarterly* 14 (53): 9–19.

Cohen, Matthew Isaac (2007), 'Contemporary Wayang in Global Contexts', *Asian Theatre Journal* 24 (2): 338–69.

Conquergood, Dwight (1985), 'Performing as a Moral Act: Ethical Dimensions of the Ethnography of Performance', *Literature in Performance: A Journal of Literary and Performing Art* 5 (2): 1–13.

Conquergood, Dwight (2013), *Cultural Struggles*, Baltimore: University of Michigan Press.

Escobar Varela, Miguel (2014), 'Wayang Hip Hop: Java's Oldest Performance Tradition Meets Global Youth Culture', *Asian Theatre Journal* 31 (2): 481–504.

Holledge, Julie, and Joanne Tompkins (2000), *Women's Intercultural Performance*, London and New York: Routledge.

Larasati, Rachmi Diyah (2013), *The Dance That Makes You Vanish. Difference Incorporated*, Minneapolis: University of Minnesota Press.

Lo, Jacqueline, and Helen Gilbert (2002), 'Toward a Topography of Cross-Cultural Theatre Praxis', *TDR* 46 (3): 31–53.

Mrázek, Jan (2002), *Puppet Theater in Contemporary Indonesia*, Vol. no. 50. Michigan Papers on South and Southeast Asia, University of Michigan, Centers for South and Southeast Asian Studies.

Pavis, Patrice, and Loren Kruger (2001), *Theatre at the Crossroads of Culture*, London and New York: Routledge.

Stepputat, Kendra (2012), 'Performing Kecak: A Balinese Dance Tradition between Daily Routine and Creative Art', *Yearbook for Traditional Music* 44: 49–70.

Taymor, Julie (1979), 'Teatr Loh, Indonesia, 1977–8', *TDR* 23 (2): 63–76.

Yong, Li Lan (2004), 'Ong Keng Sen's Desdemona, Ugliness, and the Intercultural Performative', *Theatre Journal* 56 (2): 251–73.

13 What Is the Impact of Theatre and Performance?

SRUTI BALA

Thinking the Question of Impact

'Art is not a mirror held up to reality, but a hammer with which to shape it': this well-known adage, commonly attributed to Brecht, captures the complex relationship between theatre and performance practices, the societies from which they emerge and to which they respond. It suggests that art can, indeed *ought* to, impact upon and transform reality, rather than seek to simply depict and re-present reality in a verifiable manner. It seems to contest the possibility of any simple, mimetic portrayal of reality altogether. For not only are there as many realities as there are ways of perceiving them, but something can only become a reality if we are able to first imagine its possibility. The adage invites us to reflect on who wields this hammer, and how it might be used to impact upon reality. The foundational question of theatre's social, cultural, political or ecological impact continues to productively preoccupy artists, scholars and critics. What are the ways in which we can think through theatre's impact on the world?

The notion of impact in conjunction with the arts remains an imprecise and unwieldy one, yet it seems to command significant power in the way it is repeatedly summoned in justifying the necessity of the arts. This can be explained by the way in which the idea of impact has become a core feature of determining the cultural value of the arts by policy makers and public and corporate funding bodies. This chapter addresses the question of impact in relation to theatre and performance by investigating the assumptions around it, as well as the critical and methodological challenges it poses in our field. Using the example of one performance, namely the 2012 Spanish-language production *Afuera: lesbianas en escena* (Outside: Lesbians on Stage) by the theatre collective Teatro Siluetas from Guatemala and El Salvador as a point of departure, the chapter will focus on a number of debates in theatre and performance scholarship pertaining to assessing and evaluating impact. In closing, the chapter offers a number of points of orientation and aspects to take into consideration when undertaking a study of theatre's impact.

Let us begin by examining the underlying premises of the question, 'what is the impact of theatre?' The notion of impact (from the Latin verb *impingere*, i.e. to 'press closely', 'fix firmly' or 'forcibly thrust') suggests that something leaves a perceptible mark or trace on its environment or surroundings. When used in relation to theatre and performance, impact seems to imply that they remain and resonate in some way with the world, that they have a palpable effect on those who partook of their making and presentation, especially after

Fig. 13.1 *Afuera* performance for students at the University of Mexico, 2012. Photo: Carla Molina.

they are over. This is hardly surprising, given the ephemerality of theatre, and the medium-specific difficulty of preserving or reproducing theatrical works. Precisely because theatre seemingly vanishes the moment it is performed in the here and now (unlike a book that can be reread and stored, or a film that can be copied and distributed, or even a piece of music that can, to some extent, be preserved in the form of a recording) it seems to repeatedly prompt the question of impact in manifold ways. What remains of theatre when the show is over? When someone claims that a certain performance had a great impact on them, they might be speaking of its lasting (positive or negative) impressions: images, movements, scenes, moments that left a mark on their memory, that resonated with them, or triggered visceral or emotional responses that extended well beyond the duration of the performance itself. Aristotle's conception of catharsis comes to mind as one of the earliest ideas in Western philosophy in which the relation between art and its (positive) effect on the viewer by way of a process of inner cleansing or purification is emphasized.

To ask of theatre's impact might equally imply wanting to understand what a certain production has achieved by way of contributing to public opinion, or in shaping the discourse around a possibly controversial topic. What discussions has it triggered, how has it thrown open new angles of interpretation? Impact might also suggest that a performance has a specific target audience who might be treated as beneficiaries (i.e. they benefit in certain ways from the performance), that it has ripple effects on their lives, attitudes or social relations. What are its consequences in other spheres of life? Has it contributed to or influenced any level of societal transformation? And if so, how? Impact could equally relate to those who are involved in the creative process, thus implying that the very act

Fig. 13.2 Lesbian subjectivity brought centre stage. Photo: Mathieu Hutin.

of participating in a theatrical production, regardless of the outcome, might serve an educational or other purpose.

Here it is important to note that the idea of impact is largely, but not necessarily always, positively connoted. One might, for instance, speak of the negative impact of a certain performance in its propagation of an aggressive masculinity or its misogynist representations of women. In situations of crisis and violent conflict, theatre may play a part in fortifying cultural stereotypes and thus have a negative impact, serving to polarize rather than de-escalate a latent conflict. (Consider, for instance, the role of radio plays in inciting violence during the Rwandan genocide. More recently, the use of blackfacing on stage has been heavily criticized in Germany and the Netherlands, pointing to the negative effects of caricaturing blackness and making its racist and discriminatory gestures invisible [Hoving and Essed 2014].) However, when we ask the question of theatre's impact, we tend to assume that there will be (or ought to be) one, and that it makes a positive difference, hopefully bringing about some desirable change in our lives. This assumption is wrought with its own contradictions. By emphasizing impact, theatrical practices may sometimes be valued only in terms of their so-called 'usefulness' in other spheres, and not in their own right. Does it promote social cohesion? Does it raise awareness about problems?

Such a reduction of theatrical art to its benefits for society is a false estimation of its potentials. Firstly, it is extremely difficult to trace any direct or causal link between a certain theatrical practice or event and its positive or negative social outcomes. Indeed, it would be more accurate to claim that no peace accords have been signed or ecological disasters been prevented due to the direct influence of theatre. Secondly, and more importantly, the potentials of theatre, like all art forms, are not calculable according to the logic of a benefit analysis. Rather than judging theatre and performance by the same standards of assessment that apply to, say, the impact of drinking water supply on public health, it is the very model of impact which needs to be attuned and realigned to the specific qualities of theatre and performance. We therefore need to think of the impact of art in less quantitative or effect-based and more qualitative and affective terms. As James Thompson points out, in concentrating on output or function 'we are in danger of losing sight of the art practice. We are becoming target not process orientated' (2000: 101–4). We need to rethink the assessment of impact in order to be able to pay attention to subtle, ambiguous and delicate indicators, which may not make sense in cost-and-benefit or utilitarian terms. The tools of gauging impact available to theatre and performance scholars ought not to be governed by a narrowly economic or technocratic, evidence-based rationale. Thirdly, and following from this, we can observe that even within the field, different traditions of performance practice entail different understandings of impact, which vary historically and regionally. Classical opera productions and participatory theatre workshops with children with autism operate in vastly different environments and reveal distinct interdependences between artistic and socio-political domains. Thus, when the question of the impact of a certain theatre practice is asked, it is important to examine the assumptions implicit to the question and its possible claims around usefulness, applicability, causality and measurability, in order to determine a working understanding of impact that is befitting to the practice.

Notwithstanding the various assumptions surrounding the notion of impact in relation to the arts, it continues to be an idea that holds the heady promise of transformation and affective force in the world. The artistic and cultural life of a society is often regarded as the 'barometer' of its well-being, maturity and, indeed, degree of civilization. This widely held orthodoxy, as Belfiore and Bennett point out in their study *The Social Impact of the Arts*, tends to assume that the study of impact is therefore about measuring and finding evidence for its existence, rather than interrogating its claims (2008: 7). How can we speak about the impact of theatre and performance, without falling prey to the tyranny of evidence and numbers, making use of the methods of the interpretive Humanities? This is all the more relevant given the growing necessity for artists to demonstrate and quantify the impact of their artistic ideas in order to avail of arts funding. A critical approach to impact could thus serve as a means to respond to funding policies from the grassroots level, as well as expand and shape the conception of impact in a manner that is adequate to the diversity of the arts.

Case Study: Teatro Siluetas

In order to think through this question I will introduce, by way of illustration, a performance case in point, namely the independent Latin American theatre group Teatro Siluetas from Guatemala and El Salvador, and specifically, their 2012 production *Afuera: lesbianas en escena* (Outside: Lesbians on Stage). This case invites us to reflect on several dimensions of theatre's impact. The focus in this analysis will primarily be on its social, cultural, affective and political dimensions.

Teatro Siluetas was founded in 2011 by four women from Guatemala and El Salvador, who self-identify as lesbian-feminist activists and formed a theatre collective under the name 'Siluetas' (Spanish for 'silhouettes') with the aim of using theatre as a means to reflect on the experiences of lesbian subjectivities in Central America. The members of the group were affiliated to and involved in various ways with autonomous feminist social justice movements in the continent. Following their participation in the activist initiative 'The Lesbian Feminist School' in Guatemala, they came together with the idea to continue their activism using the modalities of theatre, with which all four were familiar, or in which they were formally trained. To that extent, the formation of the theatre collective itself may be regarded as one indicator of the productive impact of their involvement in the feminist movement. Which is to say that the notion of impact is multidirectional; it is not only about theatre's impact on society but also about the way in which theatre is impacted upon by social developments.

Two characteristics of Teatro Siluetas are pertinent in relation to the question of impact: on the one hand, the choice of the organizational form of a collective and on the other hand, the foregrounding of a lesbian subjectivity in the artistic practice. Latin American experimental theatre and performance has widely embraced the tradition of autonomous theatre collectives (*creación colectiva*), often traced to the influence of theatre reformers such as Enrique Buenaventura in Colombia in the 1980s. The *creación colectiva* movement in Latin American theatre, which began in the 1950s, had a landmark impact on the way theatre groups approached their processes of working. This includes practices such as creating scripts through collective improvisation processes, modalities of establishing dialogues with audiences, feedback loops in the dramaturgical process and community outreach activities (Cortes and Barrea-Marlys 2003). The choice of the structure of a participatory collective, rather than that of a theatre company headed by an artistic director, with actors, assistants, designers, technicians and others in hierarchically lower positions, is indicative of the impact of democratic ideals on institutional practices and structures. For the members of Siluetas, it was important to organize the day-to-day practices of theatre in a way that questioned and changed the ways in which creative processes tended to be hierarchically organized, with predominantly male directors and playwrights having the voice of authority and actresses merely executing and embodying their ideas. Siluetas therefore collectively wrote and directed and produced the play through a process of experimentation and dialogical interaction, which not only included a horizontal communication between the four members of the collective, but also involved training with invited guests, including dancers, choreographers and theatre directors like Jesusa Rodriguez, and her singer-songwriter partner Liliana Felipe, with whose input they completed the final version of the play *Afuera*. Rodríguez and Felipe are known both for their lesbian-feminist performance activism and for their long-standing engagement with current political themes pertaining to the Latin American continent.

The second characteristic is the choice of foregrounding lesbian subjectivity in the work of the theatre collective. One might regard the launch of a theatre group that specifically addresses the needs and lives of subjects regarded as marginalized and underrepresented in the mainstream as an identitarian or minoritarian formation, with the purpose of gaining more visibility and acknowledgement in the public sphere. While this is true to some extent, for Siluetas the motivation in founding a lesbian collective extends beyond an identity-based politics. Rather, the category of 'lesbian' presents for the theatre collective an intersectional lens through which all systems of oppression and inequality can be approached. Thus, it is possible to sharpen one's understanding of racism, ableism or other forms of social discrimination through paying attention to the mechanisms by which women attracted to women are oppressed; for not only are different forms of oppression intertwined, but also conversely, the unique experiences of identifying with the figurations of 'lesbian' in a Central American context offers a different perspective on mainstream society, politics and public culture, and sheds light on the construction of categories such as 'homosexual' or 'heterosexual'. The theatrical representation of lesbian lives in *Afuera* can thus be read not as a direct correlate to some authentic reality or indigenous identity, but as a means of imagining and setting the terms of this reality.

The play *Afuera* addresses a range of issues, from lesbophobia, sexual violence and the role of religious institutions in the governance of sexual mores, to the prominent presence of religious conservatism in public affairs, in tandem with the strengthening of neoliberal economic policies put in place after the end of the civil wars in El Salvador and Guatemala in the 1990s. It also examines the lives of lesbians who challenge or try to escape from the binary gender construction with humour and lightness. It speaks of questions of loneliness, the absence of role models and popular cultural points of reference. In dramaturgical terms, it consists of a sequence of short scenes that combine a range of formats, from fragments of daily life experiences, monologues, dialogues, choreographed interludes, to humorous episodes, or elaborate *tableaux vivants*. The scenes sometimes involve conventional role-play, with four actresses playing characters such as a nun or a couple in love, shifting between *femme* and *butch* roles, well-wishers or people who ridicule lesbians. But there are also moments when they step out of their roles and address the audience directly in their own voices as members of the theatre collective and citizens of society. This makes it difficult to view 'the lesbian' as merely a fictional character on stage, but urges audiences in a non-didactic and non-confessional manner to acknowledge a personally experienced reality on and offstage. Layers of prejudices and unquestioned assumptions about what the idea of sexual orientation implies, are gradually peeled off, revealing the vulnerabilities and ambiguities of human existence.

The production *Afuera* toured across Guatemala and was performed not only in theatre venues, but also in schools, universities, community centres and female prisons, covering both urban and rural sites. These performances were accompanied by question-and-answer sessions with audiences, and workshops with young adults. A documentary film was made in 2013 about the performance with the financial support of the Dutch international development agency, HIVOS, and in collaboration with the network of Latin American artists *Trasbastidores* (Backstage). All these aspects of a performance's (after-) life are also pertinent to the assessment of its impact.

Critical and Creative Challenges

Having briefly sketched a performance example, a number of critical and creative challenges may be identified in discussing the impact of a performance. What counts as impact, under which conditions? How can impact be evaluated and what are the methods available to Theatre and Performance scholars in this quest?

On impact studies: In thinking through the question of impact in the arts, a brief note on the prominent influence of social and economic impact studies is in order. This domain of research gained currency in the 1980s, at a time when urban regeneration programmes in Europe, the United States and other industrially developed regions of the world increasingly looked to arts and culture to fill the gaps that were emerging from the decline of industries in cities. Artistic and cultural activities gradually came to be regarded as an 'expanding economic sector' (Reeves 2002). This led to the commissioning of studies that demonstrated how investment in the arts effectively led to greater economic growth or job creation in other sectors. Such advocacy-oriented studies departed from the premise that the arts are economically beneficial to cities and looked for evidence for the same in order to advocate public investment in the arts and in cultural activities and institutions. As Belfiore and Bennett point out, impact studies is motivated by an evidence-based approach to policy making, whereby pragmatism and an orientation towards 'whatever brings about the best results' serves as a guide to policy making rather than ideals or principles that are derived from constitutional or long-standing culturally rooted grounds (2008: 5).

The problems of such an evidence-led, economistic approach to studying impact have been widely criticized in cultural policy studies. All kinds of claims can be made about the benefits of the arts, and the search for impact can end up as a search based on indicators that are likely to produce the desired findings. In the logic of viewing the arts as an economic sector, the study of impact becomes often a matter of arguing that the arts generate employment, enhance social cohesion or reduce crime, which in turn indirectly supports economic growth. Thus, despite a rationale of searching for evidence for art's social or economic benefits, deep-seated, unquestioned cultural norms and values pertaining to what counts as beneficial or has a positive transformative potential inform the way impact is argued. Conventional impact studies tend to be commissioned by organizations that support or fund the arts, which implies that the findings of these studies tend to advocate various benefits and economically viable qualities of the arts, thus serving as advocacy reports rather than as research. A further problematic aspect of the domain of impact studies is that it tends to predominantly value the arts along instrumental lines. The problem is not, as Belfiore convincingly argues, that a certain instrumentality is applied to the arts. Rather, she argues, the problem 'lies in the way in which the attribution of value to the outcome of aesthetic encounters has become part of the technocratic machinery of cultural policy-making' (2015: 96). Mostly, quantitative understandings of value tend to determine whether or not a certain artistic practice is worth investing in. Thus, even within the economic logic, a very narrow understanding of 'more is better', underwritten by governmental policies of austerity and privatization, remains largely unquestioned (Fotiadi 2017). Economic understandings of 'impact' thus assume far more policy-related influence and importance than other, less utilitarian and more interpretive, subjective approaches.

In her study *Undoing the Demos: Neoliberalism's Stealth Revolution*, political philosopher Wendy Brown argues that neoliberalism is 'an order of rationality', that is not only a set of economic policies or an ideology, but also a political imaginary, an order of reason that seeps into all human domains in the most unexpected ways and in manifold forms of articulation (2015: 10–11). Every human need and desire becomes valued in economized terms, which doesn't necessarily only mean monetary terms, but a logic of profit, benefit, growth and expansion, and this also extends to those spheres that were historically governed by different values, such as the arts, interpersonal relationships, children's upbringing, education, health and well-being, ecology or spirituality. Impact studies in the arts, particularly those that seek to prove and rationalize the benefits of the arts and demonstrate them as worthy of receiving structural or financial support, face the risk of succumbing to a neoliberal logic, even while they may claim to be championing the arts.

In the present chapter, I take distance from such an evidence-based, economically rationalized understanding of impact, towards a more ambivalent, open-ended notion of impact, encompassing diverse dimensions and modes of interrelations between artworks and the societies they emerge from and respond to. The study of impact cannot be separated from the conditionalities and agendas of who is interested in theatre's impact and to what ends. The evaluation of impact is not an end in itself (Isar and Anheier 2007: 4). Further, impact need not only be perceived as the effect of the big on the small, the powerful on the weak, or of institutions on individuals, but can also be meaningfully addressed from a multidirectional, systemic perspective, that is how non-institutionalizable acts and collective bodies in turn transform the structures into which they are placed, and by which they may be restricted or empowered, but which never fully, entirely constitute or define them. Impact need not be only positive and beneficial, and it is also the critical task of scholars to pay attention to such negative aspects. It does not necessarily imply that it is a rejection of an artistic practice or its efforts altogether. In many senses, it may be argued that the theoretical division between the seemingly symbolic space of the theatre and the presumably real space of social and political coexistence is itself restrictive, as if the former were a mere service provider for – or pet animal offering solace and entertainment to – the latter; or as if the latter by definition could safely exclude the unruly realms of imagination and the impractical dimensions of the aesthetic (Bala 2017).

Specifying the scale and scope of the study: One of the critical challenges in the study of theatre's impact therefore lies in determining its scale, scope and intensity by paying attention to the particularities of every specific instance. We could start by asking what exactly we refer to when we speak of theatre: a single performance, a theatre group, a tour or festival, a play script, the acting skills of one actress, or a certain genre of performance? When we speak of impact, what are the time and geographical ranges we seek – or are able – to address? Are we interested in individuals or communities, in the short or long term, in the local or regional or transnational? Being explicit and specific about the grids of our frameworks is crucial, simply because different understandings of the arts, of communities and of the scope of impact will lead to different outcomes (Guetzkow 2002). In the case of Teatro Siluetas's show *Afuera*, the framework of analysis might be restricted to a single performance, or its entire production history, that is all the performances in different locations, or additionally, include the documentary film that can be viewed online (see Further Reading). If one is interested in addressing the impact of the process of performance making on the actresses and their social environments, the framework might be extended to the entire process of conceptualizing, rehearsing and producing the performance. It can be further expanded to include the ways in which the performance circulated to other parts of the world, through donor agency reports, or by way of invitations to the theatre group members to LGBTQ events, and academic scholarship. This selection depends on what we can access in depth and what we are interested in finding out. If we ask the question of the impact of Latin American lesbian feminism on the practice of collective, collaborative dramaturgy, we obviously need to attend to the rehearsal and conceptual processes as well as to the specificities of lesbian feminism in Guatemala and El Salvador far more than to audience responses. If we are interested in the impact of the performance on attitudes towards sexuality among young adults, we must look for ways to access and communicate with young adults who have seen the performance, independently from, or in addition to, what may be available to us via the documentation or reports by the theatre group.

The problem of aggregation: The next critical challenge is that of aggregation, namely how to interconnect the micro with the macro levels. How can we claim with any certainty that there is a connection between the successful ticket sales of the show and a growing acceptance and liberal attitude towards homosexuality in society? Causality is a tricky principle when it comes to studying the arts. It is a fallacy to claim, for instance, that urban audiences in Guatemala were more receptive to the topic of lesbianism than rural audiences *because* there was more laughter and applause in the former than in the latter. There is no direct causal link between applause for a show and the social openness towards a taboo topic that is the subject of the show. On the contrary, it is well known that what is widely accepted and appreciated by audiences within the imaginative space of performance may equally meet with hostility and violence on the streets (Butler 1988). Audience laughter during a scene when two women kiss on stage may well be an expression of embarrassment, ridicule or even of a sense of disgust, just as the laughter of teenage school pupils at a performance in a high school may be an indicator of a healthy emotional receptiveness and curiosity towards sexuality and love, or indeed a mix of emotions. It requires heightened caution and sensitivity as a viewer and researcher to distinguish between appreciative and disapproving responses and draw conclusions based on them.

Institutional impact: One of the possible ways to resolve the problem of aggregating the relation between the performance and society at large, is to define and delimit the analysis to specific societal institutions, and examine the points of contact between the performance and these institutions. These could include artistic and cultural venues but also community centres, schools, universities, prisons or church-run institutions. Such institutions can be regarded, in the sense of Louis Althusser, as ideological state apparatuses, which reinforce the dominant ideology without using state repressive force or violence. In an influential essay originally published in 1970, Marxist philosopher Althusser argues that the state and its subjects share not only a legal or territorial relationship, but also a psychological one, marked by ideology. A state controls its subjects not only through law-enforcement institutions and agents, like the police or the courts, but equally, and in a far more heterogeneous and decentralized manner, through cultural apparatuses, such as schools, religious bodies, the social institution of the family and the media. These so-called 'ideological state apparatuses' ensure that citizens comply with and subjugate themselves to state control by willingly and unquestioningly believing that their position within the state and its structures is a natural one. Althusser argues that through these ideological state apparatuses, subjects are hailed into being, they learn to recognize themselves and others and acquiesce to the place allocated to them, a process he terms 'interpellation'.

The performance *Afuera* premiered on 26 January 2012 in the Teatro de Bellas Artes theatre in Guatemala City, a cultural institution under the aegis of the Guatemalan Ministry of Culture and Sports. Laia Ribera Cañénguez, a member of Teatro Siluetas, describes in an interview the difficulties in finding a venue that would be willing to host this particular performance, because theatre halls did not want to risk their reputations by hosting a group that openly talked about lesbianism (2015: 256). The fact that Teatro de Bellas Artes did host the event might be interpreted as a mark of a critical capacity of the institution. In showing its support to an independent lesbian-feminist production in the face of widespread institutional caution and conservatism, it effectively took a public stance in support of reflecting on the social issues that the performance addressed. Who made the decision to include the performance in the programme? Were there prior connections to members of the theatre collective? Perhaps it lost some of its regular audience members in the process, perhaps it accessed a different public, or perhaps it led to new international connections. All these aspects might form the focus of an investigation.

Similarly, we can enquire into the impact on those institutions that hesitated or categorically refused to host the performance. Was there an internal discussion prior to the decision, how were the hesitations regarding the play formulated, how did the institutions perceive their own social responsibility? Since the performance toured to various other countries and was shown in venues such as universities, schools and church centres, the institutional responses and afterlife of the performance offer possibilities for analysing the social impact of the performance by examining the impact on institutions with which it came into contact. Since these institutions make it possible for people who would presumably never buy a ticket to go and see the show in Guatemala City to view the performance in a familiar environment, it is no exaggeration to claim that the outreach of the performance expanded greatly by virtue of being shown under the purview of these institutions. The performance also triggered some discriminatory responses from institutions. In Costa Rica, the performers were asked to leave a café, where they gathered after a show, since the owners felt that the presence of lesbians would be a bad influence on children (Cañénguez 2015: 247). In anticipation of protests or objections to the play, the theatre group took security measures at the performance venues, to prevent damage to property or personal injury. One of the performers was asked by her family to leave Guatemala, in order not to blemish the family's reputation. This indicates that performances (or public perceptions and projections of what a performance is about) can trigger very real social repercussions, which are enacted by institutions. These could come from strangers as well as from families and close networks. These impacts can consist of a motley of negative and positive responses, ranging from sentiments of moral outrage and offence on the one side to accolade and praise from the press on the other side. In all this, the performance realistically constitutes but one of several factors that impact on institutional attitudes, policies or practices.

Impact on individuals: Yet, while it might be possible to gather some statistics on the demographics of the audiences, and make qualified observations on the ways in which a performance influences, critiques or interacts with institutions, it still leaves the question open as to how to qualitatively approach a performance's impact on individuals. Audience responses have served as the primary route to assessing the individual dimensions of impact (Bennett 1990). While this chapter does not have the scope to address the methodological and theoretical complexities of audience and reception research, I would like to underline one point, at the risk of overstating the obvious: every utterance about a performance and the impact it has on an audience member needs to be carefully contextualized. It cannot be taken at face value or viewed as a validation for an external, objective reality. Precisely because our access to these contexts is likely to be limited, great caution is called for in deriving generalizations. In the case of *Afuera*, the overwhelmingly positive and supportive responses of audience members towards the performance stands in contrast to a social and political climate that is extremely hostile to those who do not conform to the norms of heterosexuality. How to make sense of this disjunction? To find an answer to this question, it is worthwhile examining some of the individual responses more closely.

The interaction with audiences, specifically with young people and women from working-class and indigenous backgrounds, was an important motivating factor for Teatro Siluetas. The performances thus regularly featured after-talks with the public. They also offered the possibility for audience members to write down their questions on a piece of paper anonymously, in case they did not feel comfortable to ask something directly. One such note they received, asked the unassuming question: 'Es bonito ser lesbiana?' (Is it nice, agreeable to be lesbian?) Cañénguez appropriately cautions against reading this remark as an indication of an innocent response from a simple, good-hearted, rural woman (2015: 249). Rather, she suggests contextualizing such positive responses against the backdrop of a society recovering from a protracted civil war, where self-pride and respect for a community's identity become important means of recovering from violent conflict. The play's choice to deliberately not depict lesbians as victims, and not to speak with echoes of self-pity and resentment, allowed for diverse forms of audience empathy and identification. This also explains responses such as the following: 'I thought I was coming to see a lesbian play and I wanted to show my solidarity, but through the play I ended up thinking about my own relations, my construction of gender and I felt that it spoke to me very personally' (Cañénguez 2015: 245). Instead of serving an identity politics, that is speaking primarily to those (few) who might self-identify with the protagonists of the performance, and thus treating lesbian subjectivity as a state of exception, *Afuera* relates to the audience through an inclusive approach. The specific loneliness that the figures in the play experience might thus be accessed as a universal, human emotion. One struggle for human dignity and recognition is not equivocal to, but also not separable from, another. When audience members say they are *touched* or *moved* by witnessing the vulnerability of another body or by the life story of another person, we are compelled to widen our understanding of impact to include not only social, political or economic *effects*, but equally also psychophysical *affects*: those forces other than or complementary to rationality, linearity, causality and cognition, which propel us in various directions in our lives and worlds (Gregg and Seigworth 2010). These cannot be measured or valued in any empirical manner, but require an interpretive register that can encompass subjective, visceral, emotional, experiential and sensorial traces.

Conclusion: Making Thinking

In thinking through the challenges of what the impact of theatre and performance might be, and how to critically approach it, I have argued against a purely policy-oriented notion of impact that is underwritten by a rationale of utility and profitability. Instead, I propose studying impact in its varied dimensions as well as in its unique contexts, while making as transparent as possible the objectives that inform us as researchers, and specifying the scope and scale of what one can realistically make claims of impact about. Such an interpretive approach also requires methodological experimentation and a stretching of disciplinary horizons. To speak of the impact of a performance such as *Afuera* in Guatemala and El Salvador requires a heightened sensitivity towards and awareness of the socio-political context, and an openness to discuss issues and events that take place outside of the theatre in the strict sense. This involves a combination of a performance analysis, supplemented by ethnographic research and audience research, as well as a close contextualization of the events that happen around and beyond the performance itself: from after-talks to press criticisms to public interventions to everyday events.

Given the extensive critique of the term 'impact' and its evidence-based positivist foundations, one wonders whether 'impact' is, after all, the best term, and whether it might better be discarded altogether in favour of a less controversial concept? Indeed, there are several related concepts in the vocabulary of theatre and performance studies, ranging from a more empirically grounded idea of 'reception' in audience research, to a philosophically argued idea of 'performative force' or 'efficacy', to sociologically cadenced terms, such as 'outreach'. Yet I am convinced that the problems related to a utilitarian, economic interpretation of impact would not go away by simply replacing the term with something else. And the question of how theatre or performance remain beyond the moment of their presence and how they might contribute to historical transformation processes will continue to be asked by practitioners, scholars and critics. The problem is thus not just a matter of terminology. Rather, the concept of impact insists on being rethought and newly formulated in as much as the discontent with it seems inseparable from the possibility it offers.

Performance Details

Afuera: lesbianas en escena (Outside, Lesbians on Stage) by theatre group Colectiva Siluetas (co-produced with Trasbastidores). Premiere: 26 January 2012 in Teatro de Bellas Artes of Guatemala City. Performers: Tatiana Palomo, Camila Urrutia, Laia Cañénguez, Lu Robles. Advisors: Liliana Felipe and Jesusa Rodriguez. Documentary film: Documental sobre la gira centroamericana de la Colectiva Siluetas con AFUERA (2012). https://youtu.be/zlym8PxUbkA. Direction: Carla Molina, Editing: Pepe Orozco, Carla Molina.

The presentation of the case study *Afuera* in this chapter is based on an interview I conducted with Laia América Ribera Cañénguez from Teatro Siluetas, as well as documentary material (Cañénguez 2015).

Further Reading

Belfiore and Bennett (2008) approach the question of the impact of the arts from a historical perspective, i.e. what has impact meant in different times and contexts? Their book also examines differences between artistic disciplines, including music, literature, theatre and the visual arts. Thompson (2009) is a critical reflection on current interventions by theatre practitioners, particularly as therapeutic or reconciliatory efforts in zones of violent conflict. It argues that effects of performance need to be considered together with their affects. Schechner (2003), especially the chapter 'From Ritual to Theatre and Back', elaborates a spectrum of effects of performance, from entertainment to efficacy. The book looks to cultural anthropology and the study of ritual and festival, in particular, to develop a theorization of impact. Etherton and Prentki's (2006) special issue consists of a number of contributions from different parts of the world that critically examine and challenge what impact assessment means in relation to applied theatre and performance. The articles reflect on the relationship between context, method and outcome in different artistic practices. Schneider's study on theatrical re-enactment (2011) theorises impact in terms of theatre's afterlives and self-referential traces.[1]

References

Althusser, Louis ([1970] 2014), *On the Reproduction of Capitalism: Ideology and Ideological State Apparatuses*, London and New York: Verso.

Bala, Sruti (2017), 'The Art of Unsolicited Participation', in Tony Fisher and Eve Katsouraki (eds), *Performing Antagonism: Theatre, Performance and Radical Democracy*, 273–87, Basingstoke: Palgrave Macmillan.

Bala, Sruti (2018), *The Gestures of Participatory Art*, Manchester: Manchester University Press.

Belfiore, Eleonora (2015), '"Impact," "value" and "bad Economics": Making Sense of the Problem of Value in the Arts and Humanities', *Arts & Humanities in Higher Education* 14 (1): 95–110.

Belfiore, Eleonora, and Oliver Bennett (2008), *The Social Impact of the Arts: An Intellectual History*, Basingstoke: Palgrave Macmillan.

Bennett, Susan (1990), *Theatre Audiences: A Theory of Production and Reception*, London and New York: Routledge.

Brown, Wendy (2015) *Undoing the Demos: Neoliberalism's Stealth Revolution*, New York: Zone Books.

Butler, Judith (1988), 'Performative Acts and Gender Constitution: An Essay in Phenomenology and Feminist Theory', *Theatre Journal* 40 (4): 519–31.

Cañénguez, Laia América Ribera (2015), 'Outside and Onstage: Experiences of the Lesbian Feminist Theater Collective Teatro Siluetas from Guatemala and El Salvador', in Ashley

---

[1]An extended version of this chapter is published in Bala (2018).

Tellis and Sruti Bala (eds), *The Global Trajectories of Queerness: Re-Thinking Same-Sex Politics in the Global South*, 241–62, Leiden: Brill/Rodopi.

Cortes, Eladio, and Mirta Barrea-Marlys (2003), *Encyclopedia of Latin American Theater*, Westport: Greenwood Press.

Etherton, Michael, and Tim Prentki, eds (2006), Special Issue on Applied Theatre and Impact Assessment, *Research in Drama Education: The Journal of Applied Theatre and Performance* 11 (2).

Fotiadi, Eva (2017), 'Von Autonomer Zu Allgemein Anwendbarer Kunst', in Matthias Warstat, Florian Evers, Kristin Flade, Fabian Lempa and Lilian Seuberling (eds), *Recherchen* 129, *Applied Theatre*: *Rahmen Und Positionen*, 251–73, Berlin: Theater der Zeit.

Gregg, Melissa, and Gregory J. Seigworth, eds (2010), *The Affect Theory Reader*, Durham and London: Duke University Press.

Guetzkow, Joshua (2002), 'How the Arts Impact Communities: An Introduction to the Literature on Arts Impact Studies' (Working Paper 20), Princeton, NJ Available online: https://www.princeton.edu/~artspol/workpap/WP20 - Guetzkow.pdf (accessed 7 May 2018).

Hoving, Isabel, and Philomena Essed, eds (2014), *Dutch Racism*, Leiden: Brill/Rodopi.

Isar, Yudhishthir Raj, and Helmut Anheier, eds (2007), *Conflicts and Tensions*, Cultures and Globalizations, Vol. 1, London: Sage Publications.

Reeves, Michelle (2002), *Measuring the Social and Economic Impact of the Arts*, London: Arts Council of England.

Schechner, Richard (2003), *Performance Theory*, revised edn, London and New York: Routledge.

Schneider, Rebecca (2011), *Performing Remains: Art and War in Times of Theatrical Reenactment*. London and New York: Routledge.

Thompson, James (2000), 'It Don't Mean a Thing If It Ain't Got That Swing: Some Questions on Participatory Theatre, Evaluation and Impact', *Research in Drama Education: The Journal of Applied Theatre and Performance* 5 (1): 101–4.

Thompson, James (2009), *Performance Affects: Applied Theatre and the End of Affect.* Basingstoke: Palgrave Macmillan.

14 Does Staging Historical Trauma Re-Enact It?

TAVIA NYONG'O

Introduction: Are You Being Triggered?

Debates over 'trigger warnings' and other content warnings on college syllabi and theatrical playbills have posed an important question for theatre and performance studies: can theatre and performance stage historical trauma without re-enacting it? Put another way, what is the responsibility of the theatre student, theatre artist and/or theatre educator to the historical and present-day realities that their art seeks to depict, particularly when the nature of that reality, and the form of that art, might, intentionally or otherwise, 'trigger' a member of the audience (or for that matter, a member of the production)? This chapter will work through this question by focusing on a particular text in performance, Jackie Sibblies Drury's 2014 play *We Are Proud to Present a Presentation About the Herero of Namibia, Formerly Known as Southwest Africa, From the German Sudwestafrika, Between the Years 1884–1915.* As the very title of the play suggests, and as I shall seek to show over the course of this chapter, contemporary theatre does not offer a straightforward, one-size-fits-all answer to the question of the ethics of representing historical trauma. Rather, at its best, theatre creates a *good enough holding environment* (to draw upon a psychoanalytical concept that I will go into more detail about later) in which trauma can be encountered, as it were, non-traumatically. Because the subject, I shall argue, is herself constituted *through* trauma, it would be unwise to promise the delivery of the impossible: a theatrical production that poses no possibility of triggering any of its audience member. But the apparent impossibility of such a 'trigger-free' theatre should not dissuade theatre artists from rigorously searching for an ethics of rehearsal, performance and after-care, based not on the absence of trauma or re-traumatizing, but upon an alert and dynamic response to triggering when and where it occurs.

The topic of this chapter suggested itself to me after I witnessed a performance of a student production of *We Are Proud to Present …* in which the actor playing Actor 2/Black Man was purportedly triggered by the climax of the play – which calls for two white characters to lynch him – and ran off stage. That evening, I had been invited to participate in a post-performance talkback with the audience (I was also witnessing this production for the first time). As I went up on stage to begin the talk back, I was informed by the director as well as another student actor that the actor playing Black Man might or might not join us for the talkback, as he had been so 'triggered' (triggered was the word used, I believe) by the scene that he required some offstage 'after-care' before he could consider rejoining the cast (I explain the concept of after-care below). It was intimated to me at the time that he had even disrupted the play, somehow, by running offstage before his cue, even though the text of the play actually *calls* for the actor playing Black Man to 'break character' and leave the stage (Drury 2014: 101). In other words, even though I was fully prepared to believe what I had just been told (that the intensity of re-enacting racial trauma had caused a member of the cast to flee the stage and to be temporarily unable to return to it), I understood that the nature of Drury's play – Drury's theatrical ingenuity, as it were – rendered the difference between this real experience and an imaginary staging or simulation of it *indiscernible*. While such a blurring of the lines between real and imagined traumas would ordinarily be understood to be highly unethical – what could be worse, in an ordinary context, than to falsely pretend that one had experienced a trauma that one had not – in the context of this student production of Drury's play (a play which is itself *about* a student production) such indiscernibility was key to creating a good enough holding environment for encountering and working through the racial past.

Doing Justice to a Traumatic Past?

According to the playwright, the idea for *We Are Proud to Present ...* emerged when the author was attending a graduate seminar on the subject of historiography in a Department of Theatre and Performance Studies. Struck by the questions that were emerging around the ethics of historical reconstruction, documentary theatre and the psychodynamics of trauma, Drury hit upon the concept for *We Are Proud to Present ...* . *We Are Proud to Present ...* is set in the contemporary period and revolves around a cast of six – three black and three white actors – all of whom are given generic names like Actor 1/White Man, Actor 5/Sarah, and Actor 3/Another White Man. These actors have been tasked, or have tasked themselves, with telling the story of a real event in the history of colonialism: the German genocide of the Herero and Namaqua peoples of Southwest Africa between 1904 and 1907. This little-known colonial genocide looms large in contemporary post-colonial theory, due to the arguments that scholars like Paul Gilroy have made regarding its prefigurative relationship to the subsequent Holocaust. The violence of the Germans against the resisting native subjects of their African colonial holdings, Gilroy has argued, provides a necessary historical context for the German genocide of Jews during Second World War. Despite arguments such as these, the genocide of the Herero and Namaqua peoples remains little known and infrequently remembered for several reasons. Primary among those reasons is the fact of Germany's loss of its colonial holdings after First World War, with the result that Germany – in contrast to France, Great Britain, Spain and the Netherlands – is not widely thought of as having a colonial past at all. The legacy of Germany's thwarted imperialistic expansion on the European subcontinent during First and Second World Wars has tended to dwarf acknowledgement of its overseas colonial holdings in modern memory. Up until the present day, for instance, memorials and museums to Germany's Nazi-era crimes against humanity are far more prominent and numerous in the nation's capital – Berlin – than are memorials or museums recording its colonial history (and even its key role, courtesy of the 1884–5 Berlin Conference, in orchestrating the colonial projects of the other major European powers).

We Are Proud to Present ... takes place in North America or the United Kingdom (I have seen productions that set the play on either side of the pond) and concerns the efforts of an interracial group of young actors to depict this German/African history accurately, given the fact that what they themselves know about this history is very limited. Furthermore, it emerges that what archival evidence they are given to work with really favours the subjectivity of the German colonialists over the African victims. They have access to letters home written by German soldiers, but nothing regarding the subjectivity of the massacred Africans. At various points in the play, this imbalance created by the historical archive becomes a bone of contention among the players, with the white actors wanting to do their characters justice, exploring their human complexity and thwarted romantic longings, whereas the black actors object that the roles they have been given to play are little more than ciphers. At issue, in other words, are two interrelated questions about historical racial trauma (questions that have perhaps been most fully articulated in the scholarship of Saidiya Hartman, see Further Reading). The first question concerns the direct representation on stage of racist and colonialist violence, in which actors are called upon, by virtue of their own racial, gender and national identities, to either enact stage violence upon other actors, or to submit to such symbolic violence at the hands of another member of the cast. As I have already suggested, *We Are Proud to Present ...* engages directly with this question in its climactic final scene, in which the white characters get carried away with their 'historical re-enactment' and lynch a black character. But even before we get to this stage, there is another valence of historical racial trauma to deal with: the paucity, infelicity and bias of the archive itself, which constrains (or seems to constrain) which stories can be told fully, and how.

It transpires over the course of the play, for example, that the white actors (who are not German) are nonetheless able to approach their German roles much more easily and straightforwardly than the black actors can hope to approach their African roles. In the second scene of the play ('Process') we learn that one actor wishes to perform his role with a German accent ('Because I can do a German accent. I have / access to several regional accents in Germany, several – ' [28]). The black actors, by contrast, have no such access to ethnolinguistic specificity regarding the Herero people, and are limited to disidentifying with varieties of a generically typified 'African' language, accent and behaviour. The one actor who is given a proper name – Sarah – receives it because this is the name of the German recipient of letters home from the colonial front. The Africans, by contrast, lack proper names, and with that lack, they are denied the same historical biographical status that Sarah is endowed with. What is important about noting these asymmetries in the archive is the fact that they seem to the cast to be necessary rather than contingent. It is not just chance or happenstance, in other words, that presents us with a small cast of white and black actors who happen to have access to regionally specific German accents, but no embodied knowledge, other than the absolutely stereotypical, about Africa or Africans. Rather than suggest a multicultural or intercultural scenario in which the Global North and Global South encounter each other in performance on an even plane, Drury instead presents us with the asymmetries and incommensurabilities of the colonial archive and its lasting legacy of planetary anti-blackness. Despite the apparent parallels in the cast – black and white, male and female, evenly paired and contrasted – Drury represents Africa as a region of the unthought within contemporary theatre making. The corps of actors in rehearsal are obliged to make up this Africa as they go along, fabricating and fabulating an image of the Herero people, rather than doing them historical or theatrical 'justice'.

Afro-fabulation – a mode of aesthetic endeavour into which I would classify Drury's play – responds to the double bind presented by archival absences and historical traumas with modes of creative invention. Fabulation in such a mode is not to be confused with falsification, nor yet with the free play of the imagination. It is a response to the shock of history, a shock that, in contrast to trauma narratives that foreground lost or unclaimed experience, sees those experiences as overfull with narrative possibility. Put in other words, while the theory of fabulation does not deny the existence of trauma (far from it!), it refuses to concede to the fact of trauma the terms of its narration. Theatre and performance are an especially fruitful space for engaging in collective and collaborative fabulation insofar as the double-consciousness of the actor (who must move between their own identity and that of their stage characters) is particularly well suited for the enactment through fabulation of the *good enough holding environment*.

Assembling and Disassembling a Theatrical Holding Environment

In speaking of theatre as a *good enough holding environment*, I am drawing, as I have said, on psychoanalytic theory, specifically the area of psychoanalytic theory known as the object-relations school associated with Melanie Klein, Donald Winnicott and others. (My account of this psychoanalytic tradition is drawn from Eve Kosofsky Sedgwick's essays, collected in *Touching, Feeling*, which I recommend in Further Reading.) Even though these theories originated in the context of psychoanalytic treatment, I bring them up here insofar as I believe that they can be broadly applicable, with appropriate caution, as insights into the workings of human culture (psychoanalysis is a theory of culture and society as much as it is a theory of the individual psyche). The good enough holding environment derives from two of Winnicott's insights into the interrelational psychoanalysis of mothering. The mother (or primary caregiver) is often cautioned to protect her child from all external threat, and is often judged harshly, by herself and society, if a child under her care comes into harm's way. Such epidemics of caution can even take such form as mothers refusing to vaccinate their children, as required by law, due to an excess of zeal at the (remote) possibility that a vaccination will injure their child (when in fact, leaving a child unvaccinated presents a far greater danger to themselves and others). In response to such excesses of protective zeal – sometimes called 'helicopter parenting' in contemporary parlance – Winnicottians speak of the 'good enough' mother who is not perfect in her attentions to her child, who has her own personality and leaves enough space in her relationship with her child for her own ego gratifications. By being 'good enough', a phrase which Winnicott rescues from its ordinary status as an epithet, the mother allows her child to foster a more realistic sense of its own independence and capacity for self-care.

The analogy proposed here would be between the director (in particular of a student production, where conventions of in loco parentis sometimes obtain) and the good enough director. Here we should be as careful as possible. In contrast to mothers, who are sometimes perceived to be excessively selfless in the cause of the protection of their children, directors are sometimes perceived as being excessively ego-driven in their demands upon actors and crew. The director (a position in the theatre that is historically gendered male) is probably more at risk of caring too little about the potential psychic harm to an actor (or audience member) by their production, than they are at risk of caring too much. Under the rubric of artistic freedom, I have even witnessed a director create a schoolwide incident by refusing to even dialogue with an audience member who had reached out to him with a complaint that no advance warning had been provided before a violent onstage rape scene. As a survivor of sexual assault, and a student at the university where the production was staged, the audience member felt it just that the production provide a content warning on the playbill. The director brusquely rebuked her and accused her of censorship. This is a very typical incident, in my experience, and I relate it here to distinguish such behaviour from the conduct I would, by contrast, describe as that of the *good enough* director.

The good enough director, like the good enough mother, presides over a rehearsal and performance space that can serve as a 'holding environment'. The holding environment is another concept from Winnicott, and it mobilizes two interrelated senses of the verb 'to hold': 1) to touch or grasp, and 2) to contain. A holding environment is an environment in which a child is held in both senses of the word. It is a space in which they can move around freely, at risk of surprise and even injury, but it must not be a terrifying, hostile or wholly alien environment. It is also an environment in which they are touched, held, stroked and even cuddled (all forms of physical contact which modern developmental psychology has shown to be necessary for the thriving of humans and other kinds of animals). A holding environment typically has many objects within it (including the mother, who is thought of as an 'object' within object-relations theory, odd as this thought might initially strike you) that provide comfort and recognition to the child, on the basis of which foreign and/or unexpected objects can be negotiated on braver terms. An urban apartment is often a holding environment for a domestic cat or dog, for instance. Calm and comfortable within their holding environment, the very same animal can become disturbed and agitated when taken outside of it. Of course, the better the holding environment, the more prepared the animal, or child, will be to leave it. This is perhaps a third connotation of the verb 'to hold': a holding environment is also place of 'storage' (the child or animal usually sleeps in their holding environment), and as such a storage space, such a space of reserve, it permits the subject so held to gather up strength for subsequent departures from it.

The psychoanalytic account of the subject I have been outlining here differs from the pop-psychological theory of the subject contained in most popular accounts of 'trigger warnings' and 'safe spaces' insofar as the psychoanalytic account, in contrast to the pop-psychological account, assumes that trauma is *constitutive* of the subject. Whether we are talking about Jacques Lacan's influential account of the 'mirror stage', or whether we are discussing object-relations accounts of the holding environment, psychoanalysis tends to see trauma as generative of subjectivity, rather than a violation that can and should be eliminated from experience. This is not to say that psychoanalytic theory wishes trauma upon the subject. It is rather to say that how a subject responds to, adapts, transforms, uses and indeed *lives* a traumatic event is the most realistic and compassionate topic a performance can impinge into. In contrast to a conception of self that encourages subjects to inform themselves and others as to a known and knowable list of 'triggers' they should be warned in advance of, this psychoanalytic approach tends to understand triggers as irreducibly unknown and unspecifiable, at least in advance. We can compare this again to a mother who might wish to prevent her child from becoming ill by removing all bacteria from the holding environment with antibacterial soap. Medical studies suggest that such a bacteria-free environment is more dangerous in the long run for the child, insofar as she then fails to build up needed immunities. The ordinary, uneventful and quotidian nature of traumatic events (and their indisputable idiosyncrasy: what one person finds traumatic may not be what another person, even of the same race, gender, nationality, finds so) means that theatrical re-enactment and re-performance need not be re-traumatizing. Under specific conditions, it can be an enlargement and recontextualization of the traumatic experience. Under those conditions it can be a pathway to subjectivity.

The concept of a holding environment may provide a more robust alternative to the more popular contemporary concept of 'safe space', insofar as it is more direct and realistic about what is offered within in it. As many commentators have pointed out, a totally safe space is impossible to achieve and dangerous to promise. By contrast, a holding environment is a basic requirement that all humans have, even if the requirements for what makes a holding environment a holding environment will differ among individuals and across cultures. There is no such thing as a one-size-fits-all holding environment, which is one reason why a holding environment can occasionally be, occasionally *should be*, unsafe for some who enters it. What the good enough director does is attend to the state of the holding environment they are co-creating with their cast and crew, ensuring that the boundaries between 'play' and 'reality' (key concepts for Winnicott) are fostered rather than prematurely overloaded and shut down.

To return to Drury's play, we can see how the playwright has written a script that engages all these questions I have been provisionally outlining here, even without ever directly employing the technical theoretical vocabulary I have proposed that we use. One facet of Drury's play that we immediately notice, when we view it through a Winnicottian lens, is that the 'good enough director' is played by Actor 6/Black Woman, who takes on the role of orchestrating and directing the 'lecture' the actors are rehearsing, as well as being featured within it as a speaker. This presents a familiar theatrical challenge, insofar as this actor is seeking to direct both herself and others. Over the course of the play, this blurring of boundaries is occasionally challenged by her fellow cast-mates, who feel at various times that she is imposing her personal needs and desires upon the production, while forgetting theirs. As written, Actor 6/Black Woman is a good example of a 'good enough director': she is aware and self-reflexive about her own needs and desires within the process (i.e. she is not excessively self-abnegating, invisible or imperious), and she is willing to get into a bit of a mess, more of a mess than she can necessarily find her way out of all by herself.

When the production degenerates into symbolic violence, Actor 6 both is and isn't responsible for what happens to Actor 2. She does, however, come to his rescue when he breaks character and pleads for help. And the text of the play calls for her to leave the stage before him (implying that she has surrendered control of what happens subsequently). Let me quote here some lines from the conclusion of the play – written entirely in stage directions – that demonstrate how the play works as a good enough holding environment:

Actor 5, 3, and 1 find laughter. The laughter starts and stops. ... But Actor 4 is not laughing. He might try. But he cannot laugh. He cannot leave. As the other Actors have their reaction, Actor 4 eventually notices the audience. And then ... Actor 4 cleans up the space. Actors 5, 3 and 1 see Actor 4. It jolts them out of whatever they were in. They watch him clean up the space. He picks up objects that have come to hold significance: Bottles of water, the bits of the mask, etc. And places them in the box of letters. Actors 5, 3 and 1 eventually remember the audience, and take them in, or they just remember Actor 4, or they remember themselves. In this remembering, they might be forced to leave the space. Actor 4 takes down the noose. It is the last object to be dealt with. (101–2)

I have quoted at some length from the conclusion of the play in order to illustrate several aspects of Drury's theatrical invention, which leans here towards both the depiction of a holding environment, and a generous distribution of the 'role' of the good enough mother/director. To understand the impact of this final scene, we should recall that Actors 5, 3 and 1 are the white actors/characters, and Actor 4 is the one black actor/character left on stage after Actors 2 and 6 depart. To also think here intersectionally in terms of gender, we should specify that Actor 4 is the black male character left on stage with two white men who have just re-enacted a lynching, while one white woman watches, and that this Actor 4 has just watched the black female director and the black male victim of the lynching leave the stage.

Actor 4's stage directions here illustrate how he takes on the unassigned role of the good enough mother/director. When the white actors laugh 'hysterically' – laughs, that is to say, as a defence against the admission that they have all just participated in the psychic enjoyment of racial terrorism committed against black bodies – the sole black actor left on stage cannot laugh, even when he tries to. Rather than dispel the reality of the violence by laughing, implying that it was all in jest, he attends to the objects that have been scattered within what is no longer a holding environment (at least not for the black actors). Drury's stage directions do not call for him to destroy or act out against these objects. She instructs the player to instead 'deal with' the noose last of all (leaving a fair amount of room in her text for directorial and actorly decisions in any given performance). To introduce a final concept to my analysis here – this time borrowed from BDSM (Bondage, Domination and Sado-Masochism) practices rather than object-relations psychoanalysis – Drury instructs Actor 4 to engage himself, his fellow cast-mates and the audience in a little ritual of 'after-care'.

After-care is a concept that arises within BDSM practices one that calls attention to the need to gently reintroduce a subject to their ordinary reality, as well as to the ordinary personality of the BDSM 'top', after a session of bondage, dominance, and/or submission. I don't pick this comparison frivolously, insofar as I would posit that the kinds of after-care required after the emotionally fraught re-enactment of racial terror and violence in *We Are Proud to Present …* are pretty close to those recommended after a session of deep BDSM 'play'. After-care is required in *We Are Proud to Present …* insofar as the play's text makes it difficult, or impossible, for the audience to find closure and catharsis through the expected ritual of applause. Applauding a near-lynching that has caused two actors to run off the stage feels pretty universally wrong to a contemporary audience; as does the hysterical laughter of the white cast members. Recognizing this impossible position, Actor 4 takes over the role of good enough director (a role abandoned by Actor 6 when she runs off stage), and begins to carefully break set. This action – akin to a BDSM top putting away their 'toys', or a mother reorganizing an infant's room after a particularly frenetic 'playdate' – is an act of care. Care is directed towards the objects that have been brought into performative life and meaning during the play. Actor 4's care calls attention to them as objects, objects that require their own holding environment, to which they will now be returned, to be held, stored and secured until they are brought out again for the next performance. His actions as the good enough director here call attention to both the unreality and artifice of the events that have mobilized these objects – allowing both cast and audience to transition back into ordinary reality – and, through the same gesture, make their material reality and fragility newly evident.

Dealing with a Noose

There is an art of cruelty to ending a play about German genocide with a stage direction given to a black male actor to 'deal with' a noose. How does one deal with a noose? How does one take care of it? In my own thinking about this play, I have had occasion to be critical of this ending, and indeed, of the general drift of the play, which tends to move away from the racial dynamics of the African setting of the play-within-the-play, and to move instead towards the racial dynamics of the Anglo American framing context. Even as I have understood this shift to be the playwright directly signalling that this is a missed opportunity (the play is about the failure to do justice to the genocide of the Herero and Namaqua peoples), I have still felt, at times, the play to be a missed opportunity. Viewing the play from the perspective of an American with first-generation African heritage, it has felt like many other attempts to represent modern Africa that end up instead in another self-representation of the West. In an earlier talkback for the student production I have discussed (not the talkback I happened to preside over), this critical reaction from the perspective of contemporary African viewers came up. Contemporary African viewers (so it was reported to me) felt excluded from the concerns of the play, insofar as its denouement shifted the scene of racial trauma from a colonial genocide, associated with Namibia, to a lynching, associated with the US South during the Jim Crow era. I want to give some space in my conclusion to these matters, insofar as they impinge upon an ongoing conversation or debate about the global reach of anti-blackness and the fraught and contested space we know as 'diaspora'.

Conclusion: Making Thinking

I have spent a fair amount of time in this chapter defending a psychoanalytically-informed theory of fabulation that contrasts with pop-psychological (and, I would add, neoliberal) discourses of harm, triggering and safe space. This alternative account of fabulation is specifically offered as a contrast and alternative to the more harsh, tough-lover and anti-politically correct perspective that asserts the right of art to shock, offend and indeed injure without consequence. I have had little to say about very volatile debates over free speech and the excessive censoriousness of so-called 'snowflakes'. In the place of such volatile (and in my view unproductive) debates, I have substituted a close description of a play that seeks to create a good enough holding environment for both its cast and its audience, one that probes a difficult and to some extent unknowable past without asserting the right of anyone to simply live their lives in full innocence of the afterlives of slavery and colonialism. Accepting that theatre and performance can be responsible – not just socially responsible but artistically responsible, responsibility as a value embedded in any collaborative and intersubjective art form – I have offered tools from the object-relations school of psychoanalysis to assist in the performance of that responsibility. Given the current academic interest in new materialism, posthumanism and related theoretical approaches, an additional advantage of the object-relations school is its willingness to think about humans as 'objects' and part-objects for other humans. That is, it is an approach that realizes the call of some new materialist and posthumanist theories to consider the human as an object among other objects, rather than as the central term and referent for all ethics and analysis. Object-relations psychoanalysis, I mean to say, can in this way be non-anthropocentric.

But how does such a non-anthropocentric approach to re-enacting historical trauma speak to the specific dynamics of diasporic memory and amnesia that I just called attention to? To answer this last question, we must look one final time at a moment in the play, this time a moment that comes about midway through. In this moment, Actor 6 is recalling for the others the impetus behind her desire to stage this 'lecture'/play, an impetus she describes in the following terms:

> Like, for me the whole idea for this whole presentation started when I sat down in my house, in my kitchen and I opened a magazine and I saw my grandmother's face in the middle of a page. So I read the story around her face, and the story was about people I'd never heard of, in a place I'd never cared about. (49)

A few pages later, Actor 6 goes on to relate:

> Do you see what I'm saying, people? The woman in that article looked just like my grandmother and that doesn't happen to me – I don't belong to a tribe I don't know where my ancestors were from I don't have a homeland where people look like me I'm just British, Black British, and people tell me I look like other women all the time but I never actually look like these other women they say I look like not really because to some people all black women look the same. But the woman in this article *She looked like my grandmother.* (53)

Actor 6 here relates how the experience of misogynoir (to borrow Moya Bailey's useful term for misogyny directed specifically at black women) shapes her reality, not in a traumatic way (if we adhere to the traditional definition of a trauma as an experience so forceful the subject cannot process it at the time), but precisely in a way that is casual and quotidian. When others routinely point out her likeness to other black women she does not consider herself to resemble, Actor 6 is reduced to an experience of feeling like an object among objects. But the point of this scene is not just to object to or protest this casual misogynoir. It is to comment upon, and I will say also to fabulate, a resemblance she herself sees, between her own grandmother and a complete stranger in a magazine article about the Herero genocide. Even as Actor 6 recognizes, indeed, insists upon, the formal symmetry between the casual mistaking of one black woman for another, she points out the productive interposition of such a misprision within her own memory and imagination, going so far as to assert that 'my grandmother came to me and told me about a genocide' (53).

In performance, this 'grandmother' comes to life when Actor 3 takes on her semblance. Even as Actor 6 goes on to specify that she never actually met her grandmother (rendering this biological ancestor nearly as distant as the total stranger in the magazine), Actor 3 goes on to impersonate her, performing *as* this partially known, partially mysterious grandmother for Actor 6. Together they stage another scene of fabulated memory – impinging on both the known unknowns of Actor 6's childhood and upbringing (the grandmother she doesn't know, the family ancestry cut off by the traumatic rupture of the Middle Passage) as well as the unknown knowns of black diasporic history. In contrasting the 'known unknowns' of this character's personal history, and the 'unknown knowns' of the colonial genocidal past, I mean to point out the specifically impersonal manner in which the transmission of memory occurs. Our memories seem to be what is most personal to us, what makes us most a person. The imagined horror of amnesia, of not being able to recognize a known and intimate face, like the face of a grandmother, is an imagined horror of depersonalization.

Saidiya Hartman, in recounting her own thwarted quest to make sense of the traumatic rupture between Africa and its diaspora caused by slavery and the Middle Passage, has encapsulated this in the telling phrase, 'lose your mother'. Actor 6, we may say, has lost her mother (in this case, her grandmother). But in losing her, she has found another, a fabulous double, through which she can live a history that is not her own. I end with this final image of black feminist afro-fabulation because I believe it helps answer the resistance experienced both in myself and in others of contemporary African descent in watching a play that purports to be about the genocide of the Herero and Namaqua people of Namibia, while actually being more about the vicarious route through which the search for memory and knowledge produces, instead, a kind of fabulated non-knowledge. I term this space of fabulation non-knowledge rather than falsehood or error, because no error, mistake or intentional falsehood occurs in the course of Actor 6 and Actor 3's collaborative and intersubjective invention of this grandmother. The critic Fred Moten has written about the importance of the mother's mother tongue, in the mode of an aspirational fidelity that, in this case, neither character can quite aspire to. Neither Actor 6 nor Actor 3 know this grandmother's tongue (they know neither the tongue of Actor 6's real grandmother, nor do they know the African tongue of the anonymous woman in the magazine that Actor 6 has intentionally mistaken for her). In this not-knowing, in this non-knowledge, they fabulate a new character, who is the very soul and spirit of theatre, and endow this character with the capacity to recount a genocide.

In the era of malicious and increasingly ubiquitous 'fake news', engaged in the active separation of whole contemporary populations from the basic facts of their present and historical circumstances, what could be more important than such an invention?

Performance Details

We Are Proud to Present a Presentation About the Herero of Namibia, Formerly Known as South West Africa, From the German Sudwestafrika, Between the Years 1884–1915 had its world premiere at Victory Gardens Theater in Chicago and its New York premiere at Soho Rep in autumn 2012.

Further Reading

You can read the play under discussion in Drury (2014). You can read a fuller account of afro-fabulation in my book *Afro-Fabulations* (Nyong'o 2018). Critical fabulation is defined in Hartman (2008: 1–14). See also her germinal study Hartman (1997). The mirror stage is discussed in Lacan (1998). And the best introductory account to object-relations criticism remains Sedgwick (2003). Black performance theory is indebted to the account of 'resistance of the object' in Moten (2003). On performance, truth and reconciliation, and activism, see Madison (2010).

References

Drury, Jackie Sibblies (2014), *We Are Proud to Present: A Presentation about the Herero of Namibia, Formerly Known as Southwest Africa, from the German Sudwestafrika, between the Years 1884–1915*, London: Bloomsbury.
Hartman, Saidiya (1997), *Scenes of Subjection: Terror, Slavery, and Self-Making in Nineteenth-Century America*, New York: Oxford University Press.
Hartman, Saidiya (2008), 'Venus in Two Acts', *Small Axe* 12 (2): 1–14.
Lacan, Jacques (1998), *The Four Fundamental Concepts of Psycho-Analysis*, New York and London: Norton.
Madison, D. Soyini (2010), *Acts of Activism: Human Rights as Radical Performance*, Cambridge: Cambridge University Press.
Moten, Fred (2003), *In the Break: The Aesthetics of the Black Radical Tradition*, Minneapolis: University of Minnesota Press.
Nyong'o, Tavia (2018), *Afro-Fabulations: The Queer Drama of Black Life*, New York: New York University Press.
Sedgwick, Eve Kosofsky (2003), *Touching Feeling: Affect, Pedagogy, Performativity*, Durham: Duke University Press.

15 How Does Theatre Think Through Politics?

JAZMIN BADONG LLANA

The Question

How does theatre think through politics? Threading this question together are three major terms: *theatre*, *politics*, *thought*. The answers depend largely and critically on how these terms are understood, how each stands in relation to the others, and the possible permutations of such relations and what they might mean – such as when we speak of 'political theatre' or, as I shall do here, of re-enactment *as* political theatre.

To state that theatre thinks suggests that the human capacity for, and activity of, thinking invests theatre with the same power, the same capacity. But how is theatre both thought and action? Or is this a given that comes organically with the idea 'theatre' – that is to say, theatre becomes itself because it thinks? That theatre thinking is a 'thinking through' emphasizes a process that is always and inevitably messy and repetitive. But true thought always comes in a flash, incalculable, unplanned. That there is some methodology signalled by the 'through' and 'how' is not always evident. That theatre and politics can be thought together or have something to do with each other – the third idea in the question being addressed – is the topic 'proper' of this chapter.

I explore answers to the question of how theatre thinks through politics by thinking through a 32-year-old practice of re-enactment of a 1985 'massacre' of demonstrators on the streets of Escalante, Negros Island, in the Philippines. Teatro Obrero, the 'cultural arm' of the Negros Federation of Sugar Workers, has been staging this re-enactment every single year since 1986, a year after the violent event. While the faithful restaging of the traumatic experience over the course of thirty-two years is thought by Teatro Obrero as a practice of 'political theatre', I want to understand the politics of the practice beyond its declaration, attentive to current discussions on or around the fraught question of politics and performance within performance studies, but also paying close attention to Escalante's specific contexts – the situation of the sugar workers and the sugar industry of Negros, the ideological and organizational affiliations of the group with the dominant Philippine Left espousing a national democratic struggle, and Teatro Obrero's genealogy of aesthetic practice within a larger historical context of political theatre making in the country.

How does this practice of political theatre think and do politics? The question shall be answered by a thinking through of the re-enactment itself, how it appears and is experienced as theatrical re-enactment and spectacle complete with the sound of gunfire and the blast of water cannons, and how the performance is organized and mobilized as community theatre performed mostly by young actors, within a programme of torch parades, Catholic rites, concerts, and street demonstrations of sugarcane farmers, the oppressed *sacadas* of Negros.

Thinking Back and Forward: The Escalante Massacre Re-Enactment

In September 1985, the Negros Federation of Sugar Workers (NFSW) participated in a national people's strike (*welgang bayan*) with street demonstrations and marches. They were fired upon by the police, resulting in the death of twenty and scores of wounded. This is the Escalante Massacre, as it is now known in the history of the national democratic protest and mass movement in the Philippines. Teatro Obrero, the 'cultural arm' of NFSW, has been staging the re-enactment every single year since the atrocity. The performance in 2017 was the thirty-second.

Why do they do it? What has kept them going? The survivors of the massacre and original actors of the re-enactment in 1986 are now in their fifties and most do not perform anymore, while the current actors only have their parents' stories or the re-enactments they saw as they were growing up as their material to do the performance. Whether the performance is something sustained by the Left, which continues to be strong in Negros, is beside the point. What stands out for me is the thirty-two years of unswerving fidelity to what they started in 1986, as well as the fidelity to a particular aesthetic of the re-enactment – redoing the converging marches and torch parades of militants on the street, chanting the same slogans, restaging the spectacular encounter with the police and military with sounds of rifle fire and police sirens and the scene of gore as bodies were felled by the water cannons and bullets and littered the street one on top of the other.

This is my illustrative example of how theatre thinks through politics. The illustration is focused on both the performance of the re-enactment – its text and theatrical staging – and the social and political context and conditions of its making as a yearly event.

Text and Staging

The 'theatre-text' culled from memory of the actual event was put together and used by the directors over time. This is what has been passed on from one generation of actors and directors to the next.

The protagonists are the people who had gathered in Escalante for the protest action against the continued state repression and economic strife thirteen years after the declaration of Martial Law. The antagonists are the police, military and paramilitary forces under the command of the governor of Negros Occidental and mayor of Escalante. The setting: the street in front of the Escalante town hall. The date: 20 September 1985.

According to the accounts, the protestors were organized into two groups that set up two assembly and barricade points: people from Old Escalante and nearby towns of Sagay and Cadiz set up Barricade 1 in front of the town hall, and those from San Carlos, Toboso, and Calatrava set up Barricade 2 in front of the market. While the majority were farmworkers from the sugar haciendas, teachers and other professionals and students had joined them, together with priests, nuns, seminarians and religious lay. They started arriving on 18

September and the plan was to build up to a total barricade of the roads and culminate on the thirteenth anniversary of the declaration of Martial Law on 21 September. The mass action was part of a 'national people's strike' and in Northern Negros, the strike had paralysed public transportation, suspended classes in the public and private schools, and closed down many business establishments. The re-enactment is focused on what happened on the second day at the site of the blood bath: in front of the town hall where Barricade 1 was massed up. The re-enactment deviates a bit from the actual events in that there is no massing up and setting up of a barricade in front of the town hall. Instead, the protestors arrive marching from the Mt Carmel Church where they had assembled in the morning.

The drama of the encounter begins with the protesting marchers' approach. The energy is high. As the marchers approach the Escalante town hall, with raised fists, banners, placards and flags, they shout the rallying calls over and over in an agitated chant: 'Bugas, bugas, hindi armas!' (Rice, rice, not arms!); 'Makibaka! Huwag matakot!' (Struggle! Do not be afraid!); 'Militarisasyon labanan!' (Resist militarization!); or 'Marcos: Hitler, Diktador, Tuta' (Marcos is Hitler, a dictator, and a dog [of the imperialists]).

A fire truck speeds past the marchers to their left, its siren screaming, and positions itself on one end of the street, blocking the path of the march. 'Paramilitary forces' (the Marcos created Civilian Home Defense Force [CHDF]) together with 'police and military personnel' already deployed in the area are joined by more troops and they train their rifles on the approaching marchers. The fire truck lurches to a stop and its powerful hoses immediately spew water on the approaching marchers, stop them in their tracks and scatter them, many falling to the ground or being thrown backwards by the violent force of the water. The din of the siren mixed with the marchers' cries is overwhelming. But the water runs out and the marchers shout for joy and get back to their feet. The 'government forces' then throw canisters of tear gas. Again, the marchers are scattered, dropping to the ground. One of the canisters does not fire. A moment of tension-filled silence follows as a young woman playing as Juvelyn Jaravelo gets to her feet, picks it up, and throws it back to the 'police forces'. Her companions react first with horrified warnings and then with jubilant cheers. But the cheers soon turn into screaming and howling as the firing begins and 'Juvelyn Jaravelo' is first to be 'hit'. The accounts say that a machine gun mounted on the rooftop of the municipal hall had fired on the marchers. This is relived in the re-enactment with simulated sound while the

Fig. 15.1 Battling the water cannons, 20 September 2016. Teatro Obrero is joined by members of theatre groups from Luzon and other parts of the Visayas. Photo: Jazmin Llana.

actors use mock rifles made of wood. The marchers run for cover in vain. When the shooting stops, bodies lie one on top of another. The 'government troops' close in on the wounded survivors and continue shooting at them. Fifteen people 'die' on the spot.

The accounts say that five more of those taken to the hospitals later on also died and that the government forces pursued the fleeing survivors even as far as the sugar farms and intimidated doctors and medical personnel tending to the wounded.

In the re-enactment, the government forces leave at this point. Then two children enter the scene crying out, 'Mother, mother'. Another young person comes to look for her father. And then more people come, play out the scene of looking for their loved ones and finding them and expressing their grief and anger. They pick their way across the ground littered with bodies.

And then the finale is played out theatrically with the bodies of the dead and wounded carried aloft by the survivors and brought in a procession to the town plaza and laid on the ground in front of a marker commemorating the massacre. Sounds of mourning. Sounds of anguish. Sounds of anger.

The re-enactment programme is capped by a few speeches by NFSW officials and 'mass leaders' condemning the massacre and agitating the audience to continue fighting for justice and advancing the national democratic cause for the sugar workers and the oppressed of the entire country. In the 2016 commemoration, the programme of speeches was extended and expanded with solidarity messages of people's organizations from all over the Philippines and song numbers from the vast repertoire of protest songs all the way back to the 1970s, ending with a rousing Tagalog version of the *Internationale*.

Context and Conditions of Performance

The main drama of re-enactment is the highlight of a three-day programme of activities organized by the NFSW and Teatro Obrero. Other than the re-enactment itself, there are other, as important, activities, some of them added in order to improve the commemoration. The director of the theatre group mentions two 'innovations': Tribute to the Martyrs on 19 September and the 'community-hopping' three days before. The community visits are made to gear up for the event highlight. Teatro Obrero performs songs and interpretative dances at various communities where the farm workers reside. On 19 September, these communities then mobilize participants for the converging torch parades that meet up at the town plaza, where on one corner a monument of three raised fists stands as a marker of the massacre. Here an ecumenical prayer tribute is offered and the martyrs' names are called out one by one. The crowd then moves to the main plaza for a programme of speeches and 'cultural numbers' contributed by the various contingents in the march. On the morning of 20 September, all participants gather at the Our Lady of Mt Carmel Church where a Mass is celebrated. At noon, they march to the site of the re-enactment.

All these activities require months of preparation and member groups of the NFSW in Escalante and the other towns, including the families of survivors that compose the organization called MARTYR (Mothers and Relatives Against Tyranny), organize themselves into committees that take care of raising resources for the commemoration, an important part of which are the meals of Teatro Obrero during the rehearsals that happen for at least a month prior to the event. The performers come from the different affiliated members of NFSW–Teatro Obrero and the cast thus changes from year to year, and therefore there is a need for training and intensive rehearsals. Some sixty young people are gathered and housed in one place for the training and rehearsals. This arrangement poses problems for those who are attending school, as well as for the families who will lose potential income because the actors, many of them also farm workers, cannot work during the rehearsals and thus would not earn. The communities therefore have to raise the needed funds to address these concerns. There is a system of taking turns that applies not only to the resource sharing but also to the matter of who will perform on a given year, but no one receives any payment; everything is voluntary. Everyone is a 'passionate amateur' (Ridout 2013) who is involved not because of money but because of love (more on this later).

Over time, in the thirty-two years that have passed (at the time of writing), many things have changed. Some of the leaders of the 1985 mass action are now officials of the town, now a city, and the 'Escam' (short for Escalante Massacre) commemoration is now part of the city's calendar of events. Our interview with survivors during the April 2015 visit was even held at the office of the city mayor, who also sponsored our overnight stay in the best hotel the city has. The co-ordinator of the 1985 barricades is now able to mobilize government resources to support the commemoration: 'I am usually the director, so I can guide the actors to depict what really happened. It is ironic that now I serve in City Hall, and I'm able to use real fire trucks for these re-enactments. For so long after the massacre, just seeing a fire truck pass by was a traumatic experience. Today I can give the direction: fire the water cannons and know that justice is on my side' (Villalon 2015).

* * *

When I returned in 2016, I was chair of the country's national committee on dramatic arts and was able to convince the committee to bring the tenth annual *Tanghal* university theatre festival to Escalante. And because Teatro Obrero was also part of a national network of activist community theatre groups in the country, the event concept was for a national community theatre festival to happen with Tanghal. The festival became a daily programme of immersion with workshops at the sugar farms during the day, and performances at night from 15 to 18 September. All of the 250 delegates would congregate to rehearse the re-enactment with Teatro Obrero on 19 September and the day would end with the converging torch parades and tribute to the martyrs. The re-enactment would be on 20 September. And so, it happened like this. The Cultural Center of the Philippines joined the collaboration by bringing in activist celebrity performers for the evening of 19 September. Visual artists and musicians from Negros and Iloilo also participated, reproducing the same mural that was used in 1985 in the course of the festival. Performance artists from Manila with guests from Japan, Mexico and the United States also joined.

But something else also happened. Organized artists and cultural activists saw the great opportunity opened up by the turn of events and decided to hold a summit on people's culture and arts alongside everything else. Additionally, in Escalante, the unprecedented influx of visitors and the conduct of a national festival in the small city proved to be of great significance to the city. City Hall thus supported the event with logistics, accommodation, free use of the city gymnasium and a dinner served in style on the evening of 19 September, personally supervised by the Tourism Officer.

Outside of the organized groups with a Leftist orientation, many of the festival delegates were young college students whose theatre practice was confined to, at most, 'progressive' plays. I got a sense of the disorientation they must have been feeling as each night of the festival performances exposed them to plays with clenched fists and chanting of slogans against 'imperialism, feudalism, and bureaucrat-capitalism', the three evils being fought by a national democratic protracted struggle that has been going on for more than forty-eight years now in both the open mass movement and the armed guerrilla zones. Outside of the theatre festival entries, many of the pieces shown were on the plight of the sugarcane workers in Negros, like *Tiempos Muertos* (Dead Season) performed by Sinagbayan, and on the struggles

Fig. 15.2 The massacre 'victims' played by the young members of the theatre group at the conclusion of the re-enactment on 20 September 2017. The backdrop is a reconstructed version of the mural used in 1985. Photo: Jazmin Llana.

of historical figures of the revolution against colonialism, like Dagohoy and Papa Isio, but performed in ways that speak to contemporary situations of poverty and oppression. The red flag was waved in many of the plays. The songs sung were paeans to the basic masses and their persistence to fight for social justice. On the day of the re-enactment, these young people joined the actors of Teatro Obrero, mostly also young people, shouted the same slogans with them, pushed forward in the march against the onslaught of the water cannons, and fell down to the ground as if they too were struck by the bullets of the 'massacre'.

The march was real. The water cannon from the town's fire truck was real. The siren's wail was real. The bullets were not, although Teatro Obrero masterfully produced the sounds of gunfire with real and powerful firecrackers and pieces of wood struck together to make the violent sounds. It was fiction. It was theatre. The participants were actors playing roles in the re-enacted drama. Everyone knew it was a show, especially the ones taking photos and videos who wove in and out of the action documenting everything, taking close-up shots of the 'carnage'. But the emotions I saw and heard and felt were all too real. The experience of bodies, minds, hearts that went through the terror was all real. With only the short rehearsal the previous day, the young actors from Dumaguete, from Bacolod, from Laguna, from Legazpi, from Manila, were transformed into the 1985 protestors but also into subjective participants through the experience of the event in the present of 2016, just as the people of Escalante themselves have made real *the event after the event*, in their time, year after year, through its continued performance.

Event and Re-Enactment

If the massacre is the historical event, then the re-enactment of the massacre can be thought to be the event after the event, a theatrical/aesthetic event that has enabled people to think it. As Adrian Kear puts it in *Theatre and Event*, 'think[ing] *theatrically* about the relationship between theatre and event in and through certain theatrical "stagings"', is 'quintessentially theatrical' thinking, a 'method of showing rather than saying' (Kear 2013: 3). It is also 'a retroactive mode of aesthetic thought conducted in order to elucidate the present as much as to illuminate the past in its historicity' (216–17). This *performative historiography* brings about that which it appears to represent, allowing 'the theatrical encounter to play a *constitutive* role in the construction of the event as such' (217, emphasis in original). What this chapter argues is that the Escam re-enactment is an instant of theatre that is also an instant of thought (Kear 2013: 217; Badiou 2008: 229), an event that 'orients us' in the confused times of the present, telling us 'where we are in history' (Badiou 2015: 63). Such a re-enactment can be thought of as an 'aesthetic inquiry undertaken in the form of the theatre event', a critically, creatively and politically affective afterwardness that enables some form of moving forwards' (Kear 2013: 217) in the 'politics of the present' (8).

Questions and Considerations

The Escalante re-enactment is, as philosopher Alain Badiou would say, a 'theatre-text', 'intended for, addressed to, a public' (2015: 55). This is the Escalante public, being addressed by the Escalante folk performing the re-enactment – in a sense, it is Escalante addressing itself. At this level, it is a question of how 'strong' the performance is. In other words, a question of its success as art – because 'the theatre-idea, as a public illumination of history and life, emerges only at the apex of art' (Badiou 2005: 73). I will only venture to say that I was 'hailed' by the 'call' and I 'responded' – as Rebecca Schneider would put it (2015: 181), which must say much about its 'efficacy'. I was 'struck' and have committed to follow the consequences of the theatre-idea that emerged from my encounter with Escalante, in the same way that I think Teatro Obrero and the people of Escalante experienced the event after the event when they did the re-enactment for the first time in 1986 and subsequently held on to their commitment.

That said, the re-enactment on the basis of how it appears, can be dismissed as Leftist propaganda, with the red flags, placards and slogans. It can also be dismissed as a performance nostalgic for a past that will not return anymore. It is 'outmoded'. Its appearance jars with images of 'Filipino' contemporary aspirations for living together in peace, 'moving on' from the horrors of the past because, after all, Martial Law is over and 1985 is a long time ago now. The re-enactment can then be appreciated as only a story that the State can now 'legitimate' but also 'put to rest in death' (Badiou 2015: 203). Escalante City Hall is on to something: the re-enactment as a touristic event that can attract visitors and bring in needed earnings for the city. But the tricky point is that there is something that bursts forth from beneath all these trappings, both leftist and rightist – the real of the struggle for past wrongs to be addressed, for injustices that claimed lives to be indemnified, for old oppressive situations that remain ever new and insidious to be resisted and changed. And, perhaps even more to the point, our 'passionate amateurs' of the Escalante re-enactment have remained passionate amateurs who are moved not by any remuneration or gain but by love (Ridout 2013: 15). By this, I truly mean not only love for the cause of justice or 'national democracy' however it is understood, or love for a relative who died in the massacre; it can also be love for a parent or a sibling or a neighbour who enjoins them to 'take their turn' in the performance.

Meanwhile, every year since 1986, the performance has operated not as explanation but as action that compels a response, a co-performance by its co-present audience. The audience would include those who join the march but whose role is to stay on the side of the road as 'audience', or those 'behind the scenes' responsible for the meals, the props, the tribute, the community visits, but also those who come to 'just watch'. The audience who just watch may be likened to a theatre audience seated in the auditorium who do nothing to move the action forward, and in the Escalante re-enactment this audience is still the majority, since the re-enactment itself is performed only by Teatro Obrero (or, in 2016, by Teatro Obrero and the festival delegates). It is not 'formally participatory' in the sense that the audience members are asked to join the actors, for instance, to brave the water cannon or fall dead or wounded to the ground. The organized mobilization from the sugar farms forms part of the march from Mt Carmel Church but they line up on both sides of the road upon arrival at the site of the performance. There is a clear line dividing actors and audience; there is a 'stage' and there are all the other elements of theatre meticulously prepared down to the last detail, required by the text which is always the same, year after year. The 2016 performance was different only in that the number of actors increased. The festival delegates rehearsed with Teatro Obrero and with them became actors of the re-enactment sharing 'the central virtue of the actor', which is 'not technical but ethical' (Badiou 2008:

220). Of course, since for most of them it was a first experience of the re-enactment, they were also present as audience, and thinking of it this way complicates and blurs the notion of participation as it happens in Escalante. My view is that what operates is participation as co-performance: 'theatre as the *putting at stake* of an ethics – and first of all an ethics of play' (195, emphasis mine). In Escalante, I would say this is very much about a sharing of the 'stakes'.

The performance 'orients us' in the now time that is still 'confused', giving rise to the thought, renewed at each instance of performance, that there is a need to continue what has been started. In Badiou's terms, the confusion is, first, a belief that the 'idea ... has gone missing' (63) and, second, that we should be reconciled to the idea of individual (and corporate) 'interests' in the dominant 'circulation of goods' (64). In the case of Escalante, the 'idea that has gone missing' comes into full visibility and hearing, jarring us back to a realization of our confused state, the confusion of the confusion. The idea lives. The struggle is not over. The material conditions of oppression of the sugarcane workers continue and have even worsened as changes in the conditions of work and system of sugar production have taken their toll against them. Marcos is not in power anymore and the old activists have taken the parliamentary path to push for reforms, but no substantial change has happened. The violence at Escalante is an old story, but elsewhere in the country there are new ones in the last five years: Hacienda Luisita, Kidapawan, the Lumads of Mindanao.

The second aspect of the confusion manifests in the way the event has precariously become an object of contesting interests. That the Escalante organizers of the re-enactment have been enjoying government support (from City Hall and national agencies for culture and arts) is instructive for our understanding of the confusion. The militant performance has become legitimated, recognized, supported by the State, and it is easy to think this is the way it is, 'life's natural state' (Badiou 2015: 65), and thus to nullify its intended effects. But perhaps this is really a creative negotiation of the interests in play. The re-enactment must go on, and if it means forming strategic alliances that cast the basis of working together in terms understandable and acceptable to the collaborators like those in government – *for as long as the Escam theatre-text remains the way it is* – then such negotiations are not only creative but productive at the very pragmatic organizational level. However, this cannot be purely and deplorably utilitarian, because at the micro level there is no questioning the sincerity of transactions between individuals working together to get the annual event on the road, whether they are from the local government or from the activist groups. As Eddie Villalon relates in his account of the massacre, the policemen and protestors knew each other, were friends or blood relations (Villalon 2015). The transactions are political, but also very personal.

The danger of not seeing the confusion of the confusion, of theatre failing to orient us in confused times, is ever present. The militants of Escalante must 'hold on to their desire' and 'declare' it with each performance, at the level of the performance.

Theatre and Politics

The Escalante re-enactment is understood and professed by Teatro Obrero as 'political theatre' and this is, using Paul Rae's words, 'brutally affirmed' (Rae 2009: 71). It is a practice of theatre but also a practice of politics – by its appearance, its lineage and affiliations, its organization. In his 'Rhapsody for the Theatre', Badiou says that 'politics ... [is not] merely blind fury or a nondiscursive impulse', which is 'only the material for politics, not its essence' (2008: 190). He speaks of 'three obligations of any politics (massive event, organizations, text-thoughts)' (191) and expands the list into: 'organizations, textual referents, thinkers, proper names, the State, contrasting points of view, and evental masses [as] the obligatory ingredients of a political situation' (192).

All these are present in the Escalante re-enactment as politics. The 1985 Escalante march was part of a nationwide protest action, a *welgang bayan* (national strike) staged in September of that year. Thirty-two years later, Teatro Obrero's efforts are still supported by the huge network of people's organizations affiliated with the Left-associated *Bayan* (Bagong Alyansang Makabayan [New Patriotic Alliance]) which is also now a political party that has won three seats in Congress. On its website, it declares itself 'a multisectoral formation struggling for national and social liberation against imperialism, feudalism and bureaucrat capitalism, [that] envisions a just society, free from foreign domination' (Bantayog 2016).

Radical theatre work in Negros can be traced to the early 1970s. From the account of this history given by Rosario Cruz-Lucero in an article titled 'Tiempos Muertos: The Radical Semiotics of People's Theater' (2014), we learn that politicized students in Bacolod, capital city of Negros Occidental, formed the theatre groups Katilingban sa Katubuhan and Gintong Silahis-Negros in 1970. When Martial Law was declared, these groups disbanded. 'Members were imprisoned, others lay low, and a number disappeared into the hills' (74). In 1975, a group called Pagbutlak was organized by a priest, Alan Abadesco, and two years later, Teatro Pangkatilingban, after Abadesco and his parish youth group attended 'a dramatics workshop run by the Community Outreach Program of the Philippine Educational Theatre Association (PETA)' (74). Teatro Pangkatilingban organized 'fifty-five community theatre groups' all across Negros but intensified state repression in 1978 'forced [its core members to work] underground'. It was then that Teatro Obrero was born, but became active only in 1981, when a workers' strike erupted at the Central Azucarera de La Carlota and 'caused a resurgence of coordinated protest action among all the organized militant groups' (75). The Negros Theatre League, an umbrella organization headed by director and playwright Joel Arbolario was set up in 1983, affiliated with other 'people's cultural groups' (75).

The re-enactment's aesthetic lineage is that of Philippine protest theatre that goes all the way back to the pre-Martial Law 'proletarian theatre' and its resurgence in the early 1980s, developed by activist groups that performed in massive rallies and demonstrations and in small guerrilla performances, mostly in urban areas. The body stances and movements of the actors in the small portable pieces that Teatro Obrero performs show the influence of protest theatre styles ranging from the Brechtian plays of PETA to Chinese political theatre (Fernandez 1996: 107): 'fists and red flags, cries against imperialism, dictatorship, fascism, and bureaucrat capitalism' (133). These styles were learnt from workshops and festivals conducted for and by a 'national theatre movement'. This period saw the theatre responding with direct answers to the call of the times: 'less subtle, directly confrontational – Philippine political theatre at its feistiest, as it had evolved from seditious theatre, contact with European and Asian political theatre, and the actual and theatrical experience of the First Quarter Storm [of 1970]' (136). The 1985 national people's strike, that in Escalante was violently dispersed by the shooting, was part of the resurgence of the open mass movement during this period.

This brings us to the idea that political theatre is 'outmoded' – another way of saying 'anachronistic' or out of its time. Perhaps it is. The Escam re-enactment is being staged the same way thirty-two years later, after 1986, and may indeed be thought of as anachronistic if the understanding of its time is that it is in the past. It is political theatre drawing from the larger 'tradition' and history of Philippine political theatre as described by Doreen Fernandez and others (Lumbera, Tiongson, Cruz-Lucero, to name a few). But this history and tradition is ongoing, its material ground both politically and theatrically is still here, now, in Negros, and in the larger Philippine society, and it continues to be a response to a call. It is in a category that Badiou describes as 'plays clearly structured by a political choice' (Badiou 2015: 72) for which he gives Brecht and Aristophanes as examples. In Escalante, the political choice has been made and is held up and kept with fidelity. I suspect that in the case of Escalante, what is needed is a 'diagonal' way of thinking, as Badiou enjoins. And such thinking can lead to a rethinking of notions like 'anachronism' or being outmoded or outdated.

Rebecca Schneider's *Performing Remains* (2011) on practices of re-enactment is instructive. Remarking on the *Port Huron Project* by artist and activist Mark Tribe, she says it 'meets the issue of outdatedness head-on' ... 'as if to ask not only how to protest, but *when* to protest ... *Of course, when playing in the crossfire of time, letting anachronism do its creative work, things can feel uncanny, or dislocated, or unsettling, or queer. They can also feel like downright bad art*.' But there is 'a kind of agency in the re-do' that is opened up for 'anyone' and not only 'the Great Man' (180, emphasis in original) – that is to say, for Escalante, the agency of the passionate amateurs of Negros and not only of the artists from 'imperial' Manila or Bacolod who can 'bring art' to the masses or teach them what art is. For the 2016 re-enactment, the visitors did not 'bring art' to Escalante but shared their work in solidarity with Teatro Obrero and learnt from and through their experience there.

Teatro Obrero's fidelity to the aesthetics of protest theatre, as its members encountered it in the 1980s, may be thought of as anachronistic, but it can also be seen as the faithful *redoing* of a time that is past but is not yet over. Schneider says that 'at re-enactments, participants fight to keep the past alive' (37) because 'it's not over' (8), very much as the Escalante re-enactors also say about their 'Escam' – and part of the 'fight' is the effort 'to get it right' as it happened in the past. 'It is as if some history re-enactors position their bodies to access, consciously and deliberately, a fleshy or pulsing kind of trace they deem accessible in a pose, or gesture, or set of acts' (37). Schneider talks lengthily about the problem and impossibility of conceptually and technically getting it right, but, more to the point, as she tells it, '[a]n action repeated again and again and again, however fractured or partial or incomplete, has a kind of staying power – persists through time – and even, in a sense, serves as a fleshy kind of "document" of its own recurrence' (37), the re-enactment serving as 'a vital mode of collective social remembering' (Connerton quoted in Schneider 2011: 43).

Conclusion: Making Theatre/Doing Politics

The difficulty of thinking politics and theatre together in terms of Escalante demonstrates what Badiou calls 'the difficulty of making theatre out of real politics', which 'never goes very far' (2008: 193). The point is that in Escalante it has gone far. As theatre. As politics. As political theatre understood, experienced and sustained in its local context. Teatro Obrero has made theatre out of real politics and both are ongoing. Thirty-two years and counting.

Schneider begins her book declaring that, in first suspending and then taking up the 'political stakes in reenactment', her aim is 'to explore the sharp, double-edged politics (and perhaps even the hazards) of affiliating ... reenactment with decidedly Left-wing art practices, as well as to ask the question of what it means to *protest* then, now' (2011: 2, emphasis in original). By the book's end, she is commenting on how her writing 'begins to sound like a protest speech – as if such speech might be infectious? As if scholarship might *muster*?' (186, emphases in original). As she concludes: 'The time to protest is Now. It is Again. It is the necessary vigilance, the hard labour, of reiterating *Nunca Mas*. Never Again' (186). The time to protest the Escalante Massacre is now. The re-enactment is not a nostalgic or melancholic gesture towards the 'idea that has gone missing'. The idea still lives. The struggle continues.

Alan Read remarks on 'an exponential rise in the material deaths, including suicide bombers and their victims, occurring outside performance's aestheticisation of politics' and 'contemporary with [the] deadly emphasis of performance studies' – that is, the field's 'crisis' and 'melancholia' (2008: 25). He asks 'performance academics to reconsider the degree to which the melancholy of the field is standing in for the conduct of politics elsewhere, where there is something real to be achieved, defended, spoken up for or identified' (65).

The claims for indemnification of the Escalante survivors which have not been granted by the Philippine government thirty-two years later can be cited as an example of that 'something real to be achieved, defended, spoken up for or identified'. There is a 'need to continue performative politics at every turn in the road of a true journey, one that really does go from A to B' (Read 2013: 44) in order to achieve a cause such as this. But the stakes are higher than financial indemnification, as I hope has been shown in the discussion. This is felt in the daily lives of the sugar workers, in the daily lives of those who went to Escalante to stand in solidarity with them in the 2016 re-enactment – the real, not anymore in 1985, but now. By 'emphasizing the need to continue and to persevere in continuing, the theatre-makers ... find a way forward by means of looking back' (Kear 2013: 221).

By all indications, the Escam re-enactments are 'political' in the way Read distinguishes the term (Read 2008: 25–6), that is, as a potential impediment to politics, especially as people give in to the pressures of the world that Ridout describes – to fear of repression, to aspirations of economic progress and social mobility, to hopes of living in peace by capitulation and meek submission, in a world 'where the impossibility of resistance has long been recognized, where oppositional interventions are folded into bureaucratic normativity' (Read 2008: 22) – to the confusion of the confusion as Badiou has theorized it. The Escalante re-enactment's ideological affiliation is a red flag of warning to not get involved, unless it is sanitized, legitimated, and thus turned into a harmless showcase of heritage of the radical past – 'something to be proud of' but essentially shorn of any real effects.

The politics emerges, *happens*, in the theatrical thinking of the event of re-enactment as an encounter that makes possible the relations of actors – at Escalante and those who decide to stand in solidarity with them – who hold on to their desire for a better future and follow the consequences of such a commitment.

Performance Details

Teatro Obrero, 'Escam' or Escalante Massacre Re-enactment, 20 September every year from 1986 to 2017, National Road in front of the Escalante City Hall, Escalante, Negros Occidental, Philippines; Artistic Director: Alejandro Deoma

Further Reading

Alain Badiou's thought on theatre and its relation or non-relation to politics can be found principally in Badiou (2005, 2008, 2015). Theatre as event that orients us in time can be seen in the theatrical thinking of Adrian Kear (2013), for whom the relationship between theatre and event is thought in and through certain theatrical 'stagings' by contemporary theatre makers in Europe. On the fraught connection between theatre and politics, Alan Read (1993, 2008) provides extensive discussion. Joe Kelleher's small but powerful 2008 volume in the 'Theatre &' series locates the connection between theatre and politics in the 'experience of encounter and appearance' that theatre enables. Nicholas Ridout calls for 'a politics of theatre' that exposes 'the form's entanglement with the constitution of political relations'. His essay 'Performance and Democracy' (2008) explains this in relation to melancholia in performance studies: 'the disappearance of politics' in a situation of 'postdemocracy' (after Rancière), where all political conflict is abolished. The idea of a possible community that would resist the nonconflictual postdemocratic totalitarian set up and its relation to melancholy is more fully taken up by Ridout in a later book, *Passionate Amateurs: Theatre, Communism, and Love* (2013).

References

Badiou, Alain (2005), *Handbook of Inaesthetics*, trans. A. Toscano, Stanford: Stanford University Press.

Badiou, Alain (2008), 'Rhapsody for the Theatre: A Short Philosophical Treatise', trans. B. Bosteels, *Theatre Survey* 49: 2.

Badiou, Alain with Nicolas Troung (2015), *In Praise of Theatre*, trans. A. Bielski, Cambridge and Malden: Polity Press.

Bantayog (2016), 'Escalante Massacre, 31 years ago today', 20 September. Available online: http://www.bantayog.org/?p=1873 (accessed 22 April 2017).

Bielski, Andrew (2015), 'Alain Badiou and the Untimely Stage: Translator's Introduction', in Alain Badiou with Nicolas Troung, *In Praise of Theatre*, vii–xxvi, Cambridge and Malden: Polity Press.

Conquergood, Dwight (2002), 'Performance Studies: Interventions and Radical Research', *TDR* 46 (2): 145–56.

Cruz-Lucero, Rosario (2014), 'Tiempos Muertos: The Radical Semiotics of People's Theater', in Jonathan Chua and Rosario Cruz-Lucero (eds), *A Reader in Philippine Theater History and Criticism: Essays in Honor of Nicanor J. Tiongson*, 73–89, Quezon City: University of the Philippines Press.

Del Mundo, Ida Anita Q. (2016), 'The City That Will Never Forget: Escalante, Negros Occidental', *The Philippine Star*, 2 October. Available online: http://www.pressreader.com/philippines/the-philippine-star/20161002/281552290353911 (accessed 22 April 2017).

Fernandez, Doreen G. (1996), *Palabas: Essays on Philippine Theater History*, Quezon City: Ateneo de Manila University Press.

Kear, Adrian (2013), *Theatre and Event: Staging the European Century*, Basingstoke: Palgrave Macmillan.

Kelleher, Joe (2009), *Theatre & Politics*, Basingstoke: Palgrave Macmillan.

Rae, Paul (2009), *Theatre & Human Rights*, Basingstoke: Palgrave Macmillan.

Read, Alan (1993), *Theatre and Everyday Life: An Ethics of Performance*, London and New York: Routledge.

Read, Alan (2008), *Theatre, Intimacy & Engagement: The Last Human Venue*, Basingstoke: Palgrave Macmillan.

Read, Alan (2013), *Theatre in the Expanded Field: Seven Approaches to Performance*, London: Bloomsbury Methuen Drama.

Ridout, Nicholas (2008), 'Performance and Democracy', in T. Davis (ed.), *The Cambridge Companion to Performance Studies*, 11–22, Cambridge: Cambridge University Press.

Ridout, Nicholas (2013), *Passionate Amateurs: Theatre, Communism, and Love*, Ann Arbor: The University of Michigan Press.

Schneider, Rebecca (2011), *Performing Remains: Art and War in Times of Theatrical Reenactment*, London and New York: Routledge.

UCAnews.com (1986), 'Negros Observes First Anniversary of Escalante Massacre in Which 21 Died', 17 September. Available online: http://www.ucanews.com/story-archive/?post_name= /1986/09/17/negros-observes-first-anniversary-of-escalante-massacre-in-which-21-died&post_id=34455 (accessed 22 April 2017).

Villalon, Eddie (2015), 'Eddie Villalon's account of the 1985 Escalante Massacre', 10 October. Available online: http://www.bantayog.org/?p=687 (accessed 22 April 2017).

16 How and Why Are Performances Documented?

HEIKE ROMS

Every autumn term these past few years, I have given a lecture to first-year students on the topic of site-specific theatre. Like many teachers in theatre studies, I refer extensively to filmed extracts from a performance to illustrate my points. In this case, my choice usually falls on *Gododdin*, devised by the (now disbanded) Welsh theatre company, Brith Gof, in collaboration with London-based industrial music group Test Department, and which premiered in Cardiff, Wales, on 1 December 1988. The work is widely considered one of the first theatre pieces to be labelled site-specific, and its director Mike Pearson, designer Cliff McLucas and others have frequently made reference to it to explain the key elements of the approach (Pearson 2010). While we sit and watch some performance footage posted on Vimeo, I try and evoke for the students my memories of watching the show live when it came to Germany in the summer of 1989, while I was a student myself at the University of Hamburg. *Gododdin* was the largest, most overwhelming piece of theatre I had ever seen. It was performed outside the vast halls of the Kampnagelfabrik, a former crane factory that had been turned into Hamburg's primary venue for experimental theatre. In a 'set' of landscape proportions and involving real cars and trees, performers hurtled themselves into a sandpit that was being slowly submerged in water. The show was an intensely visceral experience: my ears were filled with the amplified sounds of metal being thrashed rhythmically, my body was being pushed and pulled as the standing audience surrounding the sandpit tried to jostle for the best place to catch a glimpse of the action or duck away as performers hurled oil barrels in our general direction, my nose registering the smell of naked flames. The two experiences of the work couldn't be more different: here, we are neatly packed into rows in the featureless space of a lecture theatre, there, I was part of an excited crowd feeling the impact of weather, fire, water and the presence of many other bodies. There, an immersive, expansive, charged event; here, filmed footage confined to a camera's field of view and made grainy and tinny from years of repeated copying. Yet, on the night, my sightlines were also often obscured by others and my brain struggled to make sense of the density of impressions it received, so that upon each viewing of the footage, I keep discovering details about the work I hadn't noticed or had since forgotten.

This chapter is concerned with the purpose and form of performance records like the *Gododdin* video. It will consider the relationship between these records and the performance event that generated them. This relationship is generally discussed under the mantle of 'performance documentation'. The term is less straightforward than it might at first appear as it can refer to the document/s (e.g. videos or photographs), the processes of creating these documents (e.g. filming or sound-recording) or the cultural practice of compiling documentary records of past performance events (Sant 2017: 1ff). And what counts as a documentary record, too, is far from simple. The French information scientist, Suzanne Briet (known affectionately as 'Madame Documentation'), published an influential essay in 1951 in which she proposed that any kind of artefact can serve as a document, as long as it is presented and studied as such ([1951] 2006). So, while we might associate performance documentation primarily with the visual and audio-visual registrations of live events such as videos, photographs or sound tapes, it can also include things such as rehearsal diaries, reviews or props, and, I want to suggest, even immaterial forms, such as memories. Each of these types of documents can be said to have a different temporal relationship to the performance event – in their joint book *Theatre/Archaeology*, Mike Pearson and archaeologist Michael Shanks have suggested that 'Documentation is generated before, during and after the event by all orders of participants' (2001: 58). Forms of documentation that are produced during a performance comprise mainly visual and audio-visual recordings. (There have also been creative experiments with capturing live actions through forms of simultaneous writing or drawing.) Documents generated before might include proposals, scores, prompt books, lighting charts, costume designs or publicity announcements. And among the forms of documentation following a performance might be newspaper reviews and scholarly essays, but also forms we might not immediately identify as documentation, such as recollections, anecdotes and re-enactments.

In this chapter, I will follow Pearson and Shanks's distinction and look at the most common types of documentation that were made before, during and after the performances of *Gododdin* in 1988 and 1989, and I will summarize the major scholarly positions that help us make sense of their form and purpose. This summary will also roughly track the development of the debate on performance documentation from the mid-1980s to the present day, which leads from early reflections on the specifics of certain formats such as video and photography to recent discussions about performance's relationship to the archive, and about performative forms of documentation such as re-enactments. The debate on performance documentation has been so influential, I suggest, because an understanding of the relationship between performance and its material and immaterial traces is a basic concern for our discipline, whether we study theatre or make it, and whether our interests lie in historical or contemporary forms. Indeed, by aiming to understand how and why performance is documented, the debate touches the very heart of the question of what (a) performance actually is. I want to suggest in this chapter that there is no single definite answer to this question: ideas about what a performance is are not fixed but have been historically contingent and therefore subject to change. Accordingly, ideas about how documentation relates to performance have also changed, and so have judgements about the nature and quality of that relationship.

The main reason for choosing *Gododdin* as my case study, besides the deep impression it left on me personally, is that it was around the time of the making of *Gododdin* in the late 1980s that the debate about performance documentation really took hold in theatre and performance studies; and the way the company chose to document the work was reflective of this debate. In fact, *Gododdin* itself and its complex and dispersed form, which prevented any single viewing experience from being considered representative, inspired its director Mike Pearson, together with Michael Shanks, to think of documentation as a form of 'reworking and recontextualisation' of an event, rather than its faithful replication (2001: 58) – that documentation can never be (nor aspires to be) an exact copy of an event is taken for granted by many of the scholars I will mention in the following. And, although not central to my discussion here, it is important to note that *Gododdin* was itself a performance about how to record and account for a past event. The show was based on the medieval Welsh poem of the same name, which tells the story of the battle and defeat of a small band of Celtic warriors against the overpowering force of invading Angles in around 600 CE in what is now Northern England. Brith Gof employed the story as a metaphor for the decline in the 1980s of the Welsh heavy industry at the hands of the Conservative government under Prime Minister Margaret Thatcher – the Cardiff premiere of *Gododdin* was staged in a disused car factory already earmarked for demolition. The poem of *Y Gododdin*, traditionally ascribed to the bard Aneirin, is written from the point of view of a surviving eyewitness to the battle who laments the dead; in the performance, this position was embodied by company member Lis Hughes Jones, who sang and spoke extracts from the poem while being placed high above the physical action of the other performers as if a witness to their fate. How *Gododdin* chose to perform an event in Welsh history and explore its contemporary parallels is seemingly taking us a long way away from the chapter's enquiry into how and why a performance is captured in forms of documentation. But in the background to the discussion about performance documentation resonate such wider questions about how we access what is past, how we make sense of it and how we represent it for the present and the future. And exploring the issue of performance documentation may provide us with some tools for thinking through these wider questions.

'DURING' Part 1: The Video

ITEM A: Gododdin, *TV programme, produced by Green Eye Media for HTV Wales; broadcast 2 March 1990, 49 minutes.*

Gododdin was performed at five different locations over the course of a year. Following its premiere in Cardiff in the winter of 1988, it toured the following year to a quarry in Polverigi, Italy; the Kampnagelfabrik in Hamburg, Germany; an ice hockey stadium in Leeuwarden, the Netherlands; and to the Tramway in Glasgow, Scotland, a former tram depot that, like the Kampnagelfabrik, had been turned into a theatre venue. The only available recording of the work in its entirety was filmed in Hamburg by a local video production company, using two cameras – one roaming amid the standing crowd, one placed high above looking at the action from a bird's-eye view – over two nights. While seemingly a complete and authentic record of the performance, it is in effect a partial and constructed document: it offers a version that was put together in an editing suite from two separate performances; and it relies on a viewpoint unavailable to the audience on the night. The second video document of *Gododdin* – the one most easily available and therefore most often shown, including by me to my students – is a television documentary commissioned by former Welsh channel HTV Wales. It includes high-quality footage filmed in Cardiff, Glasgow and Polverigi, interspersed with location shots and interviews with performers and audience members. Again, the relationship between this document and the performance it records is not straightforward: the documentary is as much concerned with giving insights into the devising and staging process and with the impact the work made on those who saw it as it is with what happened during the live performances.

The debate about video as a method for documenting performance emerged in the 1980s and responded to the widespread use that was already being made of video technology at the time by those who created, taught or wrote about theatre. Video technology captured electronic signals onto a tape that could be played back straight away – meaning no costly and time-consuming processing in a laboratory as had to be done with film. Theatre makers could inspect immediately the work they had made in the rehearsal room that day, or cheaply put together a recording for publicity or archival purposes. In her summary of early discussions about the use of video documentation in theatre, Annabelle Melzer (1995a and b) identifies two main positions: a pragmatic approach that accepted video as a useful tool and limited itself to practical questions of camera angles or editing choices; and a theoretically informed position that was concerned with the medial differences between theatre (as a live medium) and video (as a recorded medium) and that was anxious about what would be lost by translating a performance from one to the other. The roots of these positions reach through the century-long history of debates on media technology and representation. In his famous essay of 1935, 'Das Kunstwerk im Zeitalter seiner technischen Reproduzierbarkeit' (usually translated as 'The Work of Art in the Age of Mechanical Reproduction', although a more faithful translation would be 'The Work of Art in the Age of its Technological Reproducibility'), German philosopher Walter Benjamin already noted that 'Even the most perfect reproduction of a work of art is lacking in one element: its presence in time and space, its unique existence at the place where it happens to be' ([1935] 1968: 214), a presence he called 'aura'. But Benjamin also valued the fact that reproducing an artwork (for example, through the printed copy of a painting in a catalogue, which effectively means moving it into a different time and space and thus destroying its aura) makes it accessible for the aesthetic enjoyment of a much greater number of people. When Melzer (1995a, b) speaks of video as a 'best betrayal' of performance, she recognizes what video documentation loses from the live event – the fullness of an audience's embodied and affective experience – but also what it gains in the shape of a wider accessibility and longer-term legacy for the work.

It is not the medial difference between theatre and video, but on the contrary, their relative similarity as shared time-based media that Gay McAuley identifies as a core issue because a video may be too successful a record of a performance: 'Perhaps it is the fact that the recording is relatively so complete that creates the difficulty … [V]ideo is already performance' (1994: 187). For McAuley, the difficulties with video documentation are less to do with the shortcomings of video as a recording medium than with 'our failure to develop the "reading" skills necessary to make appropriate use of video recordings' (184): educated in the conventions of Hollywood cinema and realist television drama, we are used to ignoring how 'realism' is the result of certain formal choices, including camera angles, shot composition and cuts, assuming that what we are watching is a true and transparent reproduction of the real. In the case of video recordings of performance, it is thus often the absence of filmic conventions such as close ups and edits that makes them appear deficient as documents. McAuley therefore calls for a greater attention to formal choices, both on the side of the creator and the watcher of performance recordings. Varney and Fensham have called such attention 'videocy' (2000: 94), by which they mean a set of reading skills that understands the differences between watching a live performance and watching its documentation and that is able to make full use of the document to access aspects of the work inaccessible to a live audience through the ability to stop and start, freeze frame, fast-forward, rewind and replay the tape over and over. What Melzer, McAuley and Varney and Fensham all agree on, therefore, is that performance is an event that is separate from its documentation but that requires such documentation in order for our knowledge about it to be developed, stored and shared. Varney and Fensham therefore propose that, 'Rather than killing off or replacing live performance ... the video may fulfil [sic] an additional task, protecting theatre from redundancy ... [to] ensure it is included in contemporary cultural discourse' (96).

If we apply some 'videocy' to the HTV documentary of *Gododdin*, we might be able to analyse the way in which the documentary (following televisual aesthetics) attempts to replicate the live experience of watching the performance by choosing certain camera angles and edits; how that experience is supplemented by a discussion of the artistic decision-making processes, the knowledge of which is not accessible through the live event alone; and how the inclusion of personal testimonies gives an insight into the frames of reference that were used by audience members afterwards to make sense of what they witnessed.

'DURING' Part 2: The Photograph

ITEM B: Gododdin, *three black and white photographs; photographers: André Lützen, Pete Telfer, Friedemann Simon; reproduced in Pearson and Shanks (2001) on pages 20, 34 and 94.*

A dozen or so photographers were invited to take images of *Gododdin* in its five locations, resulting in hundreds of black and white photographic prints, negatives, contact sheets and colour slides of the work. Comparatively few of these have appeared in print. Only three images are reproduced in Pearson and Shanks's *Theatre/Archaeology*, for example, where they serve to illustrate the use of the body in performance: performers are captured in the midst of a dynamic action, resulting in images full of gestural expressiveness.

Still photography continues to be the most commonly used form of performance documentation. It may seem counterintuitive that an art form that comes into existence through its unfolding in time would be documented in a medium that is defined by its arresting of time in the image of a singular moment – although the photographs of *Gododdin* clearly demonstrate that still images can nonetheless convey a sense of movement. It is, however, photography's unsurpassed capacity to persuade its viewer that what it depicts 'really happened' that makes it the recording medium of choice. A photo is often presumed to have a direct mimetic relationship with what it shows: writer Susan Sontag notes that 'The assumption underlying all uses of photography [is] that each photograph is a piece of the world' (1979: 93), even though images were already retouched, airbrushed, collaged and otherwise modified long before the advent of Photoshop.

A photograph's relationship to concepts of reality and truth has been most thoroughly examined with regard to the documentation of performance art, a performative practice that creates artworks through actions and that historically emerged in the context of the visual arts. Art historian Catherine Grant has suggested that 'Photography has an intimate history with performance, providing a mode of documentation that can appear to authenticate, and ultimately stand in for, the initial action' (2002: 34). The photographic authentication of an action – providing evidence that it really happened – was particularly important to

Fig. 16.1 Brith Gof, *Gododdin*, Leeuwarden 1989. Photo: Cliff McLucas.

the sub-category of performance art known as body art of the early 1970s. Its audacious acts, often carried out in front of very small audiences, were frequently documented in a deliberately raw aesthetic that closely resembled photojournalistic crime reportage (Warr 2003: 32) in order to underscore their authenticity. As performance historian Amelia Jones has argued, 'The body art event needs the photograph to confirm its having happened' (1997: 16). This dependency is mutual, as the photograph in return needs the rawness of the body art event to support its claim to providing an authentic, unfiltered representation of the real (as Jones puts it: 'the photograph needs the body art event as an ontological "anchor" for its indexicality'; ibid.). Grant's second point – that documentation can come to stand in for the initial action – suggests that certain images taken of performance art works have become famous images in their own right, disconnected from the action that gave rise to them. According to Grant, this is likely to be an image that immediately conveys a clear reading 'as a symbolic portrait rather than as part of a messy and active performance' (2002:

44). However, in many cases, it should be added, it was the artists themselves – trained in fine art traditions of image composition – that controlled the photographic representations of their work, often collaborating closely with the photographers.

In the case of *Gododdin*, there is not one single 'iconic' image that has come to stand in for the work as a whole – but there is a limited number of photographic motifs that immediately bring the work to mind and that are repeatedly used in print: almost all cropped to focus in on the performers, they portray their bodies flinging themselves into a sand-filled pit or hanging off a metal net, being sprayed with a jet of water (see Figure 16.1). The images underline the 'realness' of the performers' physical exertion and exhaustion that were among the hallmarks of *Gododdin*'s aesthetic. In this way, the photos are closer to performance art documentation than to classic theatre photography, where the photograph's frame often mimics that of the proscenium arch and the image is taken at middle distance (for a discussion of the conventions of theatre photography see Reason 2006: 113ff.).

It is also worth considering in what context we now mostly come across the photos of *Gododdin*: their reproductions in scholarly publications serve to illustrate academic arguments, thereby linking the experience of the work that the photographs promise to access to scholarly knowledge production. In this way, the work is multiplied across new audiences. As writer Tracey Warr has observed, 'Each performance work may have at least three layers of audience: the immediate audience, the audience that experiences the work through its distributed and fragmentary documentation, and the audiences of posterity, doing the same, but adding more layers to the discourses, texts and interpretations of the work' (2003: 31) – the latter including you as you are now reading this.

There are a number of works in the history of performance art that did not actually have an immediate audience and that were performed entirely for the camera as their only witness – or, rather, that were carried out for an 'audience of posterity' for whom the camera acted as a kind of surrogate. Performance scholar Philip Auslander has called the resulting photos of such actions 'theatrical' (which he distinguishes from 'documentary' images): 'The image we see thus records an event that never took place except in the photograph itself' (2006: 2) This does not imply that the action that is recorded did not take place at some point in time; but rather that, in the absence of a live audience, it is the photograph that frames such an action as a work of performance. Thinking through the implication of this proposition, Auslander comes to the conclusion that in such cases the photograph itself can be considered '*as a performance* that directly reflects an artist's aesthetic project or sensibility and for which we [the viewers of the photograph] are the present audience' (9). Auslander thereby uncouples an understanding of what a performance is from its equation with a live event that occurs independently of its documentation – instead, in the case of 'theatrical' performance documentation, Auslander proposes that our experience of the performance happens entirely in the event of us engaging with the photograph.

Liveness

Critical engagements with the issue of performance documentation have returned time and again to the question of what performance is, and how it relates to what documentation is. This discussion was significantly galvanized by the publication in 1993 of performance scholar

Peggy Phelan's *Unmarked: The Politics of Performance*. Phelan was able to tie discussions about the nature of documentation inextricably to those on the nature of performance itself, to what she termed the 'ontology of performance' (ontology deals with the nature of being). Phelan's succinct formulation of this ontology has been cited ubiquitously: 'Performance's only life is in the present. Performance cannot be saved, recorded, documented, or otherwise participate in the circulation of representations *of* representations: once it does so, it becomes something other than performance. ... Performance's being ... becomes itself through disappearance' (1993: 146). Phelan's powerful assertion has often been taken to be a categorical refusal to document performance, though it would probably be more accurate to say that her point is that documentation invariably alters the nature of the live experience of performance, fundamental to which for her is the awareness that that experience will be irretrievably gone when the show is over, only to be revisited in the memories of those who shared in it.

Philip Auslander's equally well-known critique of Phelan in his book *Liveness* (1999) pivots on her argument that live performance cannot be medially reproduced without changing its essential qualities. Auslander challenges this by declaring liveness to be a quality that is not essential to performance; it is in fact, he argues, produced as the very effect of the medial reproducibility of performance: 'It was the development of recording technologies that made it possible to perceive existing representations as "live." Prior to the advent of those technologies (e.g., sound recording and motion pictures), there was no such thing as "live" performance, for that category has meaning only in relation to an opposing possibility' (51).

Phelan's and Auslander's positions – summarized by art historian Jonah Westerman as the 'absence' and the 'presence' models of performance – have often been considered to be incompatible. However, Westerman has pointed out that both are united in their efforts to 'bind a performance work to an originary moment' (2017: 9); it is just that for Phelan, that moment occurs in a live event, whereas for Auslander, that moment can also occur, as we have seen, in the event of an audience encountering a piece of performance documentation, such as a photograph.

'BEFORE': The Archive

ITEM C: *Title:* Brith Gof Archive; *Author: Brith Gof (Theatre Company); Description: Papers of Brith Gof, including correspondence, papers and photographs relating to the company's site-specific and theatre productions, projects and television productions; together with administrative papers relating to company productions, and company business and information papers; and general papers relating to the company and its work, site-specific theatre and theatre in Wales. Format: 56 large boxes, 11 small boxes, 15 outsize folders, 8 rolls, 5 outsize bundles, 2 outsize envelopes, 1 item and 1 outsize volume; 8 large crates ... ; 1.723 cubic metres. Institution: National Library of Wales.* (The National Library of Wales catalogue entry)

After Brith Gof closed in 2004, the company donated its entire collection of documents and documentation to the National Library of Wales. In reference to *Gododdin* alone, the archive holds four boxes filled with correspondence, McLucas's scenographic designs, work plans, publicity materials, previews, and reviews and photographs. A great many of the materials were produced during or after the performances of *Gododdin*, such as the photographic slides, videos or reviews. But an even greater amount was created during the work's devising, rehearsal and production phases. These materials refer to a performance that hasn't yet happened. In what way can they therefore be considered performance documentation? To take one example: among the materials are the so-called '*Gododdin* workbooks', which the company produced for every venue to which it toured the work. They comprise detailed production notes, timetables and plans for each of the redesigns of *Gododdin*, conceived in response to the specific architectural and production conditions of each site. (See, for example, McLucas's design for the Hamburg version of *Gododdin*, Figure 16.2.) They break down the work, element by element, from lighting installation to sound design, building work to transport needs, performer requirements to object purchases for each venue, containing 'all the necessary information for your technical and building crews to make *Gododdin*' (*Gododdin – The Workbook*). As pieces of documentation, they are evidently very different to medial transcriptions of the live performance event, such as video recordings or photographs. Yet, read with reference to the videos and photographs, they can tell us much about how and why the work was conceived and what it took to stage it. They help us to understand certain artistic decisions and the material factors that impacted on them. They document *Gododdin* not as a live event, but as the sum of the processes and knowledges that created it.

In the early 2000s, the debate on performance documentation began to consider more seriously the role of the archive as the institution whose function it is to house documentation. The nature of the archive had, of course, long been of importance to theatre historians, who tend to spend much of their research time in one. But it now also became a concern

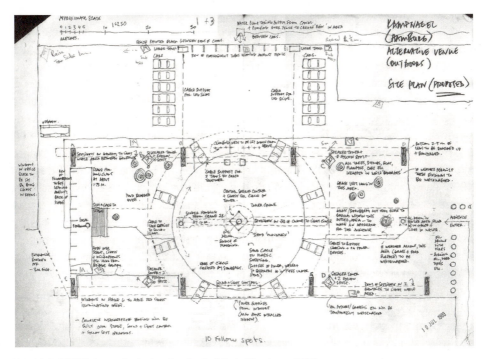

Fig. 16.2 Cliff McLucas's design for *Gododdin* in Hamburg 1989.

for scholars and artists involved in contemporary performance – although oftentimes it was the concept of an archive and what it represents rather than the actual experience of working in one that motivated this concern. Several new aspects were introduced into the debate: while the discussion on performance documentation had thus far mainly focused on singular documents, such as a video or a photograph, the question of the archive shifted the attention to collections of documents containing multiple sorts of materials, generated before, during and after performances, and to the possible cross-referencing between them. And while the discussion had previously dealt mainly with why and how to record a live event, it now began to address the issue of why and how and by whom that record is then saved, stored, accessed and used.

The issue of archiving also again helped to challenge what had become the key reference point in the debate on performance documentation, namely Phelan's definition of performance as that which disappears. In one of the first essays to consider the relationship between performance and the archive, Rebecca Schneider proposes that performance can only be said to be disappearing if looked at through the 'logic of the Archive', which merely values that which endures in material form and thus overlooks all the immaterial ways in which performance remains and reappears in the shape of memories, stories, repeated gestures or ritual re-enactments, for example (2001: 100–1). With this argument, Schneider continues a long-standing theoretical interest in the archive as a site of power, which goes back to philosophers Michel Foucault and Jacques Derrida. For Foucault, the archive is 'the law of what can be said, the system that governs the appearance of statements as unique events' (Foucault 1972: 145), meaning that it is the archive that creates the conditions and limits within which a culture can articulate itself. And Derrida (1996) has noted the essential role that the archive (as the storage space for official documents) has played in helping to establish and maintain state power.

While the particular power of theatre and performance archives may seem comparatively modest, their collection too is a reflection on what is deemed worthy of preservation and thus of cultural value and authority. In Brith Gof's case, its deposit at the National Library of Wales was confirmation of the company's status as a national asset, and the holdings of its archives not only represent parts of the cultural heritage of Wales but also provide material for the histories that will be told about it in the future: 'the question of the archive is not, we repeat, a question of the past. ... It is a question of the future', suggests Derrida (1996: 36). But if indeed the archive is the place where the remains of our past can be shaped into different future histories, then this also implies that, as historian Carolyn Steedman (1998) has pointed out, the archive is a place of creative possibilities. Theatre scholars Maggie B. Gale and Ann Featherstone, who provide a useful overview of how the archive has been written about in theatre and performance studies, have proposed that it is the archive as a place of potentiality (rather than one of power) that has made it such a popular current concern: in 'a culture dominated by the need to self-define', they state, 'the archive has become a vital cultural tool as a means of accessing versions of the past' (2011: 17). In the case of *Gododdin*, the archived workbooks may once have served as evidence to understand how site-specific performance emerged in the 1980s (Pearson 2010). Leading up to 'Brexit', though, we may now be more interested in what insights they provide into how a Welsh-language cultural product was received in Europe in the years leading up to the formation of the European Union. Supported by the archive, our understanding of and our attitudes towards a past performance can develop and change in response to the interests and desires of our present and future.

'AFTER': The Repertoire

ITEM D: Between Memory and Archive: Gododdin – A special one-day event, *Saturday 6 September 2008, Chapter Arts Centre Cardiff.*

For the twentieth anniversary of *Gododdin* in 2008, former members of Brith Gof and Test Department were reunited in Cardiff to inspect some of the archival documents that had recently been deposited at the National Library of Wales, and to share their personal recollections of *Gododdin* in front of an audience, many of whom had their own memories of seeing the work in 1988. Together they addressed the gaps in the archived records, reminding themselves of all the difficult as well as the joyful experiences of performing the work. Can this sharing of memories and anecdotes, supported by small practical demonstrations of gestures and movements, be considered a form of documenting *Gododdin*?

The question of how performance can be documented through practices that are themselves performative – demonstrations, conversations, re-enactments – has animated much of the recent debate on the subject of performance documentation. I have mentioned above Schneider's proposition that performance does not disappear only to leave behind nothing but material traces, but that it has a way of reappearing: performance remains, she argues, 'but remains *differently* ([…] history is not "lost" through body-to-body transmission)' (2001: 105). Schneider builds on the work of performance scholar Richard Schechner, who notes that 'Performance means: never for the first time. It means: for the second to the *n*th time. Performance is "twice-behaved behavior"' (1985: 36). To perform always means to repeat: whether doing a gesture done many times before, speaking a word already spoken time and again or recalling and representing an event of the past by restaging it. Performance scholar Diana Taylor has similarly argued that it is through such repetition that performance is able to transfer memory and knowledge on its own terms, which Taylor terms 'the *repertoire* of embodied practice/knowledge (i.e., spoken language, dance, sports, ritual)' (2003: 19). The repertoire passes on embodied knowledge from past to present, whether an actor trains their body through repeating physical exercises demonstrated for them by their teacher, or a community carries out the same ritual year in year out – or performers remember through words and gestures their shared experience of performing *Gododdin*. Like Schneider, Taylor emphasizes that the repertoire is an alternative form of knowledge-transfer to the '*archive* of supposedly enduring materials (i.e., texts, documents, buildings, bones)' (19). As the main mode of historical transfer, for example, in cultures without written records, for communities without access to institutions or in art forms reliant on physical expression, the repertoire tends to be marginalized and overlooked in a culture centred around the power of the archive. But Taylor also points out that the archive and the repertoire often work hand in hand: at the *Gododdin* event, memories were prompted by reading the archival documents, and the conversations in turn were recorded to be deposited alongside the papers in the National Library of Wales's collection.

The repertoire practice that has enjoyed the most scholarly and artistic attention recently has been re-enactment, where an event of the past is re-performed in the present. There are many examples of re-enactments in popular culture, such as those recreating events of the English or American Civil Wars. Re-enactment has also become a widespread artistic strategy, with artists redoing the work of other artists or of their younger selves. Re-enactments raise issues of authorship (Whose performance is it if an artist re-performs a past performance by another artist?); and whether there is such a thing as an original, authentic experience of a performance that can be recaptured. At their most critical, they examine, as Amelia Jones has suggested, '*what can be known about the event*' (2012: 17) and how such knowledge can be acquired and shared. In an extensive study of cultural and artistic practices of re-enactment, Schneider (2011) reminds us that such practices are at the very heart of theatre, which is defined by its very capacity for repetition: as I suggested at the beginning of this essay, *Gododdin* was itself a theatrical recreation of sorts of a major event in Welsh history. What interests Schneider in re-enactment is that it troubles the idea of history as a linear progression from past to present to future, and she calls the time of re-enactment a 'syncopated time', where '*then* and *now* punctuate each other' (2011: 2) – never completely then, and never merely now. In re-enactments, she notes, performance documentation therefore changes its status from past record to future script: 'Documents that had seemed to indicate *only* the past, are now pitched toward the possibility of a future reenactment as much as toward the event they apparently recorded' (28). This also means that the temporal alignment of documentation along a 'before-during-after' timeline that I have used as a convenient way to structure this chapter is not as straightforwardly linear as it seems.

    Goddodin has never been re-enacted; and the sheer scale of the work and the financial and material implications of staging it make a future re-enactment unlikely. But the potential for a future re-enactment of the performance is nonetheless always present, enabled by its material archive and its embodied repertoire: a performance is therefore never completely in the past, but continues to persist in the present and into the future.

Digital Challenges

Gododdin was conceived and performed in the late 1980s on the cusp of the development that has seen digital technology become a ubiquitous presence in our lives. The documents of the performance that I have discussed thus far were all still produced through analogue technology: VHS video tapes, photographic slides and prints, hand-drawn designs and notebooks. Since that time, digital technology has profoundly changed the way performances are documented. Take a look, for example, at the sophisticated web-based documentation of choreographer William Forsythe's piece *One Flat Thing, reproduced*. Entitled *Sychronous Objects* (2009), the website houses a range of performative documents that illuminate visually in different ways the complex structure of Forsythe's choreography. In an early essay about the potential of digital technology for performance documentation, author and director Steve Dixon (1999) highlights how such rich and multi layered documentation is enabled by the enhanced storage capacity of digital carriers and by the inherent connectivity that results from the fact that digital technology renders everything – text, images, moving footage, sound – as data. Dixon's essay, though, is also a useful reminder of the rapid evolution of this technology and the obsolescence it creates: his essay is accompanied by a

CD-ROM, which has since become unplayable on the current generation of computers and their system softwares.

The turn towards the digital has not just changed our technological tools but also altered the way we think. The fact that in the digital domain copies are the same quality as the originals from which they derive makes talking about them in terms of origin and copies in effect redundant. But how might this change our understanding of archives, for example, whose power has been founded on the fact that they store unique original objects and endow those who have access to them with certain privileges? And will the distinction between performance as an 'original' live event and its documentation as a mediated 'copy' or reproduction – that for so long dominated the debate on performance documentation – still make sense?

A distinction on which digital technology is already having a profound impact is that between author/artist and audience. If *Gododdin* were performed today, audience members would surely capture the performance in hundreds of photographs and videos on their smartphones to be widely shared on social media, removing the documentation of the performance from the relative control of its creators. Digital technology has indeed already changed the way the existing documentation of *Gododdin* is shared and engaged with: it was not its authors (Brith Gof or Test Department) but their fans that have digitized and uploaded the video documentary, the soundtrack and photographs onto video hosting platforms and websites, available to be watched and listened to, but also to be copied, edited, mashed up and reimagined. The 'reworking and recontextualisation' that Pearson and Shanks suggested (2001: 58) is afforded by documentation becomes not just the propriety of the artists but of the audience too. The live performances of a work are now only one among many possible kinds of experiences that an audience could have and can have of it. Performance scholar Gabriella Giannachi concludes therefore that 'the constantly altering reinterpretation' of performance documentation over time by the audience could 'generate a novel history of performance, one in which works are seen in a fluid or unfolding state, as processes and networks rather than products' (2017: 187).

Performance/Documentation

This chapter has aimed to provide an overview of the debate on performance documentation that has dominated theatre and performance studies for the last thirty years, and continues to do so (see the 'Further Reading' recommendations below). As I have suggested at the start, discussions about why and how performance may be documented cannot be separated from discussions about what performance is. The relationship between them has been defined differently at different times, often in response to changes in technology or artistic practice or in reflection of wider cultural or social preoccupations. Performance has been considered incompatible with documentation, or on the contrary enabled by it; documentation has been understood to stand in for performance after its disappearance or to facilitate its reappearance in the encounter between document and audience; performance has been limited to a singular live event or has been seen as an extended process that connects that live event with its continuing repetition in thought, memory, conversation, interpretation, documentary record and historical narrative. To avoid any misunderstanding:

there is no suggestion here that the past event called *Gododdin* did not take place in 1988–9; and no suggestion that experiencing it live is the same as watching a video of it (I myself can vouch for that difference). However, what the debate on performance documentation presses upon us is that the live experience of an event is not the only way to know it – any event is given meaning and value through a variety of different discourses and over time, and that process is often facilitated by documents of many kinds. It is this that will make me show the *Gododdin* documentation to my students for many years to come.

Performance Details

Brith Gof and Test Department, *Gododdin*; performers: Alistair Adams, Margaret Ames, Steve Carroll, Tony Cudlip, Graham Cunnington, Alun Elidyr, Angus Farquhar, Gus Ferguson, John E. R. Hardy, Paul Jamrozy, Lis Hughes Jones, Mike Pearson, Marc Rees, Nic Ros, Sêra Williams. Project Director: Mike Pearson; Scenography: Cliff McLucas; Music: John E. R. Hardy; Adaptation: Lis Hughes Jones. Premiere: Cardiff, December 1988. European tour: Polverigi, Hamburg, Leeuwarden, Glasgow 1989.
Gododdin, TV programme produced by Green Eye Media for HTV Wales: https://vimeo.com/80218855

Further Reading

Reason (2006) provides a comprehensive and accessible overview of the debate on the documentation of performance. The edited collection by Jones and Heathfield (2012) brings together the most important essays on the topic by scholars from performance studies and art history; Sant's collection (2017) focuses in particular on the impact of digital technology on documentation; and Giannachi and Westerman (2018) give an insight into how museums approach the documentation of performance, including interviews with curators.

References

Auslander, Philip (1999), *Liveness: Performance in a Mediatized Culture*, London: Routledge.
Auslander, Philip (2006), 'The Performativity of Performance Documentation', *PAJ: A Journal of Performance and Art* 28 (3): 1–10.
Benjamin, Walter ([1935] 1968), 'The Work of Art in the Age of Mechanical Reproduction', trans. H. Zohn, in Hannah Arendt (ed.), *Illuminations*, 214–18, London: Fontana.
Briet, Suzanne ([1951] 2006) *What is Documentation?*, trans. E. Day, L. Martinet and H. G. B. Anghelescu, Lanham, MD: Scarecrow Press.
Derrida, Jacques (1996), *Archive Fever: A Freudian Impression*, trans. E. Prenowitz, Chicago: The University of Chicago Press.
Dixon, Steve (1999), 'Digits, Discourse, and Documentation: Performance Research and Hypermedia', *TDR* 43 (1): 152–76.
Forsythe, William (2009), *Synchronous Objects*, website produced with Maria Palazzi and Norah Zuniga Shaw, https://synchronousobjects.osu.edu/ (accessed 7 May 2018).
Foucault, Michel (1972), *The Archaeology of Knowledge*, trans. A. M. Sheridan Smith, London: Tavistock Books.

Gale, Maggie B., and Ann Featherstone (2011), 'The Imperative of the Archive', in Baz Kershaw and Helen Nicholson (eds), *Research Methods in Theatre and Performance*, 17–40, Edinburgh: Edinburgh University Press.

Giannachi, Gabriella, and Jonah Westerman, eds (2018), *Histories of Performance Documentation: Museum, Artistic, and Scholarly Practices*, London and New York: Routledge.

Grant, Catherine (2002), 'Private Performances: Editing Performance Photography', *Performance Research* 7 (1): 34–44.

Jones, Amelia (1997), '"Presence" in Absentia: Experiencing Performance as Documentation', *Art Journal* 56 (4): 11–18.

Jones, Amelia, and Adrian Heathfield, eds (2012), *Perform, Repeat, Record: Live Art in History*, Bristol and Chicago: Intellect.

McAuley, Gay (1994), 'The Video Documentation of Theatrical Performance', *New Theatre Quarterly* 10 (38): 183–4.

Melzer, Annabel (1995a), '"Best Betrayal": The Documentation of Performance on Video and Film - Part 1', *New Theatre Quarterly* 11 (42): 147–57.

Melzer, Annabel (1995b), '"Best Betrayal": The Documentation of Performance on Video and Film - Part 2', *New Theatre Quarterly* 11 (43): 259–76.

Pearson, Mike (2010), *Site-Specific Performance*, Basingstoke: Palgrave Macmillan.

Pearson, Mike, and Michael Shanks (2001), *Theatre/Archaeology*, London: Routledge.

Phelan, Peggy (1993), *Unmarked: The Politics of Performance*, London and New York: Routledge.

Reason, Matthew (2006), *Documentation, Disappearance and the Representation of Live Performance*, Basingstoke: Palgrave Macmillan.

Sant, Toni, ed. (2017) *Documenting Performance: The Context & Processes of Digital Curation and Archiving*, London: Bloomsbury.

Schechner, Richard (1985) *Between Theatre and Anthropology*, Philadelphia: University of Pennsylvania Press.

Schneider, Rebecca (2001), 'Performance Remains', *Performance Research* 6 (2): 100–8.

Schneider, Rebecca (2011), *Performing Remains: Art and War in Times of Theatrical Reenactment*, London and New York: Routledge.

Sontag, Susan (1979), *On Photography*, New York: Penguin Books.

Steedman, Carolyn (1998), 'The Space of Memory: In an Archive', *History of Human Sciences* 11 (4): 65–83.

Taylor, Diana (2003), *The Archive and the Repertoire: Performing Cultural Memory in the Americas*, Durham and London: Duke University Press.

Varney, Denise, and Rachel Fensham (2000), 'More-and-less-than: Liveness, Video Recording, and the Future of Performance', *New Theatre Quarterly* 16(1): 88–96.

Warr, Tracey (2003), 'Image as Icon: Recognizing the Enigma', in Adrian George (ed.), *Art, lies and videotape: Exposing Performance*, 30–7, Liverpool: Tate.

Westerman, Jonah (2018), 'Introduction: Practical histories: How we do things with performance', in Gabriella Giannachi and Jonah Westerman (eds), *Histories of Performance Documentation: Museum, Artistic, and Scholarly Practices*, 1–12, London and New York: Routledge.

Part 4 Interventions

17 How Can Performance Disrupt Institutional Spaces?

DOMINIC JOHNSON

'How to avoid the problem of being invited or not?' asked the performance artist Christopher D'Arcangelo in 1978. His solution? 'To invite yourself' (1978a). As an artist who was generally unwelcome in the institutional spaces in which he might have had his prime sphere of relevance and effect, and with an axe to grind about the politics of such spaces, D'Arcangelo serially would present what he called 'unauthorized works'. From 1975, these unauthorized or *stealth* performances – distinctive in their unsanctioned nature, and militant in their cumulative assault on institutions – took place in a series of hallowed venues for modern and contemporary art. In New York, *Museum Pieces* included an action in the atrium of the Solomon R. Guggenheim Museum in 1975, in which he handcuffed himself at the hands and feet, a statement of anarchism emblazoned on his back, and was carried out by security guards; in another action at the Museum of Modern Art, also in 1975, he pinned a reproduction of *Guernica* (1937) to the wall next to Pablo Picasso's original, and spray-painted the former with a statement of anarchism (he was arrested and charged with disorderly conduct and trespass). The series ended abruptly when D'Arcangelo took his own life in 1979, at the age of 24.

D'Arcangelo's *Museum Pieces* provides a lens through which to pose a series of questions about the efficacy of performance; the series prompts us to explore how the social and individual effects of creating and witnessing performance is heightened when artists choose to perform without an institution's blessing. How, I ask, does performance think through – and intervene in – the locations in which it is sited? What happens when performance actions take place without authorization or invitation in institutions that might otherwise present themselves as being hospitable to experimental art and performance?

The Uninvited

In January 1975, D'Arcangelo staged the first of his *Museum Pieces* at the Whitney Museum of American Art (see Figure 17.1). On a cold Manhattan morning, D'Arcangelo removed his coat and shirt to reveal a statement of anarchism stencilled onto his back. The message read: 'When I state that I am an anarchist I must also state that I am not an anarchist, to be in keeping with the (_____) idea of anarchism. Long live anarchism' (D'Arcangelo 1977: 31). The final part, 'anarchism. Long live anarchism', is printed upside down, requiring one to read his body and its actions against the grain, or to tilt one's viewing body into an unfamiliar vantage: a *parallax* view. The artist proceeded to attach himself to the external doors of the museum, using a nine-foot steel chain, handcuffs and three padlocks. The action would last

Fig. 17.1 Christopher D'Arcangelo, action at the Whitney Museum of American Art, New York, 1975, from the *Museum Pieces* series (1975–9). Christopher D'Arcangelo Papers, MSS 264, Binder A, Fales Library and Special Collections, New York University Libraries. Photo: Cathy Weiner.

just short of two hours. In a written account, he explains that after exposing his graffitied body, and handcuffing himself, '[t]aking the remaining chain I wrapped it around the door handles and locked it in place. In so doing I was able to lock the door of the museum and also lock myself to the museum' (D'Arcangelo 1975). He continues,

> The first people to speak to me were visitors to the museum, [and] they were concerned with the statement on my back and the fact that they could no longer enter the museum. After ten minutes someone from the security department came out to speak with me. He asked if I had the keys and if the chain could be cut, [and] my answer to both questions was no.

A further security guard arrived with a chain cutter, but did not attempt to end the performance. As the performance continued, around thirty people gathered to watch. D'Arcangelo explains,

At this point the museum adopted a wait and see attitude, I believe they felt I would not stay longer, because it was only thirty degrees [Fahrenheit] and I had no shirt. For half an hour the front door was closed and now maybe sixty people had gathered on the ramp. … Two guards came around with a folding screen. They placed it in front of me, so that I could not be seen by anyone arriving at the museum. Another screen was placed on the other side of the door, completely cutting me off from the public. I stayed … for ten minutes longer, then I unlocked the door, put my shirt back on and left the museum.

Occupations of institutional spaces by stealth, as a specialized mode of performance art, arguably complement the novel formation of alternative spaces in the 1960s and 1970s. Curator Sandy Nairne explains that in these years experimental artists 'lacked sufficiently sympathetic public museums or commercial art galleries, and were also dissatisfied with the context they provided', and therefore innovated by establishing new venues, adapting 'redundant' non-art spaces, or colonizing established museums or galleries for exhibitions and performances (1996: 388). This was also a symptom of the new political and aesthetic imperatives of artists, for whom the political, critical and formal challenges instilled in their experimental work was deemed illegitimate, intolerable or irrelevant by the establishment spaces from which they were excluded. The tensions and conflicts these developments invoked were productive ones, as the proliferation of alternative spaces did not go unnoticed by institutions but, rather, laid emphasis upon the needs of artists and 'forced changes in the exhibition system', Nairne argues; however, this would not lead to a full-scale 'institutionalization of dissent' – that is, a revolution in the construction, constitution and orchestrations of institutions of art (388). Many artists thus continued to elude *or actively intervene in* institutions to critique the regulatory practices that may police – by privileging and/or excluding – what can and cannot be seen or done in such spaces. Nairne argues that artistic colonizations of space in the 1960s and 1970s directly prompted 'the making of new and complex works of art and of new forms of interaction with an audience … as a creative blur [that] frequently occurred between the making and the exhibiting of work: the spectator was self-consciously drawn into the making of the art, or at least into the making of its meaning' (391), suggesting a profound context for stealth performances, and for the heightened political and ethical demands they placed on incidental audiences.

Art historian Douglas Crimp confirms that shifting conditions of making and consuming art precipitated 'the displacement of the artist-subject by the spectator-subject', as the embodied viewer became more instrumental in the construction of meaning (1997: 17). Artists exacerbated this transformation, he writes, 'through the wedding of the art-work to a particular environment', for example through institutional critique, conceptual art, performance art or site-specific installation (17). Institutional critique designates practices that, in art historian Alexander Alberro's definition, confront 'the institution of art with the claim that it was not sufficiently committed to, let alone realizing or fulfilling, the pursuit of publicness that had brought it into being', by foregrounding – usually in stark, abrasive or combative fashions – 'the (material) actuality of the social relations that [define] it', through strategies of interference or 'gestures of negation' (2009: 3). From the 1960s to the 1990s, artist groups such as the Guerrilla Girls, the Guerrilla Art Action Group or the Art Workers' Coalition intervened with formidable efficacy in the situational characteristics of museums, including in unbidden ways (that is, without the endorsement of the institutions in which they appear). As such, they raised urgent issues about gender inequality, the ethics of corporate sponsorship and systemic racism (respectively) in institutions of art. Today, contemporary groups sustain similar agendas, perhaps most notably the Guerrilla Girls (still), Liberate Tate and Black Lives Matter. More broadly, today, institutions and public spaces are a frequent stage or canvas for unauthorized interventions by a range of creative trespassers, including the activist-artist groups Pussy Riot, Clandestine Insurgent Rebel Clown Army, Surveillance Camera Players, Space Hijackers, Yes Men, and Reverend Billy and the Church of Stop Shopping; or lone wolves and irreverent duos like Linda Mary Montano, the Disabled Avant-Garde (Katherine Araniello and Aaron Williamson), Mad For Real (Cai Yuan and JJ Xi), Jelili Atiku, and Pyotr Pavlensky.

Space is politically and socially constituted, and is thus party to oppressive and hegemonic forces. This fact enables performative contestations of public and private spaces by artists, including the creation and appropriation of alternative spaces, and the activation of urban and institutional spaces by performance interventions. When William Pope.L performs an endurance crawl through the streets of Manhattan (*Times Square Crawl*, 1978), or La Congelada de Uva (Rocío Boliver) sits on a playground swing on a crane above the Tijuana/San Diego border – and thus pivots, illegally, in and out of Mexico and the United States (*To the Rhythm of the Swing*, 2012) – their unbidden site-responsive works make visible the social, economic and spatial relations that give art its meaning, and which thus condition our encounter with a particular work. Both carry extreme risks, not least by the barely recognizable status of their works as art: concerned or enraged passers-by or the police interrupt Pope.L in his crawls; Boliver was concerned that border-patrol guards might shoot her. Theorizing site-responsiveness (or site-specificity), Crimp theorizes the *contingency* of art, namely, an object or action's essential dependency upon its site of presentation: its 'material, scale, and form intersect not only with the formal characteristics of its environment', he writes, 'but also with the desires and assumptions of a very different public from the one conditioned to the shocks of the art of the late 1960s' (1997: 154). D'Arcangelo anticipates this account when he writes that his site-responsive performances emphasize 'the nature of the relationship between a given person and their surroundings', which he terms the 'support' (equivalent, too, to Alberro's '"material" actuality'), adding that this social relation is 'more complex than rely[ing] on the use of a single object to communicate' (1978b).

Why, then, and with what effects, might artists need to intervene in, colonize and recast existing spaces of art? For performance scholar Jen Harvie, alternative or temporary art spaces 'can de-ghettoize art art itself [because] by drawing new audiences by migrating art beyond districts that are comparatively over-endowed ... they can be site-responsive; and they can model micro-utopian possibilities for cultural change' (2013: 111). However, Harvie explores how art and performance, while generally well-intentioned, can also enforce or enhance the encroachment of conservative spatial effects. Despite or because of their apparent irreverence or edginess, publicly sited art and performance practices 'may cultivate an appetite for the claiming of private space' and 'may contribute to social ghettoization, for example, by privileging an already comparatively privileged so-called "creative class" and facilitating processes of gentrification' (109–10). For example, she notes that 'pop-up performances' may create economic effects that resemble those of short-term commercial ventures, like fashionable 'pop-up' shops and restaurants (120). Harvie's account might suggest reasons why artists might resolve to re-tool existing institutions of art, so that any deleterious effects are felt by the monolithic institutions in which an artist intervenes – or by works installed legitimately within them, which are sometimes marred symbolically by their

Fig. 17.2 Christopher D'Arcangelo, action at the Musée du Louvre, Paris 1978, from the *Museum Pieces* series (1975–9). Christopher D'Arcangelo Papers, MSS 264, Binder A, Fales Library and Special Collections, New York University Libraries.

misuse by uninvited artists. The commitment to contingency and site-responsiveness has higher stakes, then, when artists find unlicensed or unbidden ways to present their work inside institutional spaces. Indeed, when performance art might seem to be on the verge of its neutralization – and, not least, its supposed institutionalization – how might it still retain a glimmer (or promise) of subversion or subterfuge? These contexts perhaps dramatize the singular capacity of D'Arcangelo's *Museum Pieces* to stage a break with the political, social and economic consolations that often limit the transgressive appeal of alternative spaces, and, so too, those limits that constrain the disruptiveness of performance art.

Museum Pieces

On 8 March 1978, D'Arcangelo entered the Musée du Louvre in Paris, and proceeded to the second-floor gallery adjoining the Henri II staircase; he removed Thomas Gainsborough's *Conversation in a Park* (1740) from the wall, placed (or reinstalled) it on the floor and attached a printed statement (in French) to the place on the wall where the painting was previously hanging (see Figure 17.2). The artist had no authority to do so: he did not seek permission before staging his intervention. As in his other *Museum Pieces*, its unbidden or stealth aspect was instrumental to the way it asks an incidental viewer to read the performance; the shape of the action also points to the potentially renewed vantage an audience might take to the existing works of art he frequently manhandled. The text on the wall translates as:

When you look at a painting
where do you look for that painting?

What is the difference between a painting installed
on the wall and a painting installed on the floor?

When I state that I am an anarchist
I must also state that I am not an anarchist,
to be in keeping with the (_____) idea of anarchism. (1978c)

The performance would attempt to transform or wilfully evade the power structures that condition the nature of the encounter with works of art that the museum both presents and sanctifies. D'Arcangelo carried a letter (also written in French) for the purpose of explanation should he be arrested. The handwritten English draft usefully maps his imperatives in the action: 'It was not my intention to steal a painting', he writes (1978d). In the remainder of the letter, he explained the content of the typed sheet he affixed to the wall: the first question sought to expose the incidental viewer to her or his immediate context, while the second question assists the viewer in exposing the relationship between the 'immediate objects' and the 'immediate context'. The third statement – his classic stencilled slogan – connects the objects in their context to the fuller social context, 'by use of a known political term', namely anarchism (1978d).

Including the statement of anarchism used in the other *Museum Pieces*, D'Arcangelo's text summoned the problem of space and the contingency of vision, asking how the locus of one's looking – inside or outside the institution, from the physical location of looking parallel or looking down, or looking with different levels of privilege, authority or entitlement – produces or changes the meaning of the object one addresses. The contingency of meaning is complicated in this action as D'Arcangelo's strategic resituating of the work of art affects how we might read Gainsborough's painting (as is true, also, to the general promise of curating). Its physical lowering heaps additional implications upon the work as it slips from the safe and secure verticality of its original placement down towards the abjection of horizontality (bodies laid out on the floor in public will always attain a sense of penury, scandal or destitution – indeed, this is part of the punch of Pope.L's incorrigible crawls, introduced earlier). This literal slippage of the painting has symbolic effects in the incidental viewer as a series of meanings become attached to *Conversation in a Park* – a frothy pastoral scene in pink, green and red – as an effect of D'Arcangelo's action: one might observe a lowering of tone, or a depleting of the painting's apparent worth, as an object now to be looked down upon, or as a work *on the slide*, on its hapless way towards dispossession. Moreover, the contingency of meaning is also operative in an equally substantial sense, as D'Arcangelo's action of removing and replacing Gainsborough's painting *is in itself a work of art*, a performance (however slight) with its own aesthetic, political and cultural qualities and effects, a new work that complements and extends a given history at the intersection of performance art, institutional critique and direct action. Being contingent, meaning is not embedded in the performance itself: as in any work of art, meaning is dependent upon the specific location (cultural, social, historical) from which we read it, and the desires, needs and assumptions that condition our encounter.

D'Arcangelo's action at the Louvre attempted to disavow or dismantle the conventions that govern one's interaction with the power of art and its institutions. Prior to his action, in an earlier visit to Paris in 1976, he sketched the ideological seed of his future intervention. On a page stapled into his notebook, under his familiar anarchist statement, he writes:

> I beleave that I have just in the last day or so, come to a new aproch to the above statement. That is to envolve the museum goer in the work, not as a viewer but as part of the work. In the past I have used my body in an art, <u>artist</u>, viewer triangel. now it is time to use the art, <u>viewer</u>, artist triangel. Still leaving the athoraties of the museum in the dark as I have done in the past. I hope to in some way change the structure of the museum. (1976a)

His phonetic, dyslexic prose captures the haste with which he set down his realization, and lends his idea a breathless urgency (the underlining and typographical errors are preserved from the original). He depicts the triangular network in which meaning is produced, namely between art/artist/viewer, which anticipates Ric Knowles's later mapping of the three mutually constituting poles between which a 'materialist semiotics' might emerge, namely between the text of performance, the material conditions of production, and reception: '"Meaning" in a given performance situation – the social and cultural work done by the performance, its performativity, and its force – is the effect of all of these systems', Knowles writes, with 'each pole of the interpretive triangle working dynamically and relationally together' (2009: 19). D'Arcangelo situates his own body as the central medium that negotiates the three operative co-ordinates, and, moreover, he suggests that his practice has developed through the realization that his stealth performances must shift the emphasis from the artist (as a privileged origin of the idea, strategy or desire) to the needs and political aspirations of the viewer, as the ideal destination of the production of meaning, efficacy and change. Doing so, he claims, will have a transformative effect on culture, namely, to 'change the structure of the museum', by using performance to interrogate – and ideally undermine, or even dismantle – the power of institutions of art.

The action was carried out without a hitch. In a letter to the editor of the French newspaper *Libération*, D'Arcangelo recounts that the scene was left uninterrupted for thirty minutes, after which museum staff were alerted to the intervention, removed the posted statement, and reinstalled the painting on the wall. The artist and photographer left the scene without being interrupted or apprehended. In a postscript to the letter he describes the performance as an attempt at the 'liberation' of the painting, by 'point[ing] out a weakness in the present controlling power', namely, the museum. His action was not merely a crime, but a performance in a series of what he termed 'contextually correct demonstrations'. Implicit in his work was a promise that the regulatory power of the state – instilled in public institutions, and in the modes of social decorum that govern our interactions with them – is open to contestation, specifically through the transformative power of performance. 'Can the present controlling power be dismantled?' he asks. 'Yes' (1978e).

An Intervention in an Archive

Held in an archive in New York, D'Arcangelo's papers – including typed and handwritten statements, photographs, legal summons and affidavits, and clippings – allow me to reconstruct an account of a performance that has otherwise been ignored in the history of performance art. My attention to D'Arcangelo's performances is entirely furnished – and thus conditioned – by my attention to their archival traces, suggesting, perhaps, that the perspicacity of stealth performance is somehow enabled or confirmed by archival research. The latter is not the only – or the best – method with which to approach stealth performances as an object of enquiry; yet, for me, the archival turn in the study of performance art allows me to seek out the details of a performance that took place in the past, in a time to which I could not hope to be present (it occurred before I was born), and prompts me to think through its provocations. Indeed, beyond the relative privacy of his archive, D'Arcangelo is hard to find. In a rare, brief discussion of his work, art historian Thomas Crow notes D'Arcangelo's wilful obscurity, as evidenced by the 'fierce reticence' of the sole example of his participation in an exhibition as an invited artist (1996: 242). At Artist's Space (a non-profit gallery) in New York in 1978, D'Arcangelo's contribution consisted of a series of wall texts, and the demand that his name be redacted from the exhibition and all the supplementary documentation produced for it, including gallery signage, wall texts, the exhibition catalogue and press releases. 'No intervention could have caused greater difficulties for the critic and historian', Crow states, 'in that any precise citation of D'Arcangelo's piece would destroy the grounds of its insistence', adding sympathetically that 'silence will be maintained here' (1996: 234). Methodologically, how might we hear and sustain D'Arcangelo's silence as a kind of call?

From the archive, I am able to piece together a survey of D'Arcangelo's performance works from 1975 until his untimely death in 1979. I learn, for example, that D'Arcangelo staged an ambitious stealth performance at the Norton Simon Museum in Pasadena, California. The archive yields a wealth of surprisingly unambiguous details. I know that he entered the museum at 1.00 pm on 8 July 1976, and that he proceeded to stencil his anarchist message of intent onto two paintings (D'Arcangelo 1976b). He had completed the stencilling of one, and was in the process of stencilling another when a security guard apprehended him. I can see (from the 'General Crime Report' prepared after his arrest and contained in his archive) that thick, reflective anti-vandalism screens protected the paintings, such that the canvases were unharmed. In this work, his characteristic attention to the ways museums warp our perception of its collections was focused on the material distortions created by the reflective screens that protect (and sanctify) certain paintings: the screen becomes a metaphor for the way our encounter is 'screened' by invisible networks of power. I also learn (from the 'Record of Property' prepared at his arraignment) that he used Bonbon Fast Dry 'Licorice stick black' spray paint and a 20-by-18½-inch stencil. I also know (from his summons) that he was arrested and charged with a misdemeanour, namely violating Section 622 of the Penal Code of the State of California, which forbids one to 'injure and disfigure a work of art', specifically, 'to wit: paintings of which he was not the owner.'

Curiously, the archive cannot tell me which paintings he attacked. However, the institutions he struck have recorded the archival traces of performative infractions: I emailed the museum, and its director of public affairs confirmed that D'Arcangelo attacked Francisco de Zurbarán's *The Birth of the Virgin* (1627) – which he successfully defaced – and Bartolomé-Esteban Murillo's *The Birth of St. John the Baptist* (1655), which he was spraying when apprehended by security (Denk 2015). I can cross-check Denk's email with a blurry photograph in D'Arcangelo's archive to identify that he stencilled his text above and across (perhaps rather provocatively) the face of Zurbarán's baby Jesus. Such gaps and inconsistencies – the lack of clarity on this issue in his papers – are fundamental to the nature of archives: as historian Carolyn Steedman argues, while orderly in its outward presentation, the archive is a site of 'mad fragmentation': 'in the Archive', she writes, 'you cannot be shocked at its exclusions, its emptinesses, at what is not catalogued … Its condition of being deflects outrage' (2001: 68). Yet we can be shocked by or outraged at the histories told by others – stories of tacit exclusions, willed oversights or biases – which demand our own attentive return to the archival traces left by acts that demand us to think again about what performance might do, in the past, and in the present.

Mona Lisa's Face, or Problems in Reading

A key critical and creative challenge of performance art is the way individual works often demand an *interdisciplinary* approach, namely, a methodology that draws from more than one scholarly tradition of knowledge and application. Throughout the preceding analysis of D'Arcangelo's action, my disciplinary contexts include theatre and performance studies, on the one hand, and art history and visual studies on the other. The following section suggests how and with what effects a foot in each discipline may prove useful for teasing out the fuller provocations of performance art, by way of explicit references by artists, as well as to the cultural histories that make a specific action readable.

As noted above, D'Arcangelo's plan to intervene in the nature of the encounter with works in the Louvre was hatched two years earlier. On his visit in 1976, D'Arcangelo noted with wry humour his (familiar) feeling of being manipulated by the museum into an emotional response. In a journal, he describes following the crowds to Leonardo's *Mona Lisa* (1503–17): 'You feel your heart pound harder', he writes, 'because in a minute you will be looking the power in the face. Ah! but what a sly old bitch[:] she looks back at you through a window and you can't touch her cause she is the power and Duchamp can never give her a moustach[e] … and neither can you' (1976a). D'Arcangelo refers to an iconic Readymade art work by Marcel Duchamp: in 1919, he acquired a souvenir postcard of the *Mona Lisa* and added a whimsical moustache and beard to her laconic face; as if to add insult to symbolic injury, he titled the work *L.H.O.O.Q*, whose letters (when read aloud in French) resemble the phrase '*elle a chaud au cul*' (she has a hot ass), a vulgarity that infers the sexual insatiability of the objectified, improbably moustachioed sitter. D'Arcangelo's own comment redoubles Duchamp's slur: she's aged since, and is now 'a sly old bitch', who revels in the additive cultural capital that has been afforded her, and the gravitas she has recouped since Duchamp's affront.

The face of the *Mona Lisa* 'looks back at you through a window and you can't touch her cause she is the power', D'Arcangelo writes, staging the museum's safeguarding of culturally important paintings. Set untouchable behind glass – a material imposition tackled by his attack on Zurbarán and Murillo – its cordons, alarms and guards protect it cumulatively from overzealous art-lovers and militant antagonists alike, and thus consecrate the work. The painting, and by extension, all 'great' art, is rendered sacred, invincible and abstracted from its potential functionality as a part of everyday life. Despite its puerility, Duchamp's gesture asks an important question of the historical avant-garde, namely, why and with what effects is art assumed to be unavailable to everyday use, and immune to quotidian, individual experience? So, while the *Mona Lisa* would have been too well guarded to allow D'Arcangelo to tamper with it, he takes the lesson he has learnt about the sacral power of individual artworks, transfers it laterally, and seeks to overcome the seemingly insuperable boundary between art and life, in contact with another painting, Gainsborough's fussy-looking *Conversation in a Park*.

Searching for further art-historical contexts for D'Arcangelo's intervention, one might look to Robert Filliou's *Dust to Dust: The Giotto Effect* (1977). The work consists of a small cardboard archival box containing a piece of cloth blemished heavily with dust harvested by rubbing the frame of Giotto's medieval painting, *St. Francis of Assisi Receiving the Stigmata* (ca. 1295), and a photographic document of the intervention (one in a series of such works under the main title *Dust to Dust* – or *Poussière de poussière* in its original French), which also involved rubbings of dusty sculptures and paintings by Veronese, Leonardo, Hals, Corrège, Soutine and Klee, at two museums in Paris). This rubbing was an unauthorized action in the Louvre that conferred a conflicted kind of love upon the painting. Without touching or damaging the panel upon which Giotto painted it – and so, like D'Arcangelo, stopping short of vandalism proper – Filliou tends to and conserves the tarnished frame, and indicts the museum for its indifference to the works it otherwise sacralizes, namely, by allowing its looted masterpiece to get so bedraggled. For James Trainor, the *Dust to Dust* series is 'seriously playful', in that Filliou transferred the sacrosanct quality of the paintings and sculptures to the 'precious particles of dust'; safeguarded in their cardboard reliquaries, and baptized with their 'funerary' titles, the artist conferred 'mock solemnity' upon these barely material traces (1999: 132). In Filliou's reliquaries, the flecks of dust function like mementoes of the great object they touched, perhaps akin to the symbolic power of a shroud from the face of Christ, or fragments of the Holy Cross. Filliou's action was distinctly avant-garde in tone. Whereas Filliou *burlesques* the sanctity of art, by worrying over (and selling) the worthless debris that cloud the work, D'Arcangelo's sacrilegious action returns to the work a playfully disempowered function as something to be intimate with, as a priceless painting rudely stripped of its station. Both strategies – as unwarranted and invited interventions – reiterate the historical avant-garde project of the *sublation* (or dialectical overcoming) of the distinction between art and life, or between the sacred (high) and demotic (low) functions of culture.

Putting a stealth performance into a broader context of similar strategies –suggested by the resonance between D'Arcangelo's *Museum Pieces* and Filliou's *Dust to Dust* series – suggests a rich history of performance art, but also signals methodological problems in terms of which discipline ought to be called into play, and how. I have attempted to pursue a set of questions with some distance from the logic of protest and direct action – that is, without rehearsing again the assumptions and arguments about cultural interventions that have been very appositely rehearsed in the intersection between theatre studies and theories of space, in terms of the efficacy of street performance, carnival and agitprop theatre (Cohen-Cruz 1998; Kershaw 1992) or cultural hijacks of public space (Thompson and Sholette 2004; Parry 2011). While, in the UK, performance art is often studied in relation to theatre, performance art also prompts secondary questions at a distinct remove from specifically *dramatic* problems of reading. What is the status of the text in stealth performance, as script, score or source? Which theatrical conventions or expectations are being fulfilled and which are being rejected? What is the status of narrative, character, persona, costume, time, process, emotional display or virtuosity? To what extent will a stealth performance give or withhold a spectator's pleasure – well beyond or below those that attend to theatre as entertainment, for example – and with what effects?

D'Arcangelo's *Museum Pieces* are limit-cases of the historically grounded attempts of artists to intervene in the social reality of art and culture. Performances such as his Louvre action broadcast a call for artists and audiences to be *bolder, riskier and more ambitious* in our encounters with culture – and especially with elite culture. They call for our refusal *to know one's place* in the normative social relations modelled by institutions. D'Arcangelo's performances help me to think through the ways the practice and theory of theatre and performance bring with them structures of decorum or propriety. What we say, think, feel or do, within a given institution – a museum, theatre, university or library – is governed by heavily coded assumptions about what is acceptable, appropriate or reasonable, and what is not. Gratuitous, promiscuous or mischievous actions and utterances are policed in all kinds of institutional spaces, and regulated by, say, disciplinary actions against students and staff in university contexts, through to charges of illegality under existing legislation, such as the Anti-Social Behaviour, Crime and Policing Act 2014 (as one among various laws by which well-intentioned cultural hijacks of public space may be criminalized).

Interventions into Institutions

In the venues associated with traditional theatre, what potential might there be for the kind of creative interventions D'Arcangelo exemplified in art museums? The theatre artist Lois Weaver recalls a suggestive anecdote of theatrical subterfuge: during a production of David Hare's *The Secret Rapture* (1988) at the National Theatre, Weaver and Peggy Shaw – partners in the feminist theatre company Split Britches – are settling into the traditional 'sea of the well behaved' constituted in its audience by such a venue. In the denouement to the play, the male protagonist threatens his female counterpart with a gun. Guessing the inevitable – the woman's murder – Shaw intervenes from the stalls at a moment when the actor puts the gun down for a moment: raising her voice to the woman onstage, Shaw shouts: 'Pick up the gun and shoot the bastard!' Weaver recalls the shock to those in the audience (including herself) accustomed to the theatre's traditional decorum, and reads the ethical quandary posed to this norm by the feeling of being 'caught between individual responsibility … and passive consumption' (2009: ix–x). Weaver is 'caught' between the need to play by the unstated rules of the institution (to think of the actors, to suspend one's disbelief and allow the rote theatrical events – however unpalatable – to unfold), on the one hand; and, on the other, a desire to speak out against the traditions (here, of formal conservatism, and passive misogyny) that hurt or enfeeble us, despite how stigmatizing it may be (as it is for Shaw) to stage our conviction, or our protest.

What kinds of interventions might be warranted in the venues to which *you* are drawn, or from which you are repelled, or in whose orbit your thinking and/or your practice might heighten its own efficacy? Short of arrest, what responses and reactions might best activate the political exigencies of your participation in culture? Such questions return me, in conclusion, to a central theme of D'Arcangelo's practice that has ghosted my account, namely, *anarchism*. David Graeber historicizes anarchism in terms of its key principles: autonomy, voluntary association, self-organization, direct democracy and mutual aid – describing it as less a political ideology than a programme for ethical discourse: anarchy is 'a kind of moral faith', he writes, 'a rejection of all forms of structural violence, inequality, or domination … and a belief that humans would be perfectly capable of [surviving] without them' (2009: 105). Graeber goes on to suggest that anarchist practice requires a distinction between militant individualism (the 'true revolutionary path') and 'vanguardism', which involves collective or 'sectarian' relations of agreement among activists and intellectuals (2009: 108). Hence, when D'Arcangelo proclaims his anarchism, refuses to grant it a style, and adds the caveat that 'I must also state that I am not an anarchist', he is suggesting that anarchism requires a refusal of all prior forms of politics, including those of anarchism itself. He performs the creative enunciation of will or agency that is definitively required of the anarchist gesture, even if it renders his situation paradoxical, unintelligible and unsustainable.

In works beyond the realized *Museum Pieces*, D'Arcangelo explored wider approaches to institutional subterfuge, including plans for reckless endangerments that would push his political and ethical imperatives to a kind of breaking point. All are of a piece with his anarchism as defined here. For example, in a journal entry written in 1976, he sketched *The Bomb Scare*: 'To place a small suitcase in the coat room … of a museum with the [anarchist] statement on the outside [and] … call the police to say there is a bomb in the case and to make a film of the activity' (1976a). In the same journal, he sketches *The Assassination of a Painting*: 'to enter a museum with a throwing knife and the statement on my back and … take the knife and throw it very close to a painting and have it stick in the wall'. Though unrealized, both scores suggest strategies for inciting fear or anxiety on the part of those who take responsibility for the contents and conventions of museums, by putting people and artefacts under the threat of serious risk (the political murder of the painting, the fear to be instilled in museumgoers and workers, or his own fate as a prospective felon). They borrow the shape of the stunt or prank, and were either too dangerous to pull off, or were politically too naïve once the *Museum Pieces* series took on its sophisticated outlines – its apotheosis being, arguably, the formal elegance of the Louvre action.

In summary, D'Arcangelo's performances were lent a guerrilla quality by the simple fact of his refusal to seek permission to interact with the found objects (priceless paintings) or found sites (museums) that he appropriated and recast in his performances. This commitment is styled as 'anarchist' in tone and effects, specifically through the written statement of intent that emblazoned his body or other surfaces in the process of his interventions. In his anarchic self-fashioning, stealth performance reminds us of the emancipatory potential of performance more broadly, at a time when self-directed political action – out in the world, where someone might see it – has not for some time felt so urgent. As such, stealth performance recalls Mark Fisher's strident call, namely, that 'emancipatory politics must always destroy the appearance of a "natural order", must reveal what is presented as necessary and inevitable to be a mere contingency, just as it must make what was previously deemed to be impossible seem attainable' (2007: 17).

Archives

All archival documents are listed individually in the bibliography. The call mark 'MSS 264' denotes that a document is located in MSS 264 Christopher D'Arcangelo Papers, Fales Library and Special Collections, New York University Libraries, New York.

Further Reading

Cohen-Cruz's *Radical Street Performance* (1998) remains a foundational and comprehensive sourcebook on relations between performance, art and activism. Thompson and Sholette's anthology *The Interventionists* (2004) pulls together a broad range of practitioners and thinkers to more fully catalogue the new interventionist possibilities in art and performance. Kershaw's *The Politics of Performance* (1992) complements these sourcebooks with an argument-driven account of how politics and/or radicalism emerges from the re-tooling of theatre as a public form of provocation. Harvie's *Fair Play* (2013) brings similar debates up to date by considering how contemporary performance interventions may challenge neoliberalism – yet may also fall foul, despite its makers' good intentions. For accounts of how these issues apply specifically to fine art and its institutions, see Alberro and Stimson's anthology *Institutional Critique* (2009).

References

Alberro, Alexander (2009), 'Institutions, Critique, and Institutional Critique', in Alexander Alberro and Blake Stimson (eds), *Institutional Critique: An Anthology of Artists' Writings*, 2–19, Cambridge and London: MIT Press.

Cohen-Cruz, Jan (1998), *Radical Street Performance: An International Anthology*, London: Routledge.

Crimp, Douglas (1997), *On the Museum's Ruins*, Cambridge and London: MIT Press.

Crow, Thomas (1996), *Modern Art in the Common Culture*, New Haven and London: Yale University Press.

D'Arcangelo, Christopher (1975), 'Documentation: The Whitney Museum of American Art', MSS 264, Series II, Box 4, Folder 5: Copies of Work, undated.

D'Arcangelo, Christopher (1976a), 'Paris 17/4/76' (unpublished journal entry), MSS 264, Series II, Box 4, Folder 4: Copies of D'Arcangelo's Notebook undated.

D'Arcangelo, Christopher (1976b), Unpublished documents, MSS 264, Series I, Box 3, Folder 15: Norton Simon Museum 1976.

D'Arcangelo, Christopher (1977), 'LAICA as an Alternative to Museums', *LAICA Journal* 13 (January–February), 31–4.

D'Arcangelo, Christopher (1978a), Unpublished note, MSS 264, Series II, Box 4, Folder 4: Copies of D'Arcangelo's Notebook, undated.

D'Arcangelo, Christopher (1978b), Unpublished note, MSS 264, Series I, Box 1, Folder 4: Artists Space 1978.

D'Arcangelo, Christopher (1978c), 'On the 8th March, 1978…', MSS 264, Series I, Box 3, Folder 5: Louvre – Writings and Statement 1978.

D'Arcangelo, Christopher (1978d), Unpublished letters, MSS 264, Series I, Box 3, Folder 5: Louvre – Writings and Statement 1978.

D'Arcangelo, Christopher (1978e), Unpublished letter in French, MSS 264, Series II, Box 4, Folder 5: Copies of Work, undated.

Denk, Leslie C. (2015), Email to the author, Friday 12 February.

Fisher, Mark (2009), *Capitalist Realism: Is There No Alternative?*, London: Zero Books.

Graeber, David (2009), 'Anarchism, Academia, and the Avant-Garde', in Randall Amster, Abraham DeLeon, Luis A. Fernandez, Anthony J. Nocella II and Deric Shannon (eds), *Contemporary Anarchist Studies: An Introductory Anthology of Anarchy in the Academy*, 103–12, Abingdon and New York: Routledge.

Harvie, Jen (2013), *Fair Play: Art, Performance and Neoliberalism*, Basingstoke: Palgrave Macmillan.

Kershaw, Baz (1992), *The Politics of Performance: Radical Theatre as Cultural Intervention*, London and New York: Routledge.

Knowles, Ric (2009), *Reading the Material Theatre*, Cambridge: Cambridge University Press.

Nairne, Sandy (1996). 'The Institutionalization of Dissent', in Reesa Greenberg, Bruce W. Ferguson and Sandy Nairne (eds), *Thinking About Exhibitions*, 387–410, London and New York: Routledge.

Parry, Ben (2011), 'Rethinking Intervention', in Ben Parry with Sally Medlyn and Myriam Tahir (eds), *Cultural Hijack: Rethinking Intervention*, 11–13, Liverpool: Liverpool University Press.

Steedman, Carolyn (2001), *Dust*, Manchester and New York: Manchester University Press.

Thompson, Nato, and Gregory Sholette, eds (2004), *The Interventionists: Users' Manual for the Creative Disruption of Everyday Life*, Boston: MIT and MASS MoCA.

Trainor, James (1999), 'Robert Filliou', in Kynaston McShine (ed.), *The Museum as Muse: Artists Reflect*, 132–3, New York: Museum of Modern Art.

Weaver, Lois (2009), 'Foreword: A Rapture Kept Secret', in Helen Freshwater, *Theatre & Audience*, Basingstoke: Palgrave Macmillan.

18 How Does Theatre Think Through Ecology?

CARL LAVERY

There is no escape from matter.

Smithson 1996: 194

Introduction

When compared to research in cognate areas such as literary studies, geography, philosophy, sociology, and media and film studies, there is little doubt that the disciplines of theatre and performance have been relatively slow in responding to Erika Munk's 1994 calls for an ecologically aware form of theatre criticism (Munk 1994: 5). However, in the wake of recent work on animals, cyborgs and objects, as well as Baz Kershaw's sophisticated 2007 text *Theatre and Ecology: Environments and Performance Events* (Kershaw 2007), there are real signs that theatre and performance scholars are finally beginning to make their own contribution to the emergent, cross-disciplinary field of the Environmental Humanities. But if theatre critics, as I am suggesting, are finally participating in the 'ecological turn', two fundamental questions bear repeating. First, what is meant by the word 'ecology'? And second, what should an ecologically inflected mode of theatre criticism focus on or purport to do? These are questions that have preoccupied me for the past few years or so, and I would like to use this chapter to argue for a concept of ecological thinking that emerges from the material impress of theatrical images as they stick to and move through the retina. My argument is composed of four parts. Part one offers a working definition of ecology; part two traces a brief genealogy of the ecological image; part three explains how the ecological image operates within the specific medium of the theatre; and part four provides an analysis of the ecological image in the work of Mike Brookes and Rosa Casado.

Ecology and Theatre

Approached philosophically as well as biologically, ecology is best understood as a way of thinking that seeks to show how human agents are always bound up with and part of their environment or *oikos* – a word which, in Greek, translates as home or hearth. Indeed, a minimum or zero-degree definition of ecology might be found in the writings of anthropologist and systems analyst, Gregory Bateson, who defines it, with minimalist elegance, as any relationship of 'organism plus environment' (Bateson 2000: 491).

At its most progressive and expansive, ecological thinking is concerned to highlight how human beings are always already part of 'nature', creatures who have evolved out of the randomness and chaos of life's impersonal processes (atoms, cells, amoebas, etc.), and whose ability to think, speak and make art are not signs of some brilliant exceptionalism granted by a transcendent sky god, but decidedly immanent to the creative expansion of life itself. To think and act ecologically, then, is to take seriously culture's etymological root as a form of 'cultivation or sowing', something that is earthbound, immanent to and dependent on the presence and play of the singularizing capacities of organic and inorganic matter (see also Williams 2014).

If this view of ecology is accepted, then everything (cities, computers, the washing machine that rumbles in the background as I write these words) is part of nature. This has important consequences for how we go about thinking and doing ecology in theatre and performance studies. For it means that the focus is no longer simply placed on works that would purport to represent ecological issues in any explicit or frontal sense. And neither does it mean that we should be concerned with producing specifically 'green' forms of eco-theatre. (The metaphorical self-evidence of the colour green in and to ecotheory is now being challenged by new prismatic ecologies; see Cohen 2013.) Such moves are not only self-defeating, they are decidedly harmful in the extent to which they, once again, assume that ecology can be delimited, cut off from the wider social and political culture.

A better, more generative way of proceeding, I think, is to renounce the desire to establish a specific category of eco-theatre and to assume, instead, that any work can be analysed for its ecological potential. There are, of course, risks associated with such an all-inclusive methodology. For if everything is potentially ecological, then how might we determine, with any accuracy, which theatre works are viable to analyse ecologically or not? The troubling answer, quite simply, is that we cannot. Any text or performance can be analysed eco-critically, even when there is no explicit environmentalist agenda proposed. Crucially, though, this excessiveness or indeterminacy does not mean that all theatre functions homogeneously, or that all performance is ecologically generative in a similar manner. My own preference is to concentrate on those performances that provoke, in the most immediate and intensive ways possible, complex forms of ecological thinking and feeling. As I will show in the final section of this chapter, such an approach has the capacity to change, quite radically, conventional ideas of what theatre's relationship with ecology is, or more importantly, might become.

Although some attention has been placed on form (see Marranca 1996; Fuchs 1996; Bottoms and Goulish 2008), the dominant ecological readings of theatre, to date, have tended to focus, somewhat predictably, on content or, alternatively, on the role that site-specificity can play in producing progressive forces of eco-awareness. This needs to change. If we are serious about responding to the expanded definition of ecology that I have outlined, then it is incumbent upon theatre and performance scholars to investigate further and in some detail the specific ways in which the theatrical medium conveys and produces ecological experience in and by itself. It is no longer enough to castigate black-box theatre, as some of our best eco-critics in theatre studies have done, for distancing us from 'nature' by establishing an anthropocentrically determined mode of looking (Kershaw 2007: 316). On the contrary, the act of looking in the theatre auditorium is always-already embodied, an activity that has the capacity, particularly when the onus placed on narrative is abandoned, to create what I have elsewhere called 'ecological images' (Lavery 2013) – stage pictures that, in their troubling immediacy or corporeal presentness, radiate beyond their frame and give rise to ecological thought and feeling through their targeting of spectatorial vision.

In keeping with recent work done on the aesthetics of visuality in the theatre by Maaike Bleeker and Joe Kelleher, I contend that the eye in the theatre is not simply an organ that sees (Bleeker 2008; Kelleher 2015). More radically, it is an organ that thinks, a machine in which the opposition between subject and object, nature and culture, mind and body, thought and matter are undone, rendered inoperable. By focusing on this one aspect of the theatrical medium, my aim in this chapter is to rethink how theatre might engage with ecological issues and, in doing so, to enhance its eco-critical repertoire, with particular respect to an ethics of matter. But again – and inevitably – other questions emerge: what exactly is an ecological image? And, more to the point, how does it work in the theatre?

Towards the Ecological Image

The first serious attempt to think through the ecological potential of images was advanced by the cultural historian Andrew Ross, in a seminal text written after the Gulf War in 1992 and the first bombing of the World Trade Centre in 1993. In 'The Ecology of Images', Ross sought to respond to Susan Sontag's somewhat underdeveloped comments about ecology made towards the end of her 1977 publication *On Photography*. Influenced by Guy Debord's critique of 'the society of the spectacle', Sontag commented that in a world dominated by cameras, 'if there can be a better way for the real world to include one of images, it will require an ecology not of real things but of images as well' (Sontag 1979: 180). In order to unfold Sontag's gnomic statement, Ross distinguishes between what he calls 'images of ecology' (burning oilfields, poisoned rivers, stranded polar bears) and 'an ecology of images' (modes of visual distribution, circuits of information, streams of funding, etc.) (Ross 1994: 171). Whereas Sontag was, by and large, suspicious of images, Ross, by contrast, is aware that 'images of ecology', especially when combined with an 'ecology of images', have the capacity to mobilize public awareness against ecological destruction.

As a cultural historian, Ross's study is notable for the way in which he *reads* various types of images both with and against the grain, in order to tease out their environmental significance. However, in his predominantly semiotic analysis, there is nothing to suggest that images work according to an autonomous and materialist ecologic, in ways that I have suggested earlier. For that more aesthetic move to be made, we have to wait for the work of film critics who, in the early 2000s, used the theories of Gilles Deleuze, especially his idea of the 'time image' in *Cinema 2: The Time Image* (2005), to advance a mode of affective seeing or 'haptic visuality'. While they do not use the word ecology in their writings – as opposed to more recent work by media and film scholars, such as Sean Cubitt (2006) and Adrian J. Ivakhiv (2013) – Steven Shaviro and Laura Marks nevertheless offer some brilliant insights into how the ecological image operates. Dissenting from (at the time) film scholarship's allegiance to Lacanian notions of psychoanalysis rooted in the inevitably of lack and loss, the image, for Shaviro and Marks, is a material signifier, a type of texture, something that touches the spectators and which draws us into its orbit. This from Marks:

> I want to emphasize the tactile and contagious quality of the cinema and cinema-going as something we viewers brush against like another body. The words contact, contingent

and contagion all share the Latin root *contingere*, 'to have contact with; pollute; befall'. The contingent and contagious circumstances of intercultural cinema events effect a transformation in its audience. (Marks 2000: xii)

Marks's reading of the haptic image is underlined by Shaviro:

> The camera does not invent, and does not even represent: it only passively records. But this passivity allows it to penetrate, or to be enveloped by, the flux of the material world. … Sitting in the dark, watching the play of images across a screen, any detachment from the immediacy of sensation or from the speeds and delays of temporal duration, is radically impossible. Cinema invites me, or forces me, to stay within the orbit of the senses. (Shaviro 1993: 31)

From Marks and Shaviro's perspective, the ecological potential of the image is not found, then, in simply producing – in Ross's terms – 'images of ecology' that would represent nature in a direct sense. On the contrary, it is found in how aesthetically composed images, that may or may not have anything to do with nature, work through texture, speed and rhythm to jump beyond themselves and so engage spectators in a relationship with the materiality of the world. According to Marks, such images come from and return to the earth; they underscore the fact that all thought is terrestrial, something that emerges from the excessive vibrancy of matter, its surplus:

> Where do images, those things that we perceive with our senses come from? From the universe, infinite and unknowable in itself. Henri Bergson calls the universe the infinite set of all images; Deleuze terms it the plane of immanence and also flowing matter. I shall call it the universe of images, and sometimes … the Earth. (Marks 2009: 88)

While their materialist concept of images is strongly influenced by the writings of Antonin Artaud (note, for instance, the emphasis placed on contagion), Shaviro and Marks tell us little about how ecological images might function within the specific milieu of the stage. For that shift to happen, greater attention has to be paid to what we might call 'unscreened experience', the sense in which the immediacy of theatre, as Artaud points out, is a 'volcanic eruption' that transmits a kind of 'nervous magnetism', which in turn provokes '*us to think*' (Shaviro 1993: 60; original italics).

In what follows, I want to build on Artaud's dynamic and sensate model of thinking to propose five characteristics of the ecological image on stage. These characteristics are not meant to be exhaustive, prescriptive and/or definitive. They are simply an attempt – no doubt too clumsy, on my part – to open up new ways of thinking about theatre's relationship with ecology that stresses the generative power of pre-linguistic affect or sensation as opposed to more axiomatic and explicit approaches that would purport to provide information or transmit messages through dialogue and rhetoric. In that respect, I propose these characteristics as the commencement of a dialogue with other thinkers and practitioners whose ideas about ecological images will surely be different from mine in terms of class, gender and race, as well as in their own specific understanding of what the meaning and practice of ecology is or should be. In other words, there is no desire on my behalf to suggest that there is a proper way to read, experience or construct an ecological image in the theatre. A final clarification: I am concerned here with visual images, not linguistic or sonic ones. But this does not mean that images have, necessarily, to be visual.

The Ecological Image on Stage

First, and in line with what I have been arguing, an ecological image, as I see it, is an image that, above all, foregrounds its own materiality. The desire is to produce, as Artaud also wanted, a series of energetic exchanges between the stage and auditorium. While I do not think that ecological images have to be images of 'nature' per se, they should nevertheless be images of matter, compositions that affirm their dependence on the earth, extracting their charge from what Marks calls the all-encompassing 'universe of images'.

Closely related to this and moving on to my second point, the function of the ecological image is not simply to provide information about environmental issues. Rather, its more effective role is to produce sensate forms of ecological perception, which encourage spectators to develop more networked and interconnected ways of thinking. The goal here is to contest theatre criticism's long-standing tendency to isolate history from natural history and to perpetuate the view of human beings as consummate agents, able somehow to exist apart from the materiality of their environments.

Third, the ecological image is an image that shows itself in its own act of appearing or staging. That is to the say, ecological images give spectators time to reflect on *how* they are seeing as well as *what* they are seeing. Audiences are thus allowed to drift, to be distracted, to follow different rhythms and to set off on heterogeneous lines of flight. As opposed to spectacular images that seek to hide themselves in their bid to capture and colonize the spectator's attention, ecological images are 'cool images', to use the language of Marshall McLuhan. They provide a space for the imagination to drift and to make associations between disparate materials and heterogeneous formations. For that to happen, the spectator has to be 'emancipated' temporally, given the opportunity to attune themselves to a different *habitus* or refrain.

Fourth, the ecological image has to be a political image, a stage picture in which ecology is posited as something produced by and bound up with politics, economics and history; that is to say, with structures of power. As Félix Guattari notes in *The Three Ecologies*:

> Ecology must stop being associated with the image of a small nature-loving minority or with qualified specialists. Ecology in my sense questions the whole of subjectivity and capitalistic power formations, whose sweeping progress cannot be guaranteed to continue as it has for the past decade. (Guattari 2008: 35)

Finally, the ecological image gains much by constructing itself in terms of what Mario Perniola terms 'an enigma' (Perniola 1995: 6–21), an image whose meaning refuses to be fathomed and exhausted, and whose infinite unfolding generates ecological thinking and feeling through the transmission of an excess of vision. (See also Marks's argument for an aesthetics based on the 'enigma' of the image, 2009: 92.) Confronted with the ecological image, the eye finds itself fascinated and bewildered, driven mad by a surface or sheen that it cannot penetrate, and which, in the words of Joe Kelleher, it is compelled 'to suffer' (Kelleher 2015: 3).

In all cases, the ecological image returns the spectator to the body, and reverses the gaze. In its presence, the spectator is undone, made passive, 'looked at' by a material world that s/he is unable to understand. The experience generated by the ecological image, in its immediacy or strange proximity, is one of unravelling. There is no metaphysical presence involved here, and the subject does not coincide with the object, in any way. Rather the object disturbs the viewer, and presents him/her with the spectacle of what is perhaps best called a 'solid void'. In this disclosure of the enigma, this moment where appearance shows itself as a limit, the image falls back into itself and remains at a distance, resistant to the scopic desire of the spectator to master or appropriate it. The ecological image, then, is an image that is always 'a-proximate', close but far away, here and elsewhere. And it is precisely here, in this reticence, in its undoing of the subject-object divide, that the ecological image has, I believe, the potential to produce new, better ways of being on the earth. By presenting us with images of objects that we are unable to know or dominate, the ecological image encourages a different relationship with the world: one in which the paranoia of absolute knowledge is replaced with a respect for some unbreachable heterogeneity and alterity. In that etymological shift, the ecological image uses the ellipsis that it opens up for more generative and creative ends. Henceforth to exist on the earth is not to manage or own it, but to participate in the dizzying adventure of matter.

While all of the five characteristics that I have tentatively proposed here are at work in the ecological image in some form or other, they are not distributed evenly. Some images might prefer, for instance, to place greater emphasis on the elemental rather than the political, or the cosmos rather than the social. Nevertheless, the important point to remember is that no single aspect dominates or excludes. The ecological image uses the enigma of matter to produce transversal connections and heterogeneous assemblages in which human and 'more than human' actors work together to produce a new world. To that degree, the ecological image offers an implicit critique of capitalist modernity's desire to mobilize the world of matter to further its own destructive ends. The thinking that the ecological image proposes is close to what Gianni Vattimo names 'weak thought' (Vattimo 2012). That is, thinking that does not attempt to police or penetrate the image, but which prefers to think with it, to become embroiled in its radiating charge, to leave oneself open to its impress. Such thinking, then, demands alternative forms of performance analysis, in which the objective is not so much to know, to penetrate the secret of the enigma, but to follow the paths that the specific mystery of the ecological image opens up and discloses. At its simplest, the ecological image is a catalyst, something which transforms spectating into a kind of journey, in which to watch is to adventure, a word which in its Latin etymology communicates a sense of arriving or becoming (advenire), of being altered by a kind of corporeal movement, even though one is seated and physically immobilized.

In the final section of this chapter, I want to demonstrate how the adventure of the ecological image works by drawing on my own experience of spectating. The example that I use is not intended to be approached as some paradigmatic case, the only way to think and write about the ecological image. Rather, it is simply one performance, among many, that uses the materiality of the image for ecological ends. I was drawn to it because it stages, in the most literal of ways, the drama of elemental matter, a theatre of molecular flows and material movements.

The Ecological Image as Elemental Image

Like Heiner Goebbels's Stifters Dinge (2007), a performance for machines, recorded music and found voices, Mike Brookes and Rosa Casado's Some Things Happen All At Once (2008–9) has no interest in character, narrative or psychology. In the piece, human beings, while not evacuated completely from the stage, are no longer the exclusive objects of attention, the only stuff that matters. What we are confronted with instead, as in Robert Smithson's entropic sculptures, such as *Partially Buried Woodshed* and *Spiral Jetty*, is a drama of living matter, a theatre where spectators are enfolded into a spatiotemporal event, and where objects lose their discreteness and participate in an elemental dramaturgy. A dramaturgy of phase states, entropy and unpredictability.

Some Things Happen All At Once is, perhaps, best described as durational performance, structured around a key image. At the centre of a darkened space, on a ten-metre square stage, two hundred individual ice trees are placed around a miniature ice-village of forty or so houses. The ice covers 3.5 metres in total, and is shot through with wires that are connected to an electronic thermometer which measures fluctuations in temperature and blinks digital red. There is also an arc of angle-poise lamps with one horticultural bulb that heats the ice and a network of plastic tubes, connected to a specially designed cooling system powered by a bike that audience members can pedal in order to generate the energy needed to prevent the ice from melting. Spectators are free to come and go as they please and to walk around the stage observing the folds and air bubbles in the ice as it moves from a solid to a liquid state. The performance lasts for around eighty minutes and only truly finishes (although this is long after the audience have left) when all the ice has melted and the illuminated space has filled with water. The performance is punctuated by sounds as the 'trees' lose their verticality and hit the floor before losing their shape and dissolving completely. The effect induces a feeling of loss and perhaps even a sense of helplessness, certainly a kind of fragility (see Figure 18.1).

The audience are disruptive agents in/to the performance. For it is their presence, especially their breath, that produces what Erika Fischer-Lichte terms 'performance's ever changing

Fig. 18.1 *Some Things Happen All At Once*, 2008, Mike Brookes and Rosa Casado. Photo: Ovidio Aldegunde.

feedback loop' – theatre's unique and always materialized refrain – in which everyone and everything is caught up, immersed in a shower of invisible molecules, energy that radiates and blows back (Fischer-Lichte 2008: 39). However, in *Some Things Happen All At Once*, the feedback loop is not, as it is for Fischer-Lichte, a process that takes place between spectators and performers alone, a decidedly anthropocentric reading of theatrical energies. Rather, it is now figured as something impersonal and abstract, a flux and reflux that posits the audience as calorific containers, energetic bodies whose warmth is always escaping from them and transforming the atmosphere of the physical space that they occupy and impact on. In this way, *Some Things Happen All At Once* discloses or unconceals theatre's hidden but persistent elementalism, highlighting the fact that theatre is a medium of air, a transductor of energy. The more audience members there are in the space, the quicker the ice melts. There is, then, a kind of tragedy at work here, a tragedy of matter, we might say, an agonistics of metamorphosis and mutation that problematizes all attempts to manage and quantify the environment for human purposes (carbon footprints, resource quotas, etc.).

The ecological aspects of the performance are underscored through Rosa Casado's delivery of a carefully composed text that uses the ideas of the designer and utopian thinker, Buckminster Fuller, and popular science writer, Philip Ball, to think through the implications of sustaining life on what Fuller termed 'Spaceship Earth'. As we listen to Casado's words, spoken initially from the bicycle, and watch the ice melt before our eyes, we are reminded that energy is not something that can be replaced or added to; rather, its function is to transform and to move elsewhere, to be in a process of continual oscillation. In *Some Things Happen All At Once*, the problematic utopianism that characterizes Fuller's thinking, his optimism about technology, is counterbalanced by the entropy of the images themselves. As the houses liquefy and crack, the randomness, chaos and violence of the earth's systems are highlighted. Technology, here, is not a transcendent system of skills and capacities that would extricate us from the fate of the planet, as Fuller's *Operating Manual for Spaceship Earth* (1968) often implies. On the contrary, it ties us ever closer to the earth's history by revealing our fragility in the face of its material processes and chaotic forces.

A conventional eco-critical reading of the performance would, no doubt, place its politics and ethics in a logic of conservation and sustainability. The presence of the bicycle, the images of ice-melting and Fuller's ideas about extending our stay on 'spaceship earth' are all standard eco-tropes that we associate with mainstream environmental thought as well as with the ecological image-making of artists and collectives, such as Stan's Cafe, Julie's Bicycle, Olafur Eliasson and Cape Farewell. Invariably, we start to think of anthropogenic or human-induced climate change, glacial melt, sea-rises, flooding, etc. However, for all the implicit critique of energy consumption, this issue is not, ultimately, where the ecological ethics of the performance reside – at least not for me.

Rather, the materiality of the image, the way in which it transforms and melts, produces a kind of exhilaration and joy in mutability and transformation. This is not performance as metaphor but as metonymy. Not only does the part stand for the whole, the signifier is radically indexical, a self-referential icon, an instance of living matter. There is something seductive about watching the ice forest crack and break, a pleasure or *jouissance* in observing the 'trees', in their always random and unexpected ways, hitting the floor, listening to their noise resonating throughout the room like a small, atonal symphony. There are other pleasures, too – pleasures of surface and sheen: the almost erotic image that folds into the retina when the ice loses its solidity and slowly flows beyond its boundary, becoming liquefied, rounded, deliquescent. In these moments far from equilibrium, a sense of intimacy is established between the spectator and the materiality that radiates outwards from the image s/he looks at. We are drawn into the refrain of movement, to the play of entropy, the drama of irreversibility. Time here is no longer linear, cyclical or causal; it is unexpected, evental, chaotic, a kind of ellipsis from which something new, something different emerges. Indeed, at times it appears that the performance operates on us at some pre-linguistic cellular level, a type of intuitive, corporeal knowledge that affirms the need for becoming other than what one is supposed, or constructed to be.

In writing these words, I am not suggesting that these materialized thoughts are unmediated by culture or somehow inherent to the ice itself. Far from it. I am simply proposing that the elemental presence of the ice in *Some Things Happen All At Once* is a material catalyst for what could otherwise be deemed a somewhat abstract form of ecological and ontological thinking. The thinking that emerged from the performance is not *in* it per se; rather, in the same way that ice itself was subject to a process of transformation, so thinking emerges *from* it. Or, better still, was done in conjunction *with* it, *through* its unfolding. The performance is generative in that sense. It allows for thinking to be posited as a 'more than human' process; something impersonal that comes upon or strikes us, as opposed to something that we craft and control from the inside, the work of a disembodied mind, *res cogitans*. And, for me, it is in this opening to the outside, this sensitivity to matter, that the more profound ecological ethics of the performance reside; in, that is, our capacity to affirm the entropic processes of agentic matter.

In an interview with Alison Sky, published three months after his death in 1973, Robert Smithson argues for an alternative way of approaching entropy, a subject that had obsessed him throughout his short career. According to Smithson, entropy is a type of disorder that binds us to the irreversibility of time, to the fact that 'Humpty Dumpty cannot be put back together again' (Smithson 1996: 301). In keeping with the Second Law of Thermodynamics, entropy, for Smithson, is a cosmic force that shows the extent to which all matter seeks to return to a state of equilibrium, in which energy or heat are equitably distributed. Since every act or activity uses energy, it follows that to keep the world as it currently is requires a commitment to 'negentropy', to infusing things with constant heat so that systemic collapse or ruination is overcome and defeated, albeit temporarily. (Negentropy is the amount of energy pumped into a system to keep it at a state of equilibrium; counterintuitively, perhaps, the negative is a positive.) The difficulty with this position, this desire to keep things as they are, Smithson reminds us, is that each time one performs an act to combat entropy, some of the energy used invariably escapes. There is always a certain amount of wastage or excess in any activity. Despite its discourses of efficiency and sustainability, a high-energy dependent society, such as in the UK, is, ultimately, a society committed to entropy, to the extent in which our addiction to fossil fuels produces excessive amounts of waste. Our attempts to maintain living standards in the Global North results in a tragic double bind: the more we seek to deny change, the more entropic we become.

Smithson's response to this situation is not to seek a limit to action, as most conservationists are wont to do. Rather he urges architects and economists to work with entropic matter, to affirm 'the unexpected and to incorporate that into the community' (305). Smithson's argument for entropy is predicated on a form of immanent materialism that realizes that all attempts to plan and manage the future are doomed to failure. This is because entropy is unpredictable; it defeats rationality and idealism. Matter moves in its own ways and is self-organizing, which, for Smithson, results in the absurdist insight that 'planning and chance almost seem to be same thing' (304). Smithson illustrates his point with an example which, although much larger in scale than *Some Things Happen All At Once*, nevertheless engages again with the flows and fluxes of water as elemental matter:

> I'd like to mention another mistake which is essentially an engineering mistake and that's the Salton Sea in Southern California, which happens to be California's largest lake. ... There was a desperate attempt to try to reroute the Colorado River. The Colorado River was always flooding and destroying the area. There was an attempt to keep the Colorado River from flooding by building a canal, in Mexico, and this was illegally done. This canal was started in the delta of the Colorado and then it was re-routed back toward Mexicali, but what happened was that the river flooded into this canal and the canal overflowed, and fed back into the Imperial Valley which is below sea level. ... [W]hole cities were inundated, the railroad was also submerged, and there were great attempts to try to fight back this deluge but to no avail. (305)

Smithson's awareness that matter cannot be controlled offers a cautionary tale at a time when geo-engineers and eco-modernists are paradoxically gearing up to terraform the planet in the futile hope of keeping the human world as it is. Smithson's example shows that there is no way to account for or predict the direction that matter will take. As such, perhaps, the better way is to explore possibilities for living with and affirming the irreversibility of entropy, for existing with change rather than trying to stop it or dam it up. It seems to me that *Some Things Happen All At Once* occupies a similar territory; one in which ecological ethics are located in a becoming with elemental materials, in opening oneself to a process of 'de-humanizing', a melting of distinctions, an indiscernibility between supposedly separated things.

There is no desire on Brookes and Casado's part to argue for an ecological ethics, to communicate it in any direct sense. Ethics emerge from the audience's confrontation with the materiality of the stage pictures that they compose for us. This offers a very different conception of environmental pedagogy than the deficit models currently promulgated by policy makers and activist artists. In *Some Things Happen All At Once*, pedagogy is not predicated on discourse, statistics or apocalyptical rhetoric; it is bound up with images that appear and disappear as the performance unfolds. Something has taken place that cannot be reconstituted or saved. This offers an interesting ecological addendum to exhausted debates about 'liveness' in theatre and performance studies. Only here, the emphasis is not so much on safeguarding the live from representation, but on realizing that the act of perception in theatre, as in, say, Marcel Proust's Bergsonian understanding of duration, is involved in numerous deaths and rebirths as the performance unfolds. We live and die a million times in the theatre, and Brookes and Casado's elemental images are perhaps made to remind us of that.

In this way, Brookes and Casado offer us a decidedly materialist way of thinking about theatre as an ecological medium rooted in entropy, an art form where loss and expenditure are affirmed rather than denied. Such an ethics of the ecological image in theatre does not mean, of course, that one is willing to comply with or condone capitalist modernity's destruction of the earth. Rather, it is best approached as a mode of thought that contests capitalisms mechanistic and inert view of matter. Where capital sees the earth as a resource

Fig. 18.2 *Some Things Happen All At Once*, 2008, Mike Brookes and Rosa Casado. Photo: Ovidio Aldegunde.

for humans to exploit for profitable ends, Brookes and Casado's images allow us to experience the planet as something we are folded into and dependent on for *everything*.

Against neoliberal and theological models of scarcity and austerity, the *everything* that I am referring to here is not simply to do with the organism's survival needs (eating, drinking, heating, etc.). More provocatively, it is a plea for harnessing those supposedly excessive and non-productive energies that, from a utilitarian perspective, serve no purpose whatsoever. Taking my cue from Allan Stoekel's ecological interpretation of dissident surrealist George Bataille's notion of 'radical expenditure', in which consumption is more important than saving, I want to propose that those excessive and useless pleasures that go by the name of art and theatre are vital to our future existence on the earth. Indeed, it is my wager that investing in such 'uselessness' might be the most useful thing that we can do (Stoekel 2007). No secret was revealed in *Some Things Happen All At Once*, no message transmitted. There was simply a series of ecological images that generated thinking – new thinking, unexpected thinking – from the vibratory quality of matter, and which embraced their status as terrestrial signifiers before melting away into *everything*.

Performance Details

Mike Brookes and Rosa Casado, *Some Things Happen All At Once* (2008–9). Brookes and Casado are two Madrid-based artists whose work explores the ecological significance of temporality and spatiality. Their performances are subtle and indirect, and while full of environmental possibility, no message is ever offered. They simply seek to provoke an encounter with matter. *Some Things Happen All At Once* was staged in art galleries, civic buildings and squares across Europe.

Further Reading

Una Chaudhuri's extensive work on ecology, environment and animals has done much to influence critics who have followed in her wake. Along with Bonnie Marranca and Elinor Fuchs, she was the first critic to introduce an environmental sensibility to theatre and performance studies in the mid-1990s. In 'There Must be a Lot of Fish in that Lake' (Chaudhuri 1994), she argues for a literalist approach to ecology and environment in the work of Ibsen and Chekhov; and in *Staging Place* (1996), she discusses the disastrous ecological consequences of what she calls 'geopathology'.

Unlike Chaudhuri, Marranca's *Ecologies of Theatre* (1996) is concerned to focus on how theatre produces forms of ecological perception. Her original and still pertinent contribution is to suggest that the landscape plays of Gertrude Stein, Robert Wilson and Heiner Müller liberate the eye so that it develops a biocentric way of looking, characterized by an awareness of relationality.

Baz Kershaw's *Theatre Ecology: Environments and Performance Events* (2007) is an important and invaluable study that offers concepts and terminologies for engaging with the ecologies of performance. Like Andrew Ross, Kershaw is concerned with how theatre and performance exist within their own ecologies of funding, distribution, reception and knowledge as well as focusing on how theatre might engage in more direct forms of environmental representation.

In their rhizomatic, collectively authored publication *Small Acts of Repair*, Stephen Bottoms and Matthew Goulish (2008) tease out and perform the ecological dimensions of Goat Island's work. The text offers a sophisticated example of how theatre makers and theorists might go about composing and writing ecologically.

A Special Issue of *Green Letters: Studies in Ecocriticism*, 'Performance and Ecology: What Can Theatre Do?' edited by Carl Lavery (2016) features contributions by Karen Christopher and Sophie Grodin, Minty Donald, Dee Heddon, Baz Kershaw, Carl Lavery and Wallace Heim. The issue looks to interrogate what theatre and performance can do ecologically, and contains essays on disappointment, 'intractivity', conflict, rehearsal process, deceleration and the performance of landscape.

References

Bateson, Gregory ([1972] 2000), *Steps to an Ecology of Mind: Collected Essays in Anthropology, Psychiatry, Evolution, and Epistemology*, Chicago: University of Chicago Press.

Bleeker, Maaike (2008), *Visuality in Theatre; The Locus of Looking*, Basingstoke: Palgrave Macmillan.

Bottoms, Stephen, and Matthew Goulish (2008), *Small Acts of Repair: Performance, Ecology and Goat Island*, London and New York: Routledge.

Chaudhuri, Una (1994), '"There Must be a Lot of Fish in that Lake": Toward an Ecological Theater', *Theater* 25 (1): 23–31.

Chaudhuri, Una (1996), *Staging Place: The Geography of Modern Drama*, Ann Arbor: University of Michigan Press.

Cohen, Jeffrey (2013), *Prismatic Ecology: Ecotheory Beyond Green*, Minneapolis: University of Minneapolis Press.

Cubbitt, Sean (2006), *Ecomedia*, Amsterdam: Rodopoi.

Fischer-Lichte, Erika (2008), *The Transformative Power of Performance: A New Aesthetics*, trans. S. Jain, London: Routledge.

Fuchs, Elinor (1996), 'Another Version of Pastoral', in Elinor Fuchs, *The Death of Character: Perspectives on Theater After Modernism*, 92–107, Bloomington, IN: Indiana University Press.

Guattari, Félix ([1989] 2008), *The Three Ecologies*, trans I. Pindar and P. Sutton, London: Continuum.

Ivakhiv, Adrian J. (2013), *Ecologies of the Moving Image: Cinema, Affect, Nature*, Waterloo, ON: Wilfred Laurier University Press.

Kelleher, Joe (2015), *The Illuminated Theatre: Studies in the Suffering of Images*, London: Routledge.

Kershaw, Baz (2007), *Theatre Ecology: Environments and Performance Events*, Cambridge: Cambridge University Press.

Lavery, Carl (2013), 'The Ecology of the Image: The Environmental Politics of Philippe Quesne and Vivarium Studio', *French Cultural Studies* 24 (3): 264–78.

Lavery, Carl, (2016), 'Introduction', in Carl Lavery (ed.), 'Performance and Ecology: What Can Theatre Do?', *Green Letters: Studies in Ecocriticism* 20 (3): 229–36.

Marks, Laura U. (2000), *The Skin of the Film: Intercultural Cinema, Embodiment and the Senses*, Chapel Hill, NC: Duke University Press.

Marks, Laura U. (2009), 'Information, Secrets and Enigmas: An Enfolding-Unfolding Ethics for Cinema', *Screen* 50 (1): 86–99.

Marranca, Bonnie (1996), *Ecologies of Theatre*, Baltimore, MD: John Hopkins Press.

Munk, Erika (1994), 'Introduction', *Theater* 25 (1): 5–6.

Perniola, Mario (1995), *Enigmas: The Egyptian Moment in Society and Art*, trans. C. Woodall, London: Verso.

Ross, Andrew (1994), *The Chicago Gangster Theory of Life: Nature's Debt to Society*, London: Verso.

Shaviro, Steven (1993), *The Cinematic Body*, Minneapolis: University of Minnesota Press.

Smithson, Robert (1996), *The Collected Writings*, ed. Jack Flam, Berkeley: University of California Press.

Sontag, Susan ([1977] 1979), *On Photography*, London: Penguin.

Stoekel, Alan (2007), *Bataille's Peak: Energy, Religion and Postsustainability*, Minneapolis: University of Minneapolis Press.

Vattimo, Gianni (2012), 'Dialectics, Difference, Weak Thought', in Gianni Vattimo and Pier Aldo Rovatti (eds), *Weak Thought*, trans. P. Carravetta, 39–52, New York: SUNY.

Williams, Raymond (2014), 'Culture', in Raymond Williams, *Keywords*, 86–92, Oxford: Oxford University Press.

19 How Does Choreography Think 'Through' Society?

BOJANA CVEJIĆ

The reason for stressing the preposition 'through' in the question chosen as a title for this chapter is twofold. First, choreography is constituted as a social practice. Like other performing arts, choreography is shaped by the social structures (discourses and institutions, customs, modes of production and relations of power) in which it operates. More than theatre or performance art, it can provide a physical model to think through (i.e. consider and analyse) various aspects of the social as they arise 'through' physical arrangements of bodies in motion within a spatiotemporal event. This calls for the second register of thinking society 'through'. When it thinks society 'through', choreography may posit another model that either revisits a historical practice or looks past the existing social structures towards a new social order. Given such considerations, the term 'social choreography' is justified. Choreography is deemed social when it accounts for how social order is not just *reflected* in choreographed movement, but also *proposed*, exercised and instilled kinaesthetically.

To address, then, the general question that opens this chapter: the capacity of choreography to think through society lies in the agency of kinaesthetic arrangements of human bodies. When they are moving, performers' bodies are contiguous with the bodies watching, as they are both subject to a kinaesthetic continuum that ranges from dancing to everyday movement. However, it will not suffice to state the kinaesthetic continuum as a fundamental law of choreography. We will have to think further if we are going to address the questions that arise from our opening one, such as: When does choreography put into practice, in an emphatic or programmatic sense, its power to think (through) the social? How does choreography conceive of itself as a way of thinking society by producing a model of society in a deliberate manner? Furthermore, what does choreography think of the social? Which ideas does it hypothesize of society? Narrowing down these lines of enquiry, the following chapter will explore how social choreography grasps 'transindividuality', the collective mode of individuation upon which society is predicated.

From 'Choreography' to 'Social Choreography'

The open call of the Austrian dance web journal *Corpus Web* (2011) around the question 'What is Choreography?' elicited a wide variety of responses from choreographers, dancers, theoreticians, presenters and dramaturgs working in contemporary dance in Europe. Many respondents agreed on a generic determination of choreography as the organization of movement in time and space, each placing emphasis on a different term or relation within the statement. In a broad gesture indicating some of the distinct registers in which the word is used, the American choreographer Jennifer Lacey submitted the following list:

choreography [kawr-ee-og-ruh-fee, kohr-]

- the art of composing ballets and other dances and planning and arranging the movements, steps, and patterns of dancers.
- the technique of representing the various movements in dancing by a system of notation.
- the arrangement or manipulation of actions leading up to an event: the choreography of a surprise birthday party.

Dear corpus

as usual, I am partial to the third meaning love Jennifer (*Corpus Web* 2011: n.p.)

The three dictionary definitions indicate the range of understandings of the concept 'choreography'. In the first and second definitions, choreography is a technical term. It designates the composition of movement and the system of visually retracing or writing various kinds of movement down, referring to choreography as the craft of dance in general. In *Contemporary Choreography: A Critical Reader*, the editors Jo Butterworth and Liesbeth Wildschut write: 'Choreography is the making of dance. Dance, however, is not confined to theatrical contexts only. Contemporary choreography is concerned with dance making in an ever-expanding field of applications' (2009: 1). This definition, like the technical, craft-oriented meanings in Lacey's response, leans on the root etymological signification: *khoreia* (dancing in unison of *khoros*, the chorus in ancient Greek drama) + *graphia* (writing). In her response to the *Corpus Web* questionnaire (2011), the Austrian choreographer Christine Gaigg emphasizes the distinction between

choreography and choreographic craftsmanship. The craft is subject to fashions and styles. 'Choreography', on the other hand, is a term as far-reaching as 'gesture'. As such, this term contains a lot (if not everything) and can stand for all kinds of things like, e.g., composition, orchestration, timing, score, structuring. Choreographing as an action means finding orientations within a sample of conditions. Those may – but don't have to be – dance movements. On the contrary, the relation to dance movement is just a tiny special case in the thought space of choreographing. (*Corpus Web* 2011: n.p.)

In the third meaning from Lacey's list, choreography is not necessarily linked to dance, nor art for that matter. The example of 'the choreography of a surprise birthday party' opens up the term to metonymic usage in the social sphere at large. When choreography is associated with any kind of action whatsoever, its disciplinary meaning from within the Western tradition of dance is nevertheless invoked: actions are prepared, arranged or manipulated in a manner comparable to how dance movements are composed and written down, not least because actions are comprised of movements. Choreography is not relegated to a social script, but related rather to language in the poststructuralist – or more precisely Derridean – sense of writing, *écriture*. According to Derrida, writing is not only language in action, movement, thought, reflection, consciousness, unconsciousness, experience and affectivity; it is all that, but also the totality of what makes it possible. In other words, writing can include a deconstruction of the assumptions, rules and values that guide it (Derrida 1976: 9). Substitute 'choreography' for 'writing' here and the concept expands to a variety of usages. *Choreography: Webster's Timeline History 1710–2007* (Parker 2009) is a peculiar case in point. This software-generated book traces all published uses of the word 'choreography' in print and news media in the period in question. If we look for the notions of 'choreography' that are furthest from dance and performance in this curious index, we find the word 'choreography' emerging in such fields as molecular biology, information technology and diplomacy:

Shirmer, S. G., 'Quantum *choreography*: making molecules dance to technology's tune?' published in *Philosophical Transactions: Series A, Mathematical, Physical, and Engineering Sciences*, vol. 364, no. 1849, on 15 December 2006.

'Patterns: serial and parallel processes for process *choreography* and workflow.' Publisher: IBM International Technical Support Organization (Research Triangle Park, NC). Published in 2004.

Iran News, 22 Feb 2005, headline, 'Bush says Notion of Attack on Iran "Ridiculous"': 'Despite the careful *choreography*, the new tone and the desire on both sides to turn the page, some European officials are still wondering if Mr. Bush means what he says.' (Parker 2009: n.p., emphasis added)

Apart from confirming the currency of the term 'choreography', the examples cited here give insight into a more precise and yet broadly accommodating notion. Choreography cannot be reduced to any particular organization or structural capacity. Moreover, it designates dynamic patterns of complicated yet seamless organization of many heterogeneous elements in motion. In the above citations, the stress falls on the design of procedures that regulate a process, be those chemical or physical processes, algorithmic, political or diplomatic. The creation of a dance performance is not excluded by this definition. On the contrary, the expansion of the meaning of choreography outside of dance chimes with current developments in dance and performance.

For choreographers in Europe (and wider afield) today, 'choreography' tends to be privileged over 'contemporary dance' (see Cvejić 2015: 5–7). This preference indicates a nominal divergence from contemporary dance in so far as the latter historically leads back to modern dance, or more specifically to its essentialist relation to the medium of dance as an ongoing movement of the body, intentionally regulated by rhythmic, gestural or other kinds of patterns. We could refer here to the canonical, albeit laconic, definition of dance as 'any patterned, rhythmic movement in space and time' (Copeland and Cohen 1983: 1). However, William Forsythe – one of the most eminent choreographers whose practice has been centred on inventing a new dance language – puts forward an argument for separating the terms 'dance' and 'choreography':

Choreography and dancing are two distinct and very different practices. In the case that choreography and dance coincide, choreography often serves as a channel for the desire to dance. One could easily assume that the substance of choreographic thought resided exclusively in the body. But is it possible for choreography to generate autonomous expressions of its principles, a choreographic object, without the body? (Forsythe n.d.)

Forsythe's 1998 proposition of choreography as 'organizing things in space and time' (Ploebst 2009: 165) anticipated later definitions that significantly omit any mention of the human body or movement, or that do not ascribe movement to the human body. Thus, for the French choreographer Xavier Le Roy, choreography is 'artificially staged action(s) and/or situation(s)' (*Corpus Web* 2011: n.p.). The British choreographer Jonathan Burrows's answer goes even further in delinking choreography from the body in movement: 'Choreography is about making a choice, including the choice to make no choice' (*Corpus Web* 2011: n.p). Vocabulary and terms aside, it is in choreographic practices of the last two decades that a weakened relation between movement and the human body can be found. This points to an argument that will prove important for our case: if choreography can be separated from the dancing body, and moreover appears as a metaphor to describe complex patterns of non-human motion outside dance, then it can serve as an instrument to analyse the social import of both dance and everyday movement. This assumption underlies the concept of 'social choreography'.

In his book *Social Choreography: Ideology as Performance in Dance and Everyday Movement* (2005), Andrew Hewitt designates social choreography as a medium for producing and rehearsing social order. Its meaning is twofold: on the one hand, it is the material practice and the discourse on movements, gestures and bodily arrangements, and on the other, it is the method of analysis of that practice and discourse. A longer quote will capture the reach of Hewitt's concept:

> My methodology of 'social choreography' is rooted in an attempt to think the aesthetic as it operates at the very base of social experience. I use the term social choreography to denote a tradition of thinking about social order that derives its ideal from the aesthetic realm and seeks to instil that order directly at the level of the body. In its most explicit form, this tradition has observed the dynamic choreographic configurations produced in dance and sought to apply those forms to the broader social and political sphere. Accordingly, such social choreographies ascribe a fundamental role to the aesthetic in its formulation of the political. (Pristaš 2007: n.p.)

The main cue for this idea that choreography can offer an aesthetic ideal for establishing a new social order comes from an image in which the German poet and intellectual of Weimar classicism, Friedrich Schiller, describes a dance. In 1794, in a letter to Christian Gottfried Körner, he writes:

> I can think of no more fitting image for the ideal of social conduct than an English dance, composed of many complicated figures and perfectly executed. A spectator in the gallery sees innumerable movements intersecting in the most chaotic fashion, changing direction swiftly and without rhyme or reason, yet never colliding. Everything is so ordered that the one has already yielded his place when the other arises; it is all so skilfully, and yet so artlessly, integrated into a form, that each seems only to be following his own inclination, yet without ever getting in the way of anybody else. It is the most perfectly appropriate symbol of the assertion of one's own freedom and regard for the freedom of others. (Schiller 1967: 300)

The aesthetic *qua* social ideal of the English ballroom for Schiller is a harmonious play of movements between people dancing at leisure, which we are to see as a model of citizens' social intercourse. The aesthetic image functions as a social ideal for a republican model of democracy, which could not be politically realized in Schiller's time. Although Schiller had sympathies for the French Revolution, his account might also promulgate the reconciliation of freedom and nature that could take place within an enlightened monarchy. While not politically viable yet, the social ideal of democracy could be culturally and aesthetically practised and instilled. The social extension of significance rests on the assumption that there exists an aesthetic continuum in bodily articulation that spans from everyday movement to dance. This continuous aesthetic spectrum is framed at the one end by the (conscious or unconscious) sensory experience of daily movements, gestures, postures and relations between bodies in time and space, and at the other by aestheticized movement in the artistic and social sense, as in social dance. It means that any expression of bodily movement can slide on that scale: from everyday functional to artistic and aesthetically isolated movement. The thesis could be paraphrased as follows: if the body I dance with and the body I work and walk with are one and the same, I must, when dancing, show unaware that all of the body's movements are, to a greater or lesser extent, choreographed. Yet the choreography becomes social only when it is embodied and performed, as there is no 'movement text' prior to it. Additionally, it is usually accompanied with a way of thinking the social, the reflection of a social or political idea that is both inspired by and instilled through dancing. This constitutes a sliding or grey zone in which discourse meets practice. Other historical examples of social choreography include the gesture of walking rehearsed by the eighteenth- and nineteenth-century bourgeoisie as a pre-revolutionary expression of freedom, and mass dancing in the early twentieth century in which the rationalization of industrial production mixes with totalitarianism. In the next section, we will probe the social choreography of *9x9*, a series of performances made between 1999 and 2001 in which the choreographing of a 'mass' of people makes the social idea of transindividuality appear on stage.

For starters, transindividuality might be briefly defined as a mode of being, doing and also – specifically here – performing that privileges social relations and processes of differentiation over the principle and goal of becoming unitary individual selves. The term 'transindividual' was coined by the French philosopher Gilbert Simondon (see Simondon 2005; Combes 2012) in his seminal theory of ontogenesis, which includes the life of minerals, plant and animal world, as well as the mode of existence of technical objects. It derives from individuation, the ontological principle that accounts for how something comes into being through a process of differentiation, without a goal or terminus. In contrast to individualization, or becoming an individual, individuation prioritizes process and difference over entity and identity. Hence, individuals, that is beings and things, are regarded as passing phases; what matters are reciprocal relations between the milieu (environment, ground) and the living being, their joint transformation. The process of individuation involves preindividual and transindividual stages, whereby the preindividual equals the potentials and the source of future changes. The preindividual is a precondition for the becoming of the individual, resulting from the psychic aspect of individuation understood as resolving one's own problematic of existence self-consciously. Yet individuation doesn't stop there, but gains a collective dimension when the individual exceeds the limits of psychic individuation as it incorporates itself into a wider system of the world and the subject. Thus, the preindividual reality that every individual inherits is conjoined to the preindividual inheritance of all other individuals. As we will see later, Simondon's metaphysical idea of preindividuality acquires the social and political meaning of the common, or what is given and shared by the human species-being (Virno 2004). And for the theorists who read Simondon's account through the lens of Marxist critique (Virno 2004; Balibar 1997), transindividuality is the primary category, determining being as social through and through.

In the following section, we will explore how transindividuation is produced choreographically. The analysis of the performance series *9x9* will demonstrate five elements, focusing on both choreography and transindividuation. Those are the aforementioned 'milieu' and 'preindividual'; 'play' and 'imagination' as they combine the aesthetic and fictive dimension of performance images; and rehearsal, which enacts a social *qua* aesthetic order. Before we embark on this interpretative endeavour, however, we might consider the choice of our approach. Could the question 'How does choreography think through society?' be addressed from an alternative theoretical perspective to social choreography? The challenge is all the greater the more counterintuitive another method of analysis might seem with regard to *9x9*. From a more standard dance studies perspective, the accent would fall on the analysis of the choreography as it appears for its onlookers, the spectators of a theatre dance. A formal and rhetorical analysis would focus on how this dance signifies, the tropes in which the kinaesthetic images produce the meanings of the social. For such an attempt, Susan Leigh Foster's *Reading Dancing* (1986) would prove a useful analytical model (Foster 1986). In her seminal study, Foster advances a combined formalist and semiotic perspective in examining various paradigms of Western dance. In particular, she elaborates modes of signification in dance in parallel to rhetorical figures, such as metonymy, synecdoche, metaphor and irony. While a formalist-semiotic perspective could yield a precise array of meanings and decode the reception of *9x9* with regard to the history of dance, it would fail to account for how the process of preparation by which a sociocultural context is probed and reshuffled – as well as the actual making of this choreography in rehearsal – are constitutive for thinking the social here. In such an approach, the collective dimension of individuation remains vague or invisible or, at best, relegated to a represented image of the social that contradicts the processual nature of *9x9*. Our preference for social choreography will be tested analytically, that is, by how far the thought of the social is engendered through the choreographic devices of transindividuation.

9×9 and the Choreography of Transindividuation

My analysis of *9x9* begins with the decisions that were taken prior to this work reaching the stage. The Belgian choreographer Christine De Smedt invited eight choreographers to join her in the project of choreographing approximately eighty 'bodies'. The formula of nine choreographers each choreographing nine performers, nine-times-nine, was however eventually relegated to the title, as the artists begin to collaborate on forming a common 'platform', 'a framework within which it is possible to formulate movement, sound, light and other parameters under one roof' (De Smedt 2017: n.p.). Horizontal relations prevailed and transferred to the performers, dissolving the initial division (9 choreographers times 9 participants). The main interest lay now in choreographing 'a mass' or 'a crowd' which 'is always moving, growing, and erupting in a singular direction' (De Smedt 2017: n.p.). In De Smedt's own words:

A crowd can be constructed through dance, but can also be a dancing body in itself, consisting of a thousand bodies. From the outside a mass is always the same, it is constructed around an agreement of sameness. From the inside however every participant strives with [their] own specificity, without any possibility to perceive the movement of the mass as a whole. (De Smedt 2017: n.p.)

The 'crowd', comprising primarily non-professional performers (referred to as 'participants'), is selected and recruited in co-operation with the venue inviting the project. In each place, De Smedt and her fellow choreographers define and study its context. They consider a specific criterion for the invitation call for local people from the neighbourhood – or for people who are in some other way linked with the venue – to participate. But they insist that they are not coming to 'colonize the context, i.e. to have an educated audience come and watch the local arena' (De Smedt 2017: n.p.). Nor has this project a mission to educate or to increase social integration in the local community. 'It is instead important that the participant in the project experience that he/she is being dealt with as an artist, or equal to the rest of the team or employees in the building' (De Smedt 2017: n.p.). In Glasgow, the criterion is the age range, from one to eighty-one years old. In Paris, it is the workers of The Pompidou Cultural Centre where the project is taking place. The programmer of the City Theatre in Rotterdam commissions the project to tackle 'multiculturalism'. The choreographers interpret the topic as an occasion to invite parents with babies of the age at which the infants cannot walk by themselves. The argument for their response was the idea of embracing the potentiality of differences in lieu of already realized and represented diversity. The result of calling for young people who frequent the cultural centre of Turnhout was a mixture of Belgian nationals and immigrants.

The contextual approach of 9x9 means that each time a certain milieu is re-hallucinated and reshuffled according to new fault lines. The milieu is the first term of the analysis. In the process of individuation – understood as being and becoming through creation of difference – the milieu is not simply a support, i.e. the precondition or the framed context from which people come. As we will see, the milieu and its participants are brought into a choreography in which they reciprocally act upon each other, in the first place through the questions that instigate movements and the arising of relations among many bodies. Questions are selected on the basis of people's belonging to the context in question. Although these people are not professional performers, asking them to learn a choreography triggers a process in which they begin to use their bodies as if they were dancers. What follows is that they are to co-operate with each other and be watched by their fellow citizens, as they make and unmake choreographic patterns in response to questions that concern everyone in the room, performers and spectators alike. The most telling image is the curious co-presence between participants and spectators: they are similar in number, which is unusual for dance to have as many people watching as there are performers dancing. All are standing and mingling in the same space, restructured by the choreography and by the activity of watching.

What the people present in this situation share are skills common to all, as stated in the call for participation: '9x9 is not searching for people with any predefined skills concerning dance. All participants should be able to perform everyday movements such as walking, crawling, running, sitting and standing' (De Smedt 2017: n.p.). In the theory of transindividuation, the common is the preindividual nature that all human beings are endowed with: language, perception and an inherited mode of production. The Italian philosopher Paolo Virno defines the preindividual through Karl Marx's notion of 'General intellect' (Marx 1973: 706). Considered a source of production and social wealth, the preindividual common (or general intellect) is the social and historico-natural ground for all individuation. Language, then, stands not only for linguistic competence, but also for thought, self-reflection and the capacity for learning; perception involves sensorial habits and customs; and the mode of production is the historical and social form of organizing labour with its knowledge and capacity. In this sense, Virno contends that perception can never be personal: 'It is never an individual "I" who hears, sees, touches; it is the whole species as such' (Virno 2004: 78). The preindividual common is put at stake here when choreography arises from tasks derived from generic capacities shared by everyone in the same room. This – after decisions on the criteria that determine the selection of participants – is the second element of the analysis. However, it is worth noting that these tasks rest on the average skills of persons who are not physically disabled. On one occasion, in the edition made for Porto with elderly habitants of that city, a significant number of participants appeared to be illiterate, which also demonstrated a difference between the potential and the actualization of the linguistic capacity.

The choreography, then, is comprised of questions and tasks to which the participants respond by simple gestures and movements (turning, lying, running, and so on), or by organizing themselves in choreographic forms such as line-ups, or by forming groups and spatial ornaments. For example, the participants are asked to form a straight line according to their age, height, weight and other personal identificatory parameters. In a special adaptation of the method of *9x9* for Tate Modern, called *Spatial Confessions*, they were asked to arrange themselves in a line according to the colour of their skin from the darkest to the brightest. Translating a biometric analysis into a choreographic image here has several effects. It ironizes the apparatus of classifying populations, by adding more criteria for sorting people out socially. The procedure asks for people to comply and they usually do. The result is complex, detailed and quirky, and – most of all – it does not end up in the records of government, but in a performance, visible to everyone.

A broad range of topics is covered, usually combining serious, existentially determining and critically reflective interrogation with lighter and more personal questions about daily life preferences and habits. Hereby, an example from the questions addressed to the elderly people who were the participants of *9x9* in Porto in 2001:

Participants who prefer swimming to politics, face the back.

Participants who consider loyalty important, face the back.

Participants who consider their neighbours' chicken better, face the back.

Participants who ever committed a crime, face the back.

Participants who broke a heart, face the back.

Participants who ever shook hands with Mario Soares, face the back. [Mario Soares (1924–2017) was the Portuguese socialist politician who served the government several times, lastly as its president 1986–96.]

Participants who know the name of the Pope, face the back.

Participants who ever read a book by José Saramago, face the back. [José Saramago (1922–2010) was a Portuguese writer, and winner of the Nobel Prize in Literature (1998).]

If you sing, take a step backward.

If you cook for somebody else, take a step forward.

If you eat dinner with somebody else, take a step backward.

Form groups with participants that practice the same leisure activities as you.

Form groups with participants with a similar political opinion to yourself.

In other cases, the questions could be grouped thematically, addressing issues such as work, money, housing and political opinions. Questions were posed so as to exhaust the stances that participants could take, and to impact upon the resulting choreographic pattern:

If you are a freelancer or self-employed, come to the middle.

If you have a monthly salary, pension or scholarship, make a ring around the freelancers.

If you consider yourself able to manage the time that you spend working, come together and keep distance from each other at arms' length.

If you go on vacation every year, sit down.

Put your arm up if you think the vacation you would like to go on would be possible in your current conditions. If not, put it down.

Now point to whom you think is the richest person in this group. If you think it is you, just raise your arm up.

If you think money is overrated, go to the left border, the others go to the right border.

If you think art is overrated, go to the right border, the others go to the left border.

If you think sex is overrated, go to the right border, the others go to the left border.

Form a line according to the degree of capitalism and socialism you live in.

If you trust your government, go to the left border, the others go to the right border.

If you believe people should better organize themselves instead of government, yes (form a group to the left), no (form a group to the right), maybe (form a group in the middle).

If you think polarization between left and right in this room is too simple as a way of positioning oneself, lie down in the middle.

Each item takes as much time as the participants need to arrange themselves, as the choreographer calling out the question waits for people to form a pattern. The time needed for each pattern is the time it takes to negotiate the answers.

In a note about *9x9* for the production in Rotterdam, the choreographers choose their words fastidiously in order to distinguish their intentions from the genre of socially engaged, community-based projects. They write:

[Mass] can be the site of dangerous, non-humanitarian opinions, but also the starting point of cultural change and motivations of enlarged empathy. Mass engages everybody as being part of community or only few as members of sects, clubs, or neighbourhoods. It is an organization in which one can disappear…

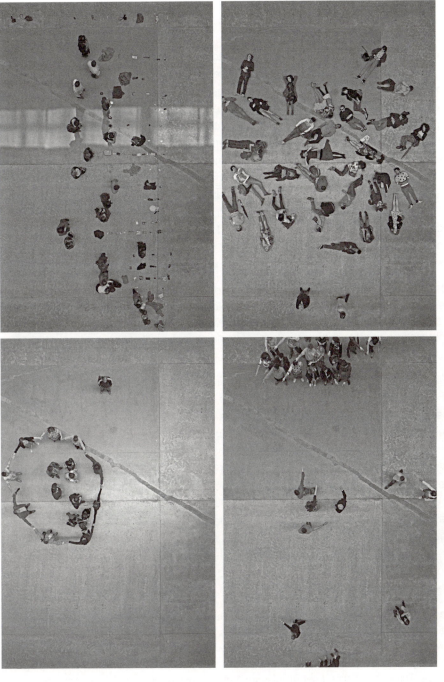

Fig. 19.1 *Spatial Confessions*, Tate Modern Turbine Hall, May 2014. Photos: Lennart Laberenz.

The last remark – that in this choreography, the individual can disappear – conceals ambivalence. When the choreographic patterns are observed from distance (and in the case of the Tate Modern edition in the Turbine Hall, seen from above) they appear similar to mass ornaments, yet without the arena of a stadium. 'Mass ornament' is the concept that the German critic, and affiliate of the Frankfurt School, Siegfrid Kracauer, coined to observe the relation between mass dancing and revue-style dancing and industrial capitalism. Kracauer writes: 'Only as parts of a mass, not as individuals who believe themselves to be formed from within, do people become fractions of a figure. The ornament is an end in itself' (Kracauer 1995: 76).

The differences in participants' responses are not so much visible in themselves, as they are instrumental to the choreographic formation on a large scale. What prevails are relations of composition, how individuals act as part of a collective image.

Yet, when the audience takes the liberty to move and mingle inside the choreography, individual choices emerge. We can see how participants 'play', how their personal answers bring them into face-to-face connection with other participants, each becoming conscious of the positions they take in public. 'Play' is another term in the analysis of this social choreography. In some editions of *9x9* (e.g. in 1999 at the Pompidou Centre in Paris), participants were involved in more complicated choreographic games. In one game, the participants moved through chains of relations based on the difference in height, which would modulate into other encounters and gestures, as the following task describes it:

> The person standing on the floor turns around and lifts/takes the other person in his/her lap (like during the wedding night) and holds the person until he or she cannot do it any longer. If the relationship is correct the person most to the right will be the one to collapse first, but due to the complexity of parameters this will not be the case (which is of course the wished for effect).

The instructions and the resulting image recall an account of transindividuation, which the French philosopher Étienne Balibar draws from the seventeenth-century rationalist philosopher Spinoza. In Spinoza, relations are necessary for the persistence and self-preservation of being. Individuals are endowed with unity; however, it is a composite one. According to Spinoza's physicalist definition, the human body is a composite individual, consisting of many parts, bodies or Individuals that enter in relations with other external bodies. These relations form a complex, nonlinear and dynamic network of modulations. 'The action of B upon any A is itself modulated by some Cs, which itself is modulated by some Ds, etc' (Balibar 1997: 15). In the choreographic games of *9x9* at the Pompidou Centre, crowds were forming such that they split and shuffled in groups that were wrestling, jumping, dancing and running. The choreography unfolded in a dynamic network of relations. The choreographic game was meant to acquire social meaning, as revealed in the choreographers' note on their intentions:

> The game-structure can be comprehended as a critique of dance composition as it introduces an open-ended flow of possibilities for new formations. This perspective of flows, breaks and resistance can also be understood as allegory for human interaction, an image of society. It also points to a difference between social dancing and concert dance. Through a defined set of rules (game) the performers can make open choices (play). There is no defined goal inscribed in the game but the intent is only to play or perform consciously.

When I 'play', I make personal choices in relation to the rules of the game, but also in relation to other players. The consciousness in which 'I' relate to 'me' arises in relation to the others, in partial likeness and partial difference. Imagination is responsible for the recognition of myself in the other, and for distinguishing the other from myself, for identification and empathy, difference and resistance. In *9x9*, this cognitive process is made explicit: as a participant takes a position in the face of their 'neighbour' taking the same or another position, both are compelled to imagine their differences and likeness. No absolute autonomy in individuals making sovereign decisions can be claimed here, and mimetic processes might occur from which new thoughts and affects arise. Do we share a common notion of empathy? How many anarchists are there in the room? What does she think about Saramago's literature? These might be the kinds of questions triggered by the curiosity that both participants and onlookers are experiencing. While the performance brings eighty strangers into rehearsing and performing a choreography together, it also generates images and provokes thoughts about who is sharing the space in the moment of performance. Imagination is the basis of sociability, a means of individuating oneself within a group that in turn individuates itself. The result is another organization of the body politic that could be regarded as transindividuation – a new social fabric of relations articulated on a formal-choreographic plane and a cognitive-social plane at the same time.

Social Choreography as Method

Social choreography has been featured as a method for examining how *9x9*, the project and its performances, are created and operate. The method propounds that choreography foregrounds and rehearses a social order. Two main forms of organization have been discerned: an associating of questions and tasks with movements, gestures and spatial patterns; and choreographic games resulting in more complex arrangements of performers and their bodies in space. Regardless of the suggestion cited, that the game structure of *9x9* might be considered an 'allegory of society', the question of *which* social order is aesthetically instilled is relevant. Were we to borrow Schiller's perspective, as in his observation of English ballroom dance, what kind of society could we see in the choreographic patterns of *9x9*?

In the period of 1999 to 2001, social democracy was the predominant political system in the countries of Western and Southwestern Europe where *9x9* was made and shown. In its mode of operation, *9x9* does not contrast or deviate much from the ideals of social democracy vested in people's participation in the public sphere. Yet, it does intervene into the prevalent mechanism of representation by which identity would be the underlying logic of the public's appearance on stage. Even if the participants of *9x9* can be identified in a more general sense (for example, according to the age group they belong to), their actions appear more important than their identity, shifting focus from who they are to how they can co-operate and make choreographies. Clearly, they belong to, and – as has been argued – they reshuffle the *milieu* from which the specific performance of *9x9* arises. The emphasis on generic capacities (such as reading, counting, walking, running, ways of working together) brings to the fore what is common to all before they are recognized as individuals. All actions, movements and gestures, or ways of arranging bodies in space, require and promote playful co-operation. Even if they are inclined to act individually by virtue of their personal choice, the participants lend themselves to games and patterns in which their bodies are only visible as parts of a joint construction. Underneath the image of the crowd choreographed as a transindividual multitude, imagination vibrates, through thoughts and images about social, political, moral and cultural issues in which people individuate as individuals and within a group.

Summing up our investigation, four parameters of this social choreography have provided its key analytical terms: *milieu* encompassed in the contextual approach; the generic skills emerging from the *preindividual* species-being of humans; performance as *play* based on personally chosen action and co-operation; and *imagination* as the cognitive and mimetic process of encounters and relations. A fifth term can be added, in order to distinguish *9x9* from flash mobs as a more appropriate example of social choreography. While flash mobs capitalize on the instant mobilization of a more or less found crowd, and therefore reduce performance to an improvised action, *9x9* is a social choreography because it invests time in mounting and *rehearsing* an aesthetic order. It is this temporality that enables people to engage in thinking through society, from learning an aesthetic towards comprehending a potentially modified social order.

Performance Details

9x9. Concept by Christine De Smedt. Developed with Alexandra Bachsetzis, Nuno Bizarro, Christine De Smedt, Staffan Eek, Tino Sehgal, Marten Spangberg, Mette Edvardsen, Lilia Mestre. Created with Alexandra Bachsetzis, Nuno Bizarro, Christine De Smedt, Mette Edvardsen, Staffan Eek, Sylvia Hasenclever, Damien Jalet, Vincent Malstaf, Lilia Mestre, Tino Sehgal, Marten Spangberg, Gerd Van Looy, Maria Clara Villa-Lobos, Eva Meyer-Keller, Ivana Müller, Carlos Pez, Bruno Pocheron, Vasco Macide, Tony Chong, Jean-Pierre Côté, Alain Francoeur, Marc Parent, Harold Henning, Heleen Vervondel, Carlo Bourguignon, Vania Gala, Vera Knolle, Yasmina Van Assche, Palle Dyrval, Kurt Verleure, Lies Vanborm and Inge Staelens

Produced by Ballets C de la B. Premiere: 7 September 2000 at Minardschouwburg, Ghent. Performed in Paris (avant-première), Ghent, Rotterdam, Berlin, Amsterdam, Porto, Montréal, Glasgow, Turnhout, Terschelling, Nantes, Vienna and Brussels
http://dev.lesballetscdela.be/en/projects/productions/9-x-9/info/

Further Reading

This essay forwards the claim that the question of how choreography thinks through society should be best approached through social choreography, as the method demonstrates how social order is thought and made aesthetically. For further study, the following literature is recommended: Hewitt (2005) for an introduction of social choreography as a form of aesthetic ideology, developed in literary and theoretical discourses and choreographic practices from 1770 until the twentieth century; Cvejić and Vujanović (2012) for more on social choreography and social drama as two complementary models of analysis of the public sphere expressed in words, deeds, movements and gestures; Kracauer (1995) for the historical precursor of the method of social choreography, elucidating a relationship between choreography and industrial production; Toepfner (1997) for a comprehensive historical study of the period in which social choreography firmly took ground from leisure to political ideology; and van Eikels (2012) for an account of collectivity in neoliberal society.

References

Balibar, Étienne (1997), *Spinoza: From Individuality to Transindividuality*, Delft: Eburon.

Butterworth, Jo, and Liesbeth Wildschut, eds (2009), *Contemporary Choreography: A Critical Reader*, London and New York: Routledge.

Combes, Muriel (2012), *Gilbert Simondon and the Philosophy of the Transindividual*, trans. T. LaMarre, Cambridge, MA: MIT Press.

Copeland, Roger and Marshall Cohen, eds (1983), *What Is Dance?*, Oxford: Oxford University Press.

Corpus Web (2011), 'What is Choreography?'. Available online, http://www.corpusweb.net/tongue-6.html (accessed 5 September 2011).

Cvejić, Bojana (2015), *Choreographing Problems: Expressive Problems in European Contemporary Dance and Performance*, Basingstoke: Palgrave Macmillan.

Cvejić, Bojana, and Ana Vujanović (2012), *Public Sphere by Performance*, Berlin: books.

De Smedt, Christine (2017), Unpublished documentation on the performance *9x9* (obtained from the author).

Derrida, Jacques (1976), *Of Grammatology*, trans. G. C. Spivak, Baltimore and London: The Johns Hopkins University Press.

Forsythe, William (n.d.), 'Choreographic Objects'. Available online: http://www.williamforsythe.com/essay.html (accessed 27 November 2017).

Foster, Susan Leigh (1986), *Reading Dancing: Bodies and Subjects in Contemporary American Dance*, Berkeley and Los Angeles: University of California Press.

Hewitt, Andrew (2005), *Social Choreography: Ideology as Performance in Dance and Everyday Movement*, Durham, NC: Duke University Press.

Hirose, Jun Fujitsa (2006), 'Reading Gilbert Simondon: Transindividuality, Technical Activity and Reification. Interview with Paolo Virno', *Radical Philosophy* 136: 34–43.

Kracauer, Siegfried (1995), *The Mass Ornament*, Cambridge, MA: Harvard University Press.

Marx, Karl (1973), *Grundrisse: Foundations of the Critique of Political Economy (Rough Draft)*, trans. M. Nicolaus, Harmondsworth: Penguin / New Left Review.

Parker, Philip M., ed. (2009), *Choreography: Webster's Timeline History 1710-2007*, San Diego, CA: ICON Group International, Inc.

Ploebst, Helmut (2009), 'Blago Bung Bosso Fataka', *Frakcija Performing Arts Journal* 51–2: 160–71.

Pristaš, Goran Sergej (2007), 'Andrew Hewitt: Choreography is a Way of Thinking about the Relationship of Aesthetics to Politics'. Available online, http://www.old.tkh-generator.net/sr/openedsource/andrew-hewitt-choreography-a-way-thinking-about-relationship-aesthetics-politics (accessed 27 November 2017).

Simondon, Gilbert (2005), *L'individuation à la lumière des notions de forme et d'information*, Grenoble: Éditions Jérôme Millon.

Schiller, Friedrich (1967), *On the Aesthetic Education of Man*, trans. E. M. Wilkinson and L. A. Willoughby, Oxford: Clarendon Press.

Toepfner, Karl (1997), *Empire of Ecstasy: Nudity and Movement in German Body Culture, 1910–1935*, Berkeley, CA: University of California Press.

Van Eikels, Kai (2012), 'From Archein to Prattein. Suggestions for an Un-Creative Collectivity', in Elena Basteri, Emanuele Guidi and Elisa Ricci (eds) *Rehearsing Collectivity. Choreography Beyond Dance*, 5–19, Berlin: Argobooks.

Virno, Paolo (2004), *Grammar of the Multitude*, trans. I. Bertoletti, J. Cascaito and A. Casson, New York: Semiotext(e).

20 How Does Theatricality Legitimize the Law?

SOPHIE NIELD

The Court: [W]ill the marshals exclude from the courtroom anyone who applauded. We don't applaud here. This isn't a theater …

29 January 1970

Many aspects of public life have what we might see as 'theatrical' qualities. Political events are often described as 'dramatic' or 'heightened' when they seem to mirror dramaturgical or narrative patterns. The actions of individuals in public life are frequently interpreted as though revelatory of their 'inner' thoughts or motivations. More foundationally, ceremonies, protests and theatrical 'actions' are understood to be making visible to the spectator concepts which may otherwise be abstract or imaginary, such as 'nation', or 'empire', or 'monarchy' or 'freedom'. And of course, the fates of rulers and those who oppose them can be read as exemplary, in the same way as the fictional destiny of a dramatic hero can 'teach' the ordinary spectator how to act. This sense of a theatrical parallel is enhanced by the use of shared vocabularies and grammars of expression such as costumes, rituals or repertoires of actions. In short, it is easy to see the likeness. But, as I will suggest in this chapter, this is not always enough. For these public performances are not fictions, nor are they imitations of actions taking place elsewhere. They are both presentation and execution; the performance of the event, and the fact of the event simultaneously.

Legal systems in particular lend themselves very readily to theatrical comparisons: there are clear rituals and routines of behaviour; roles and relationships are communicated through performance, costume and forms of speech. Again, I will suggest that these shared vocabularies, while certainly revealing strategic similarities, cannot necessarily account for their differences. In sociologist Erving Goffman's famous phrase, '[a]ll the world is not, of course, a stage, but the crucial ways in which it isn't are not easy to specify' (Goffman 1959: 78). A judge may indeed be wearing a costume. But their judgement carries material force. What lends authority to the performance of the law? In this chapter, I will investigate aspects of the 'theatricality' of law, using ideas of the theatre, and a 'theatrical' trial, to explore how thinking through theatre can illuminate our understanding of both.

The Trial of the Chicago Eight

This chapter will focus on the Trial of the Chicago Eight, which began in the autumn of 1969 and concluded in spring of 1970. These were turbulent times in the United States, as struggles for civil rights, gender and sexual equality saw mass actions and resistance taken to the streets. Youth protest, in particular against the draft and the ongoing war in Vietnam, was giving political focus to the so-called 'counterculture'. Diverse groups, including the Vietnam Veterans Against The War, socialist student organizations, the Black Panther Party, socially engaged theatre collectives such as the Living Theater and the Diggers, and the activist-prankster 'Yippies' were all staging multiple resistant actions.

In August 1968, on the occasion of the Democratic Party National Convention in Chicago, several thousand youth and anti-war activists had gathered together to hold a huge Festival of Life, featuring music, theatre performances, marches, demonstrations and protests. Participants included Yippies, anti-war protestors, student and peace protestors, and many celebrity supporters, such as the radical poet Allen Ginsberg, French playwright Jean Genet and protest singer Phil Ochs. They were met with hostility from the mayor, Richard Daley, who mobilized over 20,000 police and National Guardsmen, and refused to grant permits for protestors to gather, to march and to sleep overnight in Lincoln Park. Over the course of five days and nights, there were attempts on the part of protestors to access various venues, to which the police responded with increasing levels of violence, including the tear-gassing of the crowd.

Following these events, a federal grand jury was convened in September to consider potential criminal charges arising from the public disorder in Chicago. Under a new anti-riot act, passed by Congress in April 1968 to prohibit the crossing of state lines with intent to incite riot, eight of the perceived 'leaders' of the disparate protest groups were indicted on charges of conspiracy. The Trial of the Chicago Eight (also referred to as the Chicago Conspiracy Trial) began on 24 September 1969 and ran until February 1970. The defendants were David Dellinger, leader of MOBE (National Mobilisation Committee to End the War in Vietnam), Tom Hayden and Rennie Davis of SDS (Students for a Democratic Society), academics Lee Weiner and John Froines, Yippie activists Abbie Hoffman and Jerry Rubin, and, as a late addition to the indictment, Bobby Seale of the Black Panther Party. Known colloquially as 'the Panthers', this organization was formed in the autumn of 1966 as the Black Panther Party for Self-Defence, with the aim of resisting perceived police oppression of Black communities, and also to run community programmes such as the provision of school meals for children. The trial was heard before US District Court Judge Julius Hoffman. The prosecutors were Thomas Foran and Richard Schultz. For the defence, Charles Garry of San Francisco was, initially, the lead attorney, but he had to withdraw for reasons of ill-health and was replaced by William Kunstler and Leonard Weinglass. This substitution was to become crucial in the arguments that arose on the subject of Bobby Seale's defence.

This trial is particularly remembered for its engagement with theatricality. The participation in particular of Yippie activists Abbie Hoffman and Jerry Rubin, already renowned within the counterculture for acts of public theatre such as 'levitating' the Pentagon in 1967 in protest against the Vietnam War, and interrupting the activities of the New York Stock Exchange by throwing dollar bills onto the trading floor, meant that contemporary commentators were already primed to discuss the trial in terms of theatrical presentation and challenge. At several points in the trial transcript itself, the proceedings were described as 'good theater' by the defendants, to the recurring bafflement of Judge Hoffman. The presence of star witnesses such as Allen Ginsberg, folk singer Judy Collins, Phil Ochs and experimental writer William Burroughs (later to play Judge Hoffman himself in 1970 in a verbatim staging of the trial at the Open Space Theatre in London) exacerbated the feeling of there being simply two cultures, speaking to each other across a gulf of generational and political misunderstanding, and deploying their respective theatrical performances in the service of completely different ends. As commentator Joseph Sander noted at the time: 'The impossible circumstance in the present case of conspiracy ... is that both sides are, by this time, incapable of understanding each other' (Sander 1969: 5). This was not entirely accidental: Abbie Hoffmann, in testimony on 29 December 1969, said of the origins of the 'Yippie' name that his wife Anita had commented: 'although "Yippie" would be understood by our generation ... straight newspapers like the New York Times and the U.S. Government and the courts and everything wouldn't take it seriously unless it had a kind of formal name, so she came up with the name of the "Youth International Party." She said that we could play a lot of jokes on the concept of party because everybody would think that we were this huge international conspiracy, but that in actuality we were a party that you had fun at' (Levine et al. 1970: 144–5).

It is no surprise that the Yippies, in particular, Rubin and Hoffman, saw the trial as an opportune moment to stage their brand of spectacular resistance, for, while consciously utilizing vocabularies of symbol, myth and representation, their resistant theatrical tactics were also deployed as exercises in experience. Abbie Hoffman commented, 'action is the only reality; not only reality but morality as well ... a subjective experience' (1989: 3). This encapsulates the radical perspective of their resistant programme: the proposal that subjectivity is the only reality and is being produced by power; therefore, the only way to resist is to alter the way in which life is experienced. Furthermore, the theatricality of power should be explicitly conceived as materially constitutive of power and central to its execution. In this way, for the Yippies, the theatricality of power in America was not to be critiqued simply as 'set-dressing', or 'illusion' superimposed onto a material 'real'. It was as an actual as well as a symbolic exchange. The theatricality of resistance, both in the street and, as I shall explore, in the courtroom, was activated as part of a conscious critique of the theatricality of power. As Hoffman wrote: 'Guerrilla theatre is only a transitional step in the development of total life actors' (1989: 81). Part of the purpose of theatrical resistance was to expose the ways in which authorities maintained control of existing society through theatricalization itself.

Thus, the defendants were clear from the outset that they viewed the trial as a show trial, but where earlier 'political' trials had for the most part followed legal protocols, these defendants decided to resist the traditional imperatives: as Tom Hayden said 'we can't resist illegitimate authority in the street only to bow politely before it in the courtroom' (Barkan 1977: 325). They responded to questions in ways that baffled the judge, Abbie Hoffman claiming for example to live in a place he called 'Woodstock Nation' and giving it as his address. They opened their post at the defence table, they had birthday cake delivered, saluted the judge with clenched fists, and in many other ways would not obey the behavioural protocols of the court room. Although Tom Hayden wrote later that as a proportion of their activities in the court room these instances of guerrilla theatre only formed a fraction, it was the element widely reported in the media, and created an atmosphere of disruption to the formal performance of institutional theatricality (Barkan 1977: 325). As Joseph Sander wrote: 'this incredible conspiracy trial [is] a trial *of* the law, and not a trial, in the ordinary sense, *by* the law' (Sander 1969: 6). So, how can this highly theatricalized trial help us to investigate how the theatre thinks through law? To approach this question, I will argue that we need to explore not just the theatrical 'face' of the court – what it looks like – but also what it masks.

Thinking Through Theatre/Thinking Theatre Through

There have been several studies made of the theatricality of courtroom practice. The trustworthiness (or not) of a person giving evidence in the witness box for example, and the plausibility (or not) of the account of events that they are giving, can be seen, in a sense, to be being assessed by judge or jury in the same way that an actor's performance might be assessed: Is this person credible? Are they believable? Does their account ring true?

Furthermore, in terms of judicial 'theatre', Peter Goodrich, writing of the Royal Courts of Justice in London, noted: 'Consider the iconic order of licit representation as it is to be found in the architectural organisation of a court, in the symbolics of its physical places, in the aura of its furniture … in its modes of dress and of address, and finally in its terms, its moment of appearance and disappearance, of sitting and of dissolution.' All of these, he argues, exist to create the space of law, that will 'allow the judge to speak in the mask of the Other, to speak innocently as a mouth of the law' (Goodrich 1990: 222). The forms of dress, the modes of speech, the performance of status and respect, the ways in which the judge is addressed as the law, or the court itself ('the court, the bench, your honour, your worship, your lordship') means that when the judge sits, 'it is the Law which sits down' (Goodrich 1990: 224). These accepted forms of behaviour, in other words, imbue the process with dignity and authority; they make up the 'face' of the legal process itself, and it is through these signs and signifiers that the public recognize its legitimacy.

The process of law would also seem to rely on what I have argued elsewhere (Nield 2006) can be seen as the structural, or foundational, aspects of theatricality: a set of relationships between modes of presence, representation and spectatorship which, together, produce an effective mode of 'appearance' in public life. The doubling of presence and representation – as an explicitly theatrical model – provides a way of thinking about how we 'appear' before the institutions of the state, and how the exchanges which take place there are structurally determined by these relationships. In this example, a person accused must 'appear' before the Court. They must, under most circumstances, be 'present' to hear the case against them. They must be 'represented' appropriately (by Counsel, or by themselves) in order to be 'recognized' by the Court. The Court can decide what it will or will not 'see' according to the rules and protocols of the judicial process: it is not uncommon for a jury to be instructed to 'disregard' an intervention, or piece of evidence – literally, to 'un-see' something which they have, in actuality, seen. It is the court record which 'shows' what happened. And justice itself, of course, is something which must be 'seen' to be done.

Overall, the parallels between the performance of law, and the structures and practices of the theatre, would seem to be very clear. Nevertheless, there is, I think, a key difference which remains, and it is this: the outcome of a legal process produces an 'extra' truth effect, in that it is capable of determining, ultimately, what *is* true, not just what *seems* true. Alan Read, in his 2016 study of theatre and law, invoked J. L. Austin's (1962) work on language acts and performativity in relation to court process, particularly a category of speech act which is consequential, in the sense that it causes something further to occur (Read 2016: 15). When a person is 'found' to be guilty, they become guilty, and the court has the right to impose punishment for that guilt. When a person is 'found' to be innocent, they become innocent, and may leave without a stain on their character.

But the question remains, how is this actually working? For all this is still, as Peter Goodrich calls it, 'an aura or display of power that simultaneously hides the logic of its practice' (Goodrich 1990: 227). How can thinking through the theatre of law's process help us identify not just what it looks like, but how it works? How can it help us identify what actually invests the theatricality of the court with its power? I should at this point make clear that the ability of the court to sustain its authority is an immensely important part of the maintenance of law. Many aspects of the Trial of the Chicago Eight, as we will see, were critiqued at the time, but the 'face' of dignity which Judge Hoffman sought so hard to preserve is the same 'face' of dignity which sustains confidence in judicial processes as a whole. This does not mean, however, that we cannot use the instance of the Trial of the Chicago Eight to unpick some of the theatrical elements at work in these processes.

I'm going to focus on two of the most notorious moments of this already highly theatrical trial, drawing additionally on some key proposals on the idea of state violence from the early-twentieth-century German philosopher Walter Benjamin, to see if the differences between them can illuminate these questions. On the surface, these moments contain many similarities: both challenged the 'face' of the court; both led to moments of spectacle; both dealt with the violence which underpins the legal process. Yet, effectively, they contain two distinct theatrical modes. The first, in which Abbie Hoffman and Jerry Rubin wore disrespectful clothing, was playful, imitative, carnivalesque, but reaped a serious consequence, as the two were punished by charges of contempt of court. The other – the shackling and gagging of Bobby Seale in open court – was not playful at all but was technically a legal act of violent restraint on the part of the judge. The first event undermined the court's right to sustain its own theatricality by exposing its 'face', as the defendants produced, effectively, a site-specific performance about the superficial theatricality of justice. But 'theatre' spaces are not neutral: they cause the things that appear within them to read in particular ways, to take on symbolic functions, and speak in heightened modes, and once these appear, the court cannot control their meanings. For these reasons, the second event, I will propose, caused a more foundational rupture in the theatrical coherence of the court process, breaking apart the elements of theatrical representation, by, literally, making a spectacle out of the violence which lies beneath. The consequences here were for the efficacy of legal theatricality itself, as Justice's blindfold revealed itself as a mask.

Imitating the Law

On 6 February 1970, Abbie Hoffman and Jerry Rubin arrived at the courtroom dressed in fake judicial robes. This was not their first time wearing costume to formal public processes: appearing before HUAC (House Un-American Activities Committee) in 1968, Rubin dressed as 'a one-man international revolution, a walking conspiracy', wearing among other things 'a Black Panther beret … a Mexican bandolier, with live 303 British Infield bullets around my chest, black Viet Kong pyjamas' (Rubin 1970: 202–3). In the courtroom, as they reached the defendant's table, they removed the robes, threw them to the floor, and stamped on them. Unbeknownst to Rubin, Abbie Hoffman was wearing a Chicago police shirt under his robe. Tom Hayden observed: 'even I had to applaud their sense of theater' (Hayden et al. 2008: 250).

It is clear that such a tactic was deliberately intended to annoy and anger Judge Hoffman, who demonstrated huge anxieties about his own status, the status of the court and the constant undermining behaviour of the defendants. As Joseph Sander observed of him: 'he is on eternal guard against being made a fool of ... it is [much more] likely that his deeper concerns lie with decorum, with the traditional obsequies of those before the bench that defined a sense of dignity in the 19th Century, and sustain the illusion for men like Hoffman to this day' (Sander 1969: 4). As I mentioned earlier, there have been a number of treatments of the Trial of the Chicago Eight, many of which take aspects of its theatricality as a central focus. Legal scholar Pnina Lahav developed a detailed analysis, reading the proceedings through the theory of theatre director Peter Brook (Lahav 2004). Her proposal circulates around seeing a conflict between the deadly theatricality of court process – verbal, conventional, conservative – and the rough theatricality of Yippie and protest performance – lively, spontaneous, anarchic, spectacular. In terms of this opposition of the 'deadly' and the 'rough', it is clear that any institution dependent on efficacious theatricality is going to be resistant to, and fearful of, alternative modes of theatricality that undermine it. As well as the challenge to the seriousness of the theatricality deployed by power, there are, historically, strong reasons why elites and hierarchies have protected access to their costumes and emblems. At a time before photography or the internet, people would not necessarily know their senior officers or rulers by sight, and the use of insignia or particular fabrics or colours (as in sixteenth-century sumptuary restrictions) might determine whose word was to be obeyed, whether in a courtroom or on a battlefield. There is a paradox created in a counter-performance such as the robe wearing, which does, of course, cause the judge's robes too to appear as a costume, and does make the legal process evident as a performative practice – after all, it is one. And this revelation, evidently, did threaten the authority of Hoffman's court: ultimately, the behaviour of the defendants caused them – and also, in fact, their defence team of William Kunstler and Leonard Weinglass – to be given long sentences for contempt of court (although these were later overturned). The Michigan Law Review noted: 'criminal contempt proceedings ... are instituted primarily for the purpose of vindicating the dignity and authority of the court' (1551), against forms of behaviour which undermine it.

Nevertheless, the point still stands that the ability of a court to sustain its authority is not entirely contained in its theatrical strategies and does not depend solely on its capacity to maintain a monopoly on their deployment. Nor do I think the whole issue is contained in a conflict between two opposing modes of theatricality. Evidently, the performance staged by Jerry Rubin and Abbie Hoffman fractured the theatre of law to a certain extent. But arguably, what they made was exactly that – a performance. When Abbie Hoffman took off his judge's robe to reveal the Chicago police uniform, effectively he made a piece of theatre about the material violence that underpins the rule of law and the legitimacy of the state. It was disrespectful, it showed contempt, it gestured rudely in the face of the court; it caused the court to 'lose face'. In short, it made a powerful theatrical image of the monopoly of violence which is hidden under that face. But it did not account for that violence, nor did it bring that violence into the courtroom. For that, we must turn to the gagging of Bobby Seale.

Unmasking the Law

Bobby Seale, the eighth member of the 'conspiracy', was a key member and co-founder of the Black Panther Party. He was a late addition to the Chicago indictment, and his inclusion was widely regarded by supporters of the Eight as an attempt to 'railroad' him. The other defendants made clear they had not all met him (or for that matter all met each other) before the trial. Although acting in solidarity with the broad countercultural focus of the other defendants, the struggles of the Black Panther Party were focused particularly around civil rights issues arising for the Black community, and, as Joseph Sander summarized: 'it [is] very clear to everyone who is either young, a part of the movement, or Black, that Bobby Seale's "blackness" is the only reason he was in court' (Sander 1969: 5).

Seale had requested that he be represented by his attorney of choice, Charles R Garry, who was indisposed through ill-health. Judge Hoffmann therefore assigned William Kunstler, the lead defence attorney for the other defendants to act in Seale's defence. Both Seale and Kunstler made it clear that this was not an acceptable arrangement, and that therefore as far as they were concerned, Seale was without representation. Bobby Seale repeatedly interrupted the process of the court – for example, whenever Kunstler was called on to speak for him, or he was mentioned in testimony – in order to stage his own representation of himself. The judge, not 'recognising' this, repeatedly silenced him, and, eventually, on 29 October 1969, ordered the court ushers to bind Seale to his chair, and gag him.

This shocking decision was based in a legal ruling made in 1969 in another trial, Allen vs. Illinois (Epstein 1972: 256) which said that a defendant should be present in court in order to hear the case against them even if they were repeatedly disruptive, and the judge must therefore ensure their presence, even if it meant their being shackled and gagged. Bobby Seale details at length the treatment he received over three days in his autobiography, *Seize the Time* (1970). Of this first occasion, he notes:

> I told them 'I demand my constitutional rights'. I even banged on the table while I was talking. ... They recessed the court, then came back and Hoffman said, 'Mr Seale, are you going to disrupt this court any more?' ... Then Hoffman told the marshals, 'Take the defendant and appropriately deal with him.' ... They took me back to the lock-up right outside the courtroom. They got some tape and put it across my mouth. They handcuffed my hands down close to the legs of a metal folding chair and put the irons on my legs. They looped the chain through one of the rods running across the front of the folding part of the chair ... and clasped it to my right leg. The jury came back in, and Judge Hoffman says some kind of crazy crap. 'Disregard this and disregard that.' Some tears started rolling down one of the juror's cheeks. (Seale 1970: 376)

The other defendants tried to intervene, as Tom Hayden recorded:

> All of us jumped up. Dave Dellinger tried to put himself between the marshals and Bobby, getting knocked aside. Jerry Rubin got punched in the face as he yelled 'they're kicking him in the balls.' I tried to get the judge's attention: 'Your Honor, all he wants is to be legally represented, not be a slave here.' As each of us would speak or move, the prosecutors would excitedly declare, 'Let the record show', and then describe our behavior for future contempt citations. (Hayden et al. 2008: 222)

Needless to say, the image of Bobby Seale gagged and chained to a chair was extremely shocking: there were immediate outbursts in the court and the press, and eventually Bobby Seale's part in the trial was declared a mistrial, and the process continued with the remaining seven defendants.

The 'Face' and the 'Mask'

Unlike the carnivalesque disruption of the robe wearing, this was not an intentionally disruptive moment, in the sense of protestors deliberately undermining court process with diversionary theatricality. It was a legal act, and one intended to sustain the legal/ theatrical conditions necessary for Bobby Seale's 'appearance' in the process: a defendant must be present in order to hear what is said about them, and in order to be properly represented. Yet, as Abbie Hoffman himself observed, it was the most important image to emerge from the trial process, and one which, I will argue, disrupted the 'face' of the court and its theatricality more profoundly than the performative carnival of the Yippie protest. So, what was revealed in the image of Bobby Seale shackled and bound? And what can this tell us about the 'face' and the 'mask' of the law?

To begin to address this question, we must return to the question of legitimacy: what power lies beneath the theatre of law, which gives it force and right to act. To open up this question, I will briefly turn to the work of the early-twentieth-century German philosopher Walter Benjamin, and his essay 'On the Critique of Violence' (1921). Here, Benjamin outlines a theory of the law's essential relationship to violence. He proposes that rather than being a simple moral question, in which violence is essentially justified by the ends to which it is directed, the true relationship of violence to law is of whether its deployment is sanctioned or unsanctioned. He identifies two kinds of sanctioned violence: that which is 'law-establishing', and that which is 'law-upholding'. Law-establishing violence would underpin, for example, the formation of a state, a system of government or a legal apparatus. As Benjamin points out, it can literally 'lay down the law' (Benjamin: 9). Law-upholding violence then enables the continued existence of those structures, and would include carceral practices and legal processes whose execution, while not in any particular instance demanding the performance of violent acts, remains underpinned by their threat, and the capacity of the law to access sanctioned violence should it require to so do. I think there are two key points to draw out here: first of all, there is the question of the function of violence in the formation of systems of power and their maintenance, which would include, naturally, any legal system. Secondly, and arising from this, there is the question of why states, powers and legal structures respond so aggressively to outbreaks of unsanctioned violence – riots, civil disorder and so on.

It is evident that many of the aspects of the Trial of the Chicago Eight can be understood as struggles over the delegitimation of unsanctioned violence. For if, as Benjamin proposes, the underpinning of the authority of any particular system of power is its capacity to marshal violence, then unsanctioned violence is not simply a challenge to that system's performance of authority but is also potentially a rival law-establishing practice that could 'make possible', in the familiar phrase, 'another world'. By definition, violence outside the legal system threatens the law because it exists outside the law, which is why the state, for Benjamin, insists on holding a monopoly on legitimate violence. In many ways, the Trial of the Chicago Eight was about many aspects of public theatricality and its limits: the performance of justice and resistant actions; the articulation of legitimacy through a series of theatrical and representative practices; the idea of the public 'face' of the court, understood as both dignity, decorum and respect, and also as a form of behaviour masking or disguising the actual relations of power and right. It was also about aspects of the state's management of violence, from the police actions to control and limit the original events in Chicago, to the violence perpetrated within the legal process. So, what happened in Judge Hoffman's courtroom, when the law's foundational violence entered the theatrical space of the court as spectacle?

Theatricalizing Violence: What Appears Beneath

I'm going to start here, again, with Benjamin, who, speaking of the presence of violence under any legal contract, notes: 'Violence may not, as law-establishing, be directly present therein, but it will be represented therein to the extent to which the power guaranteeing the legal contract is itself of violent origin' (1921:14). In other words, while it is appropriate – indeed necessary – for violence to be *represented* in the theatrical appearance of justice (one thinks here of the sword carried by Justice herself), it may not be directly *present*. I am of course reading Benjamin's meaning in a particular way – that his 'may not' is an injunction, rather than a proposal – in order to make clear what I think is the rupture in theatrical structure that is taking place here. Something enters the theatrical space of the court which should only be represented – symbolized – there. The courtroom, operating as a theatrical space – one in which speech acts, emblems and costumes speak both as themselves and as metaphors for Law, Justice, Truth – deploys its capacity to render symbolic force to events that take place within it. When Judge Hoffman ordered Bobby Seale to be bound and gagged, he could not help but create a theatrical image of *in*justice. For Bobby Seale was being doubly silenced. He was silenced in his own person: gagged in order to stop him interjecting and disrupting the process of the court; restrained, Judge Hoffman argued, in order to preserve the (theatrical) conditions of his appearance, understood as the particular combination of presence and representation which must be preserved in order for a person to 'appear' before the court. But before this, he was silenced in his ability to speak before the court: by being forbidden to choose his own representative, or to represent himself, he was not able to be 'heard' or 'seen' by the court in the appropriate ways. 'I demand my constitutional rights', he said, repeatedly, through the gag; to be seen as, to be recognized as, a person with rights; a person able to be recognized by the mechanism of the law.

Furthermore, the revelation of the violence that Benjamin tells us is just underneath the performative tropes of the state, made visible as spectacularized image Bobby Seale's racialized body. Seale, as a Black man, was already widely perceived to have received differential treatment in the process of the trial: his own autobiography details the conditions of his detention and transportation to Chicago; the anti-riot laws under which all of the defendants had been indicted was originally shaped to prevent the Panthers from organizing across state lines. It goes without saying that when Judge Hoffman ordered Bobby Seale to be bound and gagged, he produced an appalling image, disturbing enough in its immediate brutality, but doubly charged in its reproduction of historical images of racist oppression, torture and enslavement.

Needless to say, Hoffman responded angrily to accusations of racist motivation on his part, claiming that it was Seale's own actions which had triggered the sanction, and that any defendant would have been dealt with in such a way had similar circumstances arisen. But justice, by admitting foundational violence into the space, was not operating in its legitimate theatrical register, and just as her sword had revealed itself to have real power and foundation, so Justice's blindfold, meant to signify fair treatment for all, had revealed itself to be no more than a mask.

As Benjamin suggests, the legitimating mechanism which enables law to be enacted (rather than just performed) is based on the monopoly of law-establishing and law-upholding violence sustained by its authorizing power. This is what was being critiqued in Abbie Hoffman and Jerry Rubin's piece of witty and carnivalesque counter-theatre. But the gagging of Bobby Seale brought that violence into the Chicago courtroom as spectacle. Although technically a legal act, it revealed the face of the court as one which regulates and manages violence on behalf of the state. This right to violence is meant to be translated, in this arena, into the acceptable theatricality of justice, in the forms of symbol and emblem, robes, wigs, scales, and the mutual enactment of 'respect' for the court and justice system. But the 'face' of the court, in this instance, could not sustain itself through the 'de-facing' of Bobby Seale. It breached the structure of its own theatrical logic, allowing its right to actual violence, with all that implies, to appear within what is meant to function only as a symbolic landscape. By allowing the performance of violence into the space where only its mask should appear, this most theatrical of trials made visible the foundational theatrical structures of the law itself.

Performance Details

United States of America, Plaintiff, vs. David T. Dellinger, Rennard C. Davis, Thomas E. Hayden, Abbott H. Hoffman, Jerry C. Rubin, Lee Weiner, John R. Froines and Bobby G. Seale, Defendants. No. 69 Crim. 180. Entitled cause before the Hon. Julius J. Hoffman and a Jury, commencing on the 26th day of September, A.D. 1969, at the hour of 10.00 o'clock am.

Present: Hon. Thomas A. Foran, United States Attorney; Mr Richard G. Schultz, Asst. United States Attorney; Mr William Kunstler and Mr Leonard I. Weinglass on behalf of the defendants.

Judge Julius Hoffman: Judge, US District Court for the Northern District of Illinois

Defendants:

Rennie Davis: community organizer and member of Students for a Democratic Society.

David Dellinger: pacifist, socialist, co-founder of *Liberation* magazine.

John Froines: chemistry professor at Goddard College, Vermont.

Tom Hayden: SDS activist and anti-war protestor.

Abbie Hoffman: political activist and theatrical prankster; Yippie.

Jerry Rubin: Yippie, anti-war protestor, counterculture activist.

Bobby Seale: co-founder, Black Panther Party for Self-Defence.

Lee Weiner: PhD student and teaching assistant, Northwestern University.

Witnesses:

William Burroughs: writer and visual artist; pioneer of postmodernism and Beat literature.

Judy Collins: singer-songwriter and social activist.

Allen Ginsberg: leading Beat poet and philosopher; author of 'Howl'.

Phil Ochs: protest singer and activist.

Further Reading

For further details of the Trial, see the defendants' own autobiographies, including Seale (1970), Rubin (1970), Hoffman (1980) and Hayden (1970). Full reports were written contemporaneously by Epstein (1972) and several versions of the transcript were also published, which would repay a close reading: see Burgess and Marowitz (1970) and Levine, McNamee and Greenberg (1970). For further thoughts on the relationship between theatre and law, see Stone Peters (2005), Read (2016), Goodrich (1990) and Lahav (2004).

References

Antonio, Robert (1972), 'The Processual Dimension of Degradation Ceremonies: The Chicago Conspiracy Trial: Success or Failure', *The British Journal of Sociology* 23 (3): 287–97.

Austin, J. L. ([1962] 1975), *How to do Things with Words,* Oxford and New York: Oxford University Press.

Barkan, Steven E. (1977), 'Political Trials and the "Pro Se" Defendant in the Adversary System', *Social Problems* 24 (3): 324–36.

Benjamin, Walter ([1921] 2008), 'On the Critique of Violence', in Walter Benjamin, *One-Way Street and Other Writings*, trans. J. A. Underwood, 1–28, London: Penguin.

Burgess, John, and Charles Marowitz (1970), *The Chicago Conspiracy* (based on a script by Jonathan Cross) presented at the Open Space Theatre, 24 August.

Epstein, Jason (1972), *The Great Conspiracy Trial (An Essay on Law, Liberty and the Constitution)*, New York: Random House.

Goffman, Erving ([1959] 1990), *The Presentation of Self in Everyday Life*, London: Penguin.

Goodrich, Peter (1990), *Languages of Law: From Logics of Memory to Nomadic Masks*, London: Weidenfeld and Nicolson.

Hayden, Tom (1970), *Trial*, London: Jonathan Cape.

Hayden, Tom, Ron Sossi and Frank Condon (2008), *Voices of the Chicago Eight: A Generation on Trial*, San Francisco: City Lights Books.

Hoffman, Abbie (1980), *The Autobiography of Abbie Hoffman*, New York and London: Four Walls Eight Windows.

Hoffman, Abbie (1989), 'Revolution for the Hell of It', in Abbie Hoffman, *The Best of Abbie Hoffman*, 3–95, New York: Four Walls Eight Windows.

'Invoking Summary Criminal Contempt Procedures: Use or Abuse? United States vs. Dellinger: The "Chicago Seven" Contempts' (1971), *Michigan Law Review* 69 (8): 1549–75.

Lahav, Pnina (2004), 'Theater in the Courtroom: The Chicago Conspiracy trial', *Law and Literature* 16 (3): 381–474.

Levine, Mark L., George McNamee and Daniel Greenberg (1970), *The Tales of Hoffman: Edited from the Official Transcript*, London, Toronto and New York: Bantam.

Nield, Sophie (2006), 'On the Border as Theatrical Space: Appearance, Dis-location and the Production of the Refugee', in Joe Kelleher and Nicholas Ridout (eds), *Contemporary Theatres in Europe*, 61–72, London: Routledge.

Read, Alan (2016), *Theatre & Law*, Basingstoke: Palgrave Macmillan.

Rubin, Jerry (1970), *Do It! Scenarios of the Revolution*, New York: Simon and Schuster.

Sander, Joseph (1969), 'Sitting in Judgement in Chicago', *The North American Review* 254 (4): 2–6.

Seale, Bobby (1970), *Seize the Time: The Story of the Black Panther Party*, London: Arrow Books.

Stone Peters, Julie (2005), 'Law, Literature, and the Vanishing Real: On the Future of an Interdisciplinary Illusion', *PMLA* 120 (2): 442–53.

Zellick, Graham (1980), 'The Criminal Trial and the Disruptive Defendant. Part One', *The Modern Law Review* 43 (2): 121–35.

21 How Does Theatre Think Through Theatricality?

ADRIAN KEAR

Staging the Question

If the question this chapter examines seems a little odd, or even deliberately obtuse, that's perhaps because its terms appear to mean the same thing. Surely theatre and theatricality are coterminous, coextensive and co-dependent? Doesn't the idea of 'theatricality' rely upon the theatre to provide its critical context and material ground, relating back to the 'theatrical matter' of dramatic performance for its meaning and explanatory purchase? When 'theatricality' is invoked as a description of a behaviour, activity, quality or property isn't it to account for a sense of 'stagey-ness' – a certain 'mode of excess' (Brooks 1976: ix) – which appears deliberate, calculated and self-knowingly 'over the top'? In other words, isn't 'theatricality' just the hyperbolic extension of the 'theatrical' – the world of pretence, exaggeration and fakery associated with the artifice and acting of 'the stage'?

The *Oxford English Dictionary* certainly follows this trajectory in defining 'theatricality' as 'the quality or character of being theatrical' while regarding the 'theatrical' simply as 'connected to the theatre or stage'. This 'cluster of concepts', as the theatre historian Tracy C. Davis casts them (2003: 127), therefore appears to rely upon theatre as its foundational term. While the dictionary definitions appear to move seamlessly from theatre, to the theatrical, to theatricality as an expanding field of terms, Davis is at pains to demonstrate that their historical emergence indicates that they mean rather different things. In an important and richly detailed analysis, she argues that the terms should be prised apart in order to account for a 'crucial distinction between *the theatrical* and *theatricality*' (128); a distinction which hinges not on staging or intention but on spectatorship and reception. Put simply, Davis argues the spectator '*creates theatricality*' through the activity of looking (141); through the *theatricalization*, so to speak, of what they see as if it were a scene appearing before them, for them to see.

Before continuing with Davis's argument, and elaborating its context, it is worth pausing to acknowledge the introduction of my own term to this 'cluster of concepts': *theatricalization*. By this, I mean the process of turning people and actions into figures within a scene, whether or not they regard themselves as on display, performing or otherwise being there to be seen. Theatricalization operates through the framing or reframing of material as 'theatrical' irrespective of its being explicitly staged as such, constituting a 'seeing as' mode of perception which produces 'theatricality' as its effect. As such, theatricalization serves as a key dynamic of power; a structure of representation rendering observable, knowable and controllable that which otherwise is simply present. It turns presence into representation, into a formalized configuration of relations of power, knowledge and visibility. It is, in other words, a political and aesthetic apparatus which produces the idea of otherness and situates the spectator as its presumed subject.

Accordingly, to examine the relationship between theatricality and theatricalization is to open up a *political* question. It is to question the politics of representation, and to see theatricality as primarily a political operation. But what does any of this have to do with *theatre*? What is the relationship between theatre and theatricality when thought of as a question of politics? How is theatre implicated in the production of otherness? What are the grounds – and the limits – of its political claim? This chapter seeks to investigate these questions directly, arguing that theatre operates as a space in which the process of theatricalization and the production of theatricality can be explicated and challenged, as well as reproduced; as the material site in which the limits of theatricality are investigated and exposed.

The argument forwarded here thereby seeks to reverse – or at least to question – the logic of extension implied by the *Oxford English Dictionary* definition of theatricality as emanating from theatre and the theatrical. It will seek to demonstrate, rather, the ways in which the institution of theatre emerged as a site in which to limit and contain generalized theatricality, and might be seen to provide a way of knowing and showing the political effects of the aesthetic framing and construction of 'otherness'. So, the question isn't really 'chicken and egg' – 'which came first, theatre or theatricality?' – but rather, one of critical and political enquiry: 'how does theatre frame, expose and delimit theatricality?'; 'how does theatre think through the problem of theatricality, as well as think through theatricality's own logic of alterity?'.

Such a shift in emphasis reflects an interdisciplinary commitment to interrogating performance as both a specific cultural *practice* (call it 'theatre', in this instance), and an important social *process* (here characterized as 'theatricalization'). In this vein, cultural archaeologist Yann-Pierre Montelle argues that 'theatricality' should be regarded primarily as the social process governing the construction of the gaze and the production of otherness, 'as the paradigm out of which the institution of the theatre emerged' (2009: 2). Theatre, for Montelle, operates as the site of the formalization of theatricality, providing a structured and sanctioned space for its practice and regulation through the development of specific codes and conventions. He charts a 'direct line of interrelated "landmarks" between the cave and the *theatron*', which link the emergence of the theatre as 'seeing place' in fifth-century-BC Athens to predecessor practices of visual, vocal and embodied display and performance 'in the deep caves of the Upper Palaeolithic, c. 30,000 years ago' (3). Theatre, then, provides a way of knowing and regulating the modes of seeing and showing attendant on the production of theatricality as a form of appearing to one another. By interrelating the examination of cultural practices/aesthetic forms and social processes/political formations, the study of performance seeks to ask fundamental questions about theatre and theatricality as modes of assembly, association and activity; and as core constituents of humans being together socially.

For the philosopher Samuel Weber, 'theatre and theatricality emerge as names for an alternative' way of knowing and understanding human beings and social behaviours to the Western conceptual tradition of thinking based on 'a certain notion of identity, reflexivity and subjectivity' (2004: 2). He suggests that theatre emerges as a practice which troubles the security of ontological categories and the distinctive boundaries of self and other, dislocating and disorienting 'the Western dream of self-identity' by always appearing only to disappear and reappear somewhere else, often *as* something else. Theatre as such therefore needs to be thought of not only as a place and a taking place – an event explicitly 'staged' in a cave or *theatron* and directed towards assembled spectators – but as a *medium* whose slipperiness and irreducibility troubles conceptual clarity and any uniform definition of reality. Weber suggests that theatrical thinking 'haunts and taunts' the philosophical project of rendering transparent by offering a kind of dirty materialist resistance to its logic (7). It is not surprising then that Plato sought to condemn and ostracize theatre from the domain of knowledge, characterizing theatricality as an artificially constructed chimera designed to hold its spectators in thrall through a fixed relation of domination, rather than as an investigative space designed to enable their thinking and self-realization. Platonic *anti-theatricality* seeks not only to reduce theatre to a primarily mimetic activity – a barely credible game of play and imitation – but to tie theatre and theatricality together in order to constrain their operation. For Weber, theatre as medium will always seek to elude and escape this tethering, refusing to be fixed either ontologically (as a form or place) or ideologically (as a specific spectatorial relation or way of seeing). Yet, what the cultural historian Jonas Barish famously called 'the anti-theatrical prejudice' – 'the ancient distrust of the stage' as duplicitous and deforming (1981: 3) – continues to over-determine our thinking about theatre and performance.

In many ways, common-sense notions of theatricality as either frivolous fakery or dangerous excessiveness rely upon this tradition of diminishing the theatre's claim to philosophical and political seriousness, and theatre itself has often been inclined to incorporate anti-theatricality into its aesthetic codes and historical conventions. Consider, for example, how the emergence of naturalism and realism in the theatre of the late-nineteenth century was predicated on the repudiation of the overtly 'theatrical' in order to appear authentically 'real', seeking in the process to produce an anti-theatrical theatre that attempted to 'render the theatrical medium absolutely transparent' and banish the stain of theatricality from the theatre as such (Williams 2001: 285). Contrastingly, in the Renaissance, the reanimation of the theatre as a significant cultural form and social practice was connected to a renewed understanding of theatricality as 'an organizing principle for society'. As theatre historian Thomas Postlewait has argued, playwrights 'often used the theatre to attack the theatrical' and to expose the 'inherent theatricality' of the 'performance of power' through critically redirecting and creatively reimagining the power of performance (2003: 100–16). In this context, the *theatrum mundi* metaphor appears as much material as it is metaphorical: if 'All the world's a stage', then the theatre seeks to demonstrate the generalized condition of theatricality in order to reveal its ideological operation and effects. Accordingly, theatre emerges as a specific, even specialized, way of knowing theatricality and questioning the process of theatricalization – and perhaps even of opening up ways of contesting its grip on the social formation.

We will return to these questions in the investigation of the critical case study deployed in this chapter – a contemporary theatrical reading of Shakespeare's *King Lear* (1606) – in order to analyse further how theatre thinks through theatricality and differentiates between them politically. Before doing so, however, it is worth returning to Tracy C. Davis's conception of theatricality as being produced through critically engaged spectatorship. Drawing on the etymological understanding of the theatre as a 'seeing place' – *theatron* – where spectators gather together to engage in the 'emotional participation' of watching something take place as performance, Davis argues that the spectator is actively involved in the construction and formalization of the event they see (2003: 141). This logic of active looking as the process of co-creating meaning, she proposes, is integral to the appearance of theatricality, whether in the specifically designated space of the theatre or on the broader public stage of which theatre is part. The intimate connection between the two suggests that theatricality is intrinsic to the constitution of the public realm and holds 'considerable importance for understanding public life' (131). Historicizing this development of the concept in the context of the Enlightenment and the French Revolution, Davis suggests that the operation of democratic civil society is dependent on a self-reflexive, 'volitional spectatorship' that enables the adoption of 'a critical stance toward an episode in the public sphere' (145). While this may include watching a theatre event, it is not limited to it, as theatricality is produced by the spectator choosing to see something as a scene taking place before them, through their participation in a practice of theatricalization. Davis is careful to point out that such a conception of theatricality might function as a highly racialized and 'masculinized form of viewing, a gender specific kind of participation in civil society' (146) which seeks to reassert the gaze of the spectator as the locus of power and arbiter of meaning. Yet at the same time, she argues that such spectators are aware 'of their own acting' – an awareness that might challenge their pre-existing 'sense of themselves' (148). In other words, the operation of theatricality might serve to disrupt and disturb the gaze as well as reaffirm it, destabilizing the security of the subject position it otherwise brings into effect.

The question of whether theatricality necessarily operates as mode of transgression or a form of normalization thereby appears as something of a false opposition. As theatre theorist Josette Féral points out, theatricality has 'no autonomous existence' or definite essence but is 'graspable only as a process' – as the continuous interplay between repetition and difference which both produces possibility and circumscribes its limits (2002: 12). Theatricality appears, then, as both normative *and* transgressive. It appears in the moment of crossing a boundary which simultaneously reaffirms its presence; in the movement between the opening up of a question and its recuperation into the existing logics of representation. While it might be seen to destabilize the boundaries of the subject, it nonetheless continues to constitute them, reproducing relations of power as well as appearing to contest them. So, if theatricality is neither one thing nor the other, but rather a mode of recognition of their interpenetration, how might it be useful as a way of 'understanding public life', as Davis suggests, as well as the spectatorial dynamics of subject formation? How might it open up the theatre of politics as well as the frame of the political? Let's try to explore this question through a readily available contemporary example.

Populist Theatricality, or Staging Donald Trump's Hair

In his critical exposition of 'The Populist Temptation', the left-wing political commentator Slavoj Žižek makes recourse to one of his signature jokes to explain the recent re-ascendance of the populist right in Western democratic societies. Commenting on that subject of much conjecture and speculation, Donald Trump's hair, Žižek notes: 'When a man wears a wig, he usually tries to make it look like his real hair. Trump achieved the opposite; he made his real hair look like a wig; and maybe this reversal provides a succinct formulation of the Trump phenomenon' (2017: 260). The joke, like most good ones, is really rather familiar. In concert with the characterization of populism it implies, it seems to trade on a certain anti-theatrical logic, re-inscribing the binary between the real/authentic and the mimetic/inauthentic through exposing the inversion of their terms. The fact that Trump's hair appears fake – even if, apparently, it is not – somehow indexes the fakery of his political showmanship, the self-evident 'inauthentic' stagey-ness, which must surely be seen to undermine itself. Although it might seem to self-deconstruct, it doesn't in fact self-implode; and the various parodies that seek to draw attention to the lack of seriousness or credibility of Trump as a political figure fall foul of their own anti-theatrical, binary thinking. So for Žižek, performing his own critical reversal of the apparent priority of the real over the imaginary, the joke reveals the populist distortion of the boundary between them: 'At the most elementary level', he writes, Trump 'is not trying to sell us his crazy ideological fictions as a reality – what he is trying to sell us is his own vulgar reality as a beautiful dream' (260). In this respect, it is not surprising that, following Alain Badiou's characterization of the emergence of Trump as 'symptom of global capitalism', Žižek sees right-wing populism as appealing to the rhetorical ground of working-class dispossession and disenchantment in order 'to prevent the dispossessed from defending themselves' (273). Žižek presents the populist 'slide into vulgar simplification and personalized aggressiveness' (241) embodied by Trump as a mask concealing yet revealing the true face of neoliberal capitalism; but the very logic of mask and face, mimetic construct and theatrical falsehood is left in place. This effectively allows the populist turn to be derided as an *intentional* manipulation – a theatrical sleight of hand or ideological conjuring trick – which *pretends* in order to persuade its audience of its own claims to truthfulness.

Something important is missing from this analysis; something apparent in the misunderstanding of theatricality demonstrated in the discussion of Trump's hair as real/fake. Populist theatricality is not a joke. If it is regarded simply as an attempt to deceive – as theatrical in the most directly 'vulgar' sense – we will continue to miss its most important ideological operation: the capacity to play with indeterminacy, to foreground the slipperiness of signification and the instability of meaning, to destabilize, disconnect and re-articulate 'the multi-accentuality of signs in discourse' (Hall 1988: 140) so that they can be combined differently in order to produce popular consent to an increasingly privatized, personalized and authoritarian mode of address. The point Žižek misses about Trump's hair – and about the Trump phenomenon, by extension – is that any attempt to limit the consideration of its theatricality to inverting the binaries of real/fake, authentic/inauthentic does not go far enough in examining its operation and effects. Rather, it reproduces and sustains them. For if, as Vološinov argued, 'everything that belongs to ideology has a semiotic value' (cited in Hall 1988: 140) – even the floating signifier of Trump's hair – we need to understand how these signs are articulated to one another performatively in constructing the authoritarian populist project.

An important starting point would seem to be the recognition that theatricality, as the eminent theatre scholar Erika Fischer-Lichte has argued, destabilizes the hierarchal organization of signifier/signified by producing 'a shift of dominance in the semiotic function' in which particular signs appear as 'signs of signs' (1995: 88). At least partially emptied of their signifying value they become mobile, malleable and ontologically 'indistinct'. While this 'theatrical' emptying of their referential 'content' might appear to render them 'void', and thereby also appears to void the concept of theatricality as having any explanatory purchase or critical power, it simultaneously makes visible the fundamental emptiness of the sign as only ever subject to the play of signification. The demonstrable theatricality of the sign thereby makes whatever it signifies appear as 'empty' or 'void', pointing to its apparently arbitrary, ideological construction. Hence the self-evident theatricality of Trump – and Trump's hair – appears to void any claim to authenticity even though it is actually real (isn't it, really?). Yet, as I've been trying to argue, it is important not to stop here. To do so would leave the concept of theatricality once again in the position primarily constructed by formalist anti-theatrical art critics such as Michael Fried (1967) who sees theatricality as simply signifying 'a nonthing, and emptiness, a void'; and reduces theatre to 'an empty term whose role it is to set up a system founded upon the opposition between itself and another term' (Krauss 1987: 62–3). More importantly, it would be to leave the discussion of theatricality (and Trump, and of politics) at the level of what it is rather than what it *does*.

The sociologist Elizabeth Burns's seminal study of the term pointed out that theatricality is not an inherent property or quality of things, people, practices or objects; it is rather a historically and culturally constructed 'mode of perception' which serves to 'frame' these through specific 'rhetorical and authenticating conventions' and discursive practices (1972: 1). As a 'mode of perception', theatricality requires and is produced by the activity of the spectator, albeit under historically and culturally constructed conditions of spectatorship. Accordingly, theatre theorist Josette Féral has argued that 'theatricality is the result of an act of recognition on the part of the spectator' – an act of seeing that opens the gaps in the current regime of representation and produces theatricality as the effect of 'making a disjunction in systems of signification' (2002: 10). In this respect, theatricality emerges as the result of a perceptual and critical operation which disturbs the distinction between reality and representation by recognizing their interpenetration and co-constitution. As such, its appearance might be seen to offer the spectator a 'critical lens' through which to gain a purchase on 'how, and why, we act' (Nield 2014: 556); and an optic through which to interrogate our own ideological production as a desiring subject. Although Féral, like Davis, tends to assume the subject as pre-existing the theatrical relation rather than being constituted by it, she usefully makes the connection between spectatorship and the construction of alterity. In her succinct formulation, 'theatricality cannot be, it must be for someone. In other words, it is for the Other' (1982: 178).

The relation between the theatricality produced by the performer yet addressed to the Other – remembering that, as the psychoanalytic theorist upon whom Féral draws, Jacques Lacan, argued, desire is often manifested as desire for the Other, as desire for the Other's desire – is crucial in attempting to understand the populist political claim. As we have seen, it is insufficient to attempt to essentialize theatricality as a critical operation that opens up a 'cleavage' in the ideological social formation and enables us to see its disjunction, as Féral suggests. For theatricality is also in play in covering over this gap, by, as Michael Taussig puts it, suturing 'the real to the really made-up' (1993: 86). Theatricality, as such, is not necessarily resistive or contestatory; it is as much inscribed in the construction of the regime of representation as in any apparent moment of its destabilization. Put simply, theatricality, as Trump shows and knows all too well, is as much a space of ideological investment and semiotic volatility as it is anything else; and, in being addressed to the desire of the Other, its effectivity resides in the construction of a range of subject-spectator positions rather than in the truthfulness of its address. Accordingly, the examination of the populist project should not be reduced to questions of intentionality, in/authenticity and the 'voiding' of affect; it must return to the politics of spectatorship as the site of the production of the subject.

In order to move this analysis forward, I want to give critical consideration to how theatre as the specific space dedicated to the task of making theatricality appear, and as the specific historical practice developed to produce a way of knowing theatricality and understanding its effects, might be approached as offering a useful mode of critique of the 'generalized theatricality' and 'vulgar' theatricalizations of the emergent authoritarian populist moment. In order to do this, I want to turn to the American philosopher Stanley Cavell's reading of *King Lear* (1967); and specifically to his argument that theatre, in its materiality as a place and practice, offers a limit to theatricality as an otherwise apparently transparent and 'diaphanous' medium by forcing its revelation as a political operation (Weber 2004: 7). In particular, I want to examine Cavell's claim that, in *King Lear*, Shakespeare's theatre offers an invitation to its audience to try to stop theatricalizing. In other words, I want to see if this argument might be reanimated and deployed in order to turn theatre against itself – or more precisely, against the theatre that has apparently already separated itself from the specificities of theatre as such: generalized theatricality. Can theatre offer resistance to theatricality? Or is it indelibly implicated in its construction and operation? How might theatre be thought of as exposing the dynamics of theatricalization, and serving as a limit point to generalized theatricality? What are the limits of its political claim?

Staging Theatricality: Trump/Lear

But what has *King Lear* got to do with populist politics, or, for that matter, with Donald Trump's hair? Some of the connections might already be found ghosting the brief commentary on the conceptualization of theatricality offered already, not least the idea that theatricality constitutes a void space, a semiotic emptiness: a 'nothing'. 'Nothing? Nothing. Nothing will come of nothing. Speak again.' Cordelia's famous refusal to engage Lear's self-regarding question, 'Which of you, shall we say, does love us most?' effectively operates as a refusal to enter the theatricality of the 'love test' set-up in Act 1 Scene 1 as an overtly performed display of obedience to his all-encompassing patriarchal, authoritarian power. Sam Mendes's 2014 production of the play for the Royal National Theatre makes this point very clearly. Antony Ward's stage design demonstrates how Lear, played as an ageing autocrat by Simon Russell Beale, constructs a theatre of his own within the theatre in which the play takes place – a meta-theatrical court theatre in which everyone and everything appears before him as subject to his gaze, and acts in accordance with his desire. Cordelia's 'Nothing, my Lord' in response to his attenuation of the obligations of intergenerational exchange to the dynamics of a property transaction – 'what can you say to draw a third more opulent than your sisters?' – is a refusal to *pretend*; a refusal to act according to the conventions of the theatre set-up and staged for Lear's spectatorial pleasure entirely from his own perspective. Her refusal to adhere to his authorial direction – 'mend your speech a little lest you mar your fortunes' – is both a refusal to play the game and a refusal to act the part: a refusal to appear to him as he would have her appear, a refusal of his *theatricalization*. Cordelia's 'Nothing' empties Lear's drama of succession of its manifest content in order to draw attention to its theatrical construction, exposing 'the utter emptiness of the ceremony and his demand for love' (Phelan 2005: 25). Her refusal to pretend is, as Cavell points out, itself already doubled – she refuses to pretend to love him because she actually does, whereas her sisters can pretend because they know how to act as if they do, even if they do not. In other words, she refuses to 'act'. Cordelia protests 'I cannot heave my heart into my mouth' not only because this would void her love and turn it into an empty signifier but because to do so would be to accept Lear's theatricalization of her as Other than herself, as only existing for him in his imaginary relation, not in her specificity. In Mendes's staging, the dynamics of this scene are explicitly sexualized: Regan's (Anna Maxwell Martin) coquettish acting-up to Lear's demands earns her a slap on the behind from her over-excited, boundary-crossing father; the demonstrable inappropriateness of which situates Cordelia's (Olivia Vinall) subsequent refusal to perform as a rejection of the sexualization of their relation at the very moment of her selecting a husband. It is clear from this that Lear's theatricalizations serve to maintain his sense of retaining ownership of his possessions – including his daughters, and his kingdom – even after he has given them away, effectively reducing his view of inter personal relations to relations of property and power that sustain his subjective sovereignty.

There are some obvious points of comparison between Lear's court theatrics and descent into the role of player King and Trump's highly personalized and increasingly privatized approach to government and the construction of authoritarian populism. Of course, there has been the uncomfortably nepotistic promotion of immediate family members, notably of Trump's daughter, Ivanka, and her husband, Jared Kushner, to positions of delegated responsibility; the awkward resonance of the inaugural cabinet meeting in which the newly appointed office-holders were required to attest their love for, and acquiescence to, the president alongside their willingness to serve; and the impetuous banishments and exclusions directed at those that fail to please. But more importantly, what Žižek euphemistically calls Trump's 'vulgarity' – his apparent racism, homophobia, misogyny and unbounded objectification of women, including his daughter – which might otherwise be termed his consistent *theatricalization of otherness*, so it only conforms to a property relation and a logic of self-extension – seem straight out of the Learean repertoire of reduction and misrecognition in order to render otherness obedient, observable and owned. In this respect, the 'mode of excess' of authoritarian populist theatricality might not only be its 'vulgarity' but its construction of 'a closed field, a theatrical stage already affixed' to a specific mode of cultural production (Said 1978: 63). And perhaps that mode of cultural production is inimical to the construction and operation of racist, sexist and proprietorial discourses and power relations. For Edward Said, accordingly, 'the notion of theatricality designates a particularly Western style of thought' whose operation is coextensive with a colonial regime of representation which delimits and circumscribes the appearance of the Other within the logic of the stage. Theatricality, in other words, plays an integral part of the perceptual production and configuration of an apparatus of alterity, rather than simply providing the grounds of its recognition.

Returning to *King Lear* for the moment, or at least to Cavell's reading of it – the complexity of which there is insufficient space to do justice to here – it is worth recalling that the play demonstrates how the theatricalization of others produces a 'refusal to acknowledge' what is in plain sight: the reality of other people existing in and for themselves and not only within the perceptual economy and epistemic violence of the construction of Otherness. For Cavell, theatricalization serves as an avoidance of recognition, of mutuality; the avoidance of being seen as well as seeing. It is, in other words, subjectivation without relation, without *love*; without the encumbrance of having to appear to other people as another person and without the need to recognize the specificity of their personhood. As such, Cavell suggests, theatricalization has to stop; and it is theatre, as the material space of seeing and being seen by other people – on stage and in the auditorium – which 'gives us the chance to stop' (1967: 334). In other words, the specific conditions of theatre enable the manifestation of the material relations of seeing through which we come to recognize the dynamics of theatricality and acknowledge alterity as the concrete reality of other people. As such, theatre's exposition and exposure of theatricality can be seen to limit and critique theatricalization more generally. As performance theorist Peggy Phelan points out, theatre 'exploits theatricality in order to defeat', delimit and deconstruct its operation (2005: 23). Accordingly, for Cavell, *King Lear* represents theatre against itself – or against the over-extension of theatricality as a way of seeing – and presents a way of knowing its effects: 'Tragedy has moved into the world, and with it the world becomes theatrical' (1967: 344).

Restaging *King Lear*: She She Pop's *Testament* (2010)

She She Pop's *Testament* – itself a version of *King Lear* – might offer a contemporary, postdramatic example of theatre working against itself, or at least with an awareness of the apparatus of theatricality it seeks to both expose and exploit. The piece was made and performed by members of the experimental theatre company in conjunction with their real-life fathers, who, rather than being represented by trained actors as if they were 'characters', were very much present on stage themselves. Although clearly 'playing a part' – occupying performance personae demonstrably mediated by the stage environment and at least in part produced by the theatrical apparatus – they nonetheless appeared as themselves rather than as fictional figures. In other words, they performed as themselves rather than as actors 'pretending' to be someone else; and, as a result, they both presented and represented themselves while fully acknowledging the artificially constructed 'reality' of the theatrical staging and scene. Their awareness of themselves performing while performing as themselves is consistent with the work of the other performers in the company who likewise eschew pretence in favour of recognizing their own and each other's presence – as well as the presence of the audience. This dual emphasis on performing rather than acting and on recognizing the specificity of the theatre event as engendering a self-aware mode of spectating is a hallmark of much postdramatic theatre. As Hans-Thies Lehmann has observed, the postdramatic 'strategy of refusal' of pretending reverses the privileging of the 'fictive reality' of the world of the drama over the theatrical reality of the world of the stage in order to reanimate and re-envisage their interrelation. In so doing, it tends to embrace overt theatricality as tacit acknowledgement of the reality of theatrical situation and formal disruption of the apparently 'illusionistic' conventions governing the construction of dramatic fiction. This enables the performers to inhabit the stage rather than simply inhabiting their role, thereby drawing attention to the reality of performing and the reality of performance over

Fig. 21.1 *Testament*, 2010, She She Pop. Photo: Doro Tuch.

and above any fictional 'reality' being performed. Accordingly, performers often address the audience directly – not as characters, as per the aside – but as people sharing the same space and time, co-present in the theatre event and therefore included in the process of its composition (Lehmann 2006: 90, 109).

In *Testament*, the performers' theatrical relation to the audience is first and foremost mediated through their material relation to one another. They are, after all, relatives: real fathers and daughters (and, in the version at the Barbican Centre, London, one son) occupying the stage in order to stage the grounds of their relation as a means of opening up the question of parental love, filial obligation, intergenerational exchange and the sustaining of personal dignity. Using the text of *King Lear* as a pretext, or perhaps an urtext underlying the construction of a new work, the company seeks to investigate the age-old problem of the shift in responsibility between parents and children as they become elderly and infirm; examining how the distribution of property and the dissipation of authority are subsidiary to the need for recognition and the renewal of respect above and beyond the bonds of 'duty'. In responding to Shakespeare's play rather than simply restaging it, She She Pop and their fathers make *Testament* an exploration of familial love and the ethics of care within as well as through a theatrical framework. The company members put themselves and their fathers on stage – under conditions of explicit theatricality – in order to interrogate their own theatricalization of (and by) the paternal relation. In other words, they use the theatre to both frame and challenge the theatricality of their lived experience, making it available to be seen under explicitly theatrical conditions so as to explicate its perceptual dynamics.

At the outset of the show, one by one the regular company performers enter stage left wearing faux Renaissance ruffs and approach stage centre to introduce their fathers to the audience by telling us how we might gain their respect. Behind them, stage left, a projector screen displays the title page of Shakespeare's play, in German. Once the introductions are complete, the text scrolls down to make visible the stage direction 'Enter King Lear', which a performer highlights in red ink. A trumpet sound is indicated in the text and so a trumpet is indeed played to mark the entrance of each 'Lear'/father onto the stage. One by one they take up their positions on the row of three armchair 'thrones' aligned stage right and look at the performer-daughter/son who has announced them. The last is in fact the trumpeter, who, by announcing his own entrance as he had the others, destabilizes any sense of a formal, fixed signification of hierarchy. The fathers stand to switch on cameras in front of their chairs that then project their faces into cardboard picture frames hung at the back of the stage, behind their children. Although they appear in a dominant, central position, we see their seeing – they are both looked at and looking. Their presence there, on stage, is shown to be mediated – literally framed – by the theatricality of the performance taking place. In other words, even in this 'postdramatic' performance, presence is always

Fig. 21.2 *Testament*, 2010, She She Pop. Photo: Doro Tuch.

cross-cut by representation; there is no 'authentic' presence without a form of mediation. The theatrical set-up of this scene draws attention to the fact that the fathers are presented as much as simply present; they are visibly 'staged' and 'framed' by an apparatus drawn to the attention of the audience, rather than rendered invisible. As a result we become aware of our own implication in the theatricalizing of these figures, how our looking at them in this context is part of their production in and as the *mise en scène*.

Not surprisingly, then, the theatricality of both the audience's encounter with these figures and the always-already mediated form of their relation to one another is underscored by the show's turn to popular song as the people on stage sing 'And so I stand in line until you think you have the time to spend an evening with me …'. The concluding lyric is of course the key: 'And then I go and spoil it all by saying something stupid like I love you'. As the performers read from the text of Act 1, Scene 1, it becomes clear that Cordelia's 'nothing' is here rendered as that 'something stupid like I love you'. The theatricality of the postdramatic performance is thereby used to explicate the theatrical context of the dramatic text without 'emptying' it of its resonance entirely. Accordingly, the text becomes the ground of negotiation between the fathers and their children, and the theatrical occasion an opportunity to investigate the dynamic of intergenerational exchange and the desire for mutual recognition. For example, one of the fathers offers a lecture-exposition deconstructing the false logic of Lear's seemingly self-interested reasoning; while one of the children responds with a calculation of care costs that questions the notion of 'inheritance' entirely. This is expounded further in a visual demonstration of the impossibility of moving the professor father's books from his three-storey house in Frankfurt to his daughter's two bedroom apartment in Berlin – showing that they would take up the totality of the floor space and leave no room for living. Here Regan and Goneril's forced reduction of Lear's entourage of a hundred knights is given a contemporary manifestation, enabling us to understand the problem of 'accommodation' as an enduring, everyday phenomenon. Once again, the dramatic and the theatrical are shown to be inter-animating and mutually deconstructing, with the reality-effects of the performers' seemingly 'authentic' presence ghosting and being ghosted by the reality of representation.

Conclusion: Endlessly Rethinking Theatricality

She She Pop and their fathers' *Testament* draws attention to the limits of attempting to separate 'reality' and 'theatricality' as if they were opposed terms. It exposes such logic as being overly reductive and simplistic, and counter to the knowledge that theatre itself makes available: that the real and the really made-up are always co-constituting and interdependent. Rather than see theatricality as artificial and 'inauthentic', as per the popular and critical anti-theatrical discourses that would dismiss it as having any significance as a way of knowing, seeing and thinking; or as necessarily politically disruptive and destabilizing, showing the gap between the real and the represented (Féral) or exposing the unavoidable emptiness of signification (Fischer-Lichte) and the fictive processes of ideological construction (Žižek); theatre demonstrates the operation of theatricality as a medium – as consisting in neither one thing nor the other but as the mode of their co-appearance and interrelation – which 'redefines' the boundaries between subject and object, self and other, presence and representation (Weber 2004: 29). As such, theatre emerges as the material space in which the apparatus of theatricality is rendered tangible and distinct. Theatre thinks through theatricality in order to make its operation visible, to force its dynamics to appear. Not simply as 'theatre', but as a mode of theatre thinking that challenges and critiques the regime of representation which it nonetheless contributes to and sustains. In this respect, theatre which thinks through theatricality is also theatre which appears to think against itself. Yet in doing so it also thinks against the grain of the generalized theatricality and politics of theatricalization it renders visible, calls into question and seeks to redress.

At the end of *Testament*, one of the father-daughter pairings reprise 'Somethin' Stupid' as a duet sung face to face rather than across the space of stage. Although it is tempting to see this as a concluding moment of recognition in which they acknowledge their love for one another as a 'relation without mediation' – without theatricality – it is important to acknowledge that this relation is as theatrically mediated as everything else on stage. How could it not be? If theatre makes theatricality appear, it also inevitably theatricalizes and re-theatricalizes the very grounds of its appearance. As the duet progresses, the other performers frame it for the audience through taking apart the set and unravelling the text, refracting the performance through its own dismantling. They end up forming a beautifully composed heap of bodies on the stage – an image, no less – which the duet singers join as the song fades along with the lights. The show stops; the theatre ends, as it must. But does the logic of theatricality ever stop, as Cavell argues it too surely should? The final image suggests that while theatre might appear to produce this demand in itself, its very nature *as theatre* necessarily theatricalizes it all the same.

Fig. 21.3 *Testament*, 2010, She She Pop. Photo: Doro Tuch.

Performance Details

King Lear by William Shakespeare. Director: Sam Mendes. Royal National Theatre, London, UK, 23 January–28 May 2014. For full production information and background materials, including cast list and programme, see: http://ntlive.nationaltheatre.org.uk/productions/4 4084-king-lear. For a clip of the scene discussed in the essay (part of Act 1, Scene 1), see: https://youtu.be/L_womZ_BE0Q

Testament by She She Pop and their Fathers, Barbican Centre, London, UK, 3–7 June 2014. For full production and touring information and a video trailer of the work, see: http://www.sheshepop.de/en/productions/archive/testament.html

Further Reading

Glen McGillivray (2009) provides a good overview of the development of 'theatricality' as a discursive formation and critical construct. In many ways, the foundational theoretical text on theatricality emerges not from theatre theory but from art criticism – specifically Michael Fried's ([1967] 1988) anti-theatrical characterization of theatricality as antithetical to genuine aesthetic experience. The key attempts to think through theatricality from a theatre perspective have been curated by Josette Féral (1982, 2002), with a special issue of the journal *SubStance* dedicated to leading theatre scholars' attempts to navigate, reclaim and reanimate the concept of theatricality in the context of theatrical performance. Tracy C. Davis and Thomas Postlewait's edited volume *Theatricality* (2003) is likewise dedicated to this task, which it extends by thinking about the development of the idea of theatricality in a historical as well as theoretical frame. Balme (2007) extends the cultural scope of theatricality to account for its role in the construction and operation of colonial relations of power and ways of seeing. The delineation of theatricality as a philosophical (anti-)concept and auto-deconstructive procedure is demonstrated most persuasively by Weber (2004).

Stanley Cavell's (1967) reading of *King Lear* is usefully taken up and examined by performance theorist Peggy Phelan (2005) and literary scholar Emily Sun (2010) to think through the relationship between theatre, theatricality and politics. Hans-Thies Lehmann's seminal work on contemporary performance which goes beyond the limits of the literary by focusing on the materiality of the theatre event, *Postdramatic Theatre* (2006), is investigated through a focus on the politics the spectatorial encounter in Jürs-Munby et al.'s *Postdramatic Theatre and the Political* (2013). A good account of She She Pop's *Testament* as an example of postdramatic theatre is given by Bredeson (2014); Massie (2015) usefully draws out the work's intertwining of the political, the personal and the performative in order to understand its affective appeal.

References

Balme, Christopher B. (2007), *Pacific Performances: Theatricality and Cross-cultural Encounter in the South Seas*, Basingstoke: Palgrave Macmillan.
Barish, Jonas (1981), *The Antitheatrical Prejudice*, Berkeley and Los Angeles: The University of California Press.

Bredeson, Kate (2014), 'The Sum of Testament is Love', *PAJ: A Journal of Performance and Art* 36 (1): 45–52.

Brooks, Peter (1976), *The Melodramatic Imagination: Balzac, Henry James, Melodrama, and the Mode of Excess*, New Haven: Yale University Press.

Burns, Elizabeth (1972), *Theatricality: A Study of Convention in the Theatre and in Social Life*, London: Longman.

Cavell, Stanley (1967), 'The Avoidance of Love: A Reading of *King Lear*', in Stanley Cavell (ed.), *Must we Mean what we Say?* 246–325, Cambridge: Cambridge University Press.

Davis, Tracy C. (2003), 'Theatricality in Civil Society', in Tracy C. Davis and Thomas Postlewait (eds), *Theatricality*, 127–55, Cambridge: Cambridge University Press.

Davis, Tracy C., and Thomas Postlewait (2003), 'Theatricality: An Introduction', in Tracy C. Davis and Thomas Postlewait (eds), *Theatricality*, 1–39, Cambridge: Cambridge University Press.

Féral, Josette (1982), 'Performance and Theatricality: The Subject De-mystified', *Modern Drama* 25 (1): 170–81.

Féral, Josette (2002), 'Foreword', *SubStance* 31 (2/3): 3–13.

Fischer-Lichte, Erika (1995), 'Introduction: Theatricality: A Key Concept in Theatre and Cultural Studies', *Theatre Research International* 20 (2): 85–9.

Fried, Michael ([1967] 1988), 'Art and Objecthood', in Michael Fried, *Art and Objecthood: Essays and Reviews*, 148–72, Chicago and London: Chicago University Press.

Hall, Stuart ([1980] 1988), 'Popular-Democratic vs Authoritarian Populism: Two ways of "Taking Democracy Seriously"', in Stuart Hall, *The Hard Road to Renewal: Thatcherism and the Crisis of the Left*, 123–49, London: Verso.

Jürs-Munby, Karen, Jerome Carroll and Steve Giles, eds (2013), *Postdramatic Theatre and the Political: International Perspectives on Contemporary Performance*, London: Bloomsbury.

Krauss, Rosalind (1987), 'Theories of Art after Minimalism and Pop', in Hal Foster (ed.), *Discussions in Contemporary Culture* (1), 56–87.

Lehmann, Hans-Thies (2006), *Postdramatic Theatre*, trans. K. Jürs-Munby, London: Routledge.

Massie, Eleanor (2015), 'Love Songs and Awkwardness: Non-professional Performers and Affective Labour', *Performance Paradigm* 11: 59–75.

McGillivray, Glen (2009), 'The Discursive Formation of Theatricality as a Critical Concept', *metaphoric.de* 17: 100–14.

Montelle, Yann-Pierre (2009), *Paleoperformance: The Emergence of Theatricality as Social Practice*, London and Calcutta: Seagull Books.

Nield, Sophie (2014), 'Speeches That Draw Tears: Theatricality, Commemoration and Social History', *Social History* 39 (4): 547–56.

Phelan, Peggy (2005), 'Reconstructing Love: *King Lear* and Theatre Architecture', in B. Hodgdon and W. B. Worthen (eds), *A Companion to Shakespeare and Performance*, 13–35, Oxford: Blackwell.

Postlewait, Thomas (2003), 'Theatricality and Antitheatricality in Renaissance London', in Tracy C. Davis and Thomas Postlewait (eds), *Theatricality*, 90–126, Cambridge: Cambridge University Press.

Said, Edward (1978), *Orientalism*, London: Penguin.

Sun, Emily (2010), *Succeeding King Lear: Literature, Exposure and the Possibility of Politics*, New York: Fordham University Press.

Taussig, Michael (1993), *Mimesis and Alterity: A Particular History of the Senses*, London and New York: Routledge.

Weber, Samuel (2004), *Theatricality as Medium*, New York: Fordham University Press.

Williams, Kirk (2001), 'Anti-theatricality and the Limits of Naturalism', *Modern Drama* 44 (3): 284–99.

Žižek, Slavoj (2017), *The Courage of Hopelessness: Chronicles of a Year of Acting Dangerously*, London: Allen Lane.

Subject Index

set. *See* scenography

sexuality 37, 67, 82, 190–7, 251

sign 47–57, 58–69, 118, 123, 300–1 (*see also* semiotics); sign-vehicle 80, 118; signifier, signification 47–57, 58–69, 154, 264, 275, 300–1, 306–7

simulation 158, 159, 201; simulacrum 150

site 119–20, 127, 233, 243, 254, 297; site-responsive 246–7; site-specific 106, 115, 119, 164, 225, 234, 245, 288

skill (*savoir faire*) 123, 124, 146, 162, 276–7, 282

slavery 13, 91–2, 95, 207, 209

social 26, 48, 66–7, 70, 75–6, 87–99, 117, 146–8, 152, 180, 245–9, 253, 297–8, 301; choreography as social practice 270–83; social dance 9, 87–99, 274; social formation, structure, institutions 16, 70, 81, 106, 195, 301; social impact 189–96, social justice 190, 217; social media 102, 155, 237

society 15, 48, 71, 138, 159, 160, 165, 186–99, 259, 270–83, 286, 298–9

space 72, 78, 245, 246, 248, 252, 264, 276 (*see also* time and space); and aura 228; and choreography 270–4, 281; courtroom as theatrical space 292; as 'holding environment' 204–6; and media 130, 137, 141–2; and objects 116–22; private space 78, 246; public space 42–3, 102, 246, 252–3, 299; safe space 204–5, 207; sonic space 93; and scenography 101–13; and signs 58; spatiotemporal 263, 270; and theatre architecture 36; and theatricality 302, 304, 305, 307, 308

spectacle 100, 112, 159–60, 161, 165, 259, 288, 292–3

spectator, spectating. *See* audience

speech 25, 287, 292; free speech 207; protest speech 222

sport 147–56, 235

stage. *See* scenography

stealth 193, 243–54

stereotype 67, 116, 150, 188, 202

student 1–3, 21–7, 179–80, 200–7, 285

subject 124, 140, 145, 152, 153, 200, 204, 274, 299, 302, 304, 307

subjectivity 12, 66, 78, 191–2, 196, 202, 204–5, 286, 297; subjectivity of researcher 154

symbol 59, 61–3, 67, 230, 286, 293. *See also* semiotics

synaesthesia 10, 137, 139, 142

task-based performance 11, 120, 159–60, 165, 166

technique 40, 77, 87, 95–6, 133, 146–9, 153–6, 177, 180, 218

technology: digital 155, 236–8; and the body 151; and ecology 264; media 130–44, 228; and performance documentation 228–38; and scenography 108, 112

temporality. *See* time

testimony 25, 30, 229, 285, 286, 287, 290

text 25–9, 40–3, 54–6, 120–1, 142, 156, 212, 248–52, 305–9; canonical text 52, 305; and focalization 36–7; movement text 274; theatre-text 212, 217, 219

theatricality (theatricalization) 15–17, 165, 167, 284–95, 296–310

time 15, 54, 58, 64, 89, 92, 102, 109, 123, 125, 150, 183, 193, 223, 261, 265; Aristotelian units (place, time, action) 39, 41; labour time and leisure time 74–6, 80, 278; real time 73, 178; temporality 13–4, 65, 73, 106, 109, 226, 236, 260, 267, 282; time and documentation 14, 229, 231, 235–7; time and re-enactment 219, 221–3; time and space 33, 66, 109, 118, 133, 137, 141, 270, 272, 273, 274, 305

tradition 64, 174, 180–2, 221

tragedy 23, 38–9, 264, 304

training 8, 10–11, 60, 64, 89, 145–57, 163, 168, 173, 175, 215

transcultural 183. *See also* intercultural; multicultural

transindividuation, transindividual 270, 274–6, 280–2

translation 47, 50, 52, 77, 102, 178

transnational 60, 75, 193

trauma 5, 9, 12–3, 16, 96–7, 200–10, 211, 215

trial 5, 16, 285–95

trigger warnings 13, 200, 204

uncanny 117, 140, 141, 221

value 3, 10–12, 87, 95, 145–6, 150, 153, 182, 186–99, 234

Verfremdung, Verfremdungseffekt. See alienation

video 130–44, 155, 217, 225–9, 233–8; videocy 228–9; video dance 87, 89

violence 13, 16, 38, 150, 188, 194, 196, 198, 201, 202, 204–6, 211, 219, 285, 288–9, 291–3, 304

virtual, virtuality 112, 133, 138, 140, 141

virtuosity, virtuosic 122, 160, 161, 162, 164, 252

visibility, visible   47–8, 116, 191, 219, 284, 292, 293, 306–8

visual   36–7, 52, 55, 102, 181, 250–60; visual art, fine art 93, 198, 215, 229, 231, 255; visuality 46, 259 (*see also* image)

voice, voicing   34–40, 43–5, 53, 55, 93, 156, 191, 253

voice-over   43–5, 120

watching. *See* audience

wayang kulit   12, 173–4, 177–8, 180, 184

weightlifting   10–11, 147, 151–6

wrestling   11, 135, 147–56

writing   4–6, 9, 21–32, 148, 154, 175, 268; choreographic 271–2; as documentation 226; scenic, spatial 102, 104

Names Index

JUNE 7